Alexander William Crawford

Etruscan Inscriptions Analysed

Alexander William Crawford

Etruscan Inscriptions Analysed

ISBN/EAN: 9783742829856

Manufactured in Europe, USA, Canada, Australia, Japa

Cover: Foto ©Andreas Hilbeck / pixelio.de

Manufactured and distributed by brebook publishing software (www.brebook.com)

Alexander William Crawford

Etruscan Inscriptions Analysed

ETRUSCAN INSCRIPTIONS

ANALYSED.

TRANSLATED AND COMMENTED UPON,

By ALEX. EARL OF CRAWFORD & BALCARRES,
LORD LINDSAY, &c.

"As those who unripe veins in mines explore
On the rich bed again the warm turf lay,
Till Time digests the yet imperfect ore;
And know it will be gold another day:"—
DRYDEN.

LONDON:
JOHN MURRAY, ALBEMARLE STREET.
1872.

TO

MRS. JAMES LINDSAY,

IN SPECIAL REMEMBRANCE

OF

TWO WHITE DAYS

SPENT MANY YEARS AGO TOGETHER

AMONG THE RUINS OF

ANCIENT ETRURIA.

PREFACE.

This volume was written and prepared for the press with a view to private circulation, and in the hope that others more competent than myself would take up the subject and work it out. My object was not (properly speaking) to give an accurate interpretation of the Etruscan inscriptions, but to shew that the language employed in those inscriptions was an ancient form of German, in corroboration of an argument derived from independent sources to prove that the Etruscans were a branch of the Teutonic race. My reason for publishing it is this, that in a work which I am about to issue on a much more important subject I have employed the ancient German as an instrument of etymological and mythological comparison and analysis in a manner which can only be justified by adduction of proof that the language stands upon a par in point of antiquity and importance with Greek and Latin, Zendic and Sanscrit, and that its written, or rather engraved monuments are centuries older than the Gospels of Ulphilas. Such proof is, I trust, afforded by the contents of the ensuing pages.

Dunecht, 18th October, 1872.

CONTENTS.

	PAGE
INTRODUCTORY ..	1
ETRUSCAN INSCRIPTIONS	14
CHAP. I.—Tyrrheno-Pelasgic Inscriptions	ib.
Sect. i. The small black pot of Cære	ib.
Sect. ii. Inscription of the 'Vinicopium'	21
Sect. iii. Inscription of Mark the Potter	24
Sect. iv. Minor Inscriptions of Cære	27
Sect. v. The formula Κόγξ ὄμπαξ	29
CHAP. II.—Inscription, purely Etruscan, in a tomb at Tarquinii	32
CHAP. III.—The 'Alcestis and Admetus' inscription ..	37
CHAP. IV.—Inscriptions on Votive offerings	41
Sect. i. 'Tinśkvil,' and the candelabrum of Cortona	42
Sect. ii. 'Alpan,' or fraud, in atonement for ..	44
Sect. iii. 'Aiseras,'—encroachment on land-marks ..	47
Sect. iv. Fraud, ut supra	48
Sect. v. 'Puantrn,'—breach of faith	49
Sect. vi. Fraud, ut supra	50
Sect. vii. Against sentence of damnum	52
Sect. viii. Pecuniary fine	53
Sect. ix. Pecuniary compensation for fraud	ib.
Sect. x. Failure of appearance to summons	55
Sect. xi. The 'Arringatore'	58
CHAP. V.—Sepulchral Inscriptions	61
Sect. i. The Bilingual Inscriptions	ib.
Sect. ii. Sepulchral Formulæ	93
Sect. iii. The Alethna Sarcophagus	97
Sect. iv. The Cæcina Inscription	102
Sect. v. The Inscription of San Manno	109
Sect. vi. Inscriptions in the tomb of the Pompeys ..	121

CONTENTS.

	PAGE
CHAP. VI.—Inscription relating to Land-Tenure	146
Sect. I. The Inscription of the 'Marmini' at Volterra	ib.
Sect. II. The great Inscription of Perugia	161
§ 1. Constitution of 'conductio,' or lease of farm ..	166
§ 2. Illegal alienation of two-thirds	176
§ 3. Action at law	179
§ 4. Proceedings in equity	186
SUMMARY	207
ENVOI	228

APPENDIX

I. Bilingual Inscriptions	233
II. Glossary (Abridged) of Etruscan words known to us otherwise than through the inscriptions	240
Group I. Words expressive of the relations of life and society ..	242
Group II. Words descriptive of dress, martial and domestic ..	243
Group III. The chariot; and amusements, public and private ..	244
Group IV. Animals, plants, the heavens, &c.	245
Group V. Matters of common life, and miscellaneous	247
Group VI. Etruscan Deities, including the Genii, Lares, &c. ..	250
Sect. I. The Gods,—general name	ib.
Sect. II. The Three great Gods	ib.
Sect. III. The Dii Complices and Dii Consentes	252
Sect. IV. The Dii Novensiles	ib.
Sect. V. The Dii Involuti	253
Sect. VI. Etruscan Gods, proper	ib.
Sect. VII. The Fates, or female demons, friendly and malignant	259
Sect. VIII. The Genii	260
Sect. IX. The Lemures, and their subdivisions, Lares, Larvæ, and Manes	ib.
Sect. X. The Dii Penates	262
Group VII. Divination, Public Worship, &c.	263
Sect. I. Revealers, teachers, and guardians of divination ..	ib.
Sect. II. Ministers of divination	264
Sect. III. The Insignia of divination	ib.
Sect. IV. The Templum, and the Pomœrium	265
Sect. V. Public and private worship; rites, ceremonies, officials, &c.	266

	PAGE
Group VIII. The Pontifices, the Pontifex Maximus, the Calends, Ides, Calendar, &c.,	268
Sect. I. The Pontifex Maximus	ib.
Sect. II. The Calendar, &c.	270
Group IX. Public civil ceremonial of Rome, as derived from Etruria	271
Sect. I. The Executive	ib.
Sect. II. The Nation	272
Sect. III. The Deliberative Assemblies; the Forum, the Curiæ, the Comitia, the Senate	274
Sect. IV. The Fetiales	276
Sect. V. The Insignia of Authority	277
Group X. The Sæculum	278
Group XI. Miscellaneous	279
Group XII. Proper Names	280
Sect. I. National surnames of the Etruscans	ib.
Sect. II. Names of Etruscan cities	282
Sect. III. Name of Rome, as an Etruscan city	304
Conclusions from the preceding Survey	306
Index	314

ETRUSCAN INSCRIPTIONS.

INTRODUCTORY.

"The origin of the Etruscans," says Mr. Dennis in his delightful work on Etruria, "has been assigned to the Greeks—to the Egyptians—the Phœnicians—the Canaanites—the Libyans—the Basques—the Celts, . . . and, lastly, to the Hyksos, or Shepherd-kings of Egypt. I know not if they have been taken for the lost Ten Tribes of Israel, but *certes* a very pretty theory might be set up to that effect, and supported by arguments which would appear all-cogent to every one who swears by 'Coningsby.'"—The surest test of ethnological affinity is to be found in LANGUAGE; but "the language of Etruria"—I again quote Mr. Dennis—"even in an age which has unveiled the Egyptian hieroglyphics and the arrow-headed character of Babylon, still remains a mystery. This 'geological literature,' as it has been aptly termed, has baffled the learning and research of scholars of every nation for ages past; and though fresh treasures are daily stored up, the key to unlock them is still wanting. We know the characters in which it is written, which much resemble the Pelasgic or early Greek; we can learn even somewhat of the genius of the language and its inflections; but beyond this, and the proper names and the numerals on sepulchral monuments, and a few words recorded by the ancients, the wisest must admit their ignorance, and confess that all they know of the Etruscan tongue is that it is unique—like the Basque, an utter alien to every known family of languages. To the other early tongues of Italy, which made use of the same or nearly the same character, we find some key in the Latin, especially to the Oscan, which bears to it a parental relation. But the Etruscan has been tested again and again by Greek, Latin, Hebrew, and every other ancient language, and beyond occasional affinities, which may be mere coincidences, such as occur almost in every case, no clue has yet been found to its interpretation,—and unless some monument like the Rosetta Stone should come to light, and some Young or Champollion should arise to decipher it, the Etruscan must ever remain a dead, as it has always emphatically been a sepulchral language. Till then, to every fanciful theorist who fondly hugs himself into the belief that to him it has been reserved to unravel the mystery, or who possesses the Sabine faculty of dreaming what he wishes, we must reply in the words of the prophet, 'It is an ancient nation, a nation whose language thou knowest not.'" *

With these eloquent and deterring words, and from such high authority, still fresh in my ears, you can well imagine, MY DEAR ANNE, that I did not venture to essay my luck—where so many had made shipwreck—without due consideration, without a very strong determining impulse. Rather, I may say, I was compelled by the conditions of an inquiry in which I was engaged to make the venture.

* *Cities and Cemeteries of Etruria*, by George Dennis, vol. I. pp. xxxvi–xlv.

You will recollect the labour I was at, some years ago, in tracing out and establishing the links of descent in the Aryan race as represented by the three great families which I styled, after the names of their respective eponymi in the ascending chain, the THORINGA, the HRUINGA, and the IOTINGA. In the course of those investigations I became convinced, by the convergence of almost every description of historical evidence, that the Tyrrheni, or Etruscans, belonged to the Thoringa family, and must consequently have been closely akin to the Tervingi, Thuringi, Tyrki (or pre-Odinite Northmen), and other Teutonic tribes, although come off from the common stock bearing the Thoringa name at an extremely remote period. The Rhæti or Rasenic branch of the great stock known to the ancients as Etruscan similarly belonged—so I inferred—to the Hruinga family,—and the general result I came to was, that the Tyrrheni and the Rhæti were the representatives, especially, in the South, of the Tervingi and Grutungi, better known latterly as Visi-Goths and Ostro-Goths, in the North and West of Europe. The question presented itself—and it could not be silenced, for none could be more important—Did the Etruscan language bear out this induction, or contradict it? Every attempt to interpret the language had hitherto failed; but I was so persuaded that it must have been Aryan and not remotely akin to the oldest Germanic dialects (especially to those spoken by the Thuringian tribes) that I should have been a faint-hearted knight indeed had I hesitated to apply this crucial test to the point of controversy. I began with the series of single words transmitted to us by

the ancients as Etruscan, and of which they have
given us the interpretations in Greek or Latin; and
I found them all to have a corresponding sense in—
not merely the Aryan and Japhetan tongues generally, but more particularly in ancient German. I
then tested the names of the Etruscan Gods and of
the old cities of Etruria, and found the latter more
particularly to correspond in repeated instances with
the natural features of the country and with the
symbolism of coins and other *indiciæ*, as reflected in
the same Teutonic idiom. I applied the same process
to the words connected with those Roman institutions
which the classical writers expressly inform us were
derived from Etruria; and the result was still the
same, although it almost proved too much—through
the conviction which the inquiry forced upon me
that the Oscan, Sabine, or Sabellian race, which contributed so much to the early development of Rome,
was also of a kindred origin.* The result however,
with every set-off, was so eminently satisfactory that
I should have contented myself with it but for the
consideration that the words analysed and founded
upon—those, I mean, distinctly recorded by the
Greek and Latin writers in their foreign Etruscan
form—could hardly be supposed to have escaped disguise and corruption through the uncritical medium
of their transmission and the subsequent accidents of
transcription. This was perhaps being hypercritical;
but I felt that the proof might be considered insufficient unless I could shew that the inscriptions,
written in the unmistakeable original dialect and

---

* The results of these investigations were embodied in a Glossary, an
abridgment of which is subjoined to the present Memoir.

character of Etruria, equally yielded to the touchstone. I tested several of them accordingly; and they too responded in a manner which gratified, although I cannot say it surprised me. I was called off, however, at this point by more pressing objects of interest; and therefore, after writing down the results arrived at, and completing my notes on the subject, I laid them aside; and the subject, if not forgotten, dropped for years into the background. The arrival, however, a few months ago, at an unoccupied moment, of a fresh batch of the 'Monumenti Inediti' of the 'Instituto Archeologico' of Rome—as well as of Fabretti's noble 'Corpus' of Inscriptions, Etruscan, Umbrian, Oscan, now in a completed form *—roused up the slumbering fire; and I have been amusing myself at intervals during this last winter † in re-examining the inscriptions formerly analysed, and applying the same process to others, with the results which—imperfect and tentative as they undoubtedly are—I now propose to lay before you. I have determined upon doing so inasmuch as I am again called off to matters which have a prior claim upon me; and it may be long ere I can resume the inquiry now a second time interrupted. It is true that I might lay these new notes aside, in the drawer which contains the old ones, till the lapse of two or three more *lustra* shall evoke them again to light; but time slips away—those *lustra* I may never see—I am no longer young—and it may be my fate to die in harness, at work which has its interest

---

* *Corpus Inscriptionum Italicarum Antiquioris Ævi,—et Glossarium Italicum, &c.* Aug. Taurinorum, 4to. 1867.
† Written in 1870.

doubtless, but in which the heart and the soul are too much engrossed to allow of that calm enjoyment which the intellect finds in the study of pure antiquity. Believing therefore that what I have to say is worth saying—or I certainly should not presume to utter it—wishing from my heart that it were better worth your hearing, more full and more precise in every way—and yet feeling strongly with Hesiod that "the half is better than the whole" in cases where, as in the present, my chief hope is to induce others more qualified than myself to take up the subject and do it justice—I have resolved to chronicle the results I have come to in black and white, and commit them to paper—on the principle of 'valeant quantum,' and at all events to preserve them thus far against the chances of perdition. Had I had leisure to accomplish my purpose of carefully going through the entire body of extant inscriptions, I have no doubt that the individual analyses I now present to you would have been more exact and the conclusions based upon them better warranted; and in that case I might have felt emboldened to offer them to the world at large, which at present I do not presume to do.*

I have only to add, in justice to myself, that I have no pretensions to speak with authority in linguistic matters. Language has not been my special study; I have merely courted her aid as a handmaid to history. It is true that I offer you translations of Etruscan inscriptions; but my object has not been to interpret these inscriptions for their own sake, but

* For the reason which has determined me to make them public, see the 'Preface,' supra.

simply in order—you will appreciate the distinction—
to ascertain what the language is in which they are
written, and to apply the argument thence arising
towards the solution of the ethnological question,
"Who were the Etruscans?" This is not more than
may be attempted by an ordinary historical student—
a general archæologist—without presumption. It
has fallen to my lot, as I believe, to discover and
open the door into the treasury of the Etruscan language; but it is for the great masters of the Linguistic Science—whom Britain delights to honour in the
person of her adopted son, Max Müller—to enter in
and take possession, to reduce the language to its
grammar, to elaborate its lexicon, and to determine
its exact place on the genealogical tree of German
speech, preparing the way for inquiries in which
jurists, mythologists, and the leaders of kindred schools
of study in Comparative Archæology, will have to
take part. Even now, from what little I have done,
some views may, I think, be formed as to the course
which inquiry will take in these directions.*

* I am by no means the first to affirm broadly that the Etruscan is an
Indo-European, or even a Teutonic language. "Suum cuique tribuito."
The following are Dr. Prichard's words upon the subject, published as long
ago as 1841, in his *Physical History of Mankind*:—"The best resource
for investigating the history of human races in general has almost entirely
failed in researches respecting the Etruscans. . . . All that can be inferred
as tolerably well established respecting the Etruscan dialect is, that it
belonged to the class of Indo-European languages." Mr. Bunbury again,
admitting—(I quote his excellent article on 'Etruria' in Dr. Smith's
Dict. of Greek and Roman Geography)—that the Etruscan has "words
and inflexions" in common with the Umbrian, and that "it contains
unquestionably a Greek or Pelasgic element," which "especially" (he
thinks) "discovers itself in some inscriptions found in the southern part of
Etruria," states that "the main ingredients of the language" are "radically
different" from either the Umbrian or Pelasgic;" and that this "third"
element, "probably the most important of all, wholly distinct from both,
and which may be called the Rasenic element," is "in all probability the

One more preliminary observation, and I have done. You must not expect to find the full development language of the Etruscans properly so called. Of this," he adds, " we can only assert, in the present state of our knowledge, that, although distinct from the Pelasgic or Greek family of languages on the one hand and from that of the Umbrians, Oscans, and Latins on the other, there are good reasons for believing it to belong to the same great family, or to the class of languages commonly known as the Indo-Teutonic. Some arguments," he concludes, " have lately been brought forward to show that its nearest affinities are with the Gothic, or Scandinavian group,"—these, I presume, being those advanced by Dr. Donaldson in his 'Varronianus,' those of Dr. Aufrecht published by Bunsen, and those of the Rev. Robert Ellis before he finally adopted his views as to the Armenian origin of the Etruscans; while Jacob Grimm had several years previously remarked upon the affinity of the Etruscan 'Æsar' and the Scandinavian 'Asen,' and Dr. Steub had connected the inscriptions with the Teutonic proper and the Lithuanian. I own that when, long after I had completely satisfied myself as to the Teutonic character of the Etruscan, I turned to the 'Varronianus,' my first impulse was to re-echo the old denunciation " Pereant qui ante nos nostra dixerunt!" inasmuch as that learned philologist distinctly pronounces the Etruscans to have been a Teutonic people, on the ground of a comparison of their language with the Scandinavian or Icelandic tongue, as existing in the ninth century." I soon found, however, that his etymologies and my own, as well as the conclusions we had respectively come to on many points of Etruscan history, were so materially different that any question of priority restricted itself (with rare exceptions) to the assertion of the broad fact of Teutonic descent; while, even in that point of view, while Dr. Donaldson found his analogies in the old Icelandic, and connected his Etruscans with the Low-German and Scandinavian race (restrictively so termed), I had resorted for mine to a more remote and comprehensive field of general Teutonic antiquity, and arrived at a distinct ethnological inference and, indeed, specific conclusion as to their origin. Dr. Donaldson's argument was, in fact, derived exclusively from comparison of language, leaving all the other prior arguments, from the patronymic 'Tyrrheni' or Thoringa, from the correspondence of religious sympathies and usages, and from national character and institutions, untouched. The fact appeared to me to be that we had approached the subject from different points of view, from two opposite poles of the compass; he, from the South, as a professed scholar, laying siege in due form to the walls and traditions of Tarquinii, with classical erudition and

---

* " The theory," says Dr. Donaldson, " that the Etruscan language, as we have it, is in part a Pelasgian idiom, more or less corrupted and deformed by contact with the Umbrian, and in part a relic of the oldest Low-German or Scandinavian dialects, is amply confirmed by an inspection of those remains which admit of approximate interpretation."—*Varronianus*, 3rd ed. p. 165.

ment of Teutonic inflection and grammar in these Etruscan inscriptions. Assuming that the Tyrrheni and other Thoringa tribes separated in remote antiquity, carrying their common language along with them, it is difficult at first sight to understand why the complex grammatical forms of (say) the Mœso-Gothic of Ulphilas do not appear in the Etruscan inscriptions, at all events in a parallel, if not identical development. So far from such being the case, the impression left upon me is a doubt whether the sin-

philological learning to which I could make no pretensions—and upon which he appeared to me in many instances to draw too readily and exclusively, when illustrations far more close and to the purpose—under one's very nose indeed—were to be found in the oldest Teutonic speech; but I myself, from the North, as a roving Viking, ranging in my galley from shore to shore, seeking out our ancient kinsmen, and perhaps too rash and precipitate in the first instance in grasping them by the hand when I thought I had recognized them—but with the advantage of starting from the cradle from which they also started in times of old, and of being preoccupied with the speech and traditions of our common Thoringa and Teuton forefathers rather than with those of the more polished races, whose claims could not have had a more learned or accomplished advocate than Dr. Donaldson. There might of course be advantages to truth from both points of view, from both modes of investigation; but, after full consideration, I felt that, without the slightest wish to claim undue credit through poaching (as it were) on another man's manor, I was entitled to set forth my views independently, as originally formed and developed—taking care, of course, to point out in the proper place every instance in which Dr. Donaldson and others (so far as I was aware) had anticipated me—it being understood that where such acknowledgment was not made, the responsibility rested (so far, again, as I was aware) with myself. I noticed consequently all these instances in the Glossary to 'The Etruscans' as originally written; and they will be found in the abridgment of that Glossary appended to this volume. Thus much I have been obliged to say in justice to myself with reference to the general theory I advocate. But as regards the special application of this theory I need fetter my lips by no such explanation. It has been allowed on all sides that it could not be asserted with absolute confidence that the Etruscan language was really and truly German till a sufficient number of the inscriptions had been analysed and found to render a clear and unmistakeable response in that sense to the test applied to them; and this test has now, I venture to say, for the first time, been effectually, however inadequately, applied—but only as the last link in a long chain of previous induction.

gularly simple character of the Etruscan arises from
its representing the ancient Teutonic in its undeveloped youth, laid up and preserved to us in a state
of crystallised immobility; or the same ancient language in a state of disintegration and decay, the
consequence of long isolation within a circle of
antagonistic dialects, with which it would not mingle,
and under whose influence it gradually withered and
died out. On the other hand, there *are* inflections
and grammatical forms in these inscriptions, quite
sufficient to vindicate the character, not only of the
language but of the people that spoke it, as Teutonic.
And perhaps more would be discernible but for the
singular disadvantage under which the Etruscan
speech comes before us, exclusively as a monumental
or lapidary language—always unfavourable to the
exhibition of inflection and grammatical structure,
and with a frequent tendency to run words into each
other, as in the inscriptions, without break or distinction, imposing on the decipherer in such cases a task
analogous to that of the augur, whose process of
meting out the heavens with his *lituus* before attempting to read the signs presented to him by each special
regio of observation, has its exact parallel in the case
of the antiquary face to face with these terrible
agglomerations of letters, and compelled to detach,
identify, and translate the separate words without
any traditionary "discipline" to guide his path, or any
grammatical help as yet from an Etruscan Rosetta
Stone, such as Mr. Dennis fondly hopes for, to assist
his quest by bilingual translation. Nor have the
grammatical inflections fared better, I suspect, under
the still further disadvantage in which the Etruscan

comes before us, "cabin'd, cribb'd, confin'd" within the trammels of an originally Semitic (Phœnician) alphabet, foreign to its genius and unfit to give its dialectic expression suitable utterance.

Nothing remains for me, then, but to estimate the comparative force and value of certain Etruscan letters, and to point out the extent of claim I intend to make upon your indulgence in regard to literal interchangeability, always rather a sore point between yourself and me. The fact that strikes one most forcibly on first grappling with the inscriptions is the varying use of two characters to denote the letter 's,'—one of them resembling the Latin capital 'S' reversed, the other the capital 'M,' being, in fact, the Greek Σ, but standing (as it were) on its feet; the former identical, I presume, with the Attic *sigma*, the latter, in its jagged, dentated form, reminding us of the name *san* by which 's' was known to the Dorians, the ethnological kinsmen of the Tyrrheni, and which would appear to represent hieroglyphically a 'dent-s,' ὀδόντ-ς, *zahn*, or tooth. In some inscriptions one of these characters is exclusively used, in others the alternate variety; but in a third class the reversed 'S,' which I shall call the *sigma*, is employed at the beginning, and the *san*, as I shall call the dentated letter, distinguishing it by an accent in transcription, at the end of words,—a distinction which becomes of importance when the inscriptions are written without any break between the component words.* Passing to the question of

* As the *san* is the Doric letter, we may presume that it was the Tyrrhenian, and the *sigma* would therefore be the Pelasgic character. It may be noted that *s* as a numeral, ς', was reckoned by the Greeks out of its alphabetic order and immediately after ε', the fifth letter of the Greek

literal interchangeability, I have to state that the
letters *b*, *d*, and *g*, which I have not a doubt were
sounded by the Etruscans as we do, are expressed in
the Etruscan alphabet by *u*, *t*, and *k*, which consequently
have frequently to 'serve double tides.' Of
the other letters or sounds, as transmutable from
Teutonic into Etruscan orthography, I need only
mention that *z* is represented by *th* and *t*, as well as
by its own Etruscan character ⸸; the compound *pf*
is expressed by θ or *ph*; the *sch* so familiar to us in
the German of all ages (as well as in the Semitic and
Egyptian tongues) is almost always expressed by the
character ↓, usually but inadequately transcribed as
ch,—a transcription however which I have not presumed
to modify, although I remark upon it when
necessary. Where two consonants occur together
for which there was no approximate single character
in the Greco-Phœnician alphabet, the Etruscan inscriptions
usually omit one of them, very frequently
the second, as in the case of *mb*, *nd*, *ng*. I must
plead guilty to an occasional intermutation of *l* and *d*
(the Etruscan *t*), of *k* and *t*, of *q* and *t*, of *su* and *k*,
of *th* and *ph*, and of *s* and *r*;[*] but I may allay your
nascent apprehension by promising that I will as far
as possible avoid all identifications based on such
recondite (though indubitable) rules as those that

alphabet, and in the place ordinarily assigned to ζ,—possibly therefore it
may have been originally that identical letter; in support of which we
have the fact that ϛ stands as a contraction for στ; and ϛ' is the numeral
for six.

[*] All these interchanges are of the simplest kind; and they may be
illustrated by the familiar examples of δάκρυμα, 'lacryma;' 'lingua,'
'dingua,' *zunge*, tongue; Ulyxes or Ulysses, Ὀδυσσεύς, &c.; 'qualuor,'
τέσσαρες, τέτταρες; *twist*, *quist*, 'ramus,' a bough; *swart*, *kiar*, black;
φήρ, θήρ; 'ara,' 'ara,' &c. &c.

prove that 'four' and 'quatuor,' 'five' and πέντε, 'twenty' and 'vigaint,' 'évêque' and 'bishop,' are absolutely one and the same word in each instance. My sceptical friends shall not charge me on the present occasion with arguing on the principle that ' the vowels go for nothing, and the consonants must look after themselves' in etymological matters. I trust therefore with the stronger assurance to their and your acceptance of the conclusions now submitted to you—based, as they are, on no such startling argument, but on the simple approximation of words and phrases in two languages, so plain in their outward presentment and combined import that (I may almost say) a very child may read them.

The inscriptions I have chosen for analysis and exposition shall now be adduced in the following order:—1. Two very ancient and interesting ones, the first of them found at the Pelasgo-Etruscan city of Agylla or Cære, and both of them generally accepted as Pelasgian; but which I shall show to be likewise fundamentally Teutonic,—and also one or two more from Cære,—2. A very archaic inscription, purely Etruscan, found near Tarquinii,—3. An inscription painted on a beautiful *amphora* representing the parting of Alcestis and Admetus,—4. A series of inscriptions on Votive offerings,—5. A selection from the Sepulchral inscriptions, including such bilingual inscriptions as have been discovered,—and, 6. Two inscriptions, of much interest, relating to the possession and occupation of land.

I may as well premise that the manual I have chiefly made use of throughout the ensuing analyses has been the ' Glossarium Germanicum Medii Ævi, potissimum dialecti Suevicæ,' of John George Scherz, as edited by Jeremiah James Oberlin, and published at Strasburg in two volumes folio, in 1781, a most useful compendium (bulky though it be) of the earlier works of Wachter, Haltaus, Schilter, and others, most of which indeed I have referred to in verifying my translations,—while I have also had beside me the 'Glossarium Diplomaticum' of Dr. Edward Brinckmeier, (Gotha, two volumes folio, 1856,) which includes the Latino-Teutonic words of the middle ages, and supplies much that the authors cited by Scherz have omitted or not been aware of. When, therefore, I simply cite an old German analogue without giving any authority, it is almost always from Scherz,—when other authorities are depended upon (as in the case of the Gothic, Scandinavian, and other dialects), I shall, as a rule, specify them.

CHAPTER I.

TYRRHENO-PELASGIC INSCRIPTIONS.

SECTION 1.—*The small black pot of Cære.*

This precious little pot, or rather "poculum," was discovered by General Galassi in his excavations at Cære, the modern Cervetri, in 1836, and is now preserved in the Gregorian Museum of the Vatican. It is of the most archaic type of the pottery of the place, and is considered by Dr. Lepsius to be of Pelasgic, pure Pelasgic—or (as he likewise calls it) "alt-tyrrhenisch," Old-Tyrrhenian — workmanship, rather than Etruscan proper.* I should add that Cære was originally a Pelasgian city, in close alliance with Greece, and bore the name of Agylla till the original name was supplanted by that of Cære, imposed by the Etruscan conquerors. An inscription runs round the pot, or cup, which the learned critic just mentioned considers to be, in language and character, Pelasgic and not Etruscan, basing his argument, 1. On the formation of certain letters as Old-Greek; 2. On the absence of other letters, such as *z* and *ch*, which are very common in Etruscan inscriptions; 3. On the preponderance of vowels over consonants; 4. On the occurrence of the diphthong *ai*; 5. On the general absence of the endings in *l*, *k*, and *r*, so characteristic of the Etruscan; and 6. On the expression of the liquid vowels throughout the inscription, which are usually suppressed in Etruscan writing. He admits, however, the use of the Etruscan *p*; and other of the characters, which he specifies, are occasionally (though seldom) found in the undoubted Etruscan inscriptions. But, with every qualification thus suggested, I do not venture to contest the conclusion come to by Lepsius; all I would contend is that, whether Pelasgian or Etruscan, the language of the inscription is substantially Teutonic. I need not remind you that the Etruscans were originally styled the " Tyrrheni-Pelasgi," previously to their settlement in Italy. The compound name denotes undoubtedly a mixture of Tyrrheni and Pelasgi; but the Pelasgic race was distinct, I think, from the Hellenic, and their language merely differed from that of the

* *Ueber die Tyrrhenischen-Pelasger in Etrurien.* Leipzig, 8vo. 1842,— pp. 39 *sqq.*

Tyrrheni by dialectic divergence. I think I can prove by independent evidence that the Pelasgic was what I call, in a broad sense, German.

The inscription is as follows, written without break from beginning to end:—

MINIKETHUMAMIMATHUMAR(A)MLIŚ;AITHIPURENAIETHEE-
RAIŚIEEPANAMINETHUNAŚTAVHELEPHU
(*Fabretti*, no. 2404, tab. xliii.)

Lepsius has rightly discerned that the inscription falls into two hexameter lines; but I differ from him slightly as to the division of the words, and in the scanning.* I should divide it as follows:—

Mīn ĭk ēthūm āmī māthū mārām lĭśīāi thīpūrēnāi;
Ēthēērāi śīēēp ānā mĭnēthū nāśt āv hēlēphū.

I proceed to analyse the inscription thus:—

1, 2. Min ik.—Two words, I think; a verb and its personal pronoun.—i. Min I take to be the first person present of *minnen, manian, minna,* 'monere,' Anglicè (or rather Scoticè), to 'mind,' or remember, in the sense of attending to.—ii. ik, again, seems to me identical with *ich, ἐγώ,* 'ego,' 'I.'†

3. ethum.—A compound, consisting of eth and um,—in relation to which I must observe that Etruscan and Teutonic compounds, otherwise identical, frequently vary in that the element which is first in place in Teutonic is placed last in Etruscan. Moreover, as observed in the Introduction *supra,* where double letters occur, such as *mb,* one of them, usually the last, is omitted in Etruscan. These are facts on which I would not of course lay undue stress here, on the theory

---

* Lepsius divides them thus:—

Mī nī kēthū mā mī māthū mārām lĭśīāi thīpūrēnāi;
Ēthē ērāi śīē ēpānā mĭnēthū nāśtāy hēlēphū.

† If taken as one word, minik may be *mein, meinige,* &c., 'meus', 'meum', mine; i.e. 'It is mine', that is, my province, or office, &c.

that the present inscription is Pelasgian; but they contribute nevertheless to what I believe to be the right understanding of the inscription. I thus read ETU-UM as UM-ETE, and compare it with *amb-acht, am-echt, amb-et, amb-t, amt*, a most ancient word, implying 'ministerium,' 'officium'—that is 'duty.' We shall find it in inscriptions purely Etruscan. MIN IK ETDUM would thus signify, 'I attend to the duty.'

4. AMI.—To be compared with ἅμα, *sam*, 'simul;' *samath* (A.-Sax.), *sam* (O. H. German), 'cum,' with; ἡμι-, *sami*, 'semi-'; or half. I think it means here simply, 'together with,' or 'with.'

5. MATHU.—Identical with the Teutonic *medo, medo, medu, meth*, implying 'mead,' the drink made from honey; and with the Sanscrit *madhu*, honey,—the Greek form, μέθυ, being applied to wine.—To be understood here as 'honey'— AMI MATHU, 'with, or mixed with honey,' perhaps half and half. The noun referred to follows. MATHU as governed by AMI—*sam*, 'with'—should be in the ablative case, which here ends in *u*, as we shall find the Etruscan ablative generally does.

6. MARAM.—The second *a* is obliterated, but I have no doubt that it has been rightly restored, and that the word is the Latin 'merum,' unmixed, that is, pure wine. The mixture of the 'merum' and honey produced the favourite drink 'mulsum,' the οἰνόμελι of the Greeks, which is here in question.

7. LIŚIAI.—I think this should be corrected to LIŚISI. According to the engraving (in Fabretti) it is LIŚIPI; but an additional stroke, where much rubbing off has already taken place, would complete the *n* and give us a word equivalent to the Teutonic *leisten*, 'præbere,' to afford or present,—the first only of the two consonants *st* being preserved, and the final vowel or diphthong of the infinitive being postponed to the final consonant, of which we shall have repeated examples in pure Etruscan—which, however, I only found upon here (*ut supra*) under reservation.

8. THIPURENAI.—To be read, I think, as *thipurendai*, or *-ntai*, by supplying (under the preceding reservation) a letter usually suppressed in Etruscan orthography, the word

being the dative singular of the present participle of a verb formed from the root διψ-, tip-, signifying 'to thirst;' from which we have, in Greek, διψάω, δίψιος, διψαλέος, διψηρὸς, and in Teutonic, *zuypilaer*, *taeplar*, *tippler*, all signifying a thirsty soul, a drinker, or (although the word is not from the same root, but from *zapf*) a toper.* This verb would be, in Teutonic form, *thipuren*; and the formation of the word (the participle) *thipurenti* would be analogous to 'sitio,' 'siti-enti,' in Latin.†—With this word the first line of the inscription—or, rather, the first of the two hexameter lines of the distich—is completed; and the sense runs thus in English,—"I attend to" (or "I fulfil") "the duty of offering pure wine mixed with honey," i. e. *mulsum*, "to the drinker." —The second verse follows :—

9. ETHEERAI.—The third person singular of the future tense of the Pelasgic (or early Teutonic) verb answering to *eiden*, 'jurare,' to swear; from *eid*, *aiths* (Gothicè), 'juramentum.' ETH would represent the transition-stage from the compound letter *ths*, *sth*, originally z, in the Gothic, to *eid*, the later German form of the word. The letters EE, in immediate sequence, are equivalent to the long e, or η. The meaning of the word would thus be, 'He'—i. e. the toper—'will swear,' &c.

10. SIEEP.—To be compared with *saufen*, *supfen*, *soepan*, *supan*, 'sorbere, bibere, immodicè bibere,' to absorb, drink down, or 'sup'—in the sense of the old English song (which is much to the purpose here)—

"But might I of Jove's nectar sup,
I would not change for thine!"

The double letter EE, as in the preceding word, represents a

---

* From *zapf*, a cork or stopple, and, *per meton.*, wine; whence *zapfenambacht*, the office of him who 'vinum promit,'—while the Thaliarchus of the feast, the "arbiter bibendi," is described as *sapfner* and *torper*, 'toper.' THIPURANAI may perhaps be derived from this latter root; but the etymology suggested in the text appears to be the closer.

† 'Esurio,' to be hungry, is the same original word (thus thoroughly Pelasgic),—the s representing the ψ, and the initial d or th being abraded. This shews that the primary sense was a general one, to long for food, the distinction between thirst and hunger being secondary.

long *e*, or *η*.—ETHEERAI SIEEP thus signifies, 'He will swear that he sups,' or 'drinks,' &c.

11. ANA.—The *an*, *ana*, *ane*, 'sine,' or 'without,' of the old German, now written *ohne*. Compare the Greek ἄνευ.

12. MINETHU.—The Teutonic *meineid*, perjury. In the ablative case, marked by *u*. The two letters ETH are much obliterated; but the accepted reading is, I doubt not, correct.

13. NAST.—Identical, if I mistake not, with the word *nest*, 'cibaria,' used in the middle ages in the compound *fart-nest*, *wegn-nest*, to express the Christian 'viaticum,' the Holy Eucharist, by which life and health are ministered to the soul,—the root being *nasan*, 'convalescere.' Long ago I came to the conclusion that the word 'nectar' was a form collateral and akin to this Teutonic *nest*; and here, I think, we must, conversely, translate NAST by 'nectar,' as by what follows:—

14. AV.—The 'ab,' ἀπό, *af*, *of*,—signifying 'de,' or 'from,' of the Indo-European languages. And lastly,

15. HELEPHU.—The ablative of 'Olympus,'—the *m*, as usual in the case of compound letters, being omitted.—This second verse therefore reads thus:—"He" (the drinker) "will swear, without perjury, that he sups nectar from Olympus!"

The result, I submit, is—and you will appreciate it more fully hereafter—that, while the above analysis exhibits some variation from pure Etruscan forms—while the word MARAM seems indubitably to be the Latin 'merum'—and while the words AMI and THIPURENAI may be set aside as common alike to German, Greek, and Latin, we have, nevertheless, in MIN IK, ETHUM, LIEINI, SIEEP, ANA MINETHU, and NAST AV, words, compounds, and forms unmistakeably Teutonic,—and thus the Pelasgic speech (if this be Pelasgic) was, like the Etruscan (as we shall see in time), a dialect of archaic German. The word MATHU is especially important in this regard, as it certainly, from the context here, signifies 'honey,' being thus identical with the Sanscrit form and sense, and closely akin in both to the German 'mead;' whereas both in Greek and Latin 'honey' is expressed by μέλι, 'mel;' and μέθυ has the full signification of 'wine.' What further is peculiarly interesting is the fact, pointed out (as has been said) by Lepsius, that the two lines are hexameters—the earliest thus existing in the German language. They may be imitated as follows in the same metre in modern English:—

"Mine is the task the honey-mix'd wine to present to the drinker,—
'Gods!' he will swear—nor falsely—'tis nectar fresh from Olympus!'"

This inscription must be (for an European one) of great antiquity. The letters *m* and *n* are written in the oldest form, the *p* and *t*, and the *ph*, likewise ancient; the letter *s* is throughout of the dentated, or serrated form, which I call *san*. In keeping with this, the style of the pottery is very ancient and Egyptian-like; and the tomb in which the "little black pot" was discovered is one of a group, the most important of which exhibits in its architecture and otherwise a striking similarity to the Cyclopic gallery at Tiryns and the Treasuries of Mycenæ and Orchomenus, works of the Tyrrheni-Pelasgi in Greece,—inducing the opinion, according to Mr. Dennis, that it "must be considered as of a remoter period" than the Tarquins, "coeval at least with the earliest days of Rome—prior, it may be, to the foundation of the city."* But for this judgment, founded mainly upon the fact that the builder was unacquainted with the principle of the arch as exhibited in the Cloaca

* *Cities, &c.*, vol. ii. pp. 45 sqq.

Maxima, we might have indulged in the speculation that the little drinking-vessel which has come down to us through so many ages may have done duty at banquets attended by Tarquin the Proud and his gallant son Aruns, when they found refuge at Cære among their kindred after the fall of the early monarchy of Rome.*

SECTION II.—*Inscription of the 'Vinicopium.'*

Another inscription which Dr. Lepsius pronounces to be Pelasgian is described by him as written upon a vase of black pottery formerly in Cardinal Borgia's Museum, and then in the Hall of Bronzes of the 'Museo Borbonico' at Naples; where, however, according to Fabretti, it is no longer now to be found —broken, I should fear, or mislaid. Where it was discovered is not stated, but the black earth of the pottery and the style of orthography suggest the idea that it may likewise have come from Cære.

* Dr. Donaldson translates the inscription thus,—" I am not dust; I am ruddy wine on burnt ashes; when" (or "if") "there is burning-heat under ground, I am water for thirsty lips." He recognises ΜΑΤΗΥ as μίθυ, madhu; but this is the only point of agreement between the versions here before the reader. He connects ΜΑΝΑΜ with "the root mar- found in Μάρων (the grandson of Bacchus), and in "Ιο-μαρος, the site of his vineyards (see Odym. ix. 198 sqq.)," and considers it as "probably signifying 'ruddy' (μαίρω, μαίρω, &c.)."—"ΛΙΣΙΑΙ is the locative of lisis, an old word corresponding to lix, 'ashes mingled with water.'—ΤΗΙΡΥΒΕΝΑΙ is an adjective in concord with lisisi, and probably containing the same root as tepidus, tephrul, teforom, &c. ... ΕΤΗΕ is some particle of condition or time. ΕΒΑΙ is the locative of ἔρα, earth." ... ΕΡΑΝΑ he connects with ἄστυ, and makes it synonymous with torres; and infers that ΝΕΤΗΥ " means water" from the name of ΝΕΤΗΥΝΣ = Neptunus. "The root is ne-, and appears under a slightly different development in the next word, ΝΑΣΤΑΥ (comp. νασμός, ναθμός, O. H. G. naz), which is probably a locative in -φι, agreeing with ΝΕΛΣΦΙΟ, and this may be referred to χυλός, Æolicè χύλλος, Latin helno, &c."—*Varronianus*, pp. 199, 200.

The inscription is as follows, written round the pot, as in the preceding instance:—

MINIMULVENEKEVELTHUIRPUPLIANA
(*Fabretti*, no. 2014.*)

Dr. Lepsius divides the words as in the preceding inscription, but not in accordance with any suggested interpretation,† and as the letters run (as he states) consecutively, without break, I am entitled to deal with it independently. I thus read it,—

MINI MUL VENEKEVELTHU IR PUPLIANA.

I may state at once that I believe the vaso to have been a cup specially used for the entertainment given on the occasion of the conclusion of bargains to the *weinkaufleuthe, weinkauffsleute*, as they are called in ancient and especially Low-German—the witnesses to the *weinkauff, wincop*, or 'vinicopium.' 'Een goede maeltydt,' a handsome supper, and 'een stoop wyn,' a *modium* of wine, are specified among the propines, or offerings, which celebrated such occasions. You must not be startled, here or hereafter, at finding customs—familiar to us as of yesterday—in full life and observance, and described to us in these inscriptions by the very same Teutonic words and combinations of words, in times long anterior to history. I render this inscription as follows:—

1. MINI.—Conf. 'manus,' good, as in the Latin title 'Cerus Manus' interpreted as 'Creator bonus' by Festus;

* He prints it according to Dr. Lepsius' division of the words; but it should have been given, as inscribed, without break.
† Lepsius writes it, (*Ueber die Tyrrhen.-Pelasger*, p. 42,)—

MI NI MULVENE KEVELSU IR PUPLIANA.

while, the letters *b* and *m* being interchangeable in the oldest tongues, 'manus' and 'bonus' are one and the same word, with a merely dialectical difference. This is the only word in the inscription which is of dubious paternity.

2. MUL.—The Teutonic *mal, mahl*, a meal, or feast. MINI MUL is thus the *goede maeltydt* above spoken of. The addition *-tydt*, tide or time, is equally involved in the word here in question, as *mal* signifies 'time' or 'tide' in one sense, as *mahl* does 'convivium' in another.

3. VENEKEVELTHU.—A compound, analysable as VENE-KEVE-LTHU,—and corresponding in Tyrrheno-Pelasgic with the *wein-kauff-leuthe* above spoken of; a name descriptive of "homines qui propinationi vinariæ in fidem ac testimonium contractus consummati interfuerunt."* The word here is, I take it, in the dative case. You will observe, in the case of compounds like this, that each several element in the compound must be reckoned henceforward as a distinct word. On the same principle every well-ascertained Pelasgian or Etruscan word suggests the existence of a host of etymological kindred, whose acquaintance we may expect some day to make, and whose lineaments we may anticipate by Teutonic analogy even before we come face to face with them.

4. IA.—The Teutonic *er, ere, ehre*, honour.—'In honour' of.—The word *ehrenwein*, 'honorarium vinum,' 'vinum quod regibus et potentibus honoris gratiâ offertur,' is in point here, although the cup of honour is offered to less exalted personages than those contemplated in modern Germany.

5. FUPLIANA.—The Etruscan 'Phuphluns,' or Bacchus,—a title compounded of i. FUPLI, 'Phuphl;' and, ii. ANA, or *ans*, 'deus,' or deity. †

The inscription thus signifies,—" A good " or handsome " feast to the bargain-witnesses," with " wine of honour," or " in honour of Phuphluns,"—

---

* See also *leikauf, litkop* (whence 'licopium'), and *leikauffe-leuthe*, in the lexicons of Scherz, Haltaus, &c.

† For the etymology of PHUPHLUNS see the abridged Glossary, in the Appendix.

the name, like that of "veteris Bacchi," being equally appropriate to the god and the liquor,—the *stoop wyn* being thus evidently the accompaniment of the *goede maeltydt*, or more substantial entertainment.* The line seems to be an hexameter.

I come to the same conclusion as regards the present homely inscription as that which I have ventured upon in regard to its more poetical sister, viz., that, whether Pelasgic or Tyrrhenian, it is fundamentally Teutonic. From the variations in orthography, strongly resembling those in the inscription of Cære (or Agylla) I have little doubt it represents the speech of the Pelasgic element in the Tyrrheno-Pelasgian race. But one important fact transpires from it, viz., that, if Pelasgic, the Pelasgi worshipped the God of Wine, not as Dionysus but as Phuphluns, the 'God of the Vine'—Φαμπλ-ος, 'pampin-us,'—that is, by his well-ascertained Etruscan name, which was quite unknown to the Hellenes and Romans. This affords additional proof that the difference in dialect between the Tyrrheni and Pelasgi must have been very slight.

The probability is that this vase of the old 'Museo Borgia' is of great antiquity.

SECTION III.—*The Inscription of Mark the Potter.*

The most important Tyrrheno-Pelasgic inscription of Cære—after those just analysed—is found scratched on the outside of a *crater*, or vase for pouring wine into smaller vessels, which has come down to us " ancor crudo," still unbaked. It runs as

* Dr. Donaldson translates it, "I am not of Mulva, nor Tolshull, but Populonia."—*Varron.*, p. 201.

follows; and you will, I think, recognise it as an hexameter likewise:—

|ᴜᴜɴᴀ ʟᴀᴘʜᴛʜɪ · ᴍᴀʀᴋᴇɪ · ᴋᴜʀɪᴇᴀꜱ ı | ᴋʟᴜᴛʜɪ · ɪᴜᴋɪᴇ · *
(*Fabretti*, no. 2400 *d*, tab. xliii.)†

The first four words run entirely round the vase; the two last are inserted in a second line below them. The sense seems to be as follows:—

1. Iᴜᴜɴᴀ.—To be compared with the Teutonic *jane, jone,* 'profecto non,'—answering to our 'Don't you?' 'Is not?' or 'Are not?' It appears to me to be formed of i. *ja*, yea, yes; and, ii. a compound analogous to the Latin 'anne,' but in the negative sense of interrogation.

2. ʟᴀᴘʜᴛʜʟ.—To be compared with *läufftig,* 'versatus in aliquâ re, peritus,' skilled as a workman.

3. ᴍᴀʀᴋᴇɪ.—This may be either the very ancient word *mark, merk,* 'signum,' sign, token, mark, monogram, &c. and perhaps in the plural; or the personal name 'Marko,' or 'Marcus,' which we shall find in one of the purely Etruscan inscriptions, *infra*. This last is the more likely alternative.

4. ᴋᴜʀɪᴇᴀꜱ.—A noun, I think, akin to κεραμεὺς, a potter, and having that signification.—Not from the O.N. and A.-Sax. *hverr, hver*, a pot or vase, which was always of metal; but from *kiar*, black,—black *ἔρα*, or earth. I am uncertain whether it is in the nominative or genitive case.

5. ᴋʟᴜᴛɪɪɪ.—From the root *hlu* (a variety of *hru*), whence *hliud*, 'sonare,' *lauten*, 'celebrare,' *hlium, hliumunt, hliuma*, 'rumor,' fame, *hliumuntig*, famous, &c. The Greek κλυτὸς has the same signification, but the υ is short. ᴋʟᴜᴛɪɪɪ is an early form, apparently, of *hliumuntig*.

6. ɪᴜᴋɪᴇ.—The familiar Teutonic *iuch*, 'vos, vobis,' *euch*. Here in the dative case.

---

* The letter *a* is of the Upper Italic type, and the *ph* of the Greek. The *s* is the *sigma*, not the dentated character. Iᴜᴜɴᴀ is printed Iᴜɴᴀ in Fabretti's text. The upright line denotes here, and elsewhere, the termination of a line in the original.

† He does not say where the vase is preserved.

I translate the inscription, alternatively, as "Is not the mark (seal or signature) of the skilled potter,"— or "Is not the skilled potter Marke"—"known to you by fame"—"famous among you?" This last appears to me the preferable, because the more special, reading, as the artist would naturally wish to record his name to posterity.*

* I suspect that Marke was accustomed to insert this verse upon the vessels he manufactured, and that they were highly prized as relics of the early art of Cære,—it is hardly likely otherwise than an unbaked vase like this should have been preserved and placed in a tomb. It strikes me too as probable that, long afterwards, when the peculiar dialect of Cære had died out or was but little understood, and the Greek and Roman antiquaries busied themselves with the subject, a misunderstanding of this inscription gave rise to the report transmitted to us by Pliny, that when Demaratus the merchant of Corinth, the alleged ancestor of the Tarquins, migrated to Italy and settled at Tarquinii, he brought with him two artists, Eucheir and Eugrammos, who introduced the potter's art into Etruria. All these names find their raison d'être in the foregoing inscription. The Pelasgic LAPHTHI, 'skilled,' and KCR-, this last misunderstood as the old Latin 'hir,' χείρ, the hand, would give precisely the same meaning as Εὔχειρ, and γράμμα has exactly the same sense as mark, understood as a noun, ut supra, and would produce Εὐγράμμος. Even LAPHTHI might be confounded in sound and signification with leute, δῆμος, the people, and with liebt-, ἀροτός, desirable or beloved,—a confusion which would be quite sufficient to produce the name 'Demaratus.' The words IOUVA, misread as jang, 'juvenis,' with the dual sense, perhaps, of 'binns,' ('bis'='duis') twin, twin or twain, and LAPHTHI conceived of as the name 'Demaratus' in the genitive case (Latin), would at once suggest the legend, "The two young men of Demaratus, Eugrammos and Eucheir," &c. I have no doubt myself that the Tarquinii were of purely Etruscan race—that their first home was Cære—that they afterwards removed to Tarquinii, but kept up friendly relations still with their former fellow-citizens, one branch of the family apparently continuing to flourish there—and that the supposed migration from Corinth was simply a migration from the 'ager Cæritanus,' from Cære to Tarquinii. Mr. Dennis remarks that the pottery of Cære has nothing in common with that of Corinth or Sicyon. (*Cities and Cemeteries*, vol. i. p. 357.) The statement of Tacitus that Demaratus taught the Etruscans alphabetic writing (*ibid.*, p. 375) may be similarly illustrated by the fact that one of the oldest Pelasgic alphabets and syllabaries existing is found on a pot of Cære (see *Fabretti's Corpus*, no. 2403), now preserved in the Vatican. The probability is that these alphabets were frequently inscribed on the pottery there; and this, in connexion with the present inscription, misread as suggested, would complete the legend.

Section IV.—*Minor Inscriptions of Cære.*

There are yet a few inscriptions of Cære which seem to belong to the Pelasgic period and dialect. They are of slight importance in themselves, but any relic of Pelasgic antiquity is precious. One of them is inscribed under the foot—" sub pede"—of a *cylix*, a cup, or goblet, now preserved in the Vatican,—

AVIPARGL

(*Fabretti*, no. 2409.)

—The 'g' is expressed by an Old-Greek and Old-Italic, but originally Phœnician character which is not to be found in the purely Etruscan inscriptions, in which 'g' and 'k' are both expressed by 'k.' AVIPARGL must be divided as AVIP ARGL; and of these two words the first, AVIP, appears to me identical with *umbi*, 'for,' and ARGL with *ergeilen*, 'lætari,' to be merry or (the identical word) 'jolly,'—the root GL, *geil*, *gul*, suggesting indeed the idea of luxury in eating rather than drinking. The general sense would seem to be, " For enjoyment." Our modern 'regalo' and 'regale' express this general sense of the root.

Two or three others, very short, inscribed on vases, appear to me to denote the names of their (intended) contents, as we constantly see on modern majolica pots, marked ' Mustarda,' ' Cicorea,' &c. in Italy. I think the measures are also sometimes indicated; but without knowing the precise capacity or weight of the respective vessels it would be too adventurous to suggest translations. The word

KUSIACH.

or, as I read the final letter (at least in the Etruscan

inscriptions proper), KUSIASCH, on the "parvus lapis (grigia e rozza)," given by Fabretti as no. 2398, but without saying where it is preserved, seems to me to indicate standard-weight,—*geeichtes gewicht*, or *aichmass*,[*]—the elements of the compound being reversed, as usual—at least, I must again say, in Etruscan.

The two names upon the bronze mirror, no. 2346 *bis d* of Fabretti, representing a youth (of an Apollinean type) seated, with the title PHAUN, and a girl standing on her toes, as if in the act of dancing, in front of him, and looking upwards, with the title of EVHPHIA, represent, as it appears to me, Favonius, the West-wind, otherwise Zephyrus, and his love Pitys, who was changed by the jealous Boreas into a pine-tree, her name being here given in the O. Northern, O. High German, and Anglo-Saxon form as *foraha, furh, fir*, that is EVRPU-IA, equivalent to the Greek Πίτυς. This word for the pine is common to the Teutonic and (in the form of *bor*) to the Slavonic languages. The lover of Pitys is variously described as Pan and Favonius, but PHAUN, equivalent to PHAVN, seems to me to indicate the latter deity. Max Müller connects 'Pan' with the Sanscrit 'pavana,' wind,—this is equally, or rather still more applicable to 'Favonius.' The antagonism of the forms *bor*, or *for-*, and πίτυς may perhaps have suggested the idea of the jealousy of 'Boreas.' The original word 'fir' may be still recognisable in the initial syllable of 'resina,' ῥητίνη, resin.

[*] It is possible that KUSIASCH may correspond exactly with the Zendic 'açperenanômazi,' signifying a measure or quantity equivalent to an 'açperena,' a weight corresponding with the 'dirhem,' and which is explained as answering to the 'dûdâ' in Huzvaresh and 'zûzâ' in Aramaic. See Justi's *Handbuch der Zendsprache*, p. 38.

Section V.—*The formula* Κόγξ ὄμπαξ.

The independent evidence which I mentioned *supra*, as proving that the Pelasgic was a Teutonic speech, may be subjoined here as ancillary to the inscriptions just dealt with. It consists of the formula κόγξ ὄμπαξ, with which, according to Hesychius, the hierophant dismissed the initiated at the close of the Eleusinian Mysteries. It has been interpreted in many ways, as involving unthought-of depths of mysterious knowledge. I read it as, simply, *Gang zu ambachs*, or *zum bachs* "Go (gang) to your (practical) duties," *i.e.* "Go about your business!" The word μπάξ, or πάξ, is the same of which we have had an example, in the first of the preceding inscriptions, in the compound ETUUM, ϹΜ-ΕΤΠ, *ambahs*, 'officium, ministerium;' and we shall meet with it more than once hereafter. It may be compared with the 'fex,' which terminates the Latin compounds 'pontifex,' 'carnifex,' &c.; and has a meaning akin to 'fac-ere,' *fyka*, &c. In all these words the initial consonant in 'f-ex,' π-άξ, represents the partially abraded *umb*, or ἀμφί. This Eleusinian form of dismissal is analogous to that with which the (Roman) priest of the Great Goddess, variously named Ceres, Diana, Venus, Isis, &c., dismisses the people after the restoration of Lucius (in the 'Metamorphoses' of Apuleius) to the human shape, turning to them on the threshold and pronouncing "sermone rituque Græciensi, ita, λαοῖς ἄφεσις." And the same general form is observed in the 'Ite: missa est!' with which, as pronounced by the priest, the Mass concludes in the R. Catholic office; where, as observed by the editor of the

Delphin edition of Apuleius, "missa est missio, ἄφεσις." The moral signification of the Eleusinian is wanting however to these more recent forms of dismissal.

In these Pelasgic inscriptions, as I think I may call them, you will notice, certainly, a marked contrast between the open and flowing style of orthography which characterizes them and the more rugged blocks (so to speak) of sound which will meet us in the inscriptions of other localities than Cære or Agylla. "Two periods," according to Mommsen, "in the history of the (Etruscan) language are clearly to be distinguished. In the older period the vocalisation of the language was completely carried out, and the collision of two consonants was almost without exception avoided. To this period belong such inscriptions as those on the earthen vases of Cære. . . . By throwing off both the vocal and consonantal terminations, and by softening down or expelling the vowels, this soft and melodious language gradually degenerated and became intolerably harsh and rugged." And he refers, as indicating the sound of the language at this later period, to the opening words of the great inscription of Perugia—the last of those which I have translated in this volume.* This Perugian inscription is doubtless comparatively recent, but I am not sure whether a softer and a harsher dialect—the Tyrrheno-Pelasgic of Agylla and the rougher Etruscan (for example) of the very ancient inscription at Tarquinii, to be discussed in the ensuing

* *Earliest Inhabitants of Italy; from* . . '*History of Rome*,'—*translated by Geo. Robinson*, 8vo. 1858, p. 52.

section—did not exist contemporaneously in Etruria. The Tyrrheni-Pelasgi may have taken up various words and adopted certain superficial modifications during the residence of those who spoke it in Greece; but the original Teutonic stamp—judging by the preceding specimens—was never effaced.

CHAPTER II.

INSCRIPTION, PURELY ETRUSCAN, IN A TOMB AT TARQUINII.

IF the hexameters dealt with in the preceding chapter betoken a Pelasgian laxity of morals in regard to wine, you shall have, in the inscription that now follows, an Etruscan homily against excess— although addressed against indulgence in eating rather than drinking. It runs thus:—

KIVESANAMATVESIKALESEKE I EURASVKLESVASPHESTHP-
CHVACHA
(*Fabretti*, no. 2301, tab. xlii.)

This inscription exists (or did so till lately) on the walls of a sepulchre discovered on the hill of Montarozzi, part of the metropolis of ancient Tarquinii, in 1827; and known now as the 'Grotta dello Iscrizioni,' and 'della Camera Finta.' It is found in immediate proximity and evident relation to a painting representing a youth leaning over a pan or vessel for the purpose of cooking a fish which he holds in his hand; an old man, holding a forked stick in his left hand, stands opposite to him on the other side, in the act of addressing him. Both are naked. The subject has been taken for a superstitious sacrifice, a magical conjuration, or a process of ordinary cookery; and the last, as it is the simplest, seems likewise to be the most correct explanation.* The tomb, when opened,

---

* Mr. Dennis observes, "It is possible that the stool"—(what I have spoken of as a pan or vessel)—"is a sort of altar, and that the boy is

was covered with scenes representing feasting and revelry. The inscription has (as you will have observed) only one break in it, the words being written, as in the preceding instances, without division except to that extent; but they stand naturally apart when submitted to analysis, and are to be divided thus,—

KIVEBAN AMAT VESIK AL ESEKE: EUNAS-VKLE SVAS PHES THP CHVACHA.

—I take them in order:—

1. KIVESAN.—To be compared and (I submit) identified with *quasen*, 'crapulari,' to feed luxuriously,—formed from *quas*, 'crapula,' 'luxuria,' gluttony; whence—the initial *q* being rubbed off and *s* read as *f*—our English 'feast.'

2. AMAT.—Compare with the Gothic *ambat*, 'servus, minister;' *ambacht*, 'qui ministerium habet, officiatus, Lat. Barb. anbactus;' *ambacht*, 'officium, cura, ministerium,'—all of them forms of the very ancient word already twice noticed. The '*b*' in the compound *mb* is dropped, according to the rule in Etruscan orthography above laid down. AMAT here means 'minister,' or 'servant.'

3. VESIK.—To be identified with *fisc*, 'piscis,' fish.

4. AL.—The root found in ancient German as *al*-, to burn; *alan* (M.-Goth.), *ala* (O. N. and Suio-Goth., or Swedish), *aelan* (A.-Sax.), 'accendere, alere;' *aeld*, fire,—and, the *l* being interchanged for *r*, 'ur-,' as in 'uror,' *wüp*, *feuer*, fire, &c.

5. ESEKE.—Compare with *aischen*, *eischen*, *heischen*, 'petere, exigere,' to demand or require.—The first half of the inscription would thus run, in its general sense, "The minister of

making an offering to the other figure, which may represent a divinity. I have heard it designated—'the God of chastity;' and there are features which favour this conjecture. It would probably be explained could we interpret a long Inscription in Etruscan characters over the head of this figure." But, he adds, "in our present ignorance of the Etruscan language, all attempts at translating this or other inscriptions, except proper names or other recurring formulæ, must be mere guess-work."—*Cities*, &c., vol. i. p. 342.

D

the banquet," either the gentleman or his cook, "requires," or orders the attendant, "to burn (boil, or roast) fish." *

The second portion of the inscription suggests the moral occasioned by this excessive pitch of epicurism,—for, as presumed, we have to deal here with feasting, not fasting:—

6. EURAS-VKLE.—A compound, identical, I think, with the Teutonic *vielfrass*, a gormandiser, or glutton,—the two elements, EURAS, or *frass*, and VKLE or *viel*, being, as is usually the case, reversed in the Etruscan.—i. EURAS would thus correspond with the old German *frass*, 'luxuria,' *frassa*, 'helluari*; (derived from a common root with *quas*, 'crapula,' *ut supra*; but retaining the *r* which has been abraded in the later form;) and, ii. VKLE would be identical with *mikil*, *meikle* (Scotticè), *viel*, or 'much,' through the interchange of *v* and *m* (as, *e.g.* in 'mad-' and 'wet,' &c.),—the Greek πολὺ forming a halfway-house between the *m* on one side and the *v*, *f*, or rather digamma, on the other. Possibly VKLE and *viel-* may be a degeneration from an earlier *bulk*, the belly (akin to *bauch*, our Scottish *buckie*), in the sense of EURAS-VKLE, *frass-bulk*, a belly-god.' †

7. SVAS.—To be compared with *sus*, *suss*, *suyss*, 'strepitus conviventium, luxuria;' *sol* (A.-Sax. and Bromisch dialect), 'fatuus;' and even *sus*, a pig.—An adjective, I think, implying 'noisy, obstreperous.'

8. PUFS.—Compare with *feist*, *faett*, 'pinguis,' fat; and the Latin 'obesus.'

9. THP.—Compare with *doup*, 'stup-idus,' *toupen*, 'stupidum

---

* I should have taken AL EBEKE as one word, ALEBEKE, answering to the peculiarly Scandinavian word *aelskn*, 'amare,' (metor. from fire,) in the sense of loving, that is, liking fish, had not the painting appeared to represent an order given by a superior to an attendant.

† Alternative meanings sometimes suggest themselves which (as in the preceding instance) are worth noticing; and in this case it is just possible that EURAS-VKLE may be read as *surash-buckler* in what I believe to have been the early signification of that word; or divided as EURA-SVKLE and read—EURA *as immer*, ever, and SVALE as *swaig*, 'helluo,' a glutton—in the dialect of Bremen.

fieri,' *toupheit,* 'surditas, stultitia,'—the Scottish 'dowff.' *Th, t,* and *d* in these words are all softened forms of the compound *st* in 'stupidus,' *st* being identical with *s.*

10. CHVACHA.—Transmutable into German orthography as SCHWASCHA, the Etruscan *ch* answering (as has been said, and will be seen), by an almost invariable rule, to the Teutonic *sch.* Compare *schwach,* 'debilis,' weak; *schwachen,* 'debilitare, deficere,' &c.—The sense of these five words therefore is,—" The glutton [is] noisy," (sottish, or like a pig,) " fat, stupid, weak."

The two portions of the inscription thus answer to each other, and agree in sense with the two portions of the painting to which they bear reference, and also with the general character of the scenes depicted in the tomb. These paintings are qualified by Mr. Dennis as the most archaic among the many existing at Tarquinii, bearing "a closer affinity than any other Etruscan paintings yet discovered, both in design and colouring, to those in the 'Grotta Campana' at Veii—unquestionably the most ancient specimens of pictorial art extant in Italy or Europe." * The 'Grotta Campana' contains no inscriptions, and the inscription above analysed may therefore be considered (so far as this collateral evidence from the paintings goes) the oldest written monument of the Etruscan proper—that is, as I hope to prove, of the German—language now in existence. The calligraphy is decidedly ancient; the *sigma* alone is used, and the *th* is in the older form, with the dot in the middle of the circle which forms the character.†

---

* *Cities and Cemeteries,* vol. L p. 343.

† I have little doubt that rules for judging of the comparative antiquity of Etruscan inscriptions may be gathered from an extended study of the varying styles of orthography, and the modifications in the shape or use of particular letters,—I have noticed some points of comparison and shall

The preceding inscription, you will allow, is very creditable to the Spartan morality of the early Etruscans—where uncorrupted by the softer associations of Agylla."

continue to do so,—the most certain indication of antiquity is when the 'm' and 'n' have one leg or fang (usually that to the right) much longer than the others. But I speak with diffidence on points of calligraphy, nor shall I make any attempt (for as yet it would be premature) to discriminate between the language of North and South Etruria, and the minor local dialects. My estimate of the antiquity of the inscriptions is mainly based upon the argument from architecture and painting, as more or less archaic.

" Some vases, found exclusively, I believe, at Vulci, of a festive or Bacchic kind, and some even of severer character, bear inscriptions in Greek characters, but at first sight totally unintelligible. These have been supposed to be either written in an "unknown tongue" or "in some cases," possibly, according to the learned Gerhard, "in Etruscan, in Greek letters." (See Mr. Dennis's *Cities and Cemeteries*, vol. i. p. lxxxvii; and the 'Annals' of the Roman 'Institute,' vol. for 1831, *passim*.) Neither of these suggestions are, I think, correct. With one exception—υαθαωοχει—which seems to represent 'Phopbion-Iacche'—such of these inscriptions as I have examined are of a description which had better not have been written—not indeed implying any revolting guilt, but such as to have induced the calligraphists to disguise their meaning (in the case of certain words) by transposition of some letters and substitution or interpolation of others, out of regard to decency. Some of the words too are written according to the phonetic pronunciation, as still current in modern Greek. These inscriptions are evidently Greek,—I mention this to vindicate the Etruscan from the discredit attaching to their authorship. There is not, so far as I can see, an Etruscan word among them. These vases of Vulci, observes Mr. Dennis, are "of the Attic type, of that severe and archaic design which is always connected with black figures on a yellow ground," and their date, according to Gerhard, is between the 74th and 124th Olympiad, B.C. 184–284. (Dennis, *Cities*, &c., vol. i. p. 425.) They must either be of Greek importation, or the work of Greek artists, perhaps a colony of them, settled at Vulci, hereditary potters.

CHAPTER III.

THE 'ALCESTIS AND ADMETUS' INSCRIPTION.

This occurs on an *amphora* described by Mr. Dennis as "in the late style; with a Bacchic dance on one side and on the other a striking scene of the parting of Admetus and Alcestis, whose names "—ATMITE, ALKSTI—" are attached between the figures of Charun armed with his hammer and another demon brandishing serpents." Mr. Dennis has given an engraving of this scene in the frontispiece to his second volume " as a very rare and curious specimen of undoubted Etruscan ceramography, in its natural colours," red, black, and white. The design is wholly Etruscan, rude, although highly graphic—very different from that on those vases and mirrors which exhibit the full influence of classical taste. The inscription must therefore be of corresponding relative antiquity. I should add that the demon brandishing serpents (NATHUM, probably, or 'Necessity') points them at Admetus as threatening death; while Charun at the other extremity of the composition is about to strike Alcestis; and the inscription is written in a narrow strip of letters between him and her. The self-devotion of Alcestis is thus clearly indicated in the composition, and the presumption must be that the inscription, occupying the particular place it does, has—not a general character but a special one, referring to her intervention and self-sacrifice. This *amphora* was discovered at Vulci, was afterwards in possession of the learned Dr. Emil Braun at Rome, and then passed into that of the Duc de Luynes. The inscription runs as follows:—

Eᴋᴀ : ᴇʀsᴋᴇ : ɴᴀᴋ : ᴀᴄʜʀᴜᴍ : ᴘʜʟᴇʀᴛʜʀᴋᴇ
(*Fabretti*, no. 2598, tab. xliv. *Dennis*, vol. i. p. 90.)

—I analyse it thus:—

1, 2, 3. Eᴋᴀ : ᴇʀsᴋᴇ : ɴᴀᴋ.—i. Eᴋᴀ-ɴᴀᴋ forms a compound, answering (but I am uncertain whether as the first person singular of the present tense of a verb, or as a derivative noun) to *nachhangen*, (from *nach* and *hang-en*,) signifying 'consectari, inhærere tergo fugientis,' that is, to pursue, hang upon, or run down,—but with the elements of the compound in the reverse order to that we are familiar with in German. The root *hang* might be traced further back, e.g. to *ag-*, as in '*ago*'—(" paratâ executione agere "),—but the above is sufficient for my purpose here.—ii. ᴇʀsᴋᴇ is a formation from *wer*, 'cautio, vades, fidejussor, sponsor securitatis,' in modern German *gewähr*,—akin to *warscipe* (A.-S.), *werschaft*, 'cautio de indemnitate et possessione tranquillâ,'—and derived from *waren*, 'cautionem adhibere'—to offer legal security on behalf either of oneself or another—'guarandia' or *guarantee*, (formed from *gWär*) being the English equivalent; while the Latin form 'caution' is still preserved in Scottish law. Eᴋᴀ : ᴇʀsᴋᴇ : ɴᴀᴋ thus signifies (to take the first of the above alternatives) 'I pursue,' or 'attach (legally) the guarantor,' or surety,—viz., in this case, Alcestis, who had offered herself, virtually, as such, in order to redeem her husband from imminent death.

4. ᴛʜʀᴋᴇ.—This word, although written consecutively to ᴘᴜʟᴇʀ, without break, is independent of it, a distinct vocable, as shown by many other examples.—Compare *durch*, 'per,' through. ᴛᴜʀᴋᴇ, written also ᴛʀᴋᴇ, constantly occurs in connection with some specified sin or penalty, and thus is not identical with *truge*, 'fraus, dolus,' as might otherwise be

CHAP. III.   ON THE ALCESTIS AND ADMETUS AMPHORA.   39

supposed.* The word immediately preceding and governed by THRKE is

5. PULES,—a word constantly found, like THRKE, TURKE, in the inscriptions upon votive offerings in atonement for various descriptions of guilt. It corresponds with *slur*, *flur* (equivalent to *verlust*), signifying 'damnum'—'damnum' being the technical Latin word for loss, hurt, fine, mulct, or penalty. I think it means loss, in the sense of forfeiture, here. The last word to be dealt with is

6. ACHRUM.—To be read ASCHRUM, the letter ↓ having (I am pretty sure) the force of *sch* in Etruscan; and divided as ASCH-RUM.—i. ASCH corresponds with *aisch-en*, *heisch-en*, 'expetere, exigere, citare,' (the word which we have met with as ESEKE in the preceding inscription,) *heisch-ung*, *aisch-ung*, *aisch-e*, 'citatio,' this last word being almost identical in form with the Etruscan ASCH:—And, ii. RUM answers to an ancient Teutonic word *rum*, *rahm*, implying 'terminus, scopus,' *gesetztes ziel*, prescribed limit (*up den rum* signifying 'tempore definito'), but including, in understanding and practice, the intervening *raum*, or space of time and opportunity allowed to the person summoned, and constituting the *guernacht*, *dwerchnacht*, or *swerehnacht* of old Teutonic law.†

* And still less (I submit) with the Icelandic *at tregu*, 'angere aut dolere,' *tregi*, 'dolor,' *threk*, 'gravis labor, molestia,' as urged in his commentary on this inscription by Dr. Donaldson; who founds perhaps his strongest plea for the affinity of the Scandinavians and Etruscans on the argument "that the words *three* and *suthi*, constantly occurring on Etruscan monuments of a funereal character, are translated at once by the Icelandic synonyms *tregi* and *sut*, both signifying 'grief' or 'sorrow.' If we had only this fact," he adds, "we should be induced by it to seek for further resemblances between the old languages of Northern Europe and the obscure fragments of the old Etruscan."—*Varron.*, pp. 209, 210.

† I at one time thought that NAK: THRKE denoted the *dwerchnacht*, and was disposed to connect it with the space of time, two days and a night, prescribed by Hercules to Admetus in the play of Sophocles as a period of silence and reserve, after the former hero had fought with Thanatos, or Death, and brought Alcestis back, and restored her to her husband, from the grave. It was then only, on the morning of the third day that her consecration to the Infernal Gods through death would have been done away. It appeared to me that the period of purification or rehabilitation corresponded thus with that of 'citatio' in the case of the voluntary victim. I gave up this view of the above passage with great reluctance.

By similar understanding and practice this *ram*, 'terminus,' seems to have acquired the additional sense of pledge or plight to appear, confirmed by the hand (*ram*, 'manus'); and it occurs with accessary words indicative of that idea in an inscription presently to be dealt with, where I shall revert to the subject.

The present inscription, therefore, reads, "I pursue, or attach, the guarantor" (Alcestis) "through breach of engagement" (on the part of Admetus, the principal) "to appear at the fixed term of citation."*

---

* Dr. Donaldson translates the inscription thus,—'This earthen vessel in the ground is a votive offering of sorrow.'—*Varron.*, p. 209. Mr. Dennis was guided, I think, by a truer instinct in reading it, 'Lo! she saves him from Acheron, and makes an offering of herself!'"—*Cities*, &c., vol. I. p. xc.

CHAPTER IV.

INSCRIPTIONS ON VOTIVE OFFERINGS.

There are a great many statues, statuettes, and other articles of Etruscan manufacture preserved in the Museums of Europe, which appear from the inscriptions upon them to have been of the nature of Votive Offerings—to what shrines or public edifices I know not—some in general expression of gratitude, others in acknowledgment of, or in atonement for, fraud or other guilt in matters of mercantile or personal dealing. Sometimes they bear the donor's name, sometimes not, but the majority have the character of fraud or *damnum*, debt or obligation, stamped upon them through the inscriptions. Under the former class I rank the few which bear the inscription TINŚKVIL, including that gem of Etruscan art, the great bronze *candelabrum* of Cortona. No correspondence is discernible (except in the second in the series of specimens now to be produced) between the effigies or subjects represented and the *delictum* specified in the inscriptions. The donors, I take it, bought them in the shops, and had the inscriptions engraved for presentation, just as votive offerings ready-made are purchasable even now by devotees in Italy. But the general concurrence of the inscriptions in specifying fraud in general, and instances of fraud in particular, constitutes a strong presumption in favour of the accuracy of the interpretation in the case of each inscription severally.

Section I.

The word TINŚKVIL—the ś invariably written with a śan—is found by itself alone on a Chimæra in the gallery at Florence, on a griffin at Leyden, on a bronze dog formerly in the possession of Signor Coltellini at Cortona, and, in association with other words, on the *candelabrum* above spoken of, and now first to be dealt with. All these monuments were found at Cortona and (one of them only) at Arezzo. The present beautiful work of art was discovered in 1840 at La Fratta, below Cortona, in a ditch, only slightly below the surface of the ground. It is now preserved in the museum of the city. The inscription is as follows:—

THAPNA : LUŚNI(Π) | INŚKVIL : ATHLIK | ŚALTHN
(*Fabretti*, no. 1050, tab. xxxv.)

1, 2. THAPNA : LUŚNI.—i. LUŚNI appears to me to be the dative case of LUSNA or LOSNA, an Etruscan title of Diana, and which I should connect with that of 'Lucina,' which was common likewise to Juno.—ii. THAPNA I take to represent 'Divana,' the early form of 'Diana,' and which we also have as THANA on an Etruscan mirror (*Fabretti*, no. 459), representing the nativity of Minerva. I think that THAPNA : LUŚNI answers here to 'Dianæ Lucinæ,' or 'Lucinæ,' the goddess protectress of women in childbirth.*

3. TINŚKVIL.—This word appears to me upon the whole, and mainly from its position in the present inscription, to be a formation from i., *denk-*, *denk-en*, to think, and thence, to

---

* THAPNA may be the Teutonic *hebamme*, *hevamma*, midwife; the *h* being here in the older form of *th*, as *e.g.* in the matronymic HAPIRNAI, THAPIRNAI, which we shall meet with hereafter. If so, the roots would be *heb-*, *theb-*? 'levare,' to raise up; and *emma*, *amma* (connected with the Greek *ἄμμα*), mother, nurse. But the analysis in the text is the simplest, and comes (so to speak) first to hand.

remember; and, ii. *skuld*, debt,—the compound signifying 'debt of remembrance' with the allied sense of thankfulness or gratitude. When found as a single word it is probably equivalent to 'In Memoriam,' although not necessarily of a dead person.

4. ATHLIK.—A compound of ATH and LIK, and identical with the old Teutonic *licht-fass, licht-vas*, 'lucerna, candelabrum,'—the component elements reversed.

5. SALTUN.—This appears to be a compound of i. SAL, answering to *sal*, 'traditio,' *sol* (O. N.), 'donum,' a gift or offering; and ii. TUN, representing *san-en*, to covenant or agree, a word which we shall meet with more than once hereafter.

The inscription would thus signify,—" To Diana Lucina," in " debt of gratitude," this "*candelabrum*" is "a covenanted offering."—I suspect it was dedicated by some noble lady in gratitude for recovery from childbirth; and this conclusion is to a certain extent in keeping with that of Mr. Dennis, who thinks " that it was suspended, perhaps in a tomb, perhaps in a temple as a sacrificial lamp, which in truth its remarkable size and beauty seem to indicate."

The letter "l" in this inscription is the Greek, not the Etruscan character; but the other letters are Etruscan, and the 'n' is in the regular form. "The style of art," says Mr. Dennis, " proves this monument to be of no very early date, yet there is a certain archaicism about it which marks it as of ante-Roman times." He places it between the Wolf of the Capitol and the Chimæra and Orator of Florence, and refers its date to "the fifth century" of Rome, "or the close of Etruscan independence." *

* *Cities*, &c., vol. II. pp. 442-4.

Section II.

V. KVINTI · ARNT⫶IAŚ · KULPIANŚI | ALPAN TURKE
V. KVINTI · ARN|TIAŚ · ŚELAN⫶ŚL TEZ · ALPAN | TURKE
(*Fabretti*, no. 1051, 1052, tab. xxxv.)

These two inscriptions are found severally on two little bronze statues which were discovered, in April 1857, both together, and, in Fabretti's words, "difese da poche tegole, .. alla distanza di braccia 54, quasi in linea dritta dall' antica porta a tre stipiti, che tuttora, abbenchè chiusa e mancante dell' architrave, si vede nelle mura di Cortona."

The first of the little statues represents a girl, wearing buskins and a necklace, but otherwise perfectly naked, and with two faces, one looking forward, the other backward,—the second statue represents the same figure apparently, but with the skin and head of some animal on the crown of her head,—I am uncertain whether or not she is doublefaced like the first. This characteristic of doublefacedness—the common symbol of deceit among mankind—naturally attracts attention; and if the inscription, as interpreted by comparison with ancient German, alludes to such a characteristic in the person represented or thing signified by the statue, such interpretation can hardly be considered otherwise than correct.

I proceed, as before, to analyse the two inscriptions. It will be observed that they are identical except in

---

* This is from Fabretti's transcript. In the engraving there is only one point or mark of division (after KULPIANŚI) in the first inscription. In the second, besides the points above given, there are others after ŚL and ALPAN. The 'san' is exclusively employed for the letter 's.'

the words KULPIANŚI in the first and ŚELANŚL TEZ in the second,—words which may therefore be presumed to stand in contrasted relation to each other. I shall take these words last in the analysis.

1, 2, 3. V. EVINTI ARNTIAŚ.—These words constitute a family name, and apparently in the genitive case, perhaps to be rendered 'Velia Quintia Arnthia's,'—or it may be 'Arnthia's, Velus Quintius's SECU,' or daughter, an Etruscan word to be noticed hereafter, abbreviated here as ś.

4. ALPAN.—To be compared with the ancient *alfans, alefants*, 'fraus, falsitas, nequitia,' a word spoken of by the brothers Grimm in their great lexicon as "ein merkwürdiges, bisher unverstandnes, in hohes alterthum zurückweichendes wort:"—From *alfuns* are derived *alfanzer*, 'nequam,' *allfunzerey*, 'valrities,' craftiness, cunning, artifice, &c.

5. TURKE,—*durch*, 'per,' through, *ut supra*. *Durch*, it may be observed, is found as *thairh* in Gothic and *thurh* in Old and Anglo-Saxon; but not in the Old-Northern or Scandinavian,—an important consideration with reference to the ethnology of Etruria.

6. KULPIANŚI.—A compound word formed from KUL and PIANŚI, as by comparison with a similar compound, but exhibiting its elements reversed in order, PUNIŚKIAL.—i. PIANŚI is, I think, the genitive case singular of PIAN, answering to *pfand, pand, pans* (in the 'Lex Salica'), the well-known word (*bond* in English) signifying a 'pignus' or pledge. The termination -*es*, -*is* of the genitive is frequently written RE, SI, (the letters being reversed,) in Etruscan.—ii. KUL presents more difficulty. It may be compared with *gelt*, 'res communtanda*, . . pensatio damni ant furti pecuniaria, . . donum, oblatio, retributio, solutio, debitum;' *chalt* (in the 'Lex Salica'), 'compensatio per solidos furti vel damni;' *guilt*, 'præstatio, debitum, satisfactio,'—*geld an einen guilten legen*, 'pecuniam fœnori apud aliquem exponere;' *guilten*, 'solvere, præstare,' &c. KUL-PIANŚI, in this point of view, would signify 'pledge-forfeit, or fine.' It is possible indeed that KUL may stand for an older *skal*, implying 'lapsus,' in the sense,

still, of lapse or falling away from engagement or plighted faith.*

7. SELANSL.—This word likewise is divisible into SELAN and SL,—the latter being frequently found in other combinations.—i. For SELAN, compare *scolen*, *sollen*, 'debere,' *sculd*, 'debitum, culpa;' *suilen*, 'contaminare.'—ii. For SL, compare *sollen*, 'tradere;' *sal*, 'traditio;' *sal* (Sueo-Goth.), fine (for homicide); *sol* (O.Northern), 'donum.'—SELAN-SL would thus imply 'debt-forfeit' or 'fine,' in near correspondence with KULPIANSL.—And, lastly,

8. TEZ may be compared with *zeichen*, 'indicare;' with 'in-*dic*-are' itself; 'con-*tig*-ere;' *testis*, &c. Or, with more probability, remembering the frequent interchange of *q* for *t*, (as, *e.g.* in *quist*, *twist*, 'ramus,' a bough,) our familiar *quit*, *quittance*, *quits*, may be the analogue here.

* While PRNIŚ-SIAL appears to correspond literally with KUL-PIANŚI, and PRNIŚ is certainly *pfand*, *pfandes*, I am inclined to think that SIAL may denote ultimately the *keule*, *pfandkeule*, *pfandkeule*, the 'clava pignorationis,' properly a club or stick, with knots, cut from a tree, which the lender delivered to the borrower at his house in token of equitable understanding (the root *ram* again coming into play here in the sense of 'ramus,' a bough), and which was to be restored to him before the judge when the debt was paid, in token of quittance,—*quits* and *quist*, *twist*, 'ramus' (or rather 'twig'), answering symbolically to each other again in this final stage of the transaction. In course of time articles of more or less value and bulk were substituted (I conceive) for this *keule*, stick, or club, some of them so small (although representing rights of hypothek over houses and property) that they were deposited in a chest or desk kept by the borrower, and hence called *kistenpfande*; while, in Etruria, works of art seem to have borne the same character, such as the bronze bas-relief in which the compound PHNIŚKIAL above noticed occurs. This bas-relief is now preserved in the Museum at Florence; a Gorgon's head is in the centre, and around it, along the margin, the legend, MI · SUTHILVELTHUSITHURA : TURKE · AU · VELTHURI PHNIŚKIAL · (*Fabretti*, no. 2603, and tav. xliv.) I take this to mean, "Aulus Velturius appoints, sets, or has set me" (MI SUTHI, unless these words signify 'I am appointed') "as the *pfandkeule*" (PHNIŚKIAL, or 'clava pignorationis,') "for" (TURKE) "the annual rent" (THURA) "due by him to L. Velturius (L · VELTHURI)."—Lantinius (as we may for convenience Latinise the name) being the lender and Aulus the debtor in respect of a sum of money lent on hypothek. THURA I take to be the Etruscan form of *steure*, *steuer*, 'tribulum, tailia,' a word synonymous with *gewerf*, which is used in Upper Alsatia for a 'tributum annuum.' In a less definite sense THURA might be connected mediately with *gewäre*, 'cautio, warandia,' or security.

SECT. III.   ON VOTIVE OFFERINGS.   47

The first, then, of these two inscriptions should be read, "The pledge"—"forfeit," "fine," or "gift," "of Velia Quintia Arnthia," or "of Velus Quintius's daughter, Arnthia," [incurred] "through fraud."— And the second, "The debt-forfeit, or fine" of the same personage, incurred "through fraud, paid and acquitted." *

SECTION III.

A species of fraud of very early prevalence would seem to be indicated in the inscription that I shall next adduce, in which the remarkable word ALPAN recurs:—

TITE : ALPNAS : TURKE : AISERAS : THUPHLTHIKLA : TRUTVEKIE
(*Fabretti*, no. 2603 *bis*.)

This is found on a little brass statue described by Fabretti as at Rome, "apud Depoletti." I analyse it as follows:—

1, 2. TITE : ALPNAS.—These words do not, I think, denote a proper name, to wit, 'Titus Alpinius,' or 'Titia Alpinia,' but the general character of the crime attaching to what is specified in the conclusion of the sentence. Their position in relation to TURKE, which always appears to follow the general charge, leads me to this opinion. TITE appears to me to answer to *that*, deed or act, and ALPNAS to *alfans*, fraud,—the word already sufficiently dealt with,—ALPNAS being in the genitive case, governed by TITE.

* It is possible that ŚELAN in ŚELAN-ŚL may have the sense of *schilling* as in *pfandschilling*, which denotes 1. the capital lent on hypothek, 2. by metoN. the *pfund* itself. ŚELAN-ŚL would thus signify redemption of the bond, payment of the debt; and TEZ, *ut supra*, 'acquittance'—not merely from the debt but from the moral culpability that had been incurred in connexion with it.

3. TURKE,—as before.

4. AISERAS.—Compare *eller,* 'terminus pagi ont urbis, sepes, septum,' *idrs* (Goth.), *eter* (Celt.), 'finem atque terminum.' The word is common to other languages not Indo-European.

5. THUPHLTHIRLA.—A compound, I think, of i. THUPHLTII-, the Teutonic *sweyfall-,* fraudful; and of ii. IRLA, a derivative from *wag-an,* 'movere,' formed analogously to 'vacill-are,' but in the active sense, and similar to *wechseln,* 'mutare.'

6. TRUTVEKIE. A compound likewise, and to be written TRUT-VEKIE.—i. TRUT appears to me to be the Etruscan form of what we have as στρωτ-ός in Greek, 'strat-us' in Latin, and *streu-en, gestreuet* in Teutonic, a word thus of most Pelasgic antiquity; and ii. VEKIE corresponds with *weg,* 'via,' or way. TRUT-VEKIE is thus the old Etruscan analogue of 'viae stratae' or *wegstrassen,* paved, that is, public roads or 'streets,' the constituent elements of the compound being reversed in order, as usual in Etruscan. A 'street' is properly a paved road running, not merely through a town, but through the country—as in the case of the old Roman road familiar to us in England as 'Watling-street.'

I read this inscription therefore as—"[Offered] through," or on account of, "an act of fraud, in altering deceitfully," or encroaching upon, "the bounds" (whether terminal stones or fences) "of the public *strata,*" or highway.

Section IV.

A general charge of fraud is expressed in three words inscribed on the fragment of a little statue in bronze preserved at Fermo in the 'Museo di Minicis,'—

UTNI : THUPHULTHAŚ:A | TURKE

(*Fabretti,* no. 801.)

Another reading gives UTIN for UTNI; and there

seems to have been a letter (now effaced) before the U.

THUPHULTHAŚA is evidently the adjectival form of the THUPHLTH-, *zweyfalt-*, above illustrated; and answers to the corresponding Latin development of the same root, 'dupl-ex.' UTNI, UTIN, read as TUTNI, would correspond to the Teutonic *that, thaten*, and the Latin 'faciu-us,' an action *in genere*, good or bad, but here qualified as the latter.* The inscription would thus signify,—"[Fine, or offering] on account of fraudulent actions," "fraudulent dealing."

Section V.

The following inscription is found on a small statue of bronze, discovered in 1864 about two miles from Castiglione Fiorentino, and now preserved in the Museum at Cortona:—

LARTHIA : ATEINEI : | ŚL : | PHLEREŚ : PUANTRN | TURKE :
(*Fabretti*, no. 1055 *bis*, tab. xxxv.)†

—The statue represents a boy, or youth, holding up a bird (apparently) in his right hand. The *r* and *t* in the inscription are both of an old type. ŚL is written at right angles opposite the first line at the foot of the inscription. An analysis of the words gives the following result:—

1, 2. LARTHIA : ATEINEI.—Apparently a female name, 'Larthia Atinia,' and in the genitive case.

---

* Compare TITE : ALPNAS, *supra*. It might also stand for *teding*, 'compositio pacis,'—a word which we shall meet with presently as TUTHINEŚ; but the rendering in the text seems to meet the construction best.

† PUANTRN is given as PUANTIRN in the engraving.

K

3. ŚL.—The ŚL, or ŚAL, which has been identified with *sal*, fine, payment, or offering.

4. PHLENEŚ.—The genitive of PHLERE, i. e. *tlur*, 'damnum,' as already shewn.

5. PUANTHN.—This word again, is a compound.—i. PUAN I take to be *pfand*, *bond*, a pledge or engagement, the word already noticed; and, ii. THN may be compared with *tara*, 'damnum, læsio,' *daru* (A.S.), 'damnum,' *terjan*, *derjan* (A.S.), 'nocere,' and *tarunga*, 'læsio.' The compound PUAN-THN would thus imply 'breach of pledge' or 'faith.'

6. TURKE,—already explained as *durch*, 'por,' or 'through.'

The inscription would thus signify, in English, "Fine" (gift, or offering) "of Larthia Atinia for guilt" (*damnum*, injury, penalty), "[manifested] through breach of pledge," or of plighted faith.

Section VI.

Yet another inscription of the character here under discussion is found upon a statue of bronze, where discovered I do not know, but now preserved in the Museum at Florence:—

LARKE I LEKN[E]: TURKE PHLEREMUTHURLAN VEITHI
(*Fabretti*, no. 255, tab. xxiii.)

The characters are rude and ancient, the *m* and *n* written in the same irregular proportions as in the Pelasgic inscription first analysed *supra*. The form of the PH, moreover, resembling two Greek capital sigmas facing each other, in a shape somewhat like an hour-glass, is nearly the same as in the sepulchral inscription of S. Manno, hereafter to be dealt with. These peculiarities point to considerable antiquity. PHLERE, MUTH, and URLAN appear to be separate words. The analysis is as follows:—

Sect. VI.   ON VOTIVE OFFERINGS.   51

1. LARRE.—To be compared with *lurk, lerk*, 'sinister, perversus.'
2. LERNE.—Compare with *laichen*, 'decipere;' *laicherey*, 'fraus, dolus;' *lugen*, 'mentiri.'
3, 4. TURRE, and PHLERE,—*ut supra*.
5. MUTH.—Conf. *muta* (S.-Goth.), 'merces,' meed, or desert; *mass*, 'macula;' *muth*, 'anima.'
6. URLAN.—Conf. *verlan*, 'repellere;' *verlan*, 'condonare, remittere, indulgere.'
7. VEITHI.—Conf. *wad, wæd*, 'pignus,' and *wâdja* (S.-Goth.), 'appellare, stipulare;' *veddan* (A.-S.), 'pacisci (in genere).' Our Scottish 'to wad,' 'wadset,' or pledge.

I read the inscription therefore as, "A pledge" (or offering) "to repel (or condone) the guilt-desert" (or stain) [incurred] "through sinister fraud."

Ihre observes in his 'Lexicon Suio-Gothicum' or Swedish Dictionary, that *wad* is the original word for 'pignus' in the Scandinavian languages, and that *pfand* has been of later introduction,—imported from Germany. *Pfand* was certainly the usual word for 'pignus' among the Etruscans,—we meet with it in the form of PIANSI, PUAN, PUNIS, PHANU, and otherwise. The inscriptions in which these occur are of various dates, some of them very ancient, others among the most recent. On the other hand, *wad* only occurs (for certain) in the present inscription (not a recent one) as VEITHI, and in another, hereafter to be discussed (one of great antiquity), as UATHA. It would thus seem that *wad* is the older word in Etruscan,—and this, like similar observations, may perhaps contribute towards solving the ethnological problems connected with the Etruscans at some future time.*

* See the article on the 'Pontifex Maximus' in the Glossary, *infra*.

Section VII.

Of a similar description is the following inscription, on a small bronze statue representing a boy in a reclining position and, as before, holding a bird (apparently),—found near the Lake Thrasymene, and now in the Etruscan Museum of the Vatican:—

PHLERESTEKSANSLKVER
(*Fabretti*, no. 1930, tab. xxxviii.)

The words, here agglutinated together, will arrange themselves to your eye at a glance in their distinct form:—

1. PHLERES,—*ut supra*.
2. TEK.—Compare *tycke*, 'sententia,' *tucka*, 'mulcta,' from *tycka* (S.-G.), 'existimare' in the sense of judgment—the *thugkjan* of the Mœso-Gothic Ulphilas,—words from the same root as *thinc-*, *think-*, and *ting* or *thing*, a court of law. See Ihre, *in voce* 'Tycka.'
3. SANÉL.—A compound, SAN-ŚL.—For i. SAN, compare *son*, *sund-*, 'debere, peccare, peccatum,' *saun* (Goth. Ulphil.), *sone* (O.N.), 'pax, reconciliatio, pacificatio,'—the modern *versöhnung*, atonement for crime.—ii. ŚL, as before, would denote forfeit or fine, with the sense of 'solutio' or payment. SAN-ŚL would thus be rendered 'Debt-fine,' or 'Fine paid in atonement,' 'for guilt.'
4. KVER.—Our Teutonic *kupfer*, the Latin 'œs, æris,' that is, copper or brass, whence anything made of brass, as vases, cups, caldrons (constantly spoken of under the title *hverr* in the Eddaic writings), down to coin, or money. This last is the most probable signification here.

The inscription reads, in its simplest and general sense, "Pecuniary fine paid [against] sentence of *damnum*."

A strong Gothic and Scandinavian tinge is apparent in the present inscription; and this may be said to apply to most of those inscribed on offerings for guilt. The orthography of this inscription is however later than that of the preceding one.

Section VIII.

The signification of the following inscription is nearly the same as that of the one just analysed :—

PHLERES TLENAKES KVER
(*Fabretti,* no. 2599.)

—It is found on a little statue of brass, preserved in the 'Museo Estenso.'

PHLERES and KVER are the same as in the preceding inscription. TLENAKES is also found as TLENACHIES in the more important inscription next to be dealt with. It appears to me to be a compound of TLEN and AKES. For i. TLEN, compare *zoll, toll,* 'vectigal,' 'tel-onium' (the first syllable short, the second long), a custom-house.—ii. AKES, ACHIES, I take to be the simple Latin 'as, assia,'—the compound thus signifying 'tax-,' 'tributo-,' that is, 'current-coin,' or money. The sentence would thus run, as before, "Pecuniary fine for *damnum.*"

Section IX.

One of the most important relics of Etruscan art is the statue of a boy, which was found, A.D. 1746, at Montecchio, near Cortona, within a niche, along with the statue of a woman and a *candelabrum,* all now preserved in the Museum of Leyden. The following inscription is engraved on the right thigh of the figure, in characters apparently of considerable antiquity, the L especially being the Greek capital 'lambda:'—

VELIAŚ · PHANAKNAL · THUPHLTHAŚ ALPAN · LENACHE ·
KLEN · KECHA : TUTHINEŚ · TLENACHEIŚ
(*Fabretti*, no. 1055, tab. xxxv.)

—By analysis we obtain the following results:—

1, 2. VELIAŚ PHANAKNAL.—i. VELIAŚ. This must either be in the genitive case—'Vele's,' or 'Velia's,' as we should write it; or it may stand short for VELIASECH, 'daughter of Vele,' or 'Velia.' I incline to the former alternative. As a rule, when two names, or two words, immediately associated, occur together, the inflection is only expressed in the case of one of them. The word VELIAŚ occurs nowhere else.—ii. PHANAKNAL,—that is, 'child of' a mother named ' Phanakn.' It has long since been ascertained through the evidence of bilingual inscriptions that the terminational -AL in proper names indicates 'natus'—son, or daughter, of such or such a mother, LARTHIAL being interpreted as 'Larthiā natus,' VANIAL as 'Vaniā natus,' &c. *

3, 4. THUPHLTHAŚ ALPAN.—'Double-dealing fraud,' *ut supra.*

5. LENACHE.—A compound, of which the first portion, LEN, may be compared with *lan*, 'mercea,' and the second, ACHE, with *ach, acht, aht,* judgment, public prosecution.†

6. KLEN.—Compare with *gelinden* (from *linden*), 'lenire' —a word implying, first, to smoothe or mollify, and thence, through a series of gradations, to mitigate, lessen, and diminish, in the course of which it associates itself with *klein*, small—if, indeed, *klein* is not a distinct derivative

---

* For an explanation of -AL by Teutonic roots I would refer to the Section on the Bilingual Inscriptions some pages further on.

† Compared with *lendmeke* (in the Westphalian and Saxon law), it would imply 'causa ad bonam finem directa, per compositionem finita.'

from the same root. In a legal sense, in which we find it here, it implies deprecation and propitiation as exercised either by an advocate on behalf of a criminal or, as in the present case, by the criminal himself. I am half inclined to identify it with *plain-*, *plaintiff*, discarding the usual signification of weeping, however early associated (and especially in its symbolism) with the idea of suing in law.

7. KECHA.—To be compared with *heischen*, 'petere, exigere,' (the word already twice met with,) and *heiza, ant-heiza,* 'votum, votivum, devotatio,'—from *heiz-* (O. H. G.), the root of *ant-heiz-*, 'votum,' *haizan, hailan,* 'vocare,' *gaheizan* 'spondere, vovere,' the modern *heissen*. You will recollect, too, our Scottish *hecht*, what is promised or offered.

8. TUTHINES.—Compare *teding, taeding, thaiding,* 'compositio pacis, pacificatio' (in a juridical sense). In the genitive case,—the *g*, as usual, being omitted.

9. TLENACHEIS.—As in the preceding section.

The inscription, in current English, would run:—
"Velia Phanaknal's votive-offering of pecuniary composition to soften" (diminish or appease) "the judicial award for double-dealing fraud."*

SECTION X.

The same compound—or rather association of words—KLEN KECHA—which gives its tone (as it were) to the character of the preceding inscription, is found in one engraved on the left thigh of a small statue of Apollo, crowned with laurel and wearing a necklace and armlet, and a bulla, formerly in the possession of the Grand Duchess of Tuscany, and now in the (originally) 'Bibliothèque Royale' at Paris:—

* I may add that the *candelabrum* which was found with the statue is inscribed A · VELS · KUS · THUFELTHAS ALFAN TURKE, (*Fabretti*, no. 1054); and if KUS be short, as is possible, for KUSLACH, the word explained

Mı : PHLEREŚ : SVULARE : ARITIMI | PHASTI : RUIPHRIM :
TRKE : KLEN : KECHA

(*Fabretti*, no. 2613, tab. xliv.)

The *m* and *n* are in the archaic form already spoken of; and this inscription has a certain Pelasgian character about it in other respects. I proceed to analysis, as usual :—

1. Mʟ—This is usually read as *eiμl*, 'sum,' I am. It was certainly an occasional usage in inscriptions to make the dedicated article speak for itself in the first person singular. Fabretti thinks that ᴍɪ means 'I,' and not 'I am.' Mɪ may perhaps be the Etruscan mode of writing what we should present as 'Im,' the letters transposed,—and this would bring Mɪ into more natural relation to *eiμl*.

2. ᴘʜʟᴇʀᴇś.—Genitive of ᴘʜʟᴇᴜᴇ, *ut supra*.

3. sᴠᴜʟᴀʀᴇ.—An early form, I think, of *fehl-*, *fehler*, failing or fault,—unless it be a compound of *fehl* and *waere*, *wer*, 'cautio' or security given. The initial s, lost in *fehl*, in the Sanscrit *kalusha*, and the Latin 'cad-ere,' is preserved in the Sanscrit *skhal*, to fall, the primitive root being *sk=ts*, expressive of separation and distinction, in the abstract. It is preserved too in the Teutonic *schwelcken*, 'flaccescere, deficere, defectum pati,' a word of cognate origin, which I have noticed as ꜱᴠᴀʟʀɪ in an Etruscan inscription (*Fabretti*, no. 2101) in the sense, if I mistake not, of *défaillance* through death.

4. ᴀʀɪᴛɪᴍʟ—Compare *warheit*, 'veritas, probatio, jusjurandum, olim manu conjuncta consacramentalium peractum,' —a compound of *war*, 'verum,' and *eid*, 'jurumentum.' ᴀʀɪᴛɪᴍɪ would thus be the accusative case, written so according to Etruscan usage, in lieu of ᴀʀɪᴛɪɪᴍ. ᴀʀɪᴛɪᴍɪ may even

supra as 'standard-weight,' the sense would be = Fine-offering of Aulus Velus for using false weights." Both offerings would appear to have proceeded from the same house and family. I do not know where the female statue which was found along with the statue of the boy and the candelabrum is now preserved. It probably commemorated the guilt of a third partner in the fraud.

SECT. X.   ON VOTIVE OFFERINGS.   57

be simply *wort-en*, word, or promise. I thought at first it had been *irrthum*.

5. FIASTI.—Compare *fast*, 'firmus,' *faesta*, 'firmare;' but with especial influence from *faust*, 'pugnus,' the fist or hand, *faesta*, 'manus jungere,' the symbolic accompaniment of assurance or confirmation. The resemblance of *faust* and *fast*—as in old Egyptian times of '*χρ*,' the fist, 'hp,' to judge, or adjust, 'hpt,' to join, unite, &c. (primitive forms of our familiar *kauf-*, *kaufen*, and of the Latin '*apt-are*')—suggested, I have no doubt, the symbolism.

6. RUIPURIM.—A compound, to be written RUIPU-RIM.—i. RUIPU is the Teutonic *ruff-*, *ruffen*, *rufen*, 'vocare,' and in legal language, 'in jus vocare citatum.'—ii. RIM corresponds with *ram*, *rahm*, implying term or defined extent of time, the word which we have already met with in the Admetus and Alcestis inscription, and in combination with a word identical in meaning with RUIPU, as ACH-RUM, 'period of citation.' But *ram*, or *rim*, is here, from the context, to be understood with the secondary and symbolical sense super-added of *ram* (S.-G. and O.N.), 'manus,' the hand. Ihre connects *ram* in this sense with the middle-age Latin *adhramire*, "quod est, imprimis, porrectâ et stipulatâ manu promittere," (this in general terms,) "et, in specie, promittere se ad condictum tempus loco duelli aut foro ad præstandum præstanda adfuturum"—that the person entering into the engagement should make his due appearance at the appointed time. "Jurisconsulti nostrates," continues Ihre, "*festa ed* dicunt, à *faesta*, manus jungere, dextram fidemque dare, . . . Isl. *hramr*, Lapp. *rabma*." All those ideas are sub-understood here; and it is on account of the connection shewn between the three words ARITIMI, FIASTI, and RUIPURIM that I have preferred the above to other interpretations which might be suggested, but which do not bear witness to each other in the remarkable manner that these do.—RUIPURIM thus signifies 'the term or limit of citation, or summons,' with the accessary sense of recognition and pledge of appearance on the part of the person summoned.

7. TEKE,—the same word, I presume, as TOUKE.

8. O. KLEN KECHA,—as in the preceding inscription.

The signification would thus be,—"I am the alleviation-offering of guilt [incurred] through failure in keeping an engagement, confirmed by striking hands, to appear within the appointed term of summons."*

Section XI.

I shall conclude this particular series of specimens with the inscription on a large bronze statue (now preserved in the Uffizj at Florence) and variously spoken of as that 'of Metellus,' of the 'Arringatore,' or Orator, and of the 'Aruspice Mediceo;' and which was found in 1566 near Sanguinetto on the site of the battle of Thrasymene, and not far from the Lake of Perugia. It is one of the most remarkable relics of pure, although not very archaic Etruscan art. The person represented is dressed in the tunic and *pallium* of the Greeks and Romans, and has his hand raised as if addressing an audience or propitiating a superior. The inscription is on the border of the *pallium*, and runs as follows:—

AULEŚI · METELIŚ · VE · VESIAL · KLENŚI | KEN · PLEREŚ · TEKE · SANŚL · TENINE | TUTHINEŚ · CH'SVLIKŚ ·
(*Fabretti*, no. 1922, tab. xxxviii.)

—The two forms of the s are here distinguished according to their respective position at the beginning or end of words. Analysed, it reads thus:—

1, 2, 3, 4. AULEŚI . METELIŚ . VE . VESIAL.—These first

* Dr. Donaldson translates this inscription, "Sum votivum donarium Apollini atque Artemidi; Fastia Rufria, Tusc. filia, faciundum curavit." *Varron.*, p. 207. He reads the initial words as MI PHLEBES EPUL APHE ARITIMI, &c.

four words are interpreted, doubtless correctly, as 'Aulus Metellus, son of Velus, mother's son of Vesia.'

5. KLENŚI.—The third person singular, present tense, of the verb *gelinden*, already noticed as having the sense of mitigation or deprecation in a forensic sense, but here, it would appear, employed to designate—not the cry of contrition of an offender, but the suit of the advocate. In KLENŚI, AULEŚI, and other Etruscan words similarly ending, the final ŚI represents, I think, IŚ, the letters being reversed.

6. KEN.—Compare with *gen*, *gein*, the modern *gegen*, 'contra,' against.

7. PLERES.—The same word, evidently, as PILERES, and in the genitive case.

8. TEKE.—The same word, likewise, as TEK, discussed *supra*.

9. SANŚL.—This compound too has been discussed already.

10. TENINE.—Compare *thinan*, *tenen*, 'tendere, ex-tendere,' to stretch out—not only in the primitive sense of thinning or attenuating, but in that of 'porrigere,' to offer anything. TENINE is either the infinitive, the vowel which precedes the final consonant in the Greek or German infinitive being here postponed to it, the I-E forming a long *ei*, or diphthong; or the gerund, which would be properly written TENTINTE, that is, TENDINDE, like the Latin 'tendendo,' its equivalent,—one only of the compound letters being given in Etruscan orthography.

11. TUTHINEŚ.—*Ut supra*, 'compositio pacis, pacificatio,'—in the genitive case.

12. CHISVLIKŚ.—More correctly transcribable, according to a rule already laid down, as SCUISVLIKŚ. This puzzling word is, I think, a compound of SCUIS and VLIKŚ. i. SCUIS I should identify with *schoss, geschoss*, 'exactio,' from *schiessen*, 'jacere, conjicere;' and, ii. VLIKŚ, with *pflicht*, 'praestatio debita,'—the compound thus answering in a very marked manner to the old Teutonic *su geschoss und pflicht bleiben*, in the sense of 'jure ac more debita.' I should take SCUISVLIKŚ to be the genitive of an adjective implying 'legal and customary,' agreeing with the noun TUTHINEŚ, *taedinges*, 'composition, or compromise.'

The inscription thus signifies,—"Aulus Metellus, son of Velus, mother's son of Vesia, sues (in mitigation)" or "pleads against the full judicial sentence of *damnum*, by holding forth" (i. e. by offering in extenuation) "the atonement-fine of legal and customary composition."

It is possible that these words may merely indicate a votive offering of the usual character; but the importance of the statue, its peculiar attitude, and the generalising character of the inscription, in which no specific offence is stated, make me think that the name 'Arringatore,' or 'Orator,' has been rightly attributed to it, and that it represents an advocate or lawyer of the old Etruscan bar, by name Aulus Metellus—a predecessor of Gaius, whose name bespeaks him of Etruscan descent, or of the equally Tuscan Pomponii.

———

Altogether—judging by the preceding series of inscriptions—the Etruscans set great store upon the virtue of honesty, and prescribed public atonement and humiliation for the breach of it. I do not think that any votive offerings of a similar character have come down to us from the Romans. The protest in behalf of temperance against luxury, as translated from the inscription found in the tomb of Tarquinii, taken along with that in favour of fair dealing against doublefacedness and fraud, which these penitential confessions give utterance to, may enable us to form an estimate of the standard of morality among these ancient Germans—of Etruria.

CHAPTER V.

SEPULCHRAL INSCRIPTIONS.

ANOTHER and a very important class, and more difficult to deal with, is that of the Sepulchral Inscriptions, some of which I shall now submit to you—always, bo it remembered, with the limited view of ascertaining whether the Etruscan language is, as I believe it to be, or is not, Teutonic. I have no doubt whatever that my translations are susceptible in many points of correction and improvement.

SECTION I.—*The Bilingual Inscriptions.*

All the bilingual inscriptions—that is, those written both in Etruscan and Latin, which have as yet been discovered—are clearly of the sepulchral class, with the exception of one, of which I must treat separately at the end of this Section, and of the fragments of another, too much mutilated to be intelligible. There are eighteen of them in all, inscribed for the most part on the lids or fronts of sarcophagi, or on funereal tablets, and consisting merely of the names of defunct personages. There is such a fascination in the very idea of a bilingual inscription that you will be disappointed, I fear, when I add that, with the exception of the last in the series, which is of a very peculiar character, the whole of them put together only furnish one single positive Latin equivalent for an Etruscan word other than a proper name. The

Rosetta Stone would turn up its nose indignantly if compared with these. Nevertheless they afford, in a different manner, very strong confirmation of the views advocated in this Memoir. Much that is quite new is unfolded by a close inspection of these curious records, and the following are the principal results which that inspection has led me to:—First,— whereas it has been taken for granted hitherto that the Latin is in every instance a version of the Etruscan inscription—that one and the same person is denoted by both writings in each instance—this is not always the case; in some of the inscriptions both husband and wife (or concubine) are separately commemorated; and when that is the case, it is the gentleman's name always which is given in the Latin and the lady's in Etruscan. It is true that the lady is not described by her own name—not (as a rule) as Tanaquil or Arnthia—but by a simple repetition of her husband's name with the addition of -SA or -SLA, —SA being equivalent in value, if you will excuse the comparison, to 'Mrs.' The title -SLA falls short of that dignity, but has a definite *status* of its own.*— 2. It is noticeable, moreover, that the name of the father is very often omitted in the Etruscan version, and only that of the mother given; whereas in the Latin the father is (as a rule) always specified, and the mother (except through indirect indication) never,—an interesting illustration of the superior importance attached to maternal descent among the Etruscans. This circumstance, as compared with

---

* The t which always precedes sa and sla in the inscriptions is, I think, the final letter of the husband's name, to which the feminine title is subjoined.

the still existing usage of Visi-Gothic (or Tervingian) Spain, made a forcible impression on my mind in favour of the consanguinity of the Visi-Goths and Etruscans before commencing my study of the inscriptions.—3. Again, where what appear at first sight to be *cognomina* occur in the Latin version, to which there are no equivalents in the Etruscan—the Etruscans, as there is reason to believe, not having used *cognomina*—I think that these can be shewn to be *agnomina*, translated from the name of the mother and attributed to the son—not as gentilitial or hereditary surnames, but as personal designations appropriate in each instance to the son alone; a fact which yet again illustrates that respect for mothers, and, it may be inferred, for the female sex in general, which forms so favourable a characteristic of the Etruscans—in common, it will be remembered, with the ancient Germans as described by Tacitus.—4. When the *prænomina* in the Etruscan and Latin inscriptions are different, it will be found that in almost every instance the Latin name and the Etruscan have precisely the same meaning, and are thus equivalents—the Etruscan being peculiarly Teutonic in character.—And 5. and lastly, in one case, where the *nomina* themselves are totally different in the two languages, it similarly turns out that they have one identical signification—that the one is an absolute equivalent for the other. The distinct nomenclature in these last-named cases dates in all probability from very early times.

It would weary you to go through the whole of the bilingual inscriptions in detail; but a selection from those which illustrate the preceding propositions may interest you; and you will find the whole series in the first article of the Appendix subjoined to this volume.

The one Etruscan word rendered by a Latin equivalent, as above spoken of—excluding two which occur in the last and peculiar inscription above spoken of—is the suffix -AL, translated 'natus' in the following epitaph:—

> KUINTE · SINU · ARNTNAL
> Q · SENTIUS L · F · ARRIA NATUS ·
> (*Fabretti*, no. 980. At Chianciano.)

—This denotes "Quintus Sentius" (the T, as usual, being omitted after N in SINU), "son of L., born of Arria." AL, as rendered by 'natus,' has here unquestionably the sense of 'born' or 'child of,' and this has long been recognised; but the peculiar force of the word consists in that it denotes derivation from the female parent—that it is used always with reference to the mother, not the father. This special restriction is vindicated, I think, by its cognate origin with the Greek ἀλέα, warmth, ἀλεαίνω, ἄλθω, to cause to grow, the Latin 'alere,' but more especially with the Teutonic *al-an* (M.-Goth.), *ael-an* (A.-S.), *al-a* (O. N.), signifying in its inherent and fully developed sense, 'gignere et procreare'—*ala*, in particular, being used in the O. Northern speech with an especial view to female progeniture; in support of which Ihre cites from the 'Hervarar Saga,' *Swawa ol barn*, *i. e.* 'Swawa genuit liberos.'[*] This is much to

---

[*] See too Mr. Cleasby's *Icelandic-English Dict.*, art. 'ala.' *Ala*, in a later sense, signifies 'educare,' to bring up a child or infant; and *alster* is the word for 'fœtus,' in Swedish. 'Ad-ol-esco,' 'ind-ol-es,' 'sub-ol-es,' are cognate forms in Latin.

the point, as the Asn and Tyrki, the ancestors of the Northmen, were a branch (as I conceive) of the Visi-Goths or Tervingi of Southern Europe, and thus, as I have inferred, closely akin to the Tyrrheni of Italy. —The 'L. F.' expressing the paternal descent, given in the Latin, is omitted in the Etruscan version, in accordance with the second of the results above laid down.*

It has been supposed that the word KLAN in another bilingual inscription denotes 'filius,' as shewn by the context of the sentence,—

C · CASSIUS · O · F · | SATURNINUS
V · KAZI · K · KLAN
(*Fabretti*, no. 460. Arezzo.)

But, although the relation indicated is real, as more satisfactorily shewn by the position of KLAN in other inscriptions, the word is also applied, although rarely, to daughters; and occasionally the word ETERA, that is *ander-*, *other*, or 'second,' as I understand it, is used in antithesis to KLAN in inscriptions relating to the children of the same parents. The suggestion of K. O. Müller is therefore, I have little doubt, correct, that KLAN denotes—' child ' indeed, but properly the ' first-born ' or ' eldest,' whether son or daughter.† I take it to be written short for KLANT, the final letter being omitted; and that it represents the very ancient Aryan word preserved in

* Similar renderings of AL by ' natus,' ' nata,' may be seen in the bilingual inscriptions consigned to the Appendix; where examples will also be found of the name of the father being omitted while that of the mother is given. See numbers XI., XII.

† *Die Etrusker*, vol. I. pp. 445-6. And for the examples, classified, see Fabretti, *Gloss. Ital.*, pp. 854 sqq.

F

Welsh as *plant*, in Irish as *cland*, and in Gaelic as *clan*, all denoting 'proles' or offspring; while it exists in Gothic in a varied form as *klahaim*,—"parvuli" or "babes" in St. Luke x. 21, being rendered by Ulphilas *niu-klahaim*; and in the *klagen*, 'parvuli,' of Berlin, cited by Wachter.*

The qualification of -SLA denotes, as I understand it, concubine—it occurs in the following inscription,—

    ARTH · KANZNA ¦ VARNALISLA
    O · CÆSIUS · C · F · VARIA · | NAT
    (*Fabretti*, no. 252, tab. xxiii. At Florence.)

—The lady is here commemorated in the Etruscan inscription, which has precedence over the Latin, and the gentleman in the latter language, the lady's quality only being given, and not her personal name. This qualification of -SLA is as common on Etruscan tombs as that of -SA, of which I shall give an example presently; and I think it denotes, not a wife *per excellentiam*, but, if I may so express myself, a legitimate concubine; and that the word represents the Teutonic *sello, sella, gesella*, companion, friend, or (for the word is the same) *fellow*—equivalent, in this acceptation for the homely Scottish word for a wife two or three hundred years ago, 'bedfellow.' There were such things as secondary wives in old times; and the word ETERA, '*other*,' or 'second,' just men-

* The *g* in *klagen*, like the *h* in *klahaim*, represents, if I mistake not, an aspirate or hard sound which is lost in *clan*, *c'land*, *plant*, KLAN, but preserved in τέκνον, *chicken*; while that hard sound, as well as the initial *l*, which is lost in both these latter words, as well as in the cognate *kinder*, *children*, is preserved in the O. N. *klekia* and S.-G. *klaecka* (the Scottish *kleck* and English *hatch*) in the sense of chickens or τέκνα,—this last vocable, *klaecka*, representing the oldest form of the root of KLAN which I shall here attempt to exhibit.

tioned, which also occasionally appears with the
seeming signification of 'wife' in the inscriptions,
denotes this -SLA, if I mistake not, when so used, and
is the equivalent of the Greek ἑταίρα, although of a
primitive and legal type, and not requiring, in the
old-fashioned phrase, to be 'made an honest woman
of.' The title AMKE (which does not, any more than
ETERA, occur in the bilingual inscriptions) may
perhaps have the same, or a kindred signification.*
These -SLAS, ETERAS, or AMKES had a distinct position,
protected by law, among the Teutonic races down to
a comparatively late period.

We have the -SA, denoting 'wife,' in the following
inscription, which supports several of the results
above laid down :—

AELCHEPHULNIAELCHES | KIARTHIALISA
Q · FOLNIUS · A · F · POM | FUSCUS

(*Fabretti*, no. 251.   Found at Arezzo.)

The top line must be divided as AELCHE PHULNI
AELCHES; while KIARTHIALISA shews that the
Etruscan inscription refers exclusively to the wife,
the Latin to the husband. We have here too the
first example of an *agnomen*, ' Fuscus,' foreign to the
Etruscan usage, but borrowed by translation from
the name of the mother of Q. Folnius, by name
KIARTHI, to augment the dignity of her son in
Roman eyes. We have even, apparently, a *cognomen*
reflected in like manner from the Etruscan *prænomen*;
and we have that Etruscan *prænomen* in a Latin form,
completely different, but presumably identical with it

---

* I shall speak further on this subject in treating of the word AMKE,
infra.

in signification—as represented by AELCHE and Q. The present record is thus very fertile in illustration of the peculiarities of the bilingual inscriptions.

The suffix -sa, with which the first line ends, has long been recognised as equivalent to 'uxor,' and may be compared with ' -issa,' signifying derivation, as of the woman's name and authority from her husband,—a form which occurs in all the German languages except (in curious contrast to the peculiarly Low-German character of AL) the Scandinavian. It may perhaps be nothing more than our simple English (but most ancient) 'she'—a special formation from the primitive *sk*, 'ish-a.' The personal name of the wife is not given.

The key to the reconciliation of the *prænomina* AELCHE and Q.—i.e. 'Quinctius' or 'Quintus'—is to be found in the fact that both names signify 'quince,' or rather 'of or pertaining to the quince,'—a derivation analogous to that of the surnames of the Fabii, Lentuli, and many other Roman families, taken from fruits or vegetables. A quince in German is *quette*, or *quette-baum*. *Quett-isch* would be 'of or belonging to a quince.' *T* and *l* are interchangeable letters; and thus *quet-* would become *quel-*, and *quett-isch quell-isch*. But there is a constant tendency in Teutonic words which begin with *q* to drop that letter, as e.g. in *quas*, which we have already shown to be the old form of *fons-t*, and in *quell*, 'fons,' the English 'well.' Our original *Quett-isch* thus becomes *Uell-isch*—that is, in Etruscan, ÆL-CH, or more properly ÆL-SCH-, the Etruscan ↓ having, I have suggested and, I think, shewn, the force of *sch*. On the other hand, the genius of the Latin dialect was less ready to part with the initial *q*, as we see in the retention of 'quatuor,' 'quinque,' 'quis,' as compared with the Celto-Gallic and Teutonic 'petor,' 'four,' the Greek and Italic πέντε, 'five,' and innumerable similar words; and thus 'Quinctius' survives; or in other words, 'Quinctius' is simply the original *quette, quecte*, with the *n* inserted for euphony, thus becoming 'quencte,' 'Quinct-ius'—the exact equivalent of ÆL-SCHE. What may perhaps confirm this explanation is the fact that a coin of the Quinctia gens engraved in Dr. Smith's *Dict. of Greek and Latin Biography and Mythology*, exhibits what I take to be a round fruit, probably an apple or a quince, between the letters 'T. Q.,' as, I presume, a family or heraldic device.*

But, as observed, a *cognomen*—POM—is given to Folnius in the Latin inscription, a most unusual thing in the case of an Etruscan. It is borrowed, I think, from the *prænomen* just discussed, and whatever its developed form, I suspect it to be derived from 'Pomum Cydonium,' the Latin name for the *quettebaum*, or quince.†

We have last to deal with the *cognomen* FUSCUS, as given in the Latin inscription; and this, in accordance with the result or rule above stated, has been

---

* Rasche (in his *Lex. . . Rei Nummariæ Vett.*) describes this as a "clipeus rotundus;" but the Roman shield, at least in comparatively modern times, was not round; and the device certainly looks more like an apple than a shield.

† It is just possible that AELCHE may represent an original MAEL-, or MAL-CHE, i. e. 'malum,' apple,—the M represented in this inscription by the initial A, as it frequently is, in various languages, by w; while it may have been wholly abraded by time, as is the case sometimes; and this would simply give us 'Malum Cydonium' or 'Cydonia,' the quince, as in the text. But for the fact that the digamma appears to be always given in Etruscan, I should have read the AEL in AELCHE as AFEL-, *apfel-*, *apple-ish*.

assigned in reference to the matronymic borne by Folnius, KIARTHIAL, i. e. 'mother's son of KIARTHI.' That the letters K and su are interchangeable in Etruscan, as in other languages, we shall find by many examples; and TH is a softened form of 'z.' KIARTH is thus simply the Teutonic *suuurz, suarz*, swart, the exact equivalent of 'Fuscus.'

A similar case, in which an *agnomen* is attributed to the Etruscan gentleman, borrowed from his mother's name, occurs in the following inscription,—

C · LICINI C · F · NIGRI
V · LEKNE V · | THAPIRNAL
(*Fabretti*, no. 253. At Florence. Found at Siena.)

The *agnomen* NIGER here is formed from the name of THAPIRN, the mother of Licinius, as shewn by his matronymic. We are at once reminded of the Greek ζοφερ-ός, 'niger, ater, tenebrosus,' black as night, or as the infernal regions; while the word and the common root are equally known in Teutonic as *zauber*, *zauberey, zaubern, zauberinn,* used for the 'black art,' or magic, and its male and female professors. Our English *sombre* (its connection with 'umbra' being merely collateral) is simply the Greek ζοφερ- or Etruscan TUAPIRN, the φ or '*p*' being written with us in the more archaic form of μφ or *mb*, which in fact is represented in the German *zauber* as *ub*.

This process is so curious that I may cite yet a further illustration from an inscription preserved at Perugia,—

PUP · VELIMNA AU KAHATIAL
P · VOLUMNIUS · A · F · VIOLENS
CAFATIA · NATUS
(*Fabretti*, no. 1496. Perugia.)

—The maternal name here was ΚΑΠΑΤΙ, or (as that name is elsewhere written) ΚΑΡΠΑΤΙ. This is simply our modern German *heftig*, violent, vehement, the older *haftig*, derived from the same root as the Etruscan CAPYS, or γύψ, hawk or vulture, viz. *hab-en*, 'cap-ere,' to seize; and Volumnius received the Latin *agnomen* of VIOLENS in consequence.

This inscription, which is on an 'arca' in form of a temple, is very full and illustrative, AU, the patronymic, being represented by 'A. F.,' and -AL being translated, as usual, 'natus.' This 'arca' forms a part of the treasures of the tomb of the Volumnii discovered on (or immediately adjacent to) the property of the Conte Benedetto Baglioni, the descendant of a family which gave sovereign 'signori' to Perugia, and, I suspect, also of the Volumnii themselves, the two names being etymologically identical. It was thus that tombs of the great and numerous Cæcina family of Volterra and Rome were discovered last century, one of them, if I recollect rightly, on the actual property of the descendant of the family near Volterra, himself an 'Aulo Cecina' by traditional family nomenclature. The direct line became extinct in the person of a learned ecclesiastic early in the present century. My belief is that many old Etruscan families are still flourishing, and recognisable.

Among the *prænomina* differing in the two languages but of identical signification, that of the Etruscan VELE or 'Velius,' as interpreted by 'Caius,' occurs most frequently. We have had an example of this in the epitaph of Licinius just discussed, and other instances may be seen in the Appendix. In all such cases the explanation must be sought for through inquiring what objects the names denote in common in the respective tongues. A proximate point of mutual connection in the present instance presents itself in the fact that while the Teutonic *wald* signifies forest, the medieval-Latin 'gaia' or 'gaium'—which I shall shew was likewise an Etruscan word—denotes the thick wood or copse on the higher slopes of hills,— the names 'Caius,' 'Caia,' 'Velius,' 'Velia' being thus tantamount, I might almost say, to 'Silvester' and 'Silvia,' names not wholly in disuse among ourselves. But the essential and ultimate point of contact is more remote; and the recollection of the old formula 'Ubi tu Caius, ego Caia,' uttered by the Roman wife on crossing her husband's threshold for the first time—the fact that all women married by 'co-exemptio' were 'Caiæ,' according to Cicero—the correspondence of one of the Sanscrit names for wife, 'gâjâ,' with the Etruscan and Latin 'Caia'—the fact that Γαῖα, Γῆ, the wife of the ancestral God Uranus, and whose name is usually understood to denote the Earth, was called so, as I conceive, originally as the 'Gâjâ' or 'Caia,' that is 'Wife' *per excellentiam*— and, lastly, the extreme antiquity of the name 'Caius' in Italy, common alike to Umbrian, Volscian, Oscan, and Roman—all contribute to refer that point of contact to very primeval antiquity. Traced to its origin, 'Caius' or 'Gaius' (for both names are the same) is, I think, identical with the old Egyptian *ka*, signifying 'husband, male,' while 'Caia' is the reflex or derivative from it, corresponding perhaps with the feminine article and affix (also in Egyptian) *t*, or *ta*,—the roots being primitive, and the same with that from which proceed the 'ish,' 'isha,' man and woman, husband and wife, in Genesis. But *ka* has (in Egyptian again) the parallel signification of 'bull,' and *ha* (also in Egyptian) that of 'cow;' and these sister words, with their varied meaning, descend collaterally through all the Aryan languages—the husband and wife, bull and cow, standing in correlative apposition to each other, the bull as the emblem of Caius and the cow of Caia, 'pater-' and 'mater-familias' respectively. On the other hand, a parallel series of words for 'bull' (more especially) likewise descends through the Aryan tongues in derivation from very remote antiquity, and of which *afl*, *Fal*, *bala*, strength, is a proximate root; and of these words—of which our English 'bull,' a word used by metonymy, like *ka*, for any male animal, is the best known representative—the alternate root must be presumed to be that of which the Canaanitish *baal* is the oldest recorded example; *baal* denoting man and husband in Canaanitish as *ishi* does in Hebrew or Semitic—*Baal* thus corresponding with 'Vel-ius' as *Ishi*, *Ka*, does with Caius, alike in sound and signification.* The result is that, traced to their *origines*, VELE in Etruscan has the same force as 'Caius' in Latin, and the two words could be used interchangeably; although, as 'Caius' was equally familiar to Roman and Etruscan while VELE was hardly known as a proper name beyond the

---

* On the signification of *baal* as man and husband, see an article by Mr. R. Stuart Poole on 'Baal' (in the geographical sense) in Dr. Smith's *Dict. of the Bible*, vol. I. p. 146.—"In Hos. ii. 16, a remarkable instance is preserved of the distinction . . between the heathen *Baal* and the Hebrew *Ish*,—'at that day, saith Jehovah, men shall call Me *Ishi* and shall call Me no more *Baali*,' both words having the sense of 'my husband.'"—*Ishi* is rendered in the Greek by ὁ ἀνήρ μου.

Etrurian bounds, the Romans used the former name by preference when the Etruscans wrote VELE.

Lastly, before passing to the bilingual inscription already spoken of as differing in character from all the others, I may pause on that referred to in the fifth of the series of results above noticed. It was discovered at Chiusi, the ancient Clusium, and is as follows:—

ATH · UNATA · VARNAL RA
M · OTACILIUS · RUFUS · VARIA · NATUS

(*Fabretti*, no. 794. Clusium.)

This inscription, a most interesting one in many respects, presents us with a case in which not only the *prænomina* but the *nomina* themselves, UNATA and 'Otacilius' differ, and may be presumed to be equivalent in the Latin and Etruscan languages. That the two versions both relate to one person can hardly be doubted, as there is no indication of wifehood in the Etruscan; while the correspondence of 'Variâ natus' with 'Varnal' almost prescribes the presumption.

I should connect UNATA, first, with the Etruscan ANDAS, interpreted 'Boreas' by Hesychius; secondly, with ANTÆ, likewise (on the same authority) Etruscan for the 'winds;' and thirdly, with ANTAR, another Etruscan word, signifying (still according to Hesychius) ἀετός, the eagle. ANTAR, as I have shewn in the Glossary in the Appendix, is a compound of *weat*, *ant*, *and*, *wint*, wind, and *ar*, to go, or travel, as a voyager on the storm, *ar* having the collateral sense of messenger, as in the Greek 'Iris' for example, and other Teutonic words—the Etruscan 'Aruns' being probably connected with it; while *ar*, *åro*, has moreover the independent sense of 'eagle.'* ANTÆ is also a variety of *wint*, wind, and ANDAS is a compound of this same *ant*, *wint*, or possibly of *andi*, 'regio,' and *eis*, ice,—while 'Boreas,' the equivalent of ANDAS, has the signification alike of the Northwind and of the God who presides over it. 'Aquilo' is his alternate title in Latin—one equally applicable to ANDAS and (as we shall find) UNATA.

Turning to 'Otacilius'—'Ὀτασίλ-, as it is written in Greek, with the initial long—and dividing the word as 'Ot-acil-,' I should identify i. 'Ot' with *weut*, wind, *ut supra*; and, ii. '-acil' with 'aquil-a,' eagle (the *vogel*, or bird, *per excellentiam*); and, further, with 'Aquilo,' Boreas, a name used indiscriminately (as just stated) for the North Wind and the deity who impersonates it; and which is etymologically one with the Old-Northern and Aryan *jökull*, the "thick-ribbed ice" of the north,—so far corresponding to ANDAS.

I should hardly venture, on this ground alone, to identify UNATA with 'Otacil-' as Etruscan and Latin equivalents of 'Boreas' or 'Aquilo,' the eagle-spirit or demon of the North-wind; but the convergence of testimony tends to that conclusion, as I shall now shew; and the result has a direct ethnological value in regard to one particular family (at least) among the Etruscans.

The detection of a common element in the eagle as connected with the two names UNATA and 'Otacil-ius,' is supported by the fact that the coins of

* *Wint*, *wwat* (the earlier form), springs from *wui-as*, to blow, as *derbe*, eagle, dors from the kindred *dæ*, ἄημι, to blow.

Marcia Otacilia Severa, wife of the Emperor Philip I., the most important personage of the Gens Otacilia, exhibit (as a rule) an eagle as their device, the bird usually holding a wreath of laurel in his beak or the thunderbolt in his claw, while a palm-branch is displayed in the field, and Otacilia's head is cinctured by the crescent moon,—the eagle being thus presumably the heraldic cognisance of the 'gens,' and the various accessories referential to its traditions. But this cognisance points, if I mistake not, to more than mere symbolic allusion,—taken in connection with other facts, it seems to indicate a claim on the part of the UNATA, ANTAR, or 'Otacilian' family to descent from the semi-divine Boreas himself—or, as I may now perhaps venture to suggest, from the great Jötun giant of the North celebrated in the Edda under the name of 'Hraesvelgr'—the 'Aquilo' or 'Boreas,' as I conceive, of the common ancestors of the Northmen and the Etruscans.

That the classical Boreas was looked upon as of the eagle kind, or invested with the qualities of the eagle, is clear from his title 'Aquilo;' and thus Ovid uses no mere metaphor when he writes,

"Excussit pennas, quarum jactatibus omnis
Afflata est tellus; latumque perhorruit aequor."*

In parallelism to this, but with more ethnological distinctness, we read in the Edda that the Jötun or giant Hraesvelgr dwells at the extremity of the North in the shape of an eagle, or indued at least with eagles' wings, by shaking which he produces

* *Metam.* vi., 703-4.

the wind which sweeps over the earth.* Reverting again to Boreas, his two sons, the Boreades, Zetes and Calais, are described as winged, in which capacity they drive away the Harpies who tormented Phineus, during the Argonautic Expedition, and act as envoys or messengers of Zeus in conveying Latona to the protection of Poseidon when threatened by Pytho,—mingling the while among men in every other respect as human beings. With these facts before us, and keeping the heraldic or medallic symbol of the eagle in recollection, I can hardly doubt that 'Hræsvelgr,' 'Boreas,' 'Aquilo,' 'Andas,' and 'Antar' are but various names for the same personage,—that the 'Otacilii' or Uṅata, claimed descent from him,—and that the eagle on the coins is assumed in token and memory of this Hyperborean pedigree. You might perhaps hesitate were I to suggest that 'Hræs-velgr'—for so, I think, the name should be etymologically divided †—is a Scandinavian form of 'Boreas-fylg,' the latter word denoting guardian spirit, 'Boreas-fylg' being thus equivalent to 'Boreas the ἄγγελος, or messenger;' and that Ὀτ-ακίλ- may be ultimately resolvable into this compound name; but the inference is palpably supported by the facts, that, by an ancient tradition, the 'Otacilii' derived their origin from Dacia, that is, Thrace, —that Boreas lived (according to mythological

---

* "Tell me,.. whence the wind comes, that over oxen passes, itself invisible to man?"—"Hræsvelg he is called, who at the end of heaven sits, a Jötun in an eagle's plumage: From his wings comes, it is said, the wind, that over all men passes."—*Lay of Vafthrudnir*, vss. 36, 37; 'Edda,' transl. by Mr. Thorpe, 1866, vol. 1. p. 16.

† It is currently divided as Aræ-svelgr, and derived from Arr, 'cadaver,' and svelg-, 'deglutire,'—'devourer of corpses.' But this etymology is in no wise supported by the legends of the North.

legend) in Thrace,—and that the 'Hraes' in 'Hraesvelgr' is etymologically the same as Ὀρᾷξ and 'Thrac-e,' on the one hand, and 'Boreas' on the other,—the Getæ moreover, the inhabitants of Dacia, being proto-Goths, or Jötuns—the 'Juthungi' being evidently one of their divisions—of the precise breed of Hraesvelgr. And I may draw a further illustration from the extremely curious but neglected record, the 'Fundinn Noregur' or 'Origines Norvegiæ,' the oldest and most precious relic of Thoringa history, or rather genealogy, anterior to Odin—a record which can be shewn to be trustworthy by the aid of traditions absolutely unknown to Scandinavia. We have there 'Frost,' otherwise named 'Jökull,' as, in the ascending line, the son of 'Kare,' the God of the Winds, and, in the descending, as the ancestor of 'Thor,' that is, of Thor, the eponymus of the Thoringa (of whom the Thrakes were a branch), and ancestor of the conqueror Odin, as distinguished from Thor, the God, the son of Odin, as identified with the *All-fader* or Supreme Deity. But 'Frost-Jökull' is evidently the same combination as 'Hraes-velgr,' 'Boreas-Aquilo,' 'Ὀτ-αχιλ-, this last being the Latin equivalent of the Etruscan UNATA, ANDAS, ANTAR. The identification of the names UNATA and 'Otacilius,' names at first sight so dissimilar, through a common etymological element, and apparently common traditional descent, may thus perhaps be considered established. And if so, my view that the Tyrrheni were of the great Thuringic, Tervingic or Tyrki stock, who must under any circumstances have held the tradition concerning 'Hraes-velgr' or 'Aquilo' in common, is confirmed in a very curious manner.

The branch of laurel and the crescent moon on the coins of Marcia Otacilia may perhaps be allusive to the good service performed to Apollo and Diana in the person of their mother Latona by Zetes and Calais, the Boreades, from one or other of whom the Otacilii, or UNATA, presumably derived their ancestry.

The *prænomina* ATH and M., and the *cognomina* RA and RUFUS, in the respective versions of the inscription may merit notice.

M., I suspect, stands for 'Marcus' or 'Marcius,' which seems to have been a favourite *prænomen* with the Otacilii. Remembering that the characteristics and names of Mars and Mercury resolve into the same in many mythologies, and that Mercury was the God of boundaries, we may perhaps assume that the root of 'Marcus' or 'Marcius' here is *mark*, a boundary or land-mark. ATH, on the other hand, may be the basis of the Etruscan AISER and Teutonic *eter*, which we have recognised as implying likewise a boundary-stone or landmark. ATH may possibly be identical, as a personal name, with 'Otho'—that of the Roman Emperor, an Etruscan, with the 'Azo' of medieval Italy, and the 'Other,' 'Auster-ius,' which we find in Gallic France—in which latter form it runs parallel with AISER, *eter*. But my impression is that ATH, 'Otho,' and 'Azo' (at least), are but abraded forms of an earlier 'Tath,' or 'Taut,' answering to 'Tet,' the ancient name of Hermes or Mercury, and which in a still earlier and fuller form was written 'Thoth' and 'Zet;' and that we thus have in ATH the actual name 'Zetes,' that of the eaglet son of Boreas himself, and whom I take to have been one of the innumerable forms in which the idea of the messenger-god was manifested—Hermes, or Mercury, it will be remembered, being winged (and with mechanical or artificial plumage) likewise. The abode of Hrmesvelgr, as dwelling at the 'end'—*andi*—of heaven, implies an *eter*, or landmark. ATΠ and M., understood as Marcus or Marcius, thus tally, as above shewn, in Etruscan and Latin.

The final RA, in the Etruscan inscription, and RUFUS in the Latin, must not be overlooked. RUFUS, by the analogy of the inscription to the memory of 'Publius Volumnius, A. F. Violens, Cafatiâ natus,' should be a formation from the name of the mother of Otacilius, VARN or 'Varia.' 'Varna,' the word for caste in Sanscrit, denotes properly 'colour,' and red being the peculiar heraldic badge of the Aryan race, RUFUS would thus supply a fitting *agnomen*. But we have, I think, a closer link between VARN, 'Varia,' and RUFUS in the Pelasgic word πυρρ-ὀς, 'burr-us,' denoting 'rufus;' and VARN, 'Varia,' has, I presume, been understood as 'burr-a' or πυρρ-ά by the epigraphist on this occasion.*

RA, on the other hand, cannot be a *cognomen*, the

---

* It is worth notice that 'aquilus,'—blackish or dusky, is explained in an ancient Glossary as μέλας, ὡς ὁ λοκυάλλιος. The Lucilii were a plebeian (i. e. a non-Roman) *gens* at Rome, celebrated only for the poet Lucilius, the father of Roman satire, a native of Suessa in Campania, once an Etruscan province. I cannot say whether 'Otacilius' was ever written 'Olacilius' or 'Lacilina,' but one of the *cognomina* of the Lucilii was 'Rufus.' The above reference is cited by Wachter from Huet, who adds, "Nos Galli dicimus *in bise* pari significatu; nam Gallicè *bis* nigrum sonat. In quibusdam Galliæ nostræ locis ventus Thracias (Thracias) *niger* vocatur." See Wachter, Gloss. Germanicum, art. '*Buiswind*, Ionice, aquilo,' &c.— *Bis*, like the Greek φαιὸς, 'fuscus,' dusky, the equivalent of 'aquilus,' is a degenerated form of *swarz*, *zwrz*, *suasus*, black, the initial *z* having been altered, as in the parallel case of '*bis*,' δίς, '*duis*' (Lat. antiq.), *zwin*, &c.

use of which was foreign to Etruscan usage; it is hardly conceivable that it should in any shape (even abridged) represent the actual name Hraesvelgr; and I would only suggest, with great hesitation, that it may be the complement of UNAT-A, AND-AS, making up the full equivalent of ANT-AR, with the matronymic interposed, although there does not appear any adequate motive for such interpolation here.[*]

I now pass to the last of the bilingual inscriptions—one which stands apart from the rest, not only through the fullness of its alternate readings but the singularities attending it otherwise, and which render it somewhat doubtful whether it be really of Etruscan origin. I cannot even affirm that it is of a sepulchral character,—but, if not so, it must at least have been of the nature of a monumental slab or epigraph, for the purpose of preserving the memory of a distinguished man before the eyes of his countrymen. It runs thus,—

[*] As this particular notice has run to greater length than I intended, I subjoin in a note that ATH, 'Zetes,' the son of Boreas, or Hraesvelgr, may perhaps be identical with the Jötun 'Thiassi,' equally celebrated for his eagle-plumage, and who carried off Iduna, as Zetes carried off Latona (although with a different motive), and Boreas himself Orithyia, as recorded in classic story. I hardly like to suggest that all these names are etymologically convertible. Through Orithyia the Boreades had intimate relations with Athens, and Calais is stated to have founded Cales in (the once-Etruscan) Campania in Italy. 'Thiassi,' on the other hand, is apparently identical with 'Thessalus,' the son of Hercules, from whose son Aleuss descended the great and (as they were denominated) 'kingly' house of the Aleuadæ of Larissa in Thessaly—a race whom I have felt strongly tempted to connect with the Jarls of Hlade in Norway. The prænomen ATH appears to point ut supra to Zetes as the ancestor of the Otacilii in preference to Calais, and Zetes being thus apparently the same as Thiassi, I think it not impossible that they,—the UNATA, or ANTAS-, in their Etruscan name—may have been one of the many branches of the Aleuadæ.

G

...F · ATIUS · L · F · STE · HARUSPE(X)
FULGURIATOR
KAPHATES · LR · LR · NETŚVIS · TRUTNVT · PHRONTAK · *

(Olivieri's *Marmora Pisaurensia*, 1738, p. 11; pp. 56 sqq.)

—Fabretti ranks it among the Umbrian inscriptions; it certainly was discovered at Pesaro in Umbria, where it is now preserved; moreover, its calligraphy exhibits many variations from the style of Etruria proper. It speaks, however, of a personage whose public offices, that of 'Fulgurator' especially, were peculiarly Etruscan; and the words appear to me to be Teutonic, or explainable at least by that language. It is of course conceivable that an inscription in honour of a man exercising an art so widely spread as that of the Haruspex might be written in a dialect not Etruscan. On the other hand, the word NETŚVIS is found in a genuine inscription of Clusium, and this sets up a counter-presumption in favour of its Etruscan origin. The inscription is engraved in very ornate characters on a block of marble; and, from the style of the Latin portion of the calligraphy, cannot be earlier than the last age of the Republic; while the form 'Fulguriator' instead of 'Fulgurator' witnesses to provincial inaccuracy.

I reserve the consideration of the surname of the subject of the epigraph, and begin with the concluding words descriptive of his public offices, NETŚVIS, TRUTNVT, PHRONTAK.

Taking the word PHRONTAK first, in connection with 'Fulguriator,' it appears to be a compound of PHRONT and AK,—i. PHRONT being comparable—not

* The dots at the bottom of the line denote missing letters.

with βροντή, thunder, the Fulgurator being the especial interpreter of the lightning, but with *brennen*, *brant*, *brand*, in the sense of a thunderbolt; while AK is connectible with 'ico, ict-us,' stroke, and more remotely with ἀκίς, a point, taken in connection with πέλεκυς, the original flint-axe or hammer (as I take it to have been) of Thor, and with the ancient idea that flint arrow-heads—elf-bolts as they were called—were thunderbolts. The name, in a Latinised form, of the Etruscan god 'Jupiter Elicius,' to whom Romulus is said to have dedicated an altar on the Aventine, and from whom the Etruscans evoked ('eliciebant') lightnings by their sacrifices, is apparently a compound of 'El' = 'Ill' = 'Hr' = 'Ερρ-ος, and 'ic-,' that is, the AK here in question. A combination to the same effect, and shewing a nearer relationship to PHRONTAK exists in the titles of 'Thor-Aku' and 'Taran-Ukko' given to the Thunder-God of the Scandinavians and Finns; Taran-Ukko more particularly being identical with the 'Perkunas,' 'Perun,' &c., of the Lithuanian, Lettish, and Slavonian branches of the Aryan race, φ and θ being always interchangeable. But PHRONTAK seems to represent here the simple idea of 'lightning-stroke,' or 'fulgur.' I do not think that it includes the active force of '-ator' in 'Fulguri-ator, the sense of which must be sought for elsewhere.

Proceeding to TRUTNVT, the word which corresponds in position with 'Haruspex,' I should divide it as TRUTN-VT. It is susceptible of two interpretations, and we must defer election between them till the remainder of the inscription has been analysed. In the later and more proximate signification, and which answers to the classical sense of 'Haruspex,' (or rather 'Haruspicium,') TRUTN appears to me to represent a word denoting the intestines—which must, I think, have existed in ancient German—derived (like *drut*, 'filum tortum,' for example) from *drehen* (remotely akin to the Greek στρέφειν), to twist or turn round and round,—the obvious superficial characteristic of the entrails. VT, again, in this proximate or secondary sense of TRUTNVT, is connectible with such words as the Homeric ἔντερα, the Ionic ἐντάμνω, the Latin 'int-estinus' and 'exta,' and the Teutonic *giuz-, giut-, gut*; while the word ἔνθ-εος, 'enth-eus,' i.e. 'numine afflatus,' has evidently an origin much older than the ἐν-θεός from which it is popularly derived, connecting itself with the ideas which placed the seat of inspiration, of the divine *trift*, or 'affectus,' in the γαστήρ, or belly, and produced the word for a false prophet, ἐγγαστρίμυθος. But, while TRUTNVT has this proximate signification, it appears to me, in its remote origin, to be a compound, in the first instance, of TRUTN, a word identical with *Druhtin, Truhtin*, 'Dominus, Deus,' in the sense of Lord and Governor—a very ancient word, familiar both to the Germans proper and Scandinavians, found even in Etruria as ἐροῦνα, DRUNA, government, according to the testimony of Hesychius, and perhaps too the same which gave their name to the 'Druids' of Gaul and Britain; and, secondly, of VT, equivalent to 'fat-,' 'fat-um,' oracle, or to 'vat-,' 'vat-es-,' φήτης, ἀσιδός, prophet,—TRUTNVT thus signifying, originally and properly, 'Prophet'—or 'Oracle'—'of God.' The words 'Haruspex,' 'Haruspicium,' exhibit precisely the same double signification—'Haruspex,' proximately, in the personal sense, as the *hiru-spih*, that is, 'Intestine-viewer,' or *hiru-spec*, 'Intestine-prophet;' and remotely, as *Hru-spih*, or *Hru-spec*, 'Seer or Prophet of Hru, 'Ἐῤῥος, or God;' while the action or activity expresses itself in the derivative 'Haruspic-ium.' *

Without pausing to determine the exact signification of THUTNVT here, I proceed to NETÉVIS, the third word from the end in the sentence. To this there is apparently no equivalent in the Latin version; for 'STE · ' must, by position and analogy, represent the *agnomen* derived from the mother's name. The fourth letter in NETÉVIS has certainly more resemblance to an 'M' than an 'Ś' in the inscription (especially as compared with the 'N,' as engraved); but the calligraphy is very peculiar, and the 'Ś' occurs unmistakeably in what is evidently the same word in the inscription above-mentioned discovered at Chiusi, viz.,—

NAE · KIKU | PETHNAL | NETÉVIS

which is translated by Fabretti† (by the aid of the present inscription of Pesaro) as 'Nævius Cocnes, Petiniæ filius, Haruspex.'† NETÉVIS, divisible as NETÉ-VIS, has likewise two significations, a proximate

---

* Dr. Donaldson thinks that "haruspex was the genuine Pelasgian form, *trutnft* being the Rasenic or Etruscan synonym."—"As *tru* in Icelandic signifies *fides* or *religio*, and *fit-la* = *leviter digitos movere* (where *-la* is merely a frequentative affix, Rask, *Old Norse Grammar*, p. 168), I recognise *trius* = *bacillus* in the middle of *tru-in-ft*, and refer the whole to the use of the *lituus* by the Etruscan haruspex. Those who are not satisfied with this analysis may compare *trutnft* with the Runic *trutin*, 'God,' (Dieterich, p. 322), and *feta*, 'invenire' (Egilsson, p. 167)."—*Varron.*, p. 187.

† *Bullettino dell' Instituto Archæol. di Roma*, &c. 1866, p. 240. He had expressed a doubt in the 'Corpus' as to the genuineness of the inscription, which he retracts in the paper referred to.

and limited, a remoter and general one. In the proximate sense, it is analysable as i. ΝΕΤΣ́, equivalent to νῆστις, 'intestinum jejunum,' so called from its being usually found empty,—νῆστις standing in parallel line with νήδυα and νηδύς, the belly, and finding its root, I suspect, in that represented by νήθω, the Gaelic *sniomh*, the Welsh *nyddu*, and the Teutonic *knyta*, *knit*, or *net*, signifying, in some cases specially, to spin, and in all, in a general sense, to twist—the root extending, in fact, into the Turanian and Semitic languages,*—and, ii. VIS, equivalent to *wis*, wise, as in *wisa* (S.-G.), *weisen*, 'ostendere' (the peculiar word used for portents, 'ostenta'), 'explicare,' &c., with the ultimate sense of 'vid-eo,' ā-έω, to see or ascertain by observation, or know. The general or remoter signification is again to be found in the identity (as I think) of ΝΗΤΣ́ and *Ana-wort*, 'word of Ana,' 'Ana,' or 'Deity' (conf. *antwort der Götter*, oracle), a compound which has been abraded and softened down into NEVERIT- and NORT-, as in the names of 'Neverita,' the 'Dea Reverentiæ' of Martianus Capella, and of 'Nortia,' the Etruscan Goddess of Fortune; and, still further, into the 'nut-,' the symbolical 'nutus,' or 'nod' of Jove (not to be confounded with *nôt*, 'necessitas,' which is derived from

---

* Νηστεύω, to fast, is usually derived from νῆστις; but the etymology is rather from *an-ezan*, 'not to eat;' and the idea conveyed by νηστεύω would associate itself, I should think, with the 'dies nefasti,' or unlucky days—dedicated, I presume, originally to the deities of counter and depressed religions, on which, as on our Friday, the priests of the dominant religion prescribed 'jejunium.' The special sense of νῆστις in the text is therefore, I think, secondary; originally it meant, simply, 'intestinum.' The idea of 'nexus,' complication, extended itself from the root illustrated in the text to the operations in magic, so familiar to students of the Black Art.

a distinct root); and last (almost) of all, into 'fatum,' that which is enounced prophetically,—NETŚ, in combination with VIS, *ueis-*, thus signifying the 'ostentator' or 'shewer forth of the response' of God—in equivalent value to what I believe to have been the primitive sense of 'au-spex,' 'au-gur,' before the idea of observing special signs, birds, or otherwise, had suggested itself. A preponderance in value is given to this last etymology from the almost isolated character of the word νῆστις, as expressing intestines, —the word being apparently Hellenic, not Pelasgian, as shewn by its being represented by a different word in Latin.*

Reviewing therefore the facts and circumstances, 1. That two Latin words, 'Fulguriator' and 'Haruspex,' express the distinct acts and personal agency of two classes of diviners, those who divined by lightning and those who divined by the entrails of the victim,—2. That among the (presumed) Etruscan equivalents, PHRONTAK expresses only the object of the observation of the 'Fulguriator,' not his activity or personality,—3. That TRUTNVT, which answers to 'Haruspex,' may be presumed therefore to have a similarly restricted signification,—4. That NETŚVIS is used in the inscription of Chiusi apparently in a general and comprehensive sense, which the derivation above suggested warrants,—and lastly, That NETŚVIS, being first among the three words, may be expected to govern the whole, while it has apparently no immediate equivalent in the Latin,—I think, on these grounds, we may be justified in reading

---

* If 'exta' be an abraded form of νῆστ-ις, ν-ῆστ-, as I have sometimes thought, this last observation would require to be modified.

NETŠVIS · TRUTNVT · PHRONTAK as 'Augur,' i.e.
'Ostentator' or declarer of the will of God, 'through
Haruspicia' and 'Lightnings,'—NETŠVIS, or 'Augur,'
being the personal title, and TRUTNVT and PHRONTAK
expressing the particular character of his divination.
The Augurs, Haruspices, and Fulguratores formed
distinct schools (as it were) among the Etruscan
prophets, but there was no reason why one man
should not exercise two or more functions; and the
title 'Augur' was etymologically, and by mythological use (as in the epithet 'Augur Apollo'), the
most generic and comprehensive title of all.

Travelling now from the end to the beginning of
the inscription, I have to suggest that the KAPHATES
of the Etruscan line should be divided as KAPH ·
ATES, and the lost letters at the commencement of
the Latin be restored as 'Naef · Atius.' That the
Etruscan name should be so divided is imperative,
first, because otherwise the title would be without
a *prænomen*, which cannot be supposed; and,
secondly, because the separation by a point in the
Latin version prescribes it. The letters preceding
'·F' in the Latin text, might undoubtedly be read
'Cnf.,' answering to KAPH · , but I suspect that they
were 'Naef.,' short for 'Navius,' or 'Nævius,' mainly
on the ground that the latter name occurs as that of
a certain 'M. Nævius, M. F. Pal., Magnus Augur,'
in another Pesarese (exclusively) Latin inscription,
shewing that the word 'Nævius,' although there
figuring as a *nomen*, was in familiar use at Pesaro.
If this be so, the two names KAPH · and 'Naef.,' or
'Nævius' would appear to be equivalents—proximately, I mean—(as in the case of VELE, 'Caius,'

KIARTH, 'Fuscus,' and others)—in the two languages,—KAPH · representing the ancient *kp*, the hand or fist, and 'Nævv-' the root from which proceeds *nam-in*, to take, i.e. by the hand—the same too that we have in the cant words, 'nimm' and 'nab,' but which may be recognised still more closely in the S.-G. *naifire* and Scottish *neive*, the fist. 'ATES' or 'Atius,' the name itself, is etymologically, I think, akin to ἀοιδός, or 'vates,' as I propose to illustrate more fully.

It remains for me to notice the two words, evidently abridged, LH · and LR ·, which follow the *prænomen* and *nomen* in the Etruscan inscription. With these must be considered the 'STE · ' in the Latin version. The first LR · is evidently the Etruscan equivalent of 'L. F.,' and must be understood, I presume, as 'Lartis filius,' 'son of Larth,' or Lars. The second LR · occupies the usual place of the matronymic, and I should read it as LARTHIAL, 'son of Larthia.' 'STE · ,' which corresponds to it in place, must represent a *cognomen* translated from 'Larthia ;' and remembering the Græcising affectations which came in during the latter days of the Roman Republic, I suspect that this cognomen was 'Stephanus,' and that the association of ideas was with 'Lar' or 'Lars,' the root of 'Larthia,' understood (whether rightly or wrongly) in connection with the 'laurus' or laurel—that tree connected so closely with the practice of augury and worship of its supreme representative, Apollo.*

* 'Sto.' in Roman Inscriptions usually stands for 'Stellatinus,' i.e. a member of the Stellatina tribe, which gave name to extensive jurisdictions in Umbria, Campania, and Etruria. Pisaurum (Pesaro) did not however lie within the limits of any of these. Had the abbreviation borne this mean-

The double inscription thus reads as a whole, according to the above restoration,—" Nævius Attus, son of Larth, mother's son of Larthia," surnamed "Stephanus; Augur" in the quality of "Haruspex" and "Fulgurator."

I would crave your indulgence for one more remark ere dismissing this very interesting record,—although, indeed, I may shelter myself by pleading that it involves the discussion of an independent inscription, that above cited as existing at Chiusi to the memory of

NAE · KIKU | PETHNAL | NETÉVIS

—Here, differently from the inscription to the memory of M. Nævius the 'Magnus Augur' of Pesaro, NAE · figures as the *prænomen*, as in the case of KAPH · ATES, or 'Naef · Atius.' What I wish to shew is, that KIKU is an Etruscan variety of a very ancient word equivalent to 'vates,' and thus, as I believe, to ATES, 'Atius,' or 'Attus,' *ut supra*. The initial *sp* in the Zendic çpaç and Teutonic *spähi*, implying to 'spae' or divine—and which, modified as *h*, gives rise to *hexe, wicki, witch*, and links itself through the associations of sound with a word of distinct origin, *bitch*, 'Canidia'—takes, according to an usage already illustrated, the form of *k* in Etruscan; and thus *spähi* at once becomes *kähi*, KIKU, the *nomen* of NAE · KIKU, the NETÉVIS, or 'augur' (as I have translated the word), of Clusium. It is in like manner that the Latin 'cicer' softens into *vetch*; but I

ing here, it would probably have implied that the personage commemorated belonged to the 'Stellatinus ager' in the neighbourhood of Capena, the colony of Veii and ally of Falerii, in South Etruria. But it must (as stated) have been formed, as a *cognomen*, from Larthia.

strongly suspect that the name of 'Cicero' (Κικέρων) was derived originally from this KIKU, or a word akin to it, implying 'Diviner' or 'Augur,' and this would tally not merely with the peculiar, perhaps hereditary interest in divination evinced by the great representative of the family—Marcus Tullius having been himself an augur—but with the obscure tradition mentioned by Plutarch, that the Tullia Gens derived its descent from a king of the Volscians, by name 'Tullus Attius'—equivalent, as you will see, 'Attius' corresponding with VT, 'vates,' and VT with *spåhi*, KIKU, to 'Tullus Kiku' or 'Tullus Ates,'—that is, 'Tullus the Augur,'—NAE · KIKU of Clusium and the great Roman orator being, I have little doubt, of the same original stock or clan.* I wish that Tully were alive that I might make this suggestion to him in verification of the old family legend, for I am sure it would please him,—but, as the three Scotsmen explained simultaneously to Charles Lamb on his expressing a similar wish with regard to Burns, the man is dead, and there is no help for it. But more follows from this approximation of KIKU and 'ATES' or 'Atius,'—we obtain in NAE · KIKU, the equivalent of the great name 'Attus Navius'—that of the "inclytus augur" so famous in the days of Tarquinius Priscus, who cut the whet-stone with a razor, according to the legend recorded by Livy.†

* Another of the family is commemorated in the following inscription on the *operculum* or lid of a sarcophagus now preserved at Florence,—ATII KIKU · ATE · TUTNAL · (*Fabretti*, no. 150).—ATII has been inferred (*supra*) to correspond with 'Marcus' or 'Marcina.' 'M.' is the *prænomen* of the 'Magnus Augur' of Pesaro. Or is ATE here 'Attus'?

† The resemblance of the roots of *wetzstein* and *hvrzjan*, to cut or 'whittle,' to 'Att-ius,' evidently suggested the legend.

names in combination (although reversed in sequence), and in such immediate connection with augury, at so late a date; and I think it may further be presumed, the practice of such divination being so widely diffused, that these Nævii and Atti of Pesaro and Chiusi must have been of the race of the great diviner who first bore the conjunct names.* It is not clear that Attus Navius was an Etruscan, although he was taught by the Etruscans; and the argument against the Roman origin of the poet Cn. Nævius from the fact of the name of Plautus, an Umbrian, being coupled with that of Nævius in the 'De Oratore,'† would tell in favour of the family being Umbrian, and thus, not impossibly, natives originally of Pisaurum.

Lastly, the title 'Navius,' or 'Nævius,' represents, as it appears to me, in its remote origin, the 'au-' in 'au-spex,' 'au-gur,' and the *avi* in the correspondent Zendic *aviçpaç*, in an older form; and I should derive all these forms therefore from the very archaic πν-μ, 'N-m,' 'N-f,' found as πνεῦμα, Num-a, Nep-, and otherwise—a root, with its derivatives, common to the Aryan, Hamitic, and Semitic stocks (the familiar *nabu, neby*, a prophet, representing it in Assyrian,

* Fabretti, in his interesting communication to the 'Instituto di Corrispondenza,' 20 Oct. 1860, in which he expresses his final adherence to the reading NETFVIS, and interprets it as "*haruspx od augur*," adds,—" Veggano ora gli Etruscisti . . se si possa credersi accidentale la presenza di *Navius* e di *augur* in una stessa urna cineraria," (that of M. Navius at Pesaro); "o veggano altresì so non sia tempo di rendere all' Etruria il monumento di Pesaro" (the inscription now discussed), "città che non appartenne alla tribù *Stellatina* (al r'erano ascritte la vicina *Urbino* e le Etrusche *Cortona, Tarquinii, e Orvieca*), come non v'appartenne certamente la città che diede i natali a l'ornenna."—*Bullettino*, 1866, p. 240.

† See Dr. Smith's *Dict. Greek and Rom. Biography, &c.*, art. *Nævius*, Cn.

Hebrew, and Arabic), and denoting the Almighty in the character of the 'Spirit,' the source of *trift* or inspiration. The combinations *avi-spas,* 'au-spex,' NAE · KIKU, KAPH · ATES, 'Navius Atius,' and conversely, 'Attus Navius,' would thus denote 'Prophet' or 'Diviner of the God-Spirit,' or 'Spirit-God.'

It is quite clear that there are Etruscan elements in this inscription,—the question is whether an Umbrian influence is also perceptible,—if so, it holds a position in regard to the great body of the Etruscan inscriptions something like that occupied by those of the Tyrrheni-Pelasgi at Cære. TRUTN connects itself as much with the Gaul and the Briton as with the Teuton. NETÉ, the root of NETSVIS, has a very marked development, in the sense of reticulation, in the Cymric languages. The claim of the poet Nævius to Roman origin is contested, as has been seen, on a ground not to be dismissed lightly. And Pesaro is in Umbria. But the Umbrians were of the Aryan stock; the argument is good, if not for the Teutonic, at least for the Aryan character of the Etruscan language; and anything which connects the NETSVIS or 'Augur' of Umbria and Etruria with our kinsmen of the Cymric and Celtic race cannot but be interesting.

I am distressed at the length to which this review of the bilingual inscriptions has run; but the subject is important, and this must be my excuse. I now proceed to the class of

SECTION II.—*Sepulchral Formulæ*.

There are several *formulæ* of constant occurrence in the sepulchral inscriptions that are not bilingual, but of which the general significance has been long recognised. The most familiar of these is the phrase RIL, RIL AVIL, AVIL, AVILS, always, either together or separately, preceding a numeral, and which has been inferred with good reason to signify 'vixit annos,' and 'ætatis.'* These words are, I think, purely Teutonic—RIL being formed from a common root with our English *roll*, to revolve—*hicarld-*, *hverfl-*, in old German—having nearly the signification of the "conversari" of the Romans—our *year* or *jahr* itself, the "revolving year" of Thomson, being of kindred origin; while AVIL, AVILS (in the genitive), correspond with *hvila* (O. H. G.), *hveila* (Goth.), *hvilr*, *hvile* (O. Sax. and A.-Sax.), our English 'while,' a word signifying an allotted portion of time, varying as a minute, an hour, a year, or a lifetime.† Sometimes RIL occurs in combination with the word LEINE, thus—RIL XIII LEINE; RIL LEINE L.; RIL XLII LEINE, &c.; and this LEINE I take to be the third person singular, present tense, of the verb *langen*, 'manum extendere, manu attingere'—*in einem ort gelangen*, to reach a particular spot; *in etwas gelangen*, to attain a certain object—that is, in the sepulchral sense, the goal, or term of life,—the Etruscan combination thus denoting, Velus or Larthia 'reached' or 'attained to thirteen years,' 'reached fifty years,' 'reached forty-two years,' and so on.

But a more difficult question is the proper interpretation of the following fuller *formula* which is

---

* See Fabretti, in his Glossary; and Dennis, *Cities*, &c., vol. i., p. xliv. AVITA occurs also as AVILA, but rarely.

† See, for illustrations, Graff's *Althochdeutscher Sprachschatz*, vol. iv. col. 1224.

frequently found over the doorways of tombs, and on sarcophagi, sometimes as EKAŚUTHI or EKA : ŚUTHI; sometimes as EKAŚUTHINEŚL, or with the component words divided, as in these two inscriptions, the first found at Castel d'Asso, the second at Toscanella,—

EKAŚUTHINEŚL · TETNIE ...
EKA : ŚUTHI · NEŚL : PAN ...
(*Fabretti*, no. 2089, 2133.)

—They may be dissected as follows:—

1. EKA.—This word, a different one from EKA in the inscription analysed in a former page, is usually identified with 'ecce,' or with 'hic,' here; and, if the latter, I should be tempted to recognise it in the Italian 'quà,' here. But, taking it in connection with all the other inscriptions (more than twenty in number), one or two of them not sepulchral, in which it occurs, I think it is an adjective or participle akin to *eig-*, *eigen*, to possess, in the sense of property, and with the sanction of *ehe*, law; and that it has a signification akin to the Latin 'proprius,' or 'own,'—special or private. In this sense it is congenital with *hag*, *hay*, 'sepes, domus,' the Greek οἰκ-ος, as from ἔχ-ω; with the -φάγ-ος in 'sarcophagus' (as I divide the word); and with -KE, which we shall meet with in an Etruscan word of nearly the same signification as 'sarcophagus,' viz., ZILACHENKE. Ἔχ-ω, *eig-*, again, is, if I am not mistaken, an abraded form of *erc-*, *arc-*, *είργ-*, implying seclusive, inclusive, or absolute possession; and thus EKA and 'arca,' a chest (the word constantly used for a coffin), are probably one and the same word originally, even as the '-aculum' in 'recept-aculum' is, I presume, a worn-down form of '-erculum,' as in 'op-erculum.' But the simple sense here, I think, is—'Legally own,' or 'Private.'

2. ŚUTHI.—This word I should compare with *setz-en*, 'statuere, ordinare,' in a general sense, *satjan*, *gasatjan* (Goth.), to set, place, or lay; whence *sezzi*, a place set apart for any one, the Suio-Gothic *kaette* and *kelti*, a grave, and the *hethio*,

'cubiculum' or bed, of Ulphilas,—all answering to the Greek idea of a κοίτη, κοιμητήριον, or sleeping-place,—ŚUTHI thus corresponding with *sezzi*, *hethio*, and signifying (specially) 'sepulchre.' 'Kit's Cotty House,' and other similarly named monuments in England, have, I should think, a similar derivation. ŚUTHI and EKA would appear to be used as a compound, judging by the single dot, or stop, which follows ŚUTHI in the second of the inscriptions here under discussion, of which I have noticed one or two other instances in the case of compounds, the single dot usually following the second word of the compound, and not interposed between them in the modern fashion.—Lastly, as regards

3. NEŚL,—my impression is, that this is the older form of *isel*, 'fomes, favilla,' the "yet glowing ashes of the dead," as interpreted by Mr. Bunbury; and *åtel* (Suio-Goth.), *as, az* (Alem.), *awasel, awesel*, 'cadaver,' a corpse. *Isel* and *åtel* would become *aselsen* through the pretty frequent literal change of *n* for *l*. The link between *isel, åtel*, and NEŚL is supplied by the Zendic *naçu, naçus*, 'cadaver,' the word so constantly met with in the Zend-Avesta, showing, I think, that *isel, åtel* have originally been *nisel, nåtel*. The root *naç* is common to Zendic and Sanscrit; and, although the word does not occur with the sense of a corpse in the latter language, *nashta*, the perfect past participle of the verb *naç*, has the sense of 'dead' or perished, and the familiar change of *t* into *l* gives us at once *nisel, nåtel*, NEŚL, as 'cadaver.' The probability is that the Zendic-Sanscrit root *naç* is the same as the Teutonic *nad-, nass*, moist or wet—our English 'nasty.' *

Coupling therefore EKA : ŚUTHI with NEŚL, we have

* A very near consanguinity to NEŚL may be recognised in the Armenian *nekheal*, a corpse, akin to *nas*, a coffin in that language. This is remarked in one of the most ingenious approximations of Mr. Ellis in his *Armenian Origin of the Etruscans*, pp. 109, 110. He compares the Armenian *ahd soozani nekhnal*, i.e. 'ecce *esso* condit putrefactus,' with EKA : ŚUTHI - NEŚL, and translates the latter 'hic conditur mortuus,' or 'cadaver.' I had not thought of the connection of *νέκυς* and *νεκρός* with NEŚL till I read Mr. Ellis's work. Dr. Donaldson translates EKAŚUTHI as 'This is the mourning,' reading ŚUTHI as the Icelandic *sut*, 'dolor;' and EKA ŚUTHINEŚL as 'This is the sorrowful inscription.'—*Varron.*, p. 209.

the sense, " Private Sepulchre" or " Private resting-place of the remains of "—for example Tetnia, Titnia, or Titinia, the lady whose name follows the *formula* in one of the inscriptions above cited—cut boldly in the face of the rock over the portal of what was once her tomb at Castel d'Asso.

SECTION III.—*The Alethna Sarcophagus.*

I shall not give you many of the longer sepulchral inscriptions, as they are full of words relating to the computation of time and the mythology of Mantus and the Etruscan Hades as to which I have not as yet satisfied myself, and which would require a very extended examination properly to identify. The following however is a comparatively short and intelligible one, and will, I think, support my general argument. It falls into two portions, the first being written on the *arca* or chest itself, the second on the *operculum* or lid of one of the sarcophagi of the Alethna family discovered in a tomb near Viterbo in 1850. This tomb contained more than forty very large sarcophagi, several of them doubtless 'bisomi,' or calculated to contain two bodies. Most of them were highly ornamented with bas-reliefs. The style of the inscriptions exhibits, if I mistake not, an expression of sentiment rarely demonstrated in those of Etruria,—beside other peculiarities.

LARTH · ALETHNAS · ATHNTHAL · RUVPHIALK · KLAN
AVILS · I X · LUPUKE · MUNISVLETH · KALUSURABI
TAMERA · ZELAVV ENVS · LURI · MIAKE
(*Fabretti*, no. 2058.) *

I analyse these inscriptions—for they are practi-

* In the first of these inscriptions, as transcribed by Orioli, the word

cally two—as follows,—taking that of the sarcophagus itself first:—

1-5. LARTH · ALETHNAS · ATHNTHAL · RUVPHIALK · KLAN.—The names and designation of the man interred, of which the three first words are clearly intelligible as 'Lars Alethnius, son of Atonia,' or 'Athnia,' and the fifth as 'eldest' son of his family. The fourth, RUVPHIALK, is more puzzling. Taking it in connection with the inscription immediately preceding it in Fabretti's 'Corpus,' viz. AE ... THNAS .. NNTHAL KLA .. THANKVIL LSK · RUVTHIAL · ZILACH .. &c., and with a short one at the foot of a sarcophagus, with the figure of a woman recumbent on it, discovered at Siena, and numbered 456 by Fabretti, viz. A · SEMNA · LK | AU · SIEN · AU ·, it is clear, 1. That RUVPHIA and LK in the present inscription are two separate words,—2. That LK is in a less full form than LSK, which last therefore furnishes the type of the word; and, 3. That in all the three cases it expresses a relationship of some sort existing between man and woman, presumably husband and wife; and as the man's name figures first in the two former and the woman's in the last of the three inscriptions, it probably expresses a relationship of affection primarily, independently of status or law. My impression is that the word answers to the German *lust*, 'joy, comfort, delight,'—the k taking the place of t, as in so many instances; and that, while the Sienese inscription reads, "A. Semna, the comfort of Aulus Sienna, the son of Aulus," and the epitaph preceding the present one as "Ael. Alethnius, the son of Arnthia, eldest son of his family, the comfort of Tanaquil, daughter of Ruvthia"—we must read here, "Lars Alethnius Athnthl, the comfort of Ruvphia"—Ruvthia, the mother of

LUPUKE is written LLPLKR. This, however, is so evidently (to my mind) a misreading of the second and third 'l's, a letter which merely differs in Etruscan from 'u' by the stroke to the left being more prolonged, that I have restored LUPUKE, a word frequently found in sepulchral inscriptions, and an example of which will be cited presently, also from the present tomb. It is to be observed that the 'm' employed is the more archaic one. The 's' used throughout is the *sigma*; the *san* does not occur. The two 'o's in EELAVV are written with a form of the digamma commonly found in Oscan and Umbrian inscriptions, but seldom in Etruscan, and different from that used in ENVS and elsewhere in the present inscription.

Tanaquil, being, I have little doubt, the same as Ruvphia, the wife of Lars, the personage whose epitaph we are now dealing with.*

6, 7. AVILS · ↑ X.—According to Fabretti ↑ stands for the Roman L., 'quinquaginta,' fifty. Taking X for 'decem,' ten (for which there is ample authority), AVILS · ↑ X would thus read 'ætatis I.X,' or 'sixty.'

8, 9. LUPUKE.—Divisible as LUPU KE.—L LUPU is, I think, the ablative of LUP, the Etruscan form of *lib*, *lif*, 'vita,' life. —iL KE I take to be the third person singular of the perfect tense (of course contracted) of *gehen*, to go. LUPUKE would thus signify 'went from life.'

10. MUNISVLETH.—Three words, or rather, three compounds, slightly differing from each other, and which require careful discrimination, appear in the Etruscan inscriptions— the present MUNISVLETH, MUNISURETH, and MUNIKLETH, or MUNIKLET. The letters sv and K (as already observed) are interchangeable, as by many examples in the Indo-European dialects (e.g. 'qualis,' *sulch*, 'such'); but I think the word MUNIKLETH is distinct from the other two. I shall notice it hereafter on two occasions. And that MUNISVLETH and MUNISURETH are distinct compounds would appear from the third and fourth syllables of each appearing (although in a different combination in the former case) on another of the sarcophagi found in the present tomb, the inscription of which runs,

1....... ALETHNASSETHRESA : NESS · SAK ······ S ····· | KLEN
.... I · MULETHSVALASI · ZILACHNUKE · LUPUKE · MUNI-
SURETHKALU,—with the additional words on the *operculum*,
AVILS↑XXLLIV (LUPUS.

(*Fabretti*, no. 2059.)

—It appears from this approximation that MUNI and SVLETH

* *Th* and *Ph*, *θ* and *φ*, were (as already remarked) frequently interchangeable, and the names of RUVPH and THANKVIL occur together, apparently as two daughters, in the inscription numbered 2069 by Fabretti, the last two letters in the former name being expressed by two Greek capital sigmas, which Fabretti reads 'SS.', but which I think are intended to represent the Etruscan variety of *ph* above spoken of as in shape like an hourglass, and which, being found in the Pelasgic Inscriptions of Caere, denote, I think, a high antiquity for this tomb of the Alethnii.

form the component elements of the present word; and towards its interpretation the first step must be to ascertain the meaning of MUNI. Taking SVLETH in *primâ facie* connection with it, and remembering that it occurs on a sarcophagus, the idea at once suggests itself that MUNI may represent 'Mantus,' the Etruscan Hades. The *d* or *t* following *n* is constantly (as has been stated) omitted in these inscriptions. And the identification is supported by comparison with the word MULETH in the parallel compound MULETH-SVALASI. The word 'Mantus' signifies the *mund*, or mouth—of Hell; whence the 'Mundus' of the Roman forum. And MULETH expresses the same idea through its root *mul*, the modern *maul*, mouth or maw—whence *mulecht*, 'oris formam vel vim habens,'—a derivative which closely resembles—even if it be not identical with—MULETH. Taking these words in connection with -SVLETH and -SVALASI, the identification becomes more complete, the latter being evidently, I think, the old Teutonic *schwelgen*, 'voracem esse,' our English 'swallow'—akin to *swalg* (in the dialect of Bremen*), 'helluo,' a glutton. The mythological character of the Etruscan Charon (more particularly) has been built up through the suggestive association of many words bearing a general resemblance to *swalg*, or of words compounded of interchangeable consonants, such as *selch*, *zwill*, *quell*, *zwerke*, *twerch*, *scherg*, *quälchen*, and others. MUNISVLETH thus means in this place, I conclude, 'to,' or 'into, the swallow,' or 'maw,' of 'Mantus,' i.e. Hades, or Orcus.

11, 12. KALUSURASI.—Divisible as KALU SURASI. For i. KALU, compare *kals*, 'cruciatus, dolor,' the modern German *qual*,—from a common root with *qualm*, death, and with the name of the Etruscan demon, KULMU, for whom I would refer you to the Glossary in the Appendix.—ii. SURASI I should compare with *swar*. 'gravis;' *scers*, 'dolor;' *sura*, 'læsio,' and our English *sorrow*, &c.—The general signification would be that of 'heavy' or 'bitter grief.'

The inscription may thus be read in English—

---

* I have frequently paused over words in this dialect as apparently akin to Etruscan.

"Lars Alethnius, the son of Atonia, the comfort of" his wife "Tanaquil, daughter of Ruvphin, passed from" this "life into the jaws of death, aged sixty years, bitterly mourned for."

The second legend, that on the lid of the sarcophagus, may be explained as follows:—

1. TAMERA.—To be compared with the Greek δάμαρ, a wife or married woman.*
2. ZELAVV.—Compare with *geleibet*, 'relictus;' *sa leibu*, 'residuum;' *ci leipu*, 'residui,'—derivatives from *leiben*, 'to linquere post se,' to leave behind one.
3. ENVS.—Compare with *enbeissen*, 'edere,' to eat; *anbeissen*, 'jentare,' to breakfast; *imbes*, *imbesse*, *imbiss*, 'jentaculum, prandium,' breakfast, dinner; *imbitz*, 'præbenda,' what is offered in tribute or otherwise, as 'jentaculum diis offerre,' &c. &c.
4. LUBI.—Compare with *lurk*, 'sinister, perversus,' (the *k* being omitted in the orthography,)—an epithet which would be in conformity with many Etruscan epithets of Hades and Charon implying transverseness, running across the path—of life. We have had this word as LARKE previously. LURK, LUBI, and *thwerch*, *dwerch*, are probably the same word, the "*l*" being used in the one form and the '*th*' or '*d*' in the other.
5. MIAKE.—Compare either with *mehto*, 'potestas;' or (in more special signification) with *mauch-*, *meuch-*, *meuchel*, 'clandestinus;' *mucker* (Saxon and Bremish), 'sicarius;' *mucken*, 'sicarium agere;' *meuchel*, 'sicarius.'

The sense would therefore be, "The perverse (or

---

* It might also have the sense of 'mourning' in the sense of blackness, *sauher*; but δάμαρ is more natural. The word TAMERA occurs, in combination, as ETVA · TAMERA, in another of these family sarcophagi, no. 2056 of Fabretti; where ETVA, I think, means 'widow,' as I shall shew in relation to the same word occurring in another Inscription, *infra*. And we have TAMERA on a sarcophagus in the Vatican, (*Fabretti*, no. 2100,) in combination with a word resembling in some respects that which we have next to deal with; to wit, ‡ TAMERA - ZELABAVAUA.

malevolent) power (or assassin) devours the wife, the survivor," or "relict." This inscription, I imagine, was added when the widow of Lars Alethnius was consigned to the same sarcophagus with her husband.*

SECTION IV.—*The Cesina Inscription.*

I may now pass to an inscription—or rather two inscriptions—which were found painted on opposite walls in a tomb of the Cesina (not Cæcina) family at Tarquinii, in 1735. Neither of them is quite complete, but, although Fabretti describes the first of them as an "intricatissima epigrafe," the sense can be arrived at with tolerable accuracy, and they are very interesting. The one seen in front, on entering the sepulchre, ran as follows:—

LARTH · KEISINIS · VELUS · KLAN · KIZI · ZILACHNKE |
MEANI · MUNIKLETH METHLM · NUPPHZI KANTHKE ·
KALUS ... LUPU
(*Fabretti*, no. 2339.)

—The signification will appear (or at least an approximation may be made to it) through the following analysis:—

1–4. LARTH · KEISINIS · VELUS · KLAN.—The name, in the nominative case, of the owner of the tomb, 'Lars Cesina, [eldest] son of Velius.' VELUS is genitive of VELE.

* Yet another interpretation might be suggested, by which TAMERA would answer to the Teutonic *dammen*, '*dommare,*' *dämmern,* to strike or slay; and ZELAVV would imply 'remains' in the sense of 'corpse,' or body,—the sense being, "The malevolent power devours the stricken remains." But this appears to me too vague and unpractical a rendering; and I have therefore preferred that in the text, although I am not altogether satisfied with it.

5. KIZI.—I take this word to be the German *dies* and English *this*, but in the primitive form as still preserved in vernacular Italian. Analogously to what we see in 'quinque, qvinqve,' πέντε, *fünf, five*, there must have been first, a primitive 'quizi' or 'kvizi,' then KIZI as here, and then, by mutation of *k* into *t* or *th* (as in 'quatuor,' τέσσαρες), *thisi, diess, this,*—the original KIZI—or rather, the older form *kvizi*—having descended to the Tuscan (Etruscan) peasant of to-day as 'questo.'

6. ZILACHNKE,—to be transcribed more correctly ZIL-ASCHNKE.—From its position in many sepulchral inscriptions this word would appear to signify, generally, tomb or coffin; and on dissection it resolves into, i. ZIL, *teil*, 'portio,' or what is separate; ii. ASCHEN, the genitive plural of *esch*, 'favilla,' ashes; and iii. KE, akin (as has been shown) to *ag-, hag-* (a 'hedge'), *hay, kau,* in the sense of fortified defence, for protection. ZIL-ASCHEN-KE would thus mean 'repository for separation of the ashes' of the dead. It is thus analogous to σαρκοφάγος—the component elements of which word are evidently, i. σάρξ, σαρκός, *hræ*, 'corpus;' and ii. *ϕvγ-, ὑγ-* (as in ὑγγός, a vase or urn), '*ag-*' (as in '*agger*'), *hag*, 'sepes,' &c. *ut supra*.

7. MEANI.—Compare with *mund*, 'tutela, potestas;' *munden*, 'asserere, defendere, tueri,'—a word closely connected in its sepulchral signification with the Etruscan MANTUS, or 'Mandua.' It here implies, I think, 'owns,' 'occupies,'—or perhaps 'tenants' would best express the whole range of signification.

8. MUNIKLETH.—Not, as I have shown, to be confounded with MUNISVLETH and MUNISUBETH—or even with another word of nearer resemblance, MUNIKLET, hereafter to be dealt with. The word here in question corresponds, if I mistake not, with *mein, ge-mein*, 'communis,' common, *gemeiniglig, gemeinlich,* implying 'in common with.'

9. METHLM,—otherwise transcribed as METHLUM, and perhaps mis-read, according to Fabretti's suggestion, for METHLNI.—A female name, that of 'Metella,' or rather 'Matulnia,' as appears from the other inscription in the tomb. I suspect it should be read 'Methl-am,'—that is (understanding '-am as ἅμα, *sam*), 'together with Metella,' or 'Matulnia.'

10. NUPPHZI.—Compare with *nöt, genoetig, genoetzam,* 'sufficiens, fecundus,'—but rather with 'nub-ere,' 'nupta.'

11. KANTNKE.—Compare with 'conjux,'—KAN answering to 'con,' or with ; and THKE to *zug,* 'ducere,' to lead, in the sense of 'ducere uxorem.'

12. KALUS . . . , some letters being lost. To be compared with *kale,* 'doloros,' grief, &c., as lately shewn. Perhaps in the genitive case.

13. LUPU.—Compare either with *lib, lif* (A.-S.), 'vita,' life ; or with *leiben,* 'linquere,' to leave ; *geleibet,* ' relictus.' TAMERA ZELAVV has thus been rendered 'uxor relicta,' or 'relict,' in the preceding epitaph of Lars Alethniu* and his wife.

The space of three letters, or of a point and two letters, is marked as illegible in the present inscription as given by Fabretti, and so too by Gori in his original publication of it in his ' Museum Etruscum,' which I have also beside me. But strict accuracy in such estimates was less regarded in 1735 than now. If five letters could be allowed for, I should fill the vacant space with URASI, reading KALUSURASILUPU, as in the inscription recently analysed. SURASI answers, as I have suggested, to *sear, schwer,* ' gravis,' heavy. In the alternative that the exact space is given by Gori, I should fill up the space with · ZE; that is, I should read KALUS · ZELUPU, ' his sorrowing relict,' or widow.

The inscription would therefore run as follows :—
" Lars Cesina [eldest] son of Velius, owns (has right of property and protection in, or tenants) this sepulchre, in common with Metella his wife, his companion in the sorrows of life ; " or " in common with Metella his wife, his sorrowing relict."

Opposite to the inscription just examined, run another, much injured, which is given as follows :—

RAMTH · MATULNEI · SECH · MARKES MATULM..........
PUIAM · AMKE · ŚETHRES KEIS...IES · KISUM · TAME....
U........| LAPH ... NASK · MATULNA SK · KLALUM · KE.
S .. S · KI KLENAR · M · A .... AVENKE · LUPUM · AVILS....
ACHS · MEALCHLSK · EITVAPIA · ME.....
(*Fabretti*, no. 2340.)

This inscription appears to me to be divisible into two portions, the first ending with NASK, the second beginning with MATULNA. I shall take them therefore separately. The first portion may be analysed as follows:—

1, 2. RAMTH · MATULNEI.—The female name, 'Ramtha' or (as Fabretti translates it) 'Aruntia Matulna'—perhaps 'Metella.'

3. SECH—This word, sometimes written SEK, but, as we have it here, to be spelt SESCH, occurs in innumerable inscriptions relating to women; and there can be little doubt that the accepted interpretation of it as 'filia,' 'gnata,' or daughter, is correct.

4. MARKES.—The genitive singular, apparently, of 'Mark,' 'Marcus.'

5. MATULM.—Fabretti thinks this a mistranscription for MATULNI, but I am unwilling unnecessarily to deviate from accepted readings. The remainder of the first line of the inscription is lost, to the extent of about ten letters, judging by the space in Gori's engraving, which I follow as the oldest authority. This space, I fancy, contained the name of the father of Metella.

6. PUIAM.—The words PUIUS, PUIUS, PUIA, and others similarly formed, are found in many inscriptions; and the accepted interpretation among Etruscan antiquaries is that of 'son' or 'daughter.' They connect them with the Greek υἱός, υἱά, in which they may be right. There must, however, be some distinction between the *status* of the two descriptions of children, KLAN and SEK, and those described by the words here in question, which I cannot as yet define. As KLAN and SEK (or SECH) appear to be the favourite words for

legitimate sons and daughters, I would suggest in the meanwhile whether PUIUS, PUIA, have not the signification of 'illegitimate,' or perhaps 'semi-legitimate' son or daughter, as derived from φύω, the root of φύσις, 'natura'—by the same process of thought through which we describe a child born out of lawful wedlock as a 'natural' child. The space between MATULM and PUIAM may have been filled up with the family name or some other qualification of the person spoken of, immaterial to the general sense of the inscription.

7. AMKE.—Substantially the same word with KANTIIKE, 'conjux'—ἄμ-, sam, 'with,' answering to KAN or 'con.' But it may correspond (and I am inclined to think this is the case) with *ameigi* (Alemannic), *amia* (Suio-Goth.), implying 'uxor secundaria,' or concubine in a legal and respectable sense, as I think I have shewn; the AMKE being thus identical with the ÉLA above spoken of.*

8, 9. ŚETHRES NEIS . . . IES,—to be written, I presume, KEISINIES, the genitive of 'Śethro Keisine.'

10. KISUM.—The same word, I think, as KIZI, 'this,' in the accusative sense.

11. TAME . . . .—The inscription is so defective here that I can only say that it seems to me probable that TAME . . may represent the Teutonic *tumbe*, the Latin 'tumulus,' from *tammen* 'munire.'

12. U . . . . | LAPU . . .—The lost space possibly contained the verb, to 'give,' or 'bequeath.' LAPU is probably to be restored as *su laphu*, answering to *su leiba*, 'ad vitam,'— *leib* itself having the derivative sense of 'usus fructuarius.'

13. NASK.—Compare with *nutz*, usufruct; *nutzen*, to enjoy (in possession). I suspect that . . LAPU - NASK denotes 'life-

---

* By the 'Lex Helsingica,' as quoted by Ihre, these secondary wives had a legal status, although inferior to that of the wife *per excellentiam*. Ihre and others have suggested a derivation of *ameigi* from the Latin 'amica,' but Brinckmeier expresses a doubt whether a Latin word could have come so extensively into use among the German and Scandinavian races, especially among the Saxons, and still more the Swedes. *Ameigi* is, I have little doubt, the old AMKE of the Etruscans, and 'amica' is a Latin form of AMKE. If PUIAM be rightly understood as illegitimate, or even half-legitimate, the lady here spoken of and the lower grade of wife-ship were possibly suited, according to an understood conventionality.

rent,' or, if the lost words had the effect of personal appointment, 'life-renter,'

If this analysis be correct, the first portion of the inscription now under consideration would import as follows:—" Ramtha Matulna, daughter of Marcus, appointed as life-rent proprietor of this tomb "—or, " bestowed," " gave," or " bequeathed " " the usu-fruct of this tomb "—to " Matulna, daughter semi-legitimate, of " a person whose name is lost, and the " secondary wife (or legitimate concubine) of Śethre Cesina."

The remainder of the inscription may be analysed thus :—

1–4. MATULNA SK · KLALUM · KE . S . . S .—These four words I read as follows :—i. MATULNA, a female name, in the nominative case.—ii. SK. For SEK, or SECTI, daughter.—iii. KLALUM. I am afraid that this denotes the qualification attaching to this Metella as born *gelle-um*,—UM answering to *um*, 'à, ab, de,' from,—that is, born from a *gelle*, 'pellex,' or illegitimate concubine.—iv. KE . S . . S.—restorable as KEISINS, or KEISNIS, unless the word originally stood, *ut supra*, as KEISINEIS,—the genitive of 'Cesina.'

5–8. KI KLENAR · M · | A . . . .—I will not attempt to explain this at present.

9. AVENKE.—Compare with *abengeh-en*, 'decedere.' It signifies ' departed.'

10. LUFCM.—To be read as LUF-CM, and interpreted, i. LCF, as *lib, lif*, 'vita,' life ; and ii. CM, *um*, from, as above,—*i.e.* 'from life.'

11. AVILS,—equivalent to ' ætatis,' or ' aged.'

12. . . . . ACHS,—the latter portion to be read as ASCHS. This denotes the age of the lady—eighteen ?

13. MEALCHSK, as in Gori, but MEALCHLSK, as given by Fabretti, who appears to refer to authority for inserting the ' L.' Both forms would express the same word, but I suspect that Fabretti's has been the original reading.—Compare with *malatsch, maletschig, muldzig, malzig,* 'leprosus,' leprous ;

maletschey, 'lepra.' The form MEALCTILSK, in which the letter ↓ must be credited, as in other cases, with the power of the German *sch*, and which, as a whole, should thus be written Teutonicè as MEALSCHALISCH, represents probably the oldest orthography of the word; and is apparently a compound of, i. *mal*, 'macula,' a spot; ii. *schalg*, a scale; and iii. the adjectival termination *-isch*,—the exact description of the disease to which MATULNA was a victim.

14. EITVAPIA.—A compound of, i. *iit*, *uit*, *yt* (whence *ent*), implying 'non,' not; and ii. *weib*, 'femina, mulier nupta,' a wife; and thus signifying 'innupta,' unmarried,—as might naturally be supposed from her illness, if attacked by it early in life.*

The rest of the inscription is very obscure. The letters ME are given by Gori. Three letters would complete the line; and MEANI, if I might suggest the emendation, might stand for 'beloved,' as representing *minnen*, *minne*,—like the 'dulcis suis' in the beautiful epitaph of Felicula at Volterra. An old MS. copy completes the inscription as MENUAAVENKE; and this might imply, 'She went away to Men[t]u,' i. e. Mantus, or Hades. But Fabretti evidently doubts the accuracy of this addition. The sense is complete without it; and it is possible that the word AVENKE was repeated by an oversight in the transcript.

The inscription would thus read, in its leading phrases,—" Matulna, illegitimate daughter of Cosina, departed this life, aged . . . , a leper, unmarried "— shall I add, " beloved " ?

The history of the tomb and of its occupants, as gathered from the comparison of these inscriptions,

---

* The compound *nuurip*, *unvip*, is found in old German, but in a bad sense. Here it can only have a good one.

may be stated thus:—It was excavated by Lars Cesina, the son of Velius, for the joint tenancy of himself and his wife Matulna,—whom I take to have been the Ramtha Matulna, daughter of Marcus, who figures in the second of the inscriptions. Ramtha Matulna survived her husband, and assigned or bequeathed the usufruct of the tomb to a second Matulna, a semi-legitimate daughter of one of her own family, and concubine (in a legal sense) to Sethre Cesina, probably a nephew or kinsman of Lars Cesina. And lastly, a third Matulna, illegitimate daughter of —— Cesina, was buried there, with the record that she died a leper and unwedded. More, it will be remarked, is said of her personally than of any of the others; and this would seem to shew that she was loved, pitied, and fondly remembered—whether or not the final and incomplete ME... have the force above suggested or not.

Section V.—*The Inscription of San Manno.*

The same tenderness that breathes throughout the inscription we have just analysed characterises another which I shall now bring before you, and which throws peculiar light incidentally on the ethnology of the Etruscans. It is to be seen in a tomb —spacious, and beautifully built (of travertine), and vaulted—at the village of La Commenda, about two miles from Perugia on the road to Florence. This tomb is now known as the 'Tempio di San Manno,' it being a disputed point whether it was intended for sepulchral or religious use.[*] A church,

---

[*] Kellermann calls it the 'Torre di S. Manno.'

dedicated to San Manno, was built above it some centuries ago by the Knights of Malta. The inscription is carved, in three lines, above, and continuously to the right and left of a magnificent arch opening into a recess, within which are two rectangular blocks of stone, which have been supposed to be altars. A view of the whole is given by Count Giancarlo Conestabile in his *Monumenti di Perugia*, tav. iv-xxx. The inscription runs as follows:—

KEHEN : SUTHI : HINTHIU : THUEŚ : SIANŚ : ETVE : THAURE : LAUTNEŚKLE : KARESRI : AULEŚ : LARTHIAL : PREKUTH-ARAŚI : *: LARTHIALIŚVLE : KESTNAL : KLENARAŚI : ETH : PHANU : LAUTN : PREKUŚ : IPA : MURZUA : KERURUM : EIN : |HEKZRI : TUNUR : KLUTIVA : ZELUR . . . . R . †

(*Fabretti*, no. 1915.)

—The inscription falls into two portions, the first ending with KLENARAŚI. It may be analysed as follows:—

1. KEHEN.—Akin to the Gothic *hethio*, a 'cubiculum,' or bed; and the Suio-Gothic *kaelte*; but a verb, not a noun, and implying to 'sleep' or 'rest,'—apparently in the third person of the plural (or perhaps dual?) number.

2. SUTHI.—Compare (as on a previous occasion) with *satjan*, to set, or lay—in a sepulchral sense, in the grave; *sezzi*, a place set apart for any one, &c.

3. HINTHIU.—A compound, I think—not of *hin*, thither, but of, i. *his*, here; ii. *in*; and iii. *thiu*, in the sense of *tief*, deep; but with the signification of 'down' or 'beneath,' as I

* This word is given as PREKUTHOBAŚI in Fabretti, but it ends as -ARAŚI in the engraving given by Conestabile; and this is probably correct, as the same termination occurs in KLENARAŚI in the following line.

† HEKZRI and TUNUR, so given in Conestabile's engraving, are written HERKZRI and TUN : UR in his text; but Fabretti gives both as in the engraving, from personal examination.

infer from the preservation of what appears to me the same word in modern Italian as 'giù.' I read HINTHU, therefore, as equivalent to *herunten*, 'here beneath' or 'below.' The phrase would read therefore thus far,—'There rest, buried, here below,' &c.*

4, 5. THUFS : SIANA.—I take these words together because they form a compound in the modern Teutonic languages, to wit (in the singular number) *stief-sohn*, 'step-son.' This title has nothing to do with the idea of a 'step;' nor do any of the ordinary derivations from *stief*, 'hard' (on the theory of the "injusta noverca"), *styva*, 'firmare,' *stiften*, 'ordinare,' or even from *stov, stow*, 'locus'—(e. g. 'in loco parentis'), meet the requirements of the case. Junius long ago pointed out the truth, viz., that *stepan, stiupan* (in the old Anglo-Saxon and Alemannic) denotes 'orbare'—that is, to deprive (of kindred); and that *steopmother* (A.-Sax.), *stiufmuather* (Alem.), thus signifies 'orphanorum matrem;' while Ihre adds in confirmation that in the Anglo-Saxon version of the New Testament ὀρφανὸν is translated *steopcild*. Starting from this idea we can easily ascend to the true signification of the first word in the present compound, viz. THUES. 'Orbus,' ὀρφανός, are evidently from the same root as 'priv-us,' 'priv-atus,' and 'priv-igous'—the Latin word for stepson; and 'priv-are' is clearly the same with *beraub-en*, to bereave, or, originally, to rob—a root equivalent to the Sanscrit *rabh*, the Latin 'rap-ere,' &c. The idea of orphanhood was therefore that of being 'bereaved' or 'deprived' of parents by death —coming upon the family like an armed man or a thief in the night. But *thiuba, theof, tiuf, thief*—'fur, latro'—is as ancient and pregnant a word as *rabh*, 'rap-,' *raub*, 'rapt-or,' *raub-er*; and its application to the case of orphaned children

---

* A word very like HINTHU, occupying a corresponding place and significatlon, and possibly of cognate origin, exists in Gaelic and Irish, viz. an so, 's an àite so, here, or in this place; with which the Dict. of the Highland Society compares the Persian *anja*, there, *ansu*, thither, 'illuc,' and *ansu*, hither. When a pillar-stone was set up over the grave of Fothadh Airgthcach, who was killed A.D. 285, this stone was inscribed '*Eochaidh Airgtheach inso*' (here), according to the 'Leabhar na h' Uidhre.'—*Journal of the Kilkenny Archæol. Society*, new series, vol. ii. p. 177.

would be equally appropriate. Hence I infer that the Etruscan THU, THUES—reading it as in other instances THS, THB-ES—is the same word as the old Teutonic *thiubs*, *theof*, *thief*, the compound *thief-son*, strange as it may sound, implying exactly the same as *step-son*, viz., 'bereaved-son,' —the child having been deprived of its parents by the theft of death. But, more even than this:—*Thief-son*, or *thief-mother*, is in reality the same word as *steop-son*, *steop-mualher*, the initial *th* and *st* being merely alternative forms of one original, a primitive *s*. It is curious and sad to perceive how an evil character has attached itself to stepmothers through oblivion of the true etymology of the title and adverse influence from the deceptive suggestions of sound. We shall find that we have to deal in the present inscription with a 'noverca' of the noblest and tenderest species.—ii. SIANS, the second element in what I here consider as a compound, is (in the nominative case) the Teutonic *sunu*, 'filius,' son,—the literal formation being akin to that which we have noticed in PIAN-SI for *pfand*-, or, as is to be seen in German itself, in the varying forms of *lean, laen, lehen, laun, lón, lohn*.—THU- or THB-SIAN is thus the Etruscan form of *step-son*; and from the context I am inclined to think that the word or words must be in the genitive case, either plural or dual— two persons, step-sons, being, as we shall see, in question here; in which alternative (of their being in the dual number) the words would represent a very rare formation—the -ES answering to the terminational -ôs in Sanscrit, which has disappeared in Zendic and Lithuanian.—THUES: SIANS signifies therefore, I conclude, 'of [her] two step-sons.'

6. ETVE.—Compare with *wittwe*, *wilawa* (*vidava* Sanscr.), 'vidua,' widow.* It is dangerous (at least for myself) to affirm such a thing in the face of the peculiar form of Etruscan orthography; but I should think this word too was in the dual number, like *duhitar-a*, θυγατέρ-ε in Sanscrit and Greek; and, if so, the words that follow are also in that number.

7. THACHE.—Compare *teur, thaur*, 'carus, pretiosus'—dear, or of great price. In agreement with ETVE.

* We have met with the word already as ETVA - TAMERA in an inscription cited in a note, p. 101.

8, 9. LAUTNEŚKLE.—Written together without break, but to be divided as LAUTNEŚ KLE.—i. LAUTNEŚ is the genitive singular of LAUTNE, or Lautinia, the name of a person more fully described in the second part of this inscription as LAUTN : PREKUŚ.—ii. KLE—analogously to *quell, well*; 'quatuor,' *petor*, four; 'quinque,' πέντε, five—must have been written originally KULE or KUILE, whence the form of KLE (abbreviated as usual) in the present inscription, and, the initial K being omitted, 'fil-e,' 'fil-ia' in Latin; while κοῦρος, κοῦρη, κόρος, κόρη (this last the name of 'the Daughter' *per excellentiam*, Persephone), are formed in parallel development in Greek, by mutation of the 'l' into 'r.'—THAURE : LAUTNEŚ KLE thus signifies, 'Lautinia's dear daughters.'

10. KABESRI.—A proper name, which is Latinized by Fabretti as 'Caresia.' It designates one of Lautinia's daughters, the widow of (we may infer) the eldest of her two step-sons. His name and her qualification as his wife follow:—

11-13. AULES : LARTHIAL : PREKUTHABAŚI—AULES LARTHIAL needs no explanation; it is in the genitive case. But PREKUTHABAŚI is a compound of PREKUTH and ARAŚI.—i. PREKUTH is part of the name, or rather the name itself, of Aulus Larthial, which is afterwards joined to Lautinia's (as above said) as LAUTN : PREKUŚ.—ii. ARAŚI, I think, means 'wife,'—and this may be gathered, first, from the context, in which the wives of the persons named are previously represented as widows; secondly, from the resemblance of the word to the old Homeric δαρ, δαρος, female companion, especially wife; and thirdly, from its appearance in a short inscription at Perugia, AR . . . . PII ARSA | LAUTNETERI, (*Fabretti*, no. 1060), which I read as '. . . , wife of Lautinius, second son,' or 'second' wife. "Oαp must have been pronounced and written oϝαp, oϝαρος; and, restoring the lost initial, we may recognise it probably as identical with δάμαρ, δάμαρτος, the Etruscan TAMERA. Oϝαp and *fras* may perhaps be the same word; and *heuraht*, *heurath*, wedlock, also suggests itself. I infer that Aulus was the eldest son from his being first named, and from his bearing the paternal name of 'Precuth.'

14, 15. LARTHIALIŚVLE.—Distinguishable as LARTHIALI ŚVLE.—i. LARTHIALI seems to be the name of the younger daughter, and ii. ŚVLE the *prænomen* of her husband. sv and κ are interchangeable in Etruscan, and therefore ŚVLE is probably the same name as KALE, which would be rendered in Latin by 'Gallus,' as ŚVLE itself is, I suspect, by 'Sulla,' 'Sylla.'

16. KESTNAL.—The matronymic of ŚVLE, Sylla, or Gallus.

17. KLENARAŚI.—Compounded of, i. KLEN, the final title or designation of ŚVLE KESTNAL ; and of, ii. ARAŚI, wife. KLEN—distinctly written so, and not ELAN—stands, I think, for *klein*, 'parvus,' in the sense of 'younger son.'

The translation of this first half of the inscription would thus run:—" Caresia, wife of Aulus Larthial Prekuz, [and] Larthiali, wife of Sylla Kestnal Klen, the dear daughters of Lautinia, widows of her two step-sons, rest in the sleep (of death) here-beneath." It is evident from the record that Lautinia was twice married, and by her first husband had two daughters. She married, secondly, a gentleman of the family of 'Prekuz,' or 'Prekuth,' himself already twice a widower, and the father of two sons, Aulus, the eldest, by his first wife Larthia, and Gallus, or Sylla, the younger, by his second wife Kestna. The two daughters married the two sons. The young men died early, possibly in battle, and the wives survived for awhile and then also died, leaving their mother desolate.—Matter equally interesting, although of a different character, follows in the second portion of the text, as I have ventured to divide it:—

1, 2. ETH : PHANU.—Much has been urged from the occurrence of the word PHANU in favour of this sepulchre 'di San Manno' having been really a 'fanum,' or 'tempio'—as it is popularly called. But the two words ETH and PHANU, taken together, and with the context, denote a totally different thing, to wit, a testamentary trust or disposition,—ETH corresponding with EID, 'juramentum,' an oath, and being fundamentally allied with 'fides,' trust; and PHANU (which would have been pronounced, I think, PHANTU, the accessory consonant being, as usual, omitted in the calligraphy) with *pfand, phant, pant,* 'pignus,' or perhaps with *gepfandet,* the participle past of *pfaenden,* 'pignorare,' to pledge,—the words, in effect, constituting a compound, and denoting—not exactly a last will and testament, in its entirety, but a provision or settlement under trust, by way of legacy. In the present case the words that follow shew that this provision was an endowment in mortmain, a grant in perpetuity. An ETH-PHANU in fuller detail, but with a more limited object, will be found in the inscription next to be analysed.*

3, 4.—LAUTN : PREKUś.—The name (in the genitive case) of Lautinia, by marriage 'Prekuz' (as the word must have been properly written, judging by the variations -ś and -TIF, which refer us to an original z)—or 'Preculia'—mother of the two ladies buried here, the constructor, I presume, of the tomb, and legatrix and institutrix of the trust just mentioned. It is the fact of this ' Lautn' bearing the name 'Prekuz,' combined with that of the step-son Aulus being also a Procuz, that obliges us, I think, to read LAUTN as a female name, 'Lautinia,' notwithstanding the presumption at starting against the legal competency of a woman, or widow, to act, as she is here represented as doing, independently.†

5, 6, 7. IPA : MURZUA : KER.—I detach KER from the word it is coupled with, as the sense evidently requires this; and Etruscan sculptors and scribes were at all times lax observers of the rules of calligraphy, constantly mixing up words and names together even in inscriptions as carefully executed as this is.—i. IPA is the German *bey,* and Greek ὑπὸ, by or

---

* It is just possible that the Etruscan ETH : PHANU and Latin 'testamentum' may be fundamentally the same (compound) word,—'test-' representing an earlier TETH, T-ETH, T-EZ, in the Etruscan, and PHANU the '-mentum.'

† Possibly ETH : PHANU may be the verb and LAUTN : PREKUś the governing noun, in the nominative case. The sense would be the same.

under.—ii. MURZUA is an adjective, which has its Teutonic
allies in *morth*, *murd*, and its derivatives, but in the sense—
not of 'murder' but of simple 'mors,' death.—And, iii. KEB
is the old Pelasgic χεὶρ, in Latin 'hir,' hand—a word only
known in the classical language from a notice preserved by
Cicero, after Lucilius, as signifying the hollow of the hand
employed in tasting wine.—IPA : MURZUA : KEB thus signifies,
'Per manum mortuam,' or *in todte hand*, the formula used
in cases where a grant is made to a church, and explained
'ad manus mortuas, seu perpetuas, legare,' that is, as we call
it in Scots, 'in mortification.' Such was the mode in which
the ETH : PHANU, or trust, was constituted in the present
instance; and it is interesting to find a symbolical phrase
and usage so familiar to the student of middle-age charters
thus carried back to extreme antiquity. I suspect from the
use of the word MURZ-, 'mors,' that these three words are a
technical formula of purely Pelasgic times, long anterior to
the date, remote as it is, of the present inscription.*

8, 9. URUM : EIN.—To be read, in conformity with Etruscan
usage in other instances which I shall notice, UM EIN-UR.
In compounds such as EIN-UR the first element in Latin and
German is often (as will be found) put last in Etruscan, whether
that last be a particle like EIN or a substantive noun. And
a relative word, or words, is occasionally moreover interposed
between such constituent parts of one compound, after a

* Although the trust by the *todte hand* and that by the *treue* or living
hand are expressed by the same word in medieval Teutonic, it will be
observed (if my identification of the latter phrase as also occurring in
Etruscan be found correct) that 'bir' is appropriated to the former and
hand to the latter,—a distinction which must have had its motive cause.
The discussion would be too long for this place, but I may observe, i. That
the association between 'hir,' χεὶρ, and death may have arisen from the
resemblance of 'hir' to *kreo*, a corpse, 'fer-' in 'fer-alia,' &c. :—ii. That as
the hollow or palm of the hand, 'hir,' is interpreted by 'vola manus,' the
latter having also the signification of the 'sole' of the foot, so 'palma' has
a close affinity with *qualm*, the Etruscan KULMU, death,—and, iii. That
δίναρ, the Greek equivalent of 'vola' appears to be fundamentally connected with θάνατος. It is similarly the 'hollow of the hand,' *kp*
(Egyptian), which lies at the root of *knuf-en*, the word expressive of contract generally, and which I shall speak of presently. The plucking off
and delivery of the shoe, as by Boaz (Ruth iv. 8 qq), seems to attach
itself rather to the alternate sense of 'vola manus.'

manner still familiar to us in modern German.—i. UM is here identical with *umb*, ἀμφὶ, &c. denoting 'on account of,' or 'for the purpose of,' that is, 'towards compassing anything.'—ii. EIN-UB corresponds with the Latin 'inferiæ,' or 'feralia,' the sacrifice for the dead,—the U standing here for 'v' or 'f,' EIN-UB thus becoming *ein-fr*, 'inferiæ.'

10. HEKZHI.—A compound, if I mistake not, of two words, the first itself a compound, HEK-Z, the second a single vocable, RI, and thus to be written, properly, HEK-Z RI.—i. Of HEK-Z, the first element, HEK, may be compared with *hoh*, high; the second must be considered in relation to the component elements of the single letter in which it appears before us, z. This letter 'z' is the representative of the letters 's' and 't' —letters that originally, I think, were sounded together as 'st,' (compare Σδεύς for Ζεύς in the Æolic dialect,)—but which are very frequently found apart, and receive a vowel between them. In old Egyptian 'st' signifies a stone, and I infer from the legend of Saturn or Cronos (the 'Set,' 'Tet,' 'Zida,' of the Eastern world, and the God of Tide or Time) having swallowed a stone, that such was the original orthography, or rather orthoepy of his name. By the same analogy *zeit*, *tid*, our Teutonic word for 'time,' must have been written originally 'st,' or 'z,' and thus, I infer, the Etruscan z in HEK-Z has that signification. HEK-Z is therefore, I think, identical with *hoh-zeit*, or *hoch-zeit*—not in the modern sense of a marriage, but that of the Saxon *heah-tide*, 'tempus festivum, festum,' or 'high festival' *in genere*, and the Suio-Goth. *högtid*, more especially now used for the great religious festivals of Christmas, Easter, and Passion-week in Scandinavia. But to complete the double compound HEK-Z+RI, we have yet to consider the final element, ii. RI.— This may be compared with the primitive Aryan 'er,' 'gr,' 'hr,' 'vr,' as in 'er-esc-ere,' *gr-öen*, 'vir-escere,' and with the Sanscrit *hari*, 'vir-idis,' green; and HI would thus appear to attach the idea of the green growth of early spring to the HEK-Z, *hoch-zeit*, or festival in question. HEK-Z HI thus signifies 'at the high festival of green things.'[*] The name of

---

[*] The word HEK, with the preceding signification, is of great antiquity, occurring in old Egyptian, and in various hieroglyphical combinations, as

the deity to whom the festival was dedicated immediately follows, viz.,

11. TUNUR.—The 'Thunaer,' or Thor, of Thuringia, otherwise written 'Donar' in Old High German, and 'Thunar' in the Old Saxon. Taking HER-Z BI TUNUR together, we have here the Etruscan equivalent of the Teutonic *Hohe Donnerstag*, or *Grüne Donnerstag*, as it was sometimes called—the 'Dies Viridium' or feast of spring, sacred to Jupiter—the great 'Dies Jovis,'—the 'Holy Thur's' or 'Thor's Day,' which we still celebrate with especial reverence in Passion-week; Pope Leo having, in A.D. 692, converted the pre-Christian festival into a Christian one, in perfect conformity with its original signification, Holy Thursday having been the day on which the Eucharist, or High Feast of the New Spring, the New Creation, was instituted by Our Saviour.[a]

12. KLUTIVA.—A compound, divisible into KLUT and IVA. —i. KLUT, I take it, represents *gold, gelt*, 'sterilis' (as rendered so artificially); and ii. IVA, the Indo-European word found in Greek as ὄϝις, ὄϊς, Lat. 'ovis,' and Sanscrit *avi*,— KLUTIV- thus signifying a wether—what used to be called a

[a] *Adh*, a time, festival, *Adhr*, a festival, and *Adhr*, a point of time. (*Birch's Dict. Hieroglyphica*, ap. Bunsen's *Egypt*, vol. v. p. 399, last English edition.) The relations of the old Egyptian and the Teutonic and Aryan languages, generally, are very close, and to be accounted for only, I think, by Japhetan conquest and intermixture at a very early period. I suspect, nevertheless, that BEK, *hash, hoch, hôg*, and even the Egyptian *Adh*, are but abraded forms of an older *herk, heurh*, akin to the A.-Saxon *haerg*, 'fanum,' and the Swedish *horg* and *horgy*, 'fanum, vel locus sacrorum, ubi victimae immolantur,'—the same word which we have in the old Latin 'arg-ei,' the name given by the Pontifices of Rome to the 'loca sacris faciendis' according to Livy (*lib.* i. c. 21). See Ihre *in voce*. If Conte O. Conestabile is correct in transcribing the word above discussed as HERKEH, these observations will shew that the interpretation offered in the text is in no wise affected. As stated, I have retained the current reading, as given in the Count's engraving, as well as in the transcript by Fabretti.

* In Conestabile's text (as stated in a previous note) he divides TUNUR as TUN : UR; whereas it is TUNUR in the engraving, as well as in the various transcripts. Even if divided as TUN : UR, the sense would remain the same; as TUN would then answer to Ζήν, Ζὰν, 'Tin-a,' 'Din,' or 'Pfing,' all of them varieties of the name of Thor (conf. Asshur = Aston); and UR would represent the additional syllable '-aer' as found in 'Thun-aer' of Thuringia, analogously to 'Sur-ar,' as compared with 'Surt,' in Scandinavia.

bell-wether, perhaps as sacred in Britain and Gaul to Baal, Thor, or Jupiter,—a creature always looked upon with respect, and his title even transferred to humanity as 'one who leads the people.'* I may be wrong, but ELUTIVA appears to me, from the termination, to be in the dual number,—we might perhaps infer this from there being the *manes* of two persons to propitiate; and the conjecture will possibly be confirmed by what I have to state after finishing this analysis.

13. ZELUR ... R.—Reading U as B, and comparing ZELUR with *zahlbar*, we should obtain the meaning of 'due, payable' at a certain time; and I should incline to fill up the deficient letters and read the remainder thus,—ZELUH : IPA : R,—the final R standing for an Etruscan word akin to *jar*, year, and to the verbal RIL already spoken of; and the passage thus signifying—'payable *per annum*,' or yearly.

The entire inscription may therefore be rendered,— i. "Carcsia, wife of Aulus Larthial Prekuś," and "Larthiali, wife of Sylla Kestnal Klen, the dear daughters of Lautinia, widows of her step-sons, rest in the sleep (of death) here-beneath :"—ii. "Legacy, (or fiduciary trust,) of Lautinia Prekutia"—or, "Lautinia Prekutia bequeaths in trust—*per manum mortuam*"—(that is, in perpetuity)—"as *inferiæ* (sacrifices to the dead), at the High Feast-day of Tunur" (the *Hohe Donnerstag* or 'Dies Viridium'), "[two] wethers, due" (or, to be offered) "yearly." † I offer this interpretation as that which the separate words analysed and the context appear to prescribe—so

---

* Two 'herbices' or 'vervices' are mentioned in the records of the Arval Brothers *passim* as a periodical sacrifice to Jupiter, that is, Tina, or Thunser.

† Dr. Donaldson translates the latter part of the inscription thus:— 'Tunur Clutiva let carve this sacred funeral prayer of Larthlalisulus, the younger son of Cestna, upon the building where the cinerary urns are deposited.'—*Varron.*, p. 223.

strongly indeed as to overrule the hesitation and doubt which the exhibition of such freedom and independence of action on the part even of a widow in Roman times suggest. But this was an Etruscan lady, and her action belonged to the times probably of her nation's independence.

I reserve any remarks upon the interesting mythological and (by implication) ethnological intimation in the second part of the inscription, and merely note here one or two circumstances which may support the preceding interpretation. I may state, in the first place, that I had translated the whole as above shewn before referring to Mr. Dennis's account of the tomb (which I have never visited); and there I read, to my satisfaction, as follows:—"About half-way down the chamber, on either hand, is a recess, also vaulted, in one of which stand, in the inner corners, two blocks of travertine resembling altars, each having a groove or channel at the upper edge as if to carry off the blood." It is obvious, I think, that these two blocks are the actual altars upon which the KLUTIVA, or two wethers, were sacrificed, as provided by the ETH PHANU of Lautinia Prekutia, to the *manes* of her two daughters—a separate altar for each victim. Mr. Dennis suggests that the sepulchre received its name of 'tempio' from the existence of these altars.* The justice of this criticism is now, I think, proved;

* "It is this," he says, "which has caused the vault to be regarded as a temple, though I think it more probably was a sepulchre, both from analogy and on account of its subterranean character. Moreover the existence of an altar is in no way inconsistent with the supposition of a tomb, for the relation between tombs and temples is well known; and a shrine where offerings might be made to the Manes was not infrequent in ancient sepulchres ... The sepulchre was, in fact, the shrine of the Manes, who were regarded as Gods."—*Cities, &c.*, vol. ii. p. 488.

while that criticism may equally be appealed to as shewing that the interpretation above given—in which bloody sacrifices are the subject-matter—is worthy of credit. The truth turns out to be that those who contend that the place was a tomb and the rival partisans of the 'tempio' theory are both right, and that this Etruscan sepulchre has been from the first an endowed mortuary chapel—thus at once temple and tomb. The further observation occurs to me (and this is more under the circumstances than mere matter of curiosity), that these sacrifices to the 'Manes' of the two ladies probably went on year after year till the introduction of Christianity; and then, I suspect, the title 'S. Manno' supplanted that of the 'Divi Manes;' and either the place was consecrated, or such a reverence continued to attach to it in the neighbourhood for centuries afterwards, that a chapel or church was built over it as over a crypt—the predecessor probably of the present building. In that case the two Etruscan ladies, votaries of TUNUR or Thor, have been the subject of an uninterrupted *cultus*, although latterly under the masculine title of 'S. Manno,' to the present time. It is remarked by Conte G. Conestabile that no traces of urns or sarcophagi exist in the tomb; nor have any notices of such having been ever there come down to us; and— judging from the force of the word ΜΙΝΤΗΙU, 'herebeneath,' as I understand it—I should not be surprised if the remains of Caresia and Larthiali were buried within or in front of the recess and altars, and might still be discovered there by excavation.

The question of the antiquity of the tomb is a matter of high interest, as bearing on that of the inscription.

Mr. Dennis compares it with the "Tanella di Pitagora' at Cortona and the 'Deposito del Gran Duca' at Chiusi,—the former built of very massive stones, but exquisitely shaped and finished—as old, he thinks, as the walls of Cortona herself, or the Cloaca Maxima of Rome, and such as he would have considered Pelasgian but for an Etruscan inscription formerly attached to it,*—the latter perfectly vaulted, like the present tomb, but of less massive workmanship, and not, he thinks, indicating a very high antiquity, although Stouart, he adds, assigns a very ancient date to a tomb in Lydia very similar to it in construction. The 'Deposito del Gran Duca' has been originally, in Mr. Dennis's opinion, built up as an independent structure, and then covered with earth in imitation of a *tumulus*, the soil being loose and friable; and Count G. Conestabile makes the same remark with regard to the 'Tempio di San Manno.' No argument against the early date of the 'Tempio' can be based on that 'beauty' and 'perfection' of its masonry which Mr. Dennis speaks of with such enthusiasm, inasmuch as he acknowledges that the like excellence is compatible with the opinion he holds as to the very ancient date of the 'Tanella di Pitagora.' The result, I should say, fairly to be arrived at from all this is, that the 'Tempio di S. Manno' is only second in date to the 'Tanella,' and certainly not later than the sixth century before Our Saviour, which Mr. Dennis assigns as the earliest in which the

---

* It is very short,—V · ECSO · ES · L · APA | PETRUAL · KLAN (*Fabretti*, no. 1040). The punctuation of the first line is represented by Castellani as somewhat doubtful; and the L in that line may perhaps be an I.

arch proper can be found to have been used in vaulting—at least, I should submit, by the Etruscans, for the Egyptians certainly knew and practised it a thousand years earlier. I own that, judging from the engraving of the interior given by Conestabile, I should have thought it far older than the date fixed on by Mr. Dennis. Whatever the date, it must be very early; and, if so, the inscription must of course represent the language as existing at the same period, when possibly the dual number, subsequently lost or almost effaced, may have been still *in viridi observantiâ* among the Etruscan Germans. I may add that both the 'Tanella di Pitagora' and the 'Deposito del Gran Duca' exhibit that "singular identity of dimensions with the multiples and divisions of the modern Tuscan *braccio*—which there is good reason to believe is just double the ancient Roman foot "—upon which Mr. Dennis founds his opinion " that the Romans took that measure from the Etruscans, and that the modern Tuscans use the very same measures as their celebrated forefathers." * Mr. Dennis does not state—nor does Conestabile, whether this identity exists likewise in the case of the 'Tempio di S. Manno'—but I suspect it does.

I should perhaps stop here, but the observation presses forward : May it not be inferred from this magnificent tomb and the memories associated with it, as well as from the preceding inscription, that happy homes, founded on the culture of domestic virtue, were as common with these, our remote Etruscan kinsmen, as with ourselves? It is remarkable that there is no allusion in the present inscription to

* *Cities*, &c., vol. ii. pp. 376, 448, 449.

the terrors of Charon and the grave,—no paintings of festivity or sorrow adorn the Puritan simplicity of the walls; while, at the same time, there is no outpouring of desolate hopeless distress (as in other cases) on the part of Lautinia, although left alone apparently in the world, husband, daughters, and step-son sons-in-law, all gone before her. The question suggests itself—'Whither,' in her estimation? Is it too much to think that the 'High Feast of Tunur,' the 'Dies Viridium' or *Grüne Donnerstag* of the Etruscans and (pre-Christian) Teutons, was in some dim way to them, as to ourselves, a pledge of renewed life and immortality? Such speculations are not always too daring. 'Non omnis moriar' was as instructive and influential a sentiment among the virtuous ancients as the belief in God, Θεός, 'Deus,' apart from His mythological representatives.

SECTION VI.—*Inscription in the tomb of the Pompeys.*

I now pass to the inscription which I referred to *supra*, under the word ETH : PHASU, as presently to be brought forward, and as exhibiting the form and substance of a *fidei-commissum*. It is, or rather was inscribed—for it is now nearly obliterated—on the great central pillar in the sepulchre of the Pompey family at Tarquinii, discovered in 1832,—a richly decorated tomb, a full description of which is given by Mr. Dennis;* while engravings of the paintings may be seen in the second volume of the 'Monumenti Inediti' of the 'Instituto Archeologico' of Rome. It runs as follows :—

* *Cities*, &c., vol. i. pp. 302 sqq.

TOMB OF THE POMPEYS.

EITH : PHANU : ŚATHEK : LAVTN : PUMPUS | SKUNU · S :
ŚUTHITP : IN : PHLENXNA | TEISNIKA : KAL : IPA : MA · ANI :
TINERI | MTISUŚ . . NAMUTNE : IPA : TR . . . . NIKLTE |
PHLEŚXNEVES . . A . . : K . K . . . . . . TAN . . . . ERKE : ATHIS |
THNAM · PHLENXNATE . . . . ATA · : ENAK · ELI :* |
KESASIN : THUNCHU . . . . M : ENAK · CHM . . . . VER : KAL · |
. RNTHAL : LA . . . . LIŚLA : CH . . . ELR . . . AS : K ·
ENS | SKUNA · •

A shorter inscription is also to be seen—or was so formerly—over the head of the principal personage in the most important of the paintings, to the following effect:—

LARIS : PUMPUS | ARNTHAL : KLAN | KECHASE.

(*Fabretti*, no. 2279, 2280, tab. xlii. And *Kellermann's paper*, '*Bullettino,*' *Archæol. Institute of Rome*, 1833.)†

The longer inscription has suffered so much injury, and its restoration and interpretation must be in many

---

* The 'ph' used in PHANU is, like the 'ph' in the Pelasgian inscriptions, different from the usual Etruscan letter, which resembles the numeral 8, or rather an hourglass; but, while the Pelasgian 'ph' is formed apparently of two sons facing each other, the 'ph' here used resembles two sigmas similarly opposed. The two forms son and sigma appear to be employed with careful discrimination throughout this inscription. The punctuation appears to be carried through with strict grammatical propriety. I doubt the inscription being of antiquity commensurate with that of the tomb. The paintings differ in character, some being archaic, others of the finest time of Etruscan art.

† I may take this opportunity of suggesting the extreme importance of accurate measurement, and comparative measurement too, of the *lacunæ* in Etruscan inscriptions,—each *lacuna* should itself be measured, and notice taken of any *indicia* of the original number of letters, even although they be no longer legible; and at the same time a measurement should be taken of the space occupied by (say) ten or twelve letters in an unbroken portion of the inscription, so as to furnish a standard for the assistance of the critic who may endeavour to restore the lost passages. My impression is that Kellermann has been wonderfully accurate in his transcript on the present occasion; I should otherwise never have been able to restore (as I trust I have done) the missing portions.

passages so conjectural, that I should hardly have selected it for the present purpose had it not appeared to be of peculiar interest on the ground above specified, and its general purport sufficiently apparent to justify my doing so. I have found it indeed less imperfect than I supposed at first from the irregularity with which the lines begin and end, as represented in the engraving. I doubt whether any words are wanting except in the central parts of the inscription. I proceed to analyse it as usual :—

1, 2, 3. EITH : PHANU : SATHER.—The words ETH : PHANU, taken in connection, have already been explained as signifying a testamentary trust; but the combination is somewhat different here, and while ZITH retains its signification of 'fides,' trust under oath, PHANU must be taken with SATHER, as a distinct compound. We have identified PHANU, warrantably, I think, with PFAND. As regards SATHER,—the Teutonic *satz*, and its derivative *satzung*, both signify 'pignus, hypotheca,' a pledge or mortgage ; *satzung*, 'testamentum, legatum,' a will or bequest,—while *setzen in pfandsweise* implies 'jus hypothecæ; alicui rem constituere,' to create a trust or mortgage,—which act, again, is expressed in composition by the noun *pfandsatz*. PHANU : SATHER, considered as a compound, would thus be the Teutonic *pfand-satz*, or rather *pfand-satzung*, the *d* and *n* being respectively omitted (as usual) in the Etruscan orthography. Taken with the preceding word, EITH, 'fides,' the signification may be accepted as 'Testamentary settlement, by *fidei-commissum*,' or in the hands of a fiduciary, or trustee.

4, 5. LAVTN : PUMPUA.—The name of the defunct who constitutes the *fidei-commissum* in question. It may be either in the nominative or genitive case, as the termination -US is common to both. The latter is more probable.

6. SRUNU.—Compare *schein*, 'testimonium,' *scheinôn*, 'ostendere, manifestare,' *gasceinôn*, 'notum facere,' to declare, set forth, or make known. SRUNU is, I think, written,

according to common Etruscan usage, for ꜱᴋᴜɴᴛᴜ, the past participle of the Etruscan verb, and signifies 'declared.' And the six words thus constitute the title of the inscription, 'The testamentary settlement by *fidei-commissum* of Lautinius Pompey,' duly 'declared and notified'—as we shall see, by 'nuncupatio.' The single dot or stop that follows ꜱᴋᴜɴᴜ, instead of the usual colon, appears to mark the termination of this title; and there are other instances of this in the record, constituting a peculiarity which distinguishes it from the practice in other cases in which the single dot sometimes marks the presence of compounded words.

7. ꜱ : .—This letter, I think, stands in abbreviation for an Etruscan word which would be, in German, *setzer*, i. e. 'mandator'—he who gives a charge or commission, to wit, the ᴇɪᴛʜ-ꜰʜᴀɴᴜ-ꜱᴀᴛʜᴇʀ or *pfand-satzung* just spoken of, and now to be set forth. ꜱ : is the nominative to what follows :—

8, 9. ꜱᴜᴛʜɪᴛᴘ.—This congeries of letters, although written unbrokenly as one word, is divisible into two, thus, ꜱᴜᴛʜɪ ᴛᴘ. —i. ꜱᴜᴛʜɪ I take to be the third person, present tense, of *setz-en*, 'ponere, constituere,' to appoint,—governed by ꜱ = *setzer*, the preceding word.—ii. ᴛᴘ represents the adjurative *dopp!*, signifying (in the imperative mood) 'Strike!' as derived from *duppen*, 'percutere,' to *dub* or strike (conf. τύπτω, 'percutio'); and addressed in ancient times in Germany by any one 'ad sponsionem provocante,' that is, calling upon another to ratify a bargain or agreement by joining— or, as we still say, 'striking'—hands.* The root of the symbolism is to be found (according to what I believe to be a fundamental law governing symbolical development) in the fortuitous resemblance of words—*dopp*, τύπτ-, being,

* Hence our phrase, to 'strike a bargain:'—"Nam sponsiones more antiquo complosis dextris (Latinè manum stipulatam vocant) percutiuntur. Et binus is qui ad sponsionem provocat dicere solet *dopp*, id est, percute. Confer *adabare*."—*Wachter*, sub voce *dopp*. So too under *handschlag*, which he derives from *hand*, 'stipulatio,' and *schlagen*, 'plodere, collidere.' . . "Unde natæ formulæ, *frieden anstossen, kaufschlagen*," &c. The idea thus expressed is that rather, superficially, of 'clapping' hands; but the sound merely expressed the junction, the essential point of the symbolism. 'Strip-' is, in fact, the same word originally as *kp*, which will be noticed immediately in the text.

through the interchangeability of *d* and *k*, a mere echo of *kp*, that very ancient word for the 'fist' or 'palm of the hand,' as found in old Egyptian, and still familiar to us in the Scottish 'gowp-en,' a handful, and in the English 'cuff,' to strike, which lies at the root of the entire family of words expressing sale and purchase, or bargains and covenants of whatever kind, and of which *kaufen* is the Teutonic representative. It was on this same principle of echoing sense by sound that, by Roman usage, in the case of a 'testamentum per æs et libram,' when a trust was constituted for the benefit of the 'familia' of the testator—which was the case to a certain extent, as we shall see, in the present instance—the 'emptor' (or fictitious purchaser) struck the scales with a piece of coin, which he gave to the 'testator'; and it was only after that ceremony had been completed that the 'testator' pronounced 'nuncupatio' or published his will, naming his (fiduciary) 'heres,' or heir,—the crowning ceremony which is expressed in the word ꜱᴋᴜɴᴜ in the title above analysed. I draw this illustration from Roman law and practice; but that the Roman ceremony was simply borrowed from the Etruscan, and that its relative terms were translated from the Etruscan or Teutonic language, is clear, I think, first, from the presumption that the Romans borrowed their law as well as their other institutions from Etruria, and secondly, from the fact that those words which denote the principle of 'nexum,' or obligation, the various forms and symbols of obligation, and the central authority which presided over Contract, the Pontifex Maximus, stand isolated, apart, and without any recognisable link of coherence, in Latin, while they appear in connection, each with a living meaning, and all in subordination to one dominant word, *pfand*, *bond*, ᴘʜᴀɴᴜ, in Teutonic and Etruscan. The convergence in signification of the different words thus far analysed, may enable us, I think, to conclude that the ᴇɪᴛʜ : ᴘʜᴀɴᴜ : ꜱᴀᴛʜᴇᴋ constituted by Lautinius Pompey and recorded in this inscription was a *fidei-commissum*, or trust, confirmed by 'cautiones' or mutual covenants, symbolised and ratified by that striking of hands which, certainly in Germany and, as we now see, in ancient Etruria, accompanied such transactions. We have seen in a former inscription that the violation of an engagement made by joining hands entailed a severe penalty. I read, in fine, 8 : ŚUTHI TP as, 'The mandator,' viz. L. Pompey, 'appoints by striking,' *i. e.* settles in trust. This conclusion will be supported by what immediately follows:—

10, 11. IN : PHLENXNA.—Of these two words, i. IN evidently has the same meaning as in Latin and English; and, ii. PHLENXNA is, with equal clearness, an Etruscan variety of the Roman 'bilanx,' a balance or pair of scales,—a word usually derived from 'bis' and 'lanx,' a plate or scale. It has not hitherto been determined, whether the letter t, sometimes transcribed 'z,' represents that letter or 'x'; but this identification decides it in favour of the latter. These two words complete the sense, in sequence to ŚUTHI TP; and the phrase ŚUTHI TP IN PHLENXNA must be read, 'appoints by striking' with a coin 'upon the scales,' thus expressing by its full technical formality a 'mancipium,' or transfer in trust 'per œs et libram.'

12. TEISNIKA.—Compare with *tusinc, tusing, tausend,* 'mille,' a thousand,—a numeral; to be followed by a noun substantive, TINERI, implying a coin, or denomination of money, presently.

13, 14, 15. KAL : IPA : MA · ANI :—With respect to these words I can only suggest that they express the time and seasons when the thousand TINERI are to be paid.—i. KAL : may represent either *sal,* 'numerare,' *sellen,* 'solvere, præstare,' to pay; or, more probably (as I think), 'kalendæ,' the kalends, or times when money due was payable.—ii. IPA represents ὑπό, *bey,* and signifies, as already shewn, 'per.'—iii. MA · ANI may be compared with *mand,* μήν, month; and the analysis of the word would give MA, 'mensure,' and ANI, 'of the annus,' or year-circle. The single dot, or point, interposed in lieu of the colon between MA and ANI confirms this suggestion by shewing that MA · ANI is a compound. I take KAL : IPA : MA · ANI thus to signify 'to be paid every month,' or 'on the kalends of each month' in the year.

16. TINERI.—This I take to represent 'denarii'—TEISNIKA TINERI, 'mille denarios.' *Danaro,* the vernacular word for

K

'money' in Tuscany, is a corruption (I presume) of 'denarius.' The value of the *denarius* as familiar to us in classical times and in the Roman territory can of course be no positive criterion of the value in Etruria at the date of this inscription.

17, 18. MTISUS.—Distinguishable, I should think, as MTIS UA.—i. MTIS may be compared with *mauth*, *mause*, 'vectigal,' toll—especially such as is levied on property transported by water—perhaps, in this instance, on the river Marta, or levied at Graviscæ, the port of Tarquinii; and further, with *mezz-an, metzen, metem*, to measure, the TIS answering to *tz*.—ii. Us probably corresponds with *uz, uss, aus*, 'ex,' out of. MTIS US may thus signify 'out of [his] revenue, or income'—or it may be the commencement of the ensuing clause, directing how the money should be spent, and readable, 'To mete out,' disburse, or pay—a word not inappropriate in connection with the balance or scales.*

19. . . . NAMUTNE.—Two letters being apparently lost at the beginning of this word, I suspect that the hiatus should be filled up with KE or KI, or perhaps ZE,—that the word was originally KENAMUTSE,—and that it is akin to the old German *benomunge*, 'defluita certa portio,'—a noun formed from *benuimen*, 'definire,' as *benuimen* is from *nenen* (the Greek νέμειν), 'nominare, specificare,'—the root being *nemen, nehmen*, to take—especially with the hand. The signification would be 'speciatim,' or rather, 'distributivè,'—to pay, that is to say, 'in defined, or prescribed sums,' or 'specifically,' as shall be indicated.

20, 21, 22. IPA : TB . . . . NL.—We have now entered on the broken ground of the inscription, and the difficulty of picking our way increases at every step. NI, I would observe, is written in connection with the succeeding word KLTE, without break, in the inscription; but KLTE is certainly, as will appear, a distinct word.—i. IPA has been already connected with ὑπό, 'per,' *bey*.—ii. iii. TB . . . . NI appears to

---

* Orioli reads it KUTISUS, which would be derivable from i. *sutz*, signifying the usufruct or 'redditus' of a property; and ii. *uz, aus*, as above. But I think the transcript originally made by Kellermann and taken as the text for this analysis is the more trustworthy.

me to stand for *treve hand*, 'fida manus, manus fiduciaria,' the final *d* or *t* in *hand* being omitted, as usual in Etruscan, and the word written ANI, HANI, or perhaps simply NI, as a dot appears in Kellermann's engraving near the top of the 'N,' as if there had been a colon before it. The clause would imply therefore 'to pay,' or 'payment in defined sums,' or 'specifically,' by the 'true' or faithful 'hand' of the fiduciary, or trustee.

23, 24, 25. KLTE : PHLESXNEVES . . ⋏ . . : K.K . . . . . .

—i. KLTE, akin to the Teutonic *geld*, the type and centre of an infinity of words connected with 'solutio' or money-payment, must be understood here as 'pecunia,' wages, or stipend, as for example in the compound *knecht-geld*, 'pecunia militi alendo' (especially in garrison), and others of the same kind.

—ii. PHLESXNEVES, although so like at first sight, is a different word from PHLENXNA, an '**s**' taking the place of the '**N**.' Proximately, it is comparable with *pflegnus*, 'famulitium,' i.e. the slaves, or servants, who compose what we call an establishment; but the two words represent, I think, both of them, an older original form in parallel descent. We may be guided to this form by the observation that the first '**s**' in PHLESXNEVES is rendered by the Etruscan *sas*, which in this inscription, as in various others, appears to be used in preference to the *sigma* at the end of words, or of the several elements of compound words. PHLES and XNEVES would thus be the component elements here; and the latter, XNEVES, at once reminds us of our Northern *enecht*, *knecht*, *knapp*, *knave*, 'famulus, servus,' which, in the bad sense of 'nebulo,' was familiar to the Etruscans as NEPOS. The resemblance of PHLES to *pflicht*, 'cura, tutela, servitio, &c., jure ac more debita,' &c. may be less apparent; but the terms *die pflichtige leute*, *sinspflichtig*, and others, used to denote 'servi,' whether servants, serfs, or slaves, and as tantamount to *pfleghaft*, a term again commutable with *pflegnus* (from *pflege*, 'tutela') *ut supra*, warrants the approximation; and my impression is, that the Etruscan compound now in question has been originally written PHLEKS-XNEVES, but that the '**K**' has been softened down and lost in use through the conjunction and attrition of so many consonants. The two words KLTE :

PILESXNEVES—the latter apparently in the genitive case—thus appear to signify, 'cost, or payment, of the servants,' or 'of the establishment,' provided by the settlement. It will not escape your notice that the Etruscan KLTE-XNEVES corresponds in form, although with a variation in special signification, with the Teutonic compound *knecht-geld*, above spoken of.*—iii. The gross amount to be thus paid must have been indicated in sequence to PILESXNEVES; and we can discern indications of numerals; but the illegible spaces and abbreviations which present themselves at this point throw us necessarily upon consideration of the context (before and after) as the only sure means of ascertaining the precise pecuniary provisions of the trust. I shall therefore postpone my interpretation of them, merely stating here that I believe that the text should run, restored, as

PILESXNEVES : I TR · : XKKXXXIII :

—the general signification being, 'Towards maintenance of the household,'—so much. A second clause in the specification of money-payments now succeeds:—

26–33. TAN . . . . ERKE : ATHIS | THNAM · PILENXNATE . . . . ATA · : ENAK.—The *lacunæ* here, as in the case of the preceding numerals, are unfortunate; the letters are written moreover (or were written) so irregularly that it is difficult to feel sure as to the number of them which ought to fill each separate gap; but I think the passage may be restored as follows, TANNA : HERKE : ATHIS | THNAM · PILENXNATE : CHAZI : UATA · : ENAK.—i. The word TANNA occurs in the great inscription of Perugia, hereafter to be dealt with; and I have therefore completed the word by adding the two letters deficient, followed by a colon. It appears to me to be the past participle passive of *zanen*, 'con-

---

* My first impression was that PILESXNEVES was the Etruscan equivalent for the Latin 'familia,' to wit, the inheritance which the 'emptor' bought *per as et libram*, but under covenant to the testator to deal with it according to his expressed wish. But I think the word, although covered by this legal sense of 'familia,' has likewise the more specific sense assigned in the text.

cordaro inter se,' to agree together, with the sense of 'indentured.' I shall speak of it again more fully. PHLENXNATE is its relative substantive.—ii. iii. HENKE : ATIIIS. HENKE I take to represent the word found in ancient law-Latin (I mean of Roman antiquity) as 'heretum' or 'foretum,' interpreted as 'hereditas,' and in a simpler form as 'here-' in 'here-isco,' to divide an inheritance, the '-isco' having the force of the old root *sk*, to divide, as a verb. I have restored the initial 'h' accordingly, to fill up the *lacuna*. ATIIIS represents the '-atis' in the genitival form 'heredit-atis,'—or HENKE : ATIIIS may represent 'heritag-ii,' i.e. 'of the heritage.'—The two next words, iv. v. TINAM · PHLENXNATE are written, as you will observe, with a dot, or full stop, and not a colon, between them, a mark which usually denotes a compound word, or words used in immediate connection, although in several instances in this inscription it also serves as an indication of distinction between successive clauses. PHLENXNATE is itself a compound, of (1.) PHLENX, which I take to mean 'money weighed out,' i.e. from the PHLENX, or 'balance;' and (2) NATE, that is, *nutz*, 'utilitas,'—money put out 'at use,' or lent on usury.* TINAM, again, is, I think, to be understood as *su-nam*, i.e. 'to the *nomen*,' in other words, 'to the debit' of the borrower or of the estate on the security of which money was lent—which I take to be the family estate of the Pompeys not conveyed by this document.—vi. vii. CHAZI : UATA · , as I have ventured to restore this word, represents the Teutonic *welleschatz* (the component elements being reversed) in one of its various significations, that viz. of redemption, or power of repurchase, in which sense, as KŚ UATHA, we shall meet with it in the more ancient inscription immediately following the present in this Memoir. The full Etruscan word for which KŚ stands (as I believe) in abbreviation, should be written CHAZI ; or, rather, spelled correctly (as I read the letter usually rendered by 'ch'), SCHAZI. A single dot follows the surviving letters ATA in the inscription, before ENAK ; and as the single

---

* It might be divided as PHLENX-ATE, ATE representing 'usus;' but *nutz* is, I think, the earlier form.

dot, when marking a compound, is sometimes found between the component elements, and sometimes after both, at the end of the compound, and this latter alternative appears to prevail here, I have placed a colon between UATA and CHAZI. Lastly, viii. ENAK is, if I mistake not, an Etruscan equivalent for the Latin 'æque atque,' 'æque et,' 'æque ac,' (the vocables being reversed, as usual, in the Etruscan compound,) implying 'in like proportion,' 'in equality with'—some other person or thing. EN, I conceive, answers to *end*, *und*, our English 'and.' ENAK may perhaps survive in the Italian 'anche.' The word is followed in the inscription by a single point, with the view (here) of marking the termination of the clause, as in the case of SKUNU · at the commencement of the record. I interpret the sentence therefore as—in sequence to the preceding—'Towards redemption of the money lent to the debit of' (or as a debt upon) 'the heritage, as secured by indentured covenant—the like sum.' The provision is not intended for payment of the interest on the debt, but to accumulate towards wiping out the principal.*

34. ELI.—From what follows I think this first word of the third distributive clause represents *elich*, *elleich*, 'legitimus, conjugalis,' as applied to cohabitation or wedlock. It may be the same word as ἄλοχος. A provision for a wife of Pompey's would appear to be here in question.†

35. KESASIN.—Compare (the letter 'k' being used for 'b') with *beysilz*, 'concubinatus,' *beysitzerin*, 'concubina,' but in a legitimate point of view, as by the preceding qualification of *elich*, and in the sense of *sitzen*, 'habitare, domicilium habere,' and *sitzin*, 'modestus.'—In the dative case apparently.

* I suspect that the financial word, 'principal,' which is not derivable from pure Latin, is a degenerate form of an old Pelasgian, Teutonic, or Thoringa word based upon POLENK, the 'l' at the beginning changed into 'r.' The word 'bilanx' is of extreme antiquity,—not, I think, originally compounded of 'bis' and 'lanx,' as currently held, but of *sphil*, *wfλ*-, and *dzis*, the word being the same originally as τάλαντε,—two axe- or spearheads, originally of flint (*sphil* = '*sil-ex*') serving for the weights of the balance; and this idea lies at the root of much of the penal severity with which debtors were punished as if homicidal criminals.

† A transverse stroke is given immediately after ELI : in Kellermann's plate, which appears to indicate a letter, possibly 's,' but so broken that I cannot pretend to explain it.

36. THUNCHU .... M.—To be read, in part at least, as THUNCHULUM, the name of the secondary wife or concubine in question, 'Thunchul,' or 'Tanaquil,' in the dative case, as agreeing with KESASIN.

37. ENAK.—'In equal proportion,' or 'the like sum,' *ut supra*. The word is followed by a single point, denoting here completion of the sentence.—The clause would thus signify, 'To his legitimate concubine, Tanaquil, the like sum.' It was only by a *fidei-commissum* of this description that posthumous provision could be made for a wife or other woman,— the law denying to women the right of inheritance or of holding independent property—at least by Roman usage. This third clause will be found to exhaust the funds of which the distribution is prescribed in these three last clauses; and the remaining portion of the inscription must therefore be of a supplementary or accessory character. The broken ground recommences unfortunately with this final sentence:—

38-47. CHM .... VEB : KAL · | . RNTHAL : LA .... LISLA : CB ... ELR ... AS : K · ENS | SKUNA.—This may be restored, I think, as CHMUN : VEB : KAL · | ABNTHAL : LAVTN · RNTHALISLA : CHLTZELB : THTAS : K · ENS | SKUNA.—i. ii. CHMUN : VER. Of these two words, VEB may be compared with *wer*, 'cautio,' security, *weren*, 'warantizare,' to warrant or guarantee, a word already met with in the Admetus and Alcestis inscription, VEB being, I think, in the verbal form here.—CHMUN, which should properly be written SCHMUN, or, if the final consonant were given, SCHMUNT (for *schmund*), is, it may (I think) be proved, the original form of *mund*, 'tutus,' *mund*, 'propugnaculum,' from whence we have *mundbar*, originally (I presume) *schmundbar*, 'tutor,' or fiduciary.*

* I thought indeed, at first, that this last word, *mundbar*, was the Teutonic equivalent of CHM....VEB; but the context appears to prescribe the construction adopted. Words beginning now with *m, b, p, v,* &c., in Teutonic or other Aryan languages, exhibit in instances innumerable the effect of the abrasion of time on older formations beginning with *sch* (to say nothing of other letters), as we see, for instance, in ב/ (Egyptian), a ram, *scaf, sheep, obis,* 'ovis;' and in the case just discussed we may recognise a trace of the same older form in the old Egyptian *χumi*, 'tutor,'— one of very many analogies between the language of the Pharaohs and that of ourselves.

CHMUN : VEB thus signifies 'warrants secure' or 'safe,' that is, 'guarantees from injury,' in his capacity of 'tutor' or fiduciary,—a construction requiring a nominative in the person of the 'tutor,' and an accusative in the person of the individual person or thing protected. The name of the former follows in the clause,—iii. iv. KAL · | . RNTHAL, i. e., restoring the lost letter, ARNTHAL, which I read as 'Gallus, the son of Arnthia,' the KAL being followed by a single point, apparently to denote a contraction, while ARNTHAL necessarily prescribes that the preceding word should be a personal name. —v. vi. vii. The latter, the individual to be protected, in the accusative case, was Tanaquil, Lautinius Pompey's 'legitimate concubine,' whose provision forms the subject of the clause immediately preceding the present. This is sufficiently indicated by the title ŚLA at the termination of the *lacuna*, ŚLA denoting a secondary wife, as I have already shown—the title in question, here given, being in conformity, it will be remarked, with the sense assigned to ELI : KESASIN, *supra*. And, as the husband's name was LAVTN, or Lautinius, and the title begins with LA, I restore it as LAVTNARNTHALIŚLA, or LAVTN . RNTHALIŚLA, that is, 'the ŚLA of Lautinius, son of Arnthia,—which last title, Arnthal, we shall find reason, I think, to conclude, was the matronymic of Lautinius Pompey, omitted in the beginning of this inscription. The clause reads therefore thus far, 'Gallus Arnthal guarantees' or 'warrants [Tanaquil], the wife-concubine of Lautinius Arnthal.'— viii. ix. x. CHLTZELR : THTAS : K · —Taking THTAS : K · first, I consider it an abbreviation of THTAS : KN · , and identical with *gegenthat-es*, the genitive case of *gegenthat*, signifying 'reciprocatio, factum reciprocum,' a reciprocal obligation or contract, the position of the elements of the compound being reversed, as usual. The K is followed by a full stop or point, apparently to indicate a contraction, as in the case of KAL · for 'Gallus,' just noticed. The phrase *gegenthat und vergeltung*' is explained by Drinckmeier as 'eine handlung, die man einer andern entgegensetzt, zur ausgleichung oder vergeltung,' an action which one man opposes, or sets as a *per contra*, to another by way of balance or requital. *Vergelten*, again, is explained by *bezahlen*,—'eine schuld durch zahlung oder sonst ausgleichen,' to settle a debt by payment or otherwise. *Gelten* signifies 'pensare,' to weigh with the *wage* or scales; *gellen*, 'emere,' to buy; and *zelen, zahlen*, to reckon, compute, or take into consideration. Moreover, *vergolten und bzalt* occurs as a commercial phrase in old German. I therefore, with the preceding words before me, read the broken phrase, in connection with THUTAS : K, as ' *ver*-GOLT-*be*-ZELT-ER *gegenthales*,' or, in the Etruscan brevity, CILTZELB : THTAS : K · , *ut supra*,—the '*t*' in *zelter* being omitted in ZELR in the usual manner—the CH in CILT, *golt*, pointing as SCH to an earlier stage in which *gelt* was *schuld*—and the phrase signifying ' of the reciprocal engagement,' or ' covenant,' ' upon the sale and purchase (*emptio*),' that is, of the *familia*, or at least of the rent-charge of twelve thousand *denarii*, which had passed *per æs et libram* between the fiduciary and the testator above narrated.— Lastly, xi. ENS | SKUNA is the Etruscan form of *entschoenen*, ' violare,' and of its kindred participles and nouns,—the violation here spoken of being necessarily, from the context, that of a contract or agreement. These four last words complete the clause, which we may thus read as, ' Gallus Arnthal guarantees,' in his capacity of ' tutor' or fiduciary, ' Tanaquil, legal concubine of Lautinius Arnthal, against any *damnum*,' or injury, ' through infringement of the mutual compact '— that is, between himself and the deceased.

All that remains for us now to do is to fix, if possible, the proper reading of the numerals represented by the broken letters and abbreviations which are represented by number 25 in the preceding analysis. The copies given us of the passage mark the largest *lacuna* by six and eight dots or points respectively—these dots usually representing so many letters. The former number is Kellermann's; but he increases the general allowance of space by interposing a dot between the two ' K's,' which appears to mark an intermediate lost letter, inasmuch as, judging by the analogy of other Etruscan numerals, it was not the custom to mark such as abbreviated. Orioli gives eight dots as representing the missing letters; and we are thus fairly entitled to assume seven lost letters as wanting. The inscription, as it stands, and the suggested restoration, may therefore be represented thus,—

PHLESXNEVES .. ⋀ .. : K.K .... TAN &o
PHLESXNEVES : I TR . : KKKXXIII : TAN &o

—Or, if you disallow the compromise, we may dispense with the final : , in accordance with the lax rules of Etruscan orthography. But I do not like doing so; and I would lay more stress on the fact that three of the numeral-letters, the 'K's, occupy frequently a very narrow space in the inscriptions, and would easily make room for the final : in question.

The inscription itself is in fact written very irregularly, the letters in some places rather straggling, in others close together. Passing, however, from this minute but necessary criticism, the English of the passage as above restored, would be (omitting the words preceding and following the numerals)—'One third of a denarius, and 333 denarii.' It appears strange that the fraction should be placed before the principal sum, and perhaps I ought to transpose them in my English rendering. In some Etruscan inscriptions (as in Arabic) the numerals are written from left to right, even in the midst of a legend running in the usual manner from right to left; on the other hand there are many in which the numerals run from right to left, in what must have been the original

Etruscan fashion. Such is the case in the present inscription,—and yet it is possible that the two groups were viewed in the light of two hieroglyphs, and, although read internally each of them from right to left, were regarded and read by the spectator, in their corporate character, as from left to right, according to the modern usage.—Perhaps you may say that the matter was sufficiently clear until I explained it; I pass on therefore to specify the process by which the preceding restoration and interpretation has been arrived at:—1. There are three separate provisions for payment; 2. The second and third end, each of them, with an order that the same sum shall be paid under them as under the first; 3. The total sum receivable monthly, as by the initiatory clause of the record, is 1000 denarii; 4. Dividing 1000 denarii by 3, we obtain 333½ denarii as the monthly payment under each head of disbursement; 5. The sum due under the first of the three provisions, and which we should expect to find where the broken letters occur, was therefore 333 denarii and one-third of a denarius; 6. In Etrurian letters the lump sum would be written ккк—i.e., in Latin, ccc—xxxiii. The first and third of these letters are still visible; and I restore the text therefore to its pristine integrity by adding the second and intermediate letter and the seven subsequent ones necessary to complete the sense. But more remains. I cannot say precisely in what manner the . Λ, or as I have ventured to write it, I Λ, expresses the fractional third of a denarius—a mere arithmetical intangibility, for there was no coin of that amount; but I have no doubt that it stands for the fraction in question. Is it too much to suggest that the modern copyist, transcribing by imperfect torch-light, in the obscurity of a tomb, from a record not engraved, but painted merely, on a damp and decaying wall, and without any suspicion of the purport of the inscription to quicken his observation, may have written ⟩ for ⟨, the Etruscan т,—especially if the right limb of the transverse stroke had been effaced? If we may suppose that the original letter was ⟨ or г (which stands in Etruscan for D) we should have the initial letter of *dritte*, or *drittheil*, that is, the 'third'—of a denarius. The I that follows, as restored, would represent 'one'—'one-third.' I have written it I тп · , with a point to mark the contraction. I can only suggest all this, and that the account would be thus completely squared. I shall venture to assume that it is so. The effect of these emendations in connection with the context will be seen from the recapitulation of the entire record, which I shall now make. I would only premise that the emendations are not capricious in themselves, either those here immediately in question, or those that I have suggested in other parts of the inscription. Its tenor *in extenso* is as follows:—

"The Testamentary Settlement by *fidei-commissum* of Lautinius Pompey," [duly] "declared" by *nuncupatio* :—"The *mandator*" (Pompey) "appoints by striking on the scales," or *per æs et libram*, i.e. settles in trust, "one thousand denarii out of his rents, payable on the Calends of each month of the year,"— i.e. 12,000 denarii *per annum*, "to be dispensed in certain (definite) portions by the true hand of the fiduciary (or trustee):"—To wit, I., "Towards the maintenance of the establishment"—the slaves and household of the individual in whose favour the trust is instituted—" 333½ denarii:"—II. "Towards redemption of the debt upon the heritage," that is, the principal estate, "as secured by indenture, or bond—the like sum:"—III. "To his lawful concubine, Tanaquil, the like sum:"—Lastly, "Gallus Arnthal," tutor or fiduciary, "guarantees" the said Tanaquil, "lawful concubine of Lautinius Arnthal, against" any injury through "violation of the mutual compact, as by sale and purchase," entered into between himself and the dead man. I think I am justified, under the circumstances, in assuming that the mother of Lautinius was Arnthia, seeing that Gallus bore that matronymic; and the presumption is, that the office of 'tutor' would be borne by a brother of the defunct, which I take Gallus to have been.

If the general sense of this important inscription be rightly given—if indeed its character as the record of a testamentary disposition be correctly ascertained—the identification thus effected may be useful hereafter as indicating with some *primâ facie* probability the character of similar inscriptions, should they be discovered, in corresponding positions in Etruscan tombs. No similar one to the preceding is as yet known; and few of the words above analysed occur in other inscriptions, which has of course enhanced the difficulty of interpretation.

It must not, in fine, be taken for a will conveying the whole property of the testator, but merely as a testamentary provision, executed, as all such conveyances were, *per æs et libram*, on an emergency probably, when either at the point of death, or about to start on a military campaign. The reference to the debt encumbering the 'hereditas' seems to prove this, independently of the opulence testified to by the magnificence of the tomb. The document here analysed is simply a testamentary deed intended to serve a special purpose, and based upon rights involving a much larger property than the portion which is the subject of the settlement. It is a most curious fact that it should have been inscribed— 'enrolled' as it were—in a tomb; for such enrolment of wills or testamentary covenants was not usual, at least in Roman practice. I reserve the more general remarks suggested by the transaction for a future page.

The shorter inscription mentioned at the beginning of this section will not occupy us long. It is written over the head of the principal figure in a long painted procession which runs along one of the walls of the sepulchre—that of 'Lars Pompeius.' Pompey is in the act of being—as Fabretti expresses it—"afferrato dal Caronte"—Charon's lion's-paw resting on his shoulder in the stroke of death. The legend runs thus,—

LARIS : PUMPUS | ARNTHAL : KLAN | KECHASE .

KECHASE is the dominant word in the sentence, requiring explanation. It may be compared either with *schach*, 'homicidium, latrocinium, debilitatio;' *skaeka* (O. N.), 'interficere;' *schaecken*, 'rapere;' *geschachen*, 'vincere,'—with which may be taken the words *schaecker*, 'nebulo, sicarius, praedo, latro,' all of them expressive of the onslaught of the demon of death, arriving like a thief in the night, with his fatal hammer, to stun and crush out life :—Or, it may be read as *schatz*, 'pecunia, exactio publica;' *schaetzen*, 'pecuniâ taxare,'—a word used alike in a commercial and a moral sense, and not inappropriate to Lars Pompey thus 'called to account'—*geschätzt*—by the great 'telonarius' of the unseen world.

There can be little doubt (and Mr. Dennis takes it for granted) that this ' Laris Pumpus Arnthal' is the same person as Lautinius Pompey—'Laris' being used (I think) as a formal title—'Lord' or 'Laird,' while 'Lautinius' was his *prænomen*. The matronymic corresponds with what I have assigned to him in the longer inscription.

This title LARIS—'Lars, Lartis' (gen.), in Latin—demands a word in conclusion. It certainly seems to be used, as in the case of Porsena, Tolumnius, and other distinguished personages, in an honorific or titular sense, but it must be fundamentally the same word as the more frequent LARTH, although the latter was applied indiscriminately, and the former only (to all appearance) in the case of very high rank. It is thus that 'Lord,' 'Laird,' in English and Scots, is applied to persons in almost every grade of society; and I feel a strong persuasion that LARTH, 'Lord,' and 'Laird' are the same word,—the approximation is not new; but the identity can be established by proof ascending to very remote antiquity. I take 'Lord,' 'Lar-ts,' to be a much abraded form of the Zendic and old Aryan *thwôrest-*, *thwôrestára*, 'creator,'—a title given to Deity, and which, worn down to *thword-*, would by the familiar change of *d* to *l*, become *Lword*, *lord*, *laird*, *larth*, *lar-ts*, and *lar*.* Fürst, prince, I may observe, has

---

* 'Lorn' is a provincial form of 'Lord' in England, now familiarised to us by the 'Mill on the Floss.' This dialectic form reminds us of 'Lars.'

the same origin. LARTHIA, the female form of LARTH, *Lord*, is (I believe) the original form in like manner of 'Lady'—the *r* having been rubbed down and lost. In this latter form—(which we may recognise in the *latu, lala,* 'uxor,' of the Lycian inscriptions, a word Mr. D. Sharpe has identified with the English *lady*) —LARTHIA, *lathia, lady* becomes associated with the idea of the procession of the wife, led by the husband, to her new home; and she is thus (as already stated) the *-leitu,* 'ducta,' in the sense of the 'ducere uxorem' of the Romans. But this is travelling beyond the strict borders of the present record—although not beyond the limits of Etruscan philology.

The date of the tomb is fixed by Mr. Dennis as "hardly earlier than the latter days of the Roman republic"—this judgment being based on the style of the paintings, which are (or were) of a very grand character, evidently (as Mr. Dennis expresses it) by "the Michael Angelo of Etruria." At the same time, "there are paintings" (he says) "on a block of stone of a more archaic character" than those on the sides of the column and on the walls of the tomb.* The inscriptions are probably contemporary with those first spoken of. I have noticed such indications of comparative antiquity as are afforded by the letters used, the punctuation, &c., in a note *supra*. An inference as to date may perhaps be drawn from the use of the Latin, or Pelasgic, form PHLENX for 'bilanx,' instead of *waye*, the more usual Teutonic word for scales, or balances, at least in the North of Europe. It is only wonderful that these Etruscan inscriptions, even of late date, preserve the

---

* *Cities*, &c., vol. i. pp. 305, 308.

native language so free from Latin admixture. The mention of reciprocal covenants in the record of the *fidei-commissum* might further fix the date as prior to the 'senatus-consultum Trebellianum,' in the time of Nero, which rendered such covenants—at least on the part of the 'fidei-commissarius' in favour of the 'heres'—superfluous.

CHAPTER VI.

INSCRIPTIONS RELATING TO LAND-TENURE.

I PASS from the class of Sepulchral Inscriptions to those which I conceive to relate to the Tenure of Land; selecting two specimens,—the last of which is the longest and most important inscription as yet discovered in Etruria. The two inscriptions have this in common, that they are inscribed, each of them, on the front and on one of the side-faces of a quadrangular block of stone, thus shewing that the stones served originally as corner-stones—in the case of the former probably, and in the case of the latter certainly—of buildings. It follows that the subject of the inscriptions must have been matter of public notoriety and permanent importance, either to the State or to individuals.

SECTION I.—*The Inscription of the 'Marmini' at Volterra.*

The stone on which the first and shorter of the two inscriptions is engraved was found in 1855 in a tomb near Volterra, on a spot traditionally called 'I Marmini.' Some workmen, digging for stone in the summer of that year, came to a layer of lime, and below it a hewn stone, which proved to be the architrave of the door of a subterranean tomb or *hypogæum*, of circular form, full of sepulchral vases. To the right of the entrance, and on one of the *gradini* or benches (cut in the rock) running round the walls, stood the inscribed stone, surrounded by various vases, one of them a *gutturariu*, in shape Greek, the workmanship of exquisite taste, and two large *tazze*, with red figures on a black ground,—all of very ancient character. There were many other vases, of different form and style; and in some of them were found coins, all from Roman mints, and belonging to the earliest times of consular Rome. This is but an imperfect and second-hand account, obtained by Fabretti and published by him in the 'Archivio Storico Italiano;'* but it may suffice to explain the position in which the inscribed stone was discovered.

The place known as the 'Marmini' occupies the slope of the hill, a little below the 'Porta di Diana,' and is "marked," Mr. Dennis states, "by a clump of cypresses." I think I remember them; but it is long since I was at Volterra. From the multitude of sepulchres existing there, (such, at least, is Mr. Dennis's explanation of it,) the spot was known till recently by the name of the 'Campo Nero,' a name now become "almost obsolete." The present tomb—which was discovered several years after the publication of the 'Cities and Cemeteries of Etruria,' must not be confounded with that described by Mr. Dennis under the name of the 'Grotta de' Marmini,' but which has its relative importance here, inasmuch as it is "said to be a type in form and character of the tombs of Volterra," (all of which have been filled up and closed),—circular, like this, with a square pillar in the centre, three tiers of benches covered with miniature sarcophagi, and with "two large pino-

* *Archivio, &c.; Nuova Serie,* tom. iv. p. 137.

cones of stone, common funereal emblems, lying one on each side of the entrance."* Although the brief account given by Fabretti does not mention these pine-cones as existing in the sepulchre which disclosed the inscription now to be analysed, I think it very probable that similar emblems existed there, forming, as they seem to have done, one of the features common to the tombs of the locality.

My belief is, that the tomb in question, and not only it, but the whole district of the 'Marmini,' belonged to one of the religious Fraternities or Colleges—consisting normally of twelve Fellows, one of them designated as 'Master,' and variously known as 'Salii,' 'Fratres Aterii' or 'Ateriates,' 'Fratres Arvales,' and 'Sodales Titii,' 'Titienses,' or 'Titiales,' which, with varying functions, as perambulators and lustrators of fields and boundaries, offerers up of the 'fruges' or first-fruits of the year, sacrificers of the Arval lamb at harvest-time, or as perpetuating the *sacra* of the respective nationalities, Pelasgian, Umbrian, Latin, and Oscan, to which they originally belonged, all agreed apparently in worshipping the Supreme God under variations of his early Pelasgic name of 'Deus,' Θεός, his Æolic title 'Ἐῤῥος, and his Teutonic name ' Dôd,' or 'God,'— the form 'Deus' being perpetuated in the masculine form as 'Deus Dius' and in the feminine as 'Dea Dia,'—the 'Deus Dius' melting into the character of the mythological 'Ju-piter' and 'Ja-nus,' and the 'Dea Dia' into that of 'Di-ana,' 'Deo,' 'Deione' (Demeter and Persephone), and thence by insensible gradation into that of the Phrygian 'Cybele,' whose

* *Cities and Cemeteries*, &c., vol. ii. pp. 150 sqq.

name links the East with the West in this extended connection through its identity with that of 'Ερρα, Rhea, and Juno in Etruscan, to wit, 'Cupra,'— 'Cybel-' and 'Cupr-' being etymologically identical. There cannot be a doubt, I think, that the 'Bona Dea' was worshipped in Italy ages before the importation of the more orgiastic form of her worship into Rome in the third century before Our Saviour. I have only to add that the title 'Salii,' that of the priests of Mars Gradivus ('Ἡρυ,' 'Ερρ-, or 'Herrdeus') at Rome, is identical with that of the 'Selli' or 'Helli' of Pelasgian Dodona, and that of the 'Galli,' the priests of Cybele at Pepinus in Asia Minor, although the representatives of the name presented a very different aspect to the eyes of Homer and those of Horace. The name of 'Titius,' the *eponymus* of the Titiensian College, is, I conceive, of cognate origin with that of 'Dodona,' of the river 'Titaresius,' and of the 'Campus Dotius,' in Pelasgian Thessaly.* The fraternity to whom the present inscription relates was, I think, the 'Sodales Titii,' or 'Titienses;' and the inscribed stone is the record, the title-deed (as it were), of their property at Volterra. It is engraved in very ancient characters; and must certainly, from the very fact recorded in the inscription, be older than the sepulchre—old as that

* The 'Dodona' of Homer was certainly in Thessaly, as shewn not only by internal evidence (for which see Mr. Gladstone's *Homer and the Homeric Age*, vol. i. p. 106), but from the name 'Campus Dotius' and that of the Lake 'Bœbeis.' The only Dodona known to positive geography is beyond Thessaly; and I think the worship must have been transferred thither, the neighbouring lake receiving the name 'Pambotis,' which is etymologically the same as 'Bœbeis.' Perhaps the Western Dodona may have been a colony of that in Thessaly, as affirmed by Stephanus Byzantinus.

is—in which it was discovered. I may suggest hereafter how it got there.

The inscription runs as follows,—the column here represented on the right of the vertical line being of course on the left in the original, the Etruscan language being written (I need not say) in the Oriental fashion, from right to left :—

TITEŚI : KALE	ŚI
KINA : KŚ : MEB	TLEŚ
HUTH : NAPER	LESKAN
LETEM : THUI	
ARAŚA : THEN	TMA
SELAEI : TRE	KŚ
THENŚT : ME	UATHA

(*Fabretti*, no. 340 ; and tab. xxv.)

—The letters (as above observed) are archaic in form. The 'h' is represented by a circle with two cross-lines within it, but it seems doubtful whether the second cross-line is not accidental. The circles representing the letter 'th' have each the point within them, which is understood (with reason, I think) to indicate an older form. The 'm' is of the ancient type, with one leg longer than the other two. The 'r' is very peculiar, resembling a triangle with the apex truncated. The 'p' too is peculiar,—but all the letters seem to be Etruscan. The initial *sigma* and final *san* seem to be carefully discriminated. They are better seen in Fabretti's large engraving in the 'Archivio' than in the reduced copy in the 'Corpus.' Fabretti and Migliarini both view the inscription as written continuously—KALEŚI and MESTLEŚ, for example, forming each one word ; but I think that each column is to be read separately,—which might be inferred, in fact, from the space left between the last three lines of the narrower column on the side-face of the stone, and the others. These last three lines, or words, TMA KÉ UATHA, form, it will be seen, an independent paragraph, in completion of the record.— I proceed to analysis, as usual :—

1, 2. TITEŚI : KALE.—Read according to the usual practice of Etruscan paleographers, this would imply 'Titius Gallus,' —and such reading would be as admissible as it is natural were there nothing in the context to suggest a different interpretation. The anxious desire to extract some sense, at least, out of the inscriptions, some sunbeams out of these very obscure cucumbers, has, I am convinced, not unfrequently occasioned an unwarranted assumption that words bearing in reality a very different signification are nothing more than proper names. My impression is that TITEŚI : KALE stands here for 'Titii' or 'Titiensibus Sodalibus,' in the dative case plural,—the terminational -EŚI being, in fact, very like the -εσσι of Homer. KALE receives no addition according to a frequent Etruscan (and modern) usage, of only subjoining inflections to one word where two are in grammatical agreement. I have sufficiently dealt with the title 'Titienses' in the paragraphs introductory to this analysis; and that KALE is the Etruscan equivalent of 'Sodales' will appear from the fact that KALE, GALLI, SALII, SODALES are all of them varieties, in successive stages of disintegration, of a very early word which must originally have been written 'ZFal-' or 'ZFel-,' and of which geSello is the German, 'ConSul' the Latin, and 'fellow' the English representative. The process has been analogous to that through which 'Queen,' kuna, γυνή, has been softened down to bean in Erse, βαν-ῆκες (wives) in Bœotian Greek, and 'Ven-us' in Latin; and zwanzig or twenty, 'quatuor,' quelle, 'Quain,' 'Guasc-ones' (and innumerable other cases could be cited), to vigaint or 'viginti,' 'petor,' or 'four,' 'well,' 'Finn,' and 'Vasc-ones,' or 'Basques.' 'Fellow' has thus been pronounced originally as 'gFellow' or 'kFellow'; but while in

England and Scandinavia we have dropped the 'k,' in Etruria and Phrygia they retained it, and wrote KALE, 'Galli.' Collaterally with this, the Greeks and Romans, dropping the 'k' and exchanging 'ꜰ' for 's,' wrote 'Salii,' 'Selli'—'Helli' occupying a middle place—and the Germans, *sello*. I may note in collateral illustration, i. That the idea of 'fellow'—as of the *falls*, 'socius,' of the people of Scania—is involved in the O. N. verb *falda, faella*, signifying 'coapture, committere,' to fit, or, in the general sense of the word, to 'fold' together, whether it be as the leaves of a book in binding, or as the parts of a *fald*-stool, or as parties in a bargain or lawsuit, or as friend with friend in society,—the word *fald*, be it observed, corresponding exactly with the Latin 'sodalit-as,' with the exception that 'sod-,' representing the lost initial 'z' or 'st,' has been rubbed off:—ii. That *faella* connects itself by this link of transition with *glied*, a joint, whether of the human body or of anything else,—*glied der kirche, mitglied eines kollegium, rathsglied*, having the analogous signification of member of the Church, fellow of a College, member of Council, &c.:—And, iii. that this again leads us to *gelenk* and *gleich*, each having the like sense of a joint, link, or articulation; while *gleich*, as an adjective, (a form parallel to that of ʙᴀʟᴇ,) is constantly used for 'fellow' in modern German. All this appears to me to support the identity of the TITESI KALE in the present inscription with the 'Titiensian Fellows, Brothers, or Companions.' And the word KALE, or something very like it, was actually used in Germany to express the idea thus suggested, in the case of the *Kalandsbruder* of the middle ages, the association called in Latin the 'Fratres Calendarii,' and who derived their name—not assuredly from the classical 'kalends,' as has been conjectured, but from the words above-mentioned, implying 'sodalitas,' 'societas,'—even if they were not (as I think it probable they were) the 'Titienses' or Arval Brothers themselves, surviving through the middle ages. I do not know whether their origin can be historically established; but it is quite as probable that the Arval Brothers or Titienses passed from Paganism into Christianity through a natural transfer of their superficial religious rites from the old to the new religion, as that the Pontifex Maximus and the Pontifical College of ancient Rome became (as I believe they were) absorbed into and identified with the Pope and the 'Cardinales' (as representing the 'cardines' or hinges, *gleich, gelenk, glied, fall*) of the Sublician Bridge, under the Popedom. The interest of the point here discussed may be my apology for dwelling so long on these initial words TITESI : KALF.

3. KINA.—This I take to be the name of a man, Cinna, with whom the Titienses had the dealings recorded in this inscription.

4. KÉ.—This word appears to me to be written in an abridged form. Taking it in conjunction with the KÉ : UATHA at the end of the sentence, I think it stands for *schal, schatzen*, in the sense of 'pignus,' pledge; and that it means here, 'gives in pledge,' or 'in satisfaction.'

5. MES.—Compare *messen*, 'metiri,' to measure—in the sense of payment or consideration. It seems to answer to the Latin 'modo' and the modern Italian 'mediante.'

6. HUTH.—Apparently a numeral. Fabretti thinks it means 'quat-uor,' four; and certainly it bears the same resemblance to 'q-uat-uor' that the old and very abraded Egyptian *ftu* does. But, pending further enlightenment, I would suggest *hund-*, 'cent-um,' as more probable,—HUTH representing the word in its primitive form (as in the Gaelic and Irish *cead*) before the 'n' was introduced in accordance with the rule of 'anuswara.'

7. NAPER.—From the relation in which this word stands to others in various inscriptions I am inclined to think it is Etruscan for 'nummi'—which would be, in Latin, so many 'nummi sestertii,' or 'sestertii.' But the monetary value of the Etruscan need not necessarily have been the same as that of the Roman, or even the Greek 'nummus,'—indeed, from the numerals attached to the word here and elsewhere I should think it was a conventional term used for the higher descriptions of coin—perhaps the Latin 'aureus' or Greek 'mina.' The word appears to me, proximately, a compound of i. NAP, the same root which has produced *knaepp*, a blow, *knaeppa*, to strike and resound (as in S.-Goth.); and ii. ER, identical with *er*, 'aes, aer-is,' or perhaps 'aur-,' gold,—NAP-ER thus

signifying 'struck' or 'coined money.' Through the interchange of *p* and *k*, *knaeppa* is the same word as *knacken*, 'crepitare;' and we have *gnack*, and *knack*, as 'nummus,' —names for medieval German coins. The *schnappan*— which comes nearer to NAPES, an initial *sch* having perhaps been rubbed off—was similarly an ancient coin, marked by the device of a horse—perhaps a *gnack* or *nag*, thus connecting *schnappan* and *knack*; while the 'rostrum' or beak of a ship, found on many very ancient coins—*schnabel* in old Teutonic, *neb*, whence *nibble*, in English, in its primitive sense as applied to birds, sheep, &c.—connects that device too with *schnappen*, the older form (as I conceive) of NAP-ES. Both these devices lead us, if I am not mistaken, to the original root of the word in 'Num,' π-νεῦμ-α, 'K-neph,' 'Neb-,' the title found, as already in part intimated, in the Latin, Etruscan, and Hellenic names 'Nept-unus,' 'Neth-uns,' and 'Pos-eidon,' as that of the Spirit-Deity of the Japhetan race; and the compound NAP-ER would thus signify ' the money of Neptune,' that is of commercial, especially maritime, exchange.

8. LETEM.—The accusative singular of *lul*, the earlier form of *last*, *land*.

9, 10. THUI ARASA.—My first impression was that these two words were to be read as 'Divæ Cereri,' *i.e.*, 'ΕΡΕΣΙ, 'ΕΠΕΡΙ; or as 'Diæ ad aras,' according to a form, used in Umbrian inscriptions, of 'arasa' for 'ad aras.' But the inscription records an act, or process of acts, of commercial dealing, not a gift from motives of devotion. I should read therefore i. THUI, as *zwey*, 'duo,' *two*, and, ii. ARASA as *akrs* (Goth.), *achar*, 'ager,' or perhaps 'vorsus,' the Etruscan and Umbrian word for a field one hundred feet square, as by the testimony of an ancient fragment 'De Limitibus.' The ground dealt with, although for the greater part wild uncultivated forest, would naturally be divided by the 'agrimensores' for the purposes of sale or mortgage.

11, 12. THENSELAEI.—Divisible as THEN and SELAEI.—i. For THEN, compare *tann*, 'pinus,' fir, or fir-wood.—ii. For SELAEI, compare *holz*, ὕλη, ἄλσος, 'sylva,' 'sylvestris.' THUI ARASA THEN SELAEI would thus mean 'two versi' or 'acres, of wild or natural pinewood.'

13. TRE.—Compare *tri*, 'tree,' three.

14, 15. THENŚT.—Resolvable into THEN and ŚT,—ŚT representing *sad*, sown, or planted; and thus THEN ŚT would signify 'planted pine-wood' as contrasted with the wild or uncultured growth. The fir-crop, as we know in Scotland, requires peculiar culture to produce timber—far less picturesque than the wild growth, but fitter for use. THEN-ŚT, written as a compound, and '*pin-et*-um' are, I have no doubt, the same word. The convertibility of *th* and *p* or *ph*, need hardly be insisted upon when we remember the identity of 'Thraetaona' in India and 'Feridun' in Persia, or even the alternate writing of the surname 'Throckmorton,' 'Frogmorton,' in MSS. of Queen Elizabeth's time.—The wood thus described as pledged, mortgaged, to the Titienses became subsequently, I imagine, after consecration, the sacred 'Lucus' or grove of the Brotherhood; and thenceforward the trees planted, as well as those of natural growth, would be hallowed from the axe, and their fall from age or tempest expiated by the ceremonies which we read of in the sculptured 'Acta' of the Arval Brothers as usual on such occasions.

16. MEŚI.—The same (substantially) as MES,—in the sense of consideration,—'modo,' 'mediante,' or 'by way of.'

17, 18. TLEŚ LESKAN.—i. TLEŚ is, I think, the genitive of TL, i.e. *zol*, 'debitum' or obligation; and, ii. LESKAN I take to be *leist-ung*, from *leisten*, implying the act of becoming security, on bond or bail, for a debt or obligation—the 'jus ostagii.' MEŚI TLEŚ LESKAN would thus mean 'by way of security for settlement.'* The clause finishes here, in completion of the recital that Cinna had pledged the property to the 'Titienses,' or 'Sodales Titii,' as a security for the consi-

---

* The letters *l* and *k* are often interchanged, as I assume them to have been in LESKAN, *leistung*. A nearer literal resemblance to TLEŚ LESKAN would be found in reading LESKAN as *leschung*, 'extentio solutio, extinctio,' from *löschen*, to extinguish—alike in the case of a conflagration or a debt. But in this case there would have been no occasion for the last three words in the record; and the property would have remained with Cinna; whereas, as I think we shall see reason to conclude, it lapsed to the College. I duly considered the compounds *teil-losung*, and *los-theilung*; but the interpretations they suggested would not suit the context, at least as I read it.

deration of 100 *nummi*. A new sentence, marked by the space of a line being left blank, begins with

19. TMA.—This word may be compared with *tuom, tuomo,* 'judicium,' 'judex,'—with *tum,* 'matricula, collegium,' a word used for a convent, religious house, or Collegiate Church,—with *temmen, dämpfen,* 'sedare, extinguere,' to extinguish or settle anything,—and with our Scottish *toom,* empty or void. Something may be said for each of these readings, but I have no hesitation in taking the last as at once the simplest and most agreeable to the analogy of speech. It means here 'void' in the sense in which we say, 'the agreement is void,' 'the bubble' (analogous to 'tumor,' that which is swelled up) 'has burst.'

20. KÁ.—As before, and standing for *schats*; but here to be taken in special connection with the last word in the inscription, namely,

21. UATUA.—For this, compare *wette,* 'pignus,' and the compound *wetteschatz* (from *schat,* also signifying 'pignus,') explained by Scherz as 'pignus simplex, vadium, vadimonium,' and "pignus juris Germ. in re immobili aut incorporali, quæ, una cum possessione, usum fructum proportionatum et æqualis ferè æstimationis (v. *widerlegung*) fert et proprietatem atque etiam jus alienandi, unde *ein freyer* WETTESCHATZ dicitur." *Wetteschatz* is further explained as "redemptio, retrovenditio,"—*wetteschatzen,* "impignorare, .. item emere hoc tali titulo, .. redimere hoc tali titulo pignoratum." The simple sense of 'security given' is sufficient for our purpose here; and thus the three words, or rather TMA and the compound KÁ-UATIIA, signify, 'The security, pledge, or bond is void,'— that is, the property pledged has escheated to the creditor through non-redemption of the obligation. The use of the word UATIA, *wette,* may perhaps infer a considerable antiquity for this inscription on the grounds specified in the fifth section of the chapter on 'Inscriptions on Votive Offerings,' *supra.*

I read the entire inscription, in its two portions, thus:—I. "To the 'Sodales Titii' Cinna gives in pledge, for the consideration of One Hundred *nummi,* land,—[to wit] two *rorsi*, or acres of natural pinewood, and three of planted, or cultivated *pinetum*, by way of security for debt:"—II. "The security is void"—that is, the pledged property has eschcated.

It is interesting to note that time and tradition have preserved, if I mistake not, many memorials of this ancient Fraternity in connection with the spot which once owned their beneficent power and influence. The subject of the grant, or record, was, as we have seen, a grove of pines, which, as surmised, became the sacred 'Lucus' of their worship. The pine— πίτυς—was sacred, generally, to 'Dea Dia,' the 'Bona Dea,' or Cybele, in Phrygia and Lydia, consecrated to her, I presume, in consideration of the title— 'Çpenta' in Zendic, signifying 'Holy' and 'White' —which she must have borne in Asia Minor, judging by that of 'Bendis,' the same word, her designation in the intermediate and kindred Thrace,—'Bend-' or 'Çpent-' being simply the Goth. *hveits* (*çveta*, Sanscr.), with the 'n' inserted by 'anuswara,' and πίτυς being thus adopted as the echo-emblem of 'Çpenta.' But, specially, it was the κυπάρισσος, 'pinus cupressus,' or cypress, which, I take it, her European votaries honoured, through the resemblance of the root 'cupar-' to 'Cybel-,' the words being identical through the interchangeability of 'r' and 'l,'—while this is rendered still more probable through Cybele being the same personage in the estimation of the Arval and other brotherhoods with Juno, the female 'genius' or reflex of the Supreme Deity, and who (as I may repeat here) was styled by the Etruscans, emigrants moreover from Lydia, 'Cupra.' All this throws an interesting light on the facts now before us, that the ground which the Titienses became possessed of through the transaction recorded in the present inscription was a wood of pines; that sculptured pine-cones appear to have been placed in the sepulchres of Volterra, and are still to be seen in the one and typical tomb described by Mr. Dennis; and that a clump of cypresses still crowns the eminence of the 'Marmini'—lineal descendants perhaps (it is pleasant, at least, to imagine it) of those recorded on the venerable stone here in question.—Again, it seems not improbable that the 'Porta di Diana' by which you approach the 'Marmini,' and which looks down on the scene of the old festivities of the 'Sodales Titii,' may have derived its name by corruption from that of 'Dea Dia,' or Deó, lengthened into Deione, as in the person of her daughter, or alternate self, Cora or Persephone—Diana herself being a mere form of 'Dia.'—Once more, the name 'Campo Nero'—conjecturally explained by reference to the many sepulchres, but which seems to me to require some special elucidation to account for its being affixed to this particular spot and not to other of the necropolises of Etruria—appears to bear direct reference to the old proprietors. While the Arval Brothers, the especial votaries of 'Dea Dia,' appear from their records to have worn white more especially, at least in their great festivals,[*] it is natural to suppose that the Salii, who attached themselves more peculiarly to 'Deus Dius' (although indeed the shades of varying honour were but slight) wore dark-coloured raiment;

[*] See Marini's 'Atti e Monumenti de' Fratelli Arvali,' Rome, 2 vols. 4to, 1795, and Supplement,—the great repertory of information on the subject. It is not improbable that the Arval Brothers may have worn black as their usual dress, and white only on their great ceremonies.

partly because the Supreme Deity, in his male character, was symbolised by the colour black in token of his inaccessibility and unknown character, and partly through the resemblance of their name 'Salii' to *salo*, 'fuscus,' 'niger.' It may even be questioned whether this did not attach to all the 'Sodalitates' as distinguished from the 'Fraternitates,' thus associating the Titienses at once with the Salii. 'Tit-', moreover, is in one line of descent, a worn-down form of *zwarz*, swart, black,—the name of the 'Galli' connects itself with *zwarz* through the Sanscrit form of *kâla*, the Etruscan KIARTII,—while 'Ater-' in 'Aterii,' 'Ateriates,' represents an intermediate stage of verbal degeneration. My impression therefore is that, while the 'Arvales' were the 'White,' the 'Titienses' and their con-sodalities were the 'Black Friars' (so to speak) of the ancient world; and the name 'Campo Nero' traditionally assigned to their ancient heritage thus receives an intelligible signification. The word 'Campo' itself arrests attention. The idea of 'campi,' or fields, is closely connected with these ancient brotherhoods or colleges, but in the sense, I suspect, of fields or places of combat, such as would be in harmony with the traditions of Mars Gradivus and the Salii. As applied to the hilly district of the 'Marmini,' the word is by no means appropriate in its usual signification, and must therefore have had some such other and technical meaning as that suggested.—Once more, and lastly, the name 'I Marmini' bears consentient testimony. There are two channels through which it may be traced upwards to the fountain-head, and while hesitating which to prefer, I feel confident that one of the two should conduct us to the truth. 'Marmar,' the name of Mamers, Mars, or Mars Gradivus, akin evidently to 'Mamurius Veturius,' the hero of the 'axamenta,' or commemorative songs, of the Roman Salii, the priests of Mars, is invoked with emphasis also in the ancient song of the Arval Brothers,—by a not unfamiliar change of 'n' for 'r,' 'Marmar' would become 'Marman,' and thus we should have 'I Marmini' at once restored to Etruscan antiquity:—Or, as an alternate solution, the name would equally derive from the 'ambarvalis hostia,' the 'ambarvale sacrificium,' offered up yearly by the Fratres Arvales, and the 'ambarvalia,' or perambulation of boundaries, one of the peculiar duties of the brotherhood,—the word 'ambarval-' softening down into 'mbarval,' 'marval,' and then by the usual change of 'v' into 'm' and 'l' into 'n,' into 'Marman,' 'Marmini,' to the same result as that above suggested. Both these suggestions may appear to proceed on an unwarranted assumption that the rites of the Arval Brothers, the Salii, and the Titienses were identical; but, with certain special peculiarities, the presumption is that they were so; and if we had as many documents illustrative of the traditions and practice of the Titienses as we have of the Arval Brothers we should, I think, find this to be the case. It is to be remembered too that while the various brotherhoods or religious orders above spoken of represented the Umbrian, Sabine, and Roman populations, that now under discussion represented the Etruscan; and it is impossible to say whether they may not have exercised functions which elsewhere were appropriated otherwise.

My impression, in fine, is, that the stone which bears the inscription which has detained us so long was originally built, as a corner-stone, into the wall of a chapel or temple in the sacred grove, and remained there during the flourishing times of paganism; but that when the Emperors became Christian and the old worship, although tolerated, was nodding to its fall, it was concealed for security in the tomb from which it has since emerged—that tomb being in all probability one sacred to the ashes of the Fellows of Titius. Those who concealed it probably thought that times might change and the old religion once more recover its power; and they sought to preserve it, in the meanwhile, as the precious title-deed of the chief seat of their worship, from the risk of destruction.

SECTION II.—*The great Inscription of Perugia.*

Turning to the second and last of the specimens that I propose to produce of Etruscan Inscriptions relating to Land—and which I must now formally introduce to you as the great inscription of Perugia, preserved in the Museum of that most interesting city,—I have to observe, first, that the same observation applies to it as to the preceding record, viz., that, the writing being on the front and side-face of a quadrangular block of stone, we must presume that the block in question formed the angle- or corner-stone of a building, and that the inscription related to matters requiring public notification. It is probable moreover that the building on which the inscription appeared was a farm-house or 'villa,' and not a temple, inasmuch as the block was found, not within the walls of Perugia, but at some distance from it, where it is not known that any temple existed. The inscription related therefore, it may be assumed, to private not to religious matters. It was discovered in 1822,—to the north of the city—a sufficiently meagre account.* Before analysing the inscription I had better say at once that I believe it to be the record of a series of transactions, legal and otherwise, connected with the 'conductio' or lease of the property on which it was discovered. The laws and customs in such matters were as follows among the Romans,—and, considering the influence exerted by Etruria on Rome, as well as the Pelasgic element common to both nations, I do not think that it is unreasonable to expect light towards its interpretation from that quarter:—An owner or landlord, who did not choose to cultivate the soil himself, leased it to a tenant described as the 'conductor' or 'colonus,' who paid rent for it, partly in kind and partly in money, or wholly in kind or wholly in money, as might be agreed upon. In course of time, and under the influence of the Prætors, the practice grew up of presuming a sort of subordinate property in the land, described by a Greek word as 'emphyteusis,' in favour of the tenant, who was thus placed upon a footing in relation to the landlord of very considerable independence. By this custom, gradually consolidating into law, the tenant acquired at last a perpetual right in the possession or usufruct of the land under the Dominus, conditional on fulfilling the obligations of

* Conte Giancarlo Conestabile's *Monumenti di Perugia, Etrusci e Romani*, parte IVta, p. 4.

the contract. This right was transmissible to his descendants, and by ordinary law the 'conductor' could transfer or assign the 'possessio' to a third party on a fine to the Dominus, the Dominus having no power of eviction unless the tenant injured the property, failed in payment of rent, alienated without giving due notice, or otherwise infringed the conditions of tenure. Of course, such rights could be limited by private arrangement. The 'Lar,' 'Dominus,' or Superior in the case before us was, if I read it rightly, a lady of the name of 'Aphuna,' or in Latin form, 'Aponia,' and the ground leased is described as the 'Salic' or Dominical land,—land originally wild and uncultivated, but which had been (as in other cases) newly fenced in (so I presume) for cultivation, and which was now made over to the 'conductor'—by name 'Lautn Velthina,' or 'Lautinius Veltinius'—with the reservation of feudal rights to the proprietor. I use the word 'feudal' advisedly; for I think there can be little doubt that what we call the feudal system as distinguished from the allodial was in force among the Etruscans at a period long anterior to history, and derived from a common source with the corresponding system among the Teutonic race North of the Alps.* These brief observations will make the analysis of this great Perugian inscription more intelligible during its progress, and enable me to dispense with much comment while laying the results before you.

* The local tenures and special feudal and customary law of Germany would probably throw great light on the legal antiquities of Etruria. It is singular how often the dialect of Bremen (as already observed) and the names of Holstein have cropped up in my Etruscan researches.

The inscription runs as follows,—I give it line by line, as in the original:—

EULAT·TANNA·LAREZUL	VELTHINAŚ
AMEVACHRLAUTN·VELTHINAŚ·E	ATENAZUK
ŚTLAAPHUNAŚSLELETH·KARU	I·ENEŚKI·IP
TEZANPHUŚLERI TEŚNŚTEIŚ	A·ŚPELANE
RAŚNEŚIPAAMAHENNAPER	THI·PHULUMCH
XIIVELTHINATHURAŚARAŚPE	VAŚPELTHI·
RAŚKEMULMLEŚKULZUKIEN	RENETHIEŚT
EŚKIEPLTULARU	AKVELTHINA
AULEŚI·VELTHINAŚARZNALKL	AKILUNE·
ENŚI·THII·THILŚKUNA·KENU·E	TURUNEŚK
PLK·PHELIKLARTHALŚAPHUNEŚ	UNEZEAZUK
KLENTHUNCHULTHE	I·ENEŚKI·ATH
PHALAŚ·CHIEMPHUŚLE·VELTHINA	UMIKŚ·APHU
HINTHAKAPEMUNIKLET MAŚU	NAŚ·PENTHN
NAPER·ŚRÁNKZLTHIIPHALŚTIV	A·AMAVELTH
ELTHINA·HUT·NAPER·PENEZŚ	INA·APHUN
MAŚU·AKNINA·KLEL·APHUNAVEL	THURUNI·EIN
THINAMLERZINIA·INTEMAME	ZERIUNAKCH
R·KNL·VELTHINA·ZIA ŚATENE	A·THILTHUNCH
TEŚNE·EKA·VELTHINATHURAŚTH	ULTHL·ICH·KA
AURAHELUTEŚNE RAŚNE KEI	KECHAZICHUCH
TEŚNŚTEIŚ RAŚNEŚCHIMTHŚP	E
ELTHUTAŚKUNAAPHUNAMENA	
HEN·NAPER·KI KNLHAREUTUŚE	

(*Fabretti*, no. 1014, tab. xxxviii.; and *Conestabile*, iv. p. 3.)

This congeries of words, at first appearance hopelessly conglomerated—written certainly with an anxious regard to economy of space, and in some instances evidently abbreviated—would appear to be divisible into separate words as follows, the sense in most cases determining the division; while the discriminative use of the *san* and *sigma*, observed throughout the inscription, is a further element of guidance. Each column must be read separately, as in the case of the inscription of the 'Marmini.' I add the punctuation, use capital letters for proper names, &c., exactly as if I was writing it in English:—

E-ulat. Tanna. Laro-zul:—Amovachr Lautn. Velthinaś, eśtla, Aphunaś sleleth, karu tezan, phuśleri; tesnś teiś raś-neś, ipa ama hen. naper XII:—Velthina thuraś, araś, peraś, kc, mul, mlc-skul, zuki eneski, eplt ularu.
Auleśi Velthinaś, Arznal, kleuśi thii-thilś, kana konu, ep-[k-phelik Larthalś aphuneś.
Klen thunchul thephalaś chiemphuś-le . Velthina hintha--kape.. Muniklet masu,—naper ś, rank-zl, thiiphalśti Velthina; hut naper, pcne-zś; masu akninn. Klel . Aphuna Velthinam. Ler-zinia in tem amer. Knl Volthina. Zia--ś atene tesne. Eka Velthina thuraś Thaura hel n-tesne; raś-ne ke I:—Tesnś teiś, raś-neś, chimth śpelt hnt, aś kuna aphuna mena, hen; naper, ki. Knl har eut-uśc. Velthina śatena zuki eneski ipa śpelane, thi; phulum-chvu-śpel, thi̇̂; rene, thi,— eś tak. Velthina akil une tur un-eśkune-zea zuki eneski, ath-nn-ikś Aphunaś penthna. Ama Velthina aphun-thur-uni ein, zeriun akcha.—Thil thunchul-thl, ich, kakechazi chuch e.

The inscription will be found, I think, to fall into four sections, each narrating a distinct act in the dramatic history of the farm. The first (prefaced by a short title) records its original constitution,—the second, a step taken by the heir of the original grantee in violation of the terms of the contract,—the third, an action at (strict) law, brought by the superior against the tenant in consequence, followed by the judgment,—the fourth, a consequent but distinct action before the Prætor, or chief judge in equity, the superior summoning the vassal, the vassal demurring,—the award in each instance following the narrative of the suit or appeal. The fact that the suit in equity proceeded immediately upon that in law may be a reason why the two are recorded in sequence, without break, on the inscription—if indeed any explanation be required of this peculiarity. The first section is as follows:—

§ 1.—*Constitution of the 'Conductio,' or Lease.*

1. EULAT.—A compound word, I think,—E-ULAT,—equivalent to E-BLAT, the *u* having frequently the force of *b* in Etruscan.—i. E is the old Teutonic word *é, ehe*, 'lex;' and ii. ULAT I should connect with *blasen, Bluten*, to proclaim or 'blazon' as a crier or public herald—the 'blast' of whose horn symbolically echoed his function. I take E-ULAT, *é-blat*, to be a noun signifying 'Legal Notice.'

2. TANSA.—This is the word, in full, which I have taken the liberty of restoring in the inscription in the tomb of the Pompeys at Tarquinii. It is the participle past, passive, of *zanen*, 'concordare inter se,' whence *cinsanen*, 'inserere,' and the modern 'indenture'—the root being *zahn*, 'dens,' a tooth, in reference probably to a symbolical application of the teeth in ratification of a contract, which has (I imagine) been preserved to the present day in the jagged or saw-like edge of a deed of indenture. TANNA stands for TANN-T-A, originally, I conceive, *zanen-ta*, the final consonant being omitted, as is so constantly the case in Etruscan inscriptions. This interpretation appears to me preferable to that which might be derived from TENINE, 'extendere'—the word found in the inscription on the statue of the 'Arringatore,' above dealt with. TANNA I take to be the participle used in the sense of a noun substantive, and equivalent to 'Indenture' or 'Agreement.' It is, you will recollect, as a simple participle that it stands in the restored ETU-PHANU of Lautinius Pompey.

3. LAREZUL.—A compound, divisible as LARE-ZUL.—i. LARE must be referred to LAR, 'dominus'; and ii. ZUL may either represent *zoll*, τέλ-ος, 'vectigal,' in which case LARE-ZUL would signify 'Lord's rent;' or, more probably, *zal, sal*, 'mansio, curtis, curia dominicalis, aula,'—*sal, saal*, 'aula,' 'hall,' being softened forms of the Teutonic word. LARE-ZUL thus signifies 'the Lord's Court,' or 'Hall,' the Manor-Court

(*sal-hof*, 'curia dominica'); and the clause E-ULAT TANNA LARE-ZUL would read in English, in brief lapidary style, 'Legal Notice. Indenture' or 'Agreement. Manor-Court.' This completes the title of the record.*

4. AMEVACUR,—or, as it might be written, AMEFACUR; the *v* and *f* equally representing the digamma. Compare the Teutonic *empfacher*, 'conductor' or 'colonus,' a tenant-farmer, and the cognate words *empfangnuss*, 'investitura, traditio,' *empfangen*, 'conducere aliquid titulo locationis,' to farm a property by the title of 'locatio'—the precise words being used to express the German or feudal and the Latin and the Etruscan contract. EMPFACHER or AMEVACUR, like *ambacht*, 'officium' or ministerial duty, is derived (I would say once more) from i. *umb, ἀμφί*, and ii. the root *-ahts, -ax, -ac-ere*, implying action, which—with the consonant retained from *umb, ἀμφ-*, and the initial vowel of *umb, ἀμφ-*, elided—appears before us now as *-bahts, -pax, -fix, -facere*, and in the compounds 'ponti-fex,' 'carni-fex,' and other old Latin words,—to say nothing of the Eleusinium ὄμπαξ, as above illustrated, or—to link the past with the present in the etymological chain—our Scottish *ambachter* or 'factor.' The force of the Etruscan cu, read as scu—through which the word here under discussion should more properly be written AMEVASCHER—is preserved in the Italian 'ambasciatore,' a mere Latinisation of *ambacht-âri*.† The word here may be simply a noun-substantive, in accordance with the lapidary style which prevails so markedly in the present inscription; but it is not impossible that it may in this instance be a verb, the third person singular of the present tense active, corresponding to the Swedish *fiker*, implying '*in re rustici*, terram colere,' according to Ihre, and

---

* Under the former alternative LAREZUL would be the same word as LARTHALS which occurs further on in the inscription; and the sense would be, 'Proclamation:—Covenanted Lord's rent,' &c.

† The act is equally recognisable in the French 'se fâcher,' and the Scottish *fash*, the latter implying annoyance by small cares, otherwise expressed (in nearer accordance to the Scandinavian) by *fykes*. It is singular how often Scottish forms are identical with Etruscan. The varying pronunciation of *ch* in German, as purely guttural, or in the softer form of *sch*, is equally in point.

governed by LAUTN VELTHINAŚ, the name of the 'Conductor,' in the nominative case, which follows. The formation of the third person singular in question in -r is peculiar (so far as existing proof goes) to the Scandinavian tongues, and is understood to be by mutation of a final s, t, or th. If AMEVACHR be thus understood, it affords a strong *primâ facie* argument for the Scandinavian affinities of the Etruscan; but it does not necessarily follow that such form may not have existed also in the dialects of Germany proper, although traces of it do not survive.*

5, 6. LAUTN VELTHINAŚ.—The name (as stated) of the 'Conductor' or tenant,—in the nominative case apparently. Latinised, it reads, as has been stated, 'Lautinius Veltinius.'

7. EŚTLA.—This word has been corrected as EŚTAL and interpreted as the matronymic of L. Veltinius; but this supposes an error in orthography which should not be presumed without sufficient cause. Moreover the *san* in EŚTLA suggests that it should be read as EŚ TLA, either as two words or a compound word. I think that it is a compound, to wit, of i. EŚ, that is, *heisse*, from *heischen*, 'quærere, exigere;' and ii. TLA, to be read as *toll*, τέλ-ος, *zählen*, &c.; and that it is identical with the Lombardic and medieval *gastold, gesteald* (A.-Sax.), 'gastaldus,' 'castaldus,' denoting, generally, any one placed in charge by the Dominus, but, specially and immediately, one set over the collection and administration of his rents and revenues—his steward or seneschal, in short, in this proximate capacity, and his 'actor,' 'factor,' or 'doer,' in a more extensive sense. That the title 'gastald-us' is analysable as *gas-tald*, not *gast-ald*, and is formed—not of *gast* and *alde* ('servus vel minister'), or *halten*, (still less from *gestellen*,) as commonly supposed, but of the component elements above indicated, would appear from the use of the peculiar ś or *san* in the Etruscan text; while we have a parallel compound (although reversed), proving the same fact, in the ancient *schuld-heisse*, or *scult-heisse*, the Latin

* 'The Greek or Pelasgic ἐμφύτευσις is derived, I should think, from the same root as AMEVACUR,—a mere variety, in fact, of *andercht*, *ambahts*, ἐμφύτ-ευσις; although a special sense has been induced upon it collaterally from ἐμφύω.

'scult-ctus,' explained as 'quæstor, villicus,' the officer who exacted the rent and other dues of the feudal lord, and in whose title *schuld* is convertible with *-tald-* and -TLA, while *heisse* corresponds with *gas-* and ES. I take it that L. Veltinius was 'Mayor of the Palace' in every sense of the word, and 'Major-domûs' (in one of the Latin interpretations of 'gastaldus'), to the Dominus or Etruscan 'Lar'—the lady whose name immediately follows; and that he obtained the 'conductio' from her on extremely favourable terms.*

8. APHUNAS.—The genitive case, I think, of APHUNA, 'Aponia,' the proper name of the Lar in question. That she was the 'dominus,' superior, or landlord, appears alike from the reservation of rights presently to be shewn, and from the fact that in a subsequent readjustment of the lease, in consequence of contention between herself and the heir of L. Veltinius, the arbiter decrees that the latter should hold an additional portion of land from Aponia, which could not have been thus prescribed unless Aponia had been the possessor and superior over the whole. Members, some of them ladies, of the family surnamed 'Aphuna' appear in many sepulchral inscriptions at Perugia and Clusium.†

9. SLELETIL.—Divisible as SLE-LETIL.—Compare *salland, saalland,* 'terra Salica,' or 'Dominicalis,'—that is, land held in lordship or superiority, independently of tax or tribute.

* The process by which the office of ESTLA, 'gastaldus,' or *schuldheisse* passed down, as I conceive, into the designation of the humble *stagliere* or *ostler* of our 'hospitium' or inn—the *stall* of the horse answering to the tripod *stul* of the palace on which the *schuldheiss* invested a tenant in Germany—the *ostler* receiving the payment still, I conceive, on behalf of the landlord—would be too long to trace, and irrelevant here. One link of the process may be discerned through the *stadtelhof*, contracted into *stdhof*, 'curtis domini,'—*stadel* through the interchange of *d* and *p* or *b* becoming *stabul-*, or stable. This subject might be pursued much further. —Let me add that I at first thought that ESTLA APHUNAS signified 'of the Vestal Aponia's,' and only gave up that view (with great reluctance) through the conviction that ESTLA would have been written in that case with a *sigma*, not a *sun*.

† Words almost identical with APHUNA occur elsewhere in this inscription with a different sense; but that APHUNA here is a proper name will appear from the unmistakeable significance of the word in the third and fourth divisions, or paragraphs, of the record.

In Christian times the word was, through an easy association, applied to the territories of religious fraternities—as it may indeed anciently have been in Italy and Greece to the lands of the Selli of Dodona and the Salii, Titii Sodales, and the Arval Brothers of Rome and Etruria, so lately spoken of. The Salic law of the Franks is of course familiar to us; but I apprehend that the idea of 'Salic' or Dominical land, as here described, is as old as any custom of the Teutonic race —under which I rank the Etruscan. The last four letters of SLE-LETU represent, I think, the older form of *lant*, or land, viz., *lat*, 'solum,' or land in a state of nature, i.e. uncultivated,—a form akin (in the use of the letter E instead of 'A') to that of *lethum* and the Greek 'Letho.' The word might have been explained as *seli-lat*, 'terra sylvestris,' or woodland, and understood as in the record of the dealings of Cinna with the Titienses (where it is also spelt with E as LETHEM); but it will be seen that the forests are in this instance specially excepted from the grant. *Sal-land* is sometimes used in a more restricted sense for the land attached to a farm; but in this case it is clear that it included the entire land granted for the future farm, properly fenced round, of course, in the usual manner in such cases. The root is *sal*, *zal*, 'aula,' the Lord's 'hall,' or court; and the modern English equivalent would be, I suppose, 'the demesne-land.'

10, 11. KABU TEZAN.—Of these two words the first, i. KABU, may be compared with *hure*, 'conductio, merces conditionis,' i.e. *hire* or price; and the second, ii. TEZAN, with *setzen*, *kusezzan*, 'statuere, ordinare,' to settle or fix, the initial s having been rubbed off, as in the Greek form of the word, τάττειν, τάσσειν, which must originally have been written τάτσειν or τάξειν like TEZAN, the primitive form being (as inferrible) *stetzen*, στάζειν, STEZAN. KABU TEZAN thus answers to the technical formula 'ad pretium fixum,' or the later Latin 'ad fictum,' whence the Italian *affitto*—viz., the fixed price, 'canon,' 'pensio,' or 'redditus' always agreed upon with the Conductor in cases either of 'emphyteusis' or of simple lease.

12. FRUSLERI. This word implies, I think, 'as a vassal,' or 'in vassalage;' and may be compared proximately with the middle-age Latin 'vassaleria,' 'vassallagium,' 'vassalli

feudum,' 'vassallus, *pro* feudatorius,' 'vassallus indominicatus,' 'vassallus simplex,' &c. &c. &c.,—the root being 'vass-us,' the shorter form of 'vassallus.'* This analysis suggests that the form 'vassallus' implies more than merely 'vassus;' and we accordingly find a distinction (as above illustrated) among vassals, some being specially described, as in a charter cited by Ducange—" coram *vassis dominicis*, tam Romanis quam Salicis "—the latter holding under the Salic law. My impression is that the title ' Vassalli '—properly divisible perhaps as ' Vas-salli '—denotes ' vassi ' of the ' *sal*,' or ' *aula*,' the ' curia dominica '—literally ' Vassi Dominici.' I incline upon the whole to think that PHUŚ-LEBI should be divided, not as PHUŚL-EBI but as PHUŚ-LEBI; and that LEBI represents either *leria* as in ' vassalleria,' or a substantive noun, having nearly the same signification with ' aula,'. or *sal*, and which we may recognize in the Old High German *lâr*, a forgotten word denoting house or ' mansion ' (as *e. g.* the " many mansions " in the kingdom of heaven),† and which had the same signification too, I suspect, in Etruscan. That PHUŚLEBI is a compound is almost certain from the use of the *san* to express the ' s '; and we find the same division indicated in the like manner in a word presently to be dealt with, CHIEMPHUŚLE. The ceremony of ' traditio '—in German, *sal*, *sala*—by the 'caspes,' ' waso,' *wase*, turf or sod, was a symbolical reflex of the original compound title ' vas--sal,' ' vassal,' as in so many other cases.

13, 14. TESNŚ TEIŚ.—For i. TESNŚ, compare *zins*, ' prædium de quo merces accipi potest,' a farm lettable for hire; and for ii. TEIŚ, *zeyss, zyss, ziese*, ' vectigal, telonium, accisa ' (this last being the Latin form of *ziese*, TEIS), tribute or rent. The older form of *zins* would be, I suspect, *zaun, zun*, ' sepimentum,' an enclosure, used like the Latin ' sepes ' for any enclosed place—*zaun* being the original form of the word *town*, as used to this day in Scotland to denote a farm-steading.‡

* See Ducange's Glossary of Medieval Latin, and Supplement.
† See Graff's *A. H. D. Sprachschatz*, vol. ii. col. 243.
‡ I suspect that *husband*-, in the compound *husbandman*, is under a modified exterior the same word as *zaun* = *tabn*,—*husband* having been originally written *thusband*, or *zusband*, and gradually softened down to *husb-n*, precisely as *zaun* = *tsaun* has been to TESN.

TESNŚ is probably here in the genitive case. I understand TESNŚ TEIŚ therefore as 'income of the farm.'

15. RAŚ-NEŚ,—a word distinguishable as a compound by the peculiar ś, and which has only as yet been found in this Perugian inscription. Probably from the same root as *raseria, raserium,* 'mensura annonaria,'—'annona' signifying the year's increase or produce, in grain or otherwise; and as the early Italico-Latin *rasenga,* which constantly occurs in the charters as a measure of corn paid in kind—so many *rasengæ* of 'frumentum,' so many of spelt—in recording the revenue of landed property. But although *rasenga* has the nearer superficial resemblance to RAŚ-NE, and may probably be derived from it in direct descent, RAŚ-NE is nearer in sense to *raseria;* and I should compare i. RAŚ with *gras,* in the sense of growth, *cresc-, in-crease,* or even with the Latin 'res' (of kindred origin, I suspect), understood as wealth, estate, substance—'res frumentaria' for example; and ii. NEŚ (elsewhere, in a different case, NE, as in RAŚ-NE), with 'annu-ns,' in the genitive case singular, formed in the Etruscan and Teutonic manner from the noun which we have already met with as ANI. RAŚ-NEŚ would thus be equivalent to 'annonæ' ('-ons' *per se* denoting augmentation in Latin), and signify 'of the year's produce.' If *raseria* be analysable (by a mere conjecture) as *ras-jahr-ia,* it would be identical in every respect with RAŚ-NE, RAŚ-NEŚ. We use almost the same compound words in speaking of 'this year's grass,' for example.

16, 17, 18. IPA AMA HEN.—These three words also have already come before us, in a slightly different orthographical form, as IPA: MA · ANI, and explained as 'every month' or 'measure' 'of the year.'

19, 20. NAPER XII.—Equivalent to 'nummi,' or pieces of money, in number twelve, payable, as we have just seen, monthly, making up a money-rent of 144 'nummi' yearly. The conditions of the lease having been thus far stated,* the reservation of rights by the proprietor follows in a clause

---

* There is a dot or point after XII in Fabretti's engraving which may mark the termination of a clause. But it is not in his transcript, nor in that of Conestabile.

precisely parallel in character, although the order of the subjects is different, to those which appear in old Italian charters of the ninth and tenth centuries, and which may be seen in great numbers in Muratori's 'Antiquitates Italicæ Medii Ævi:' —

21. VELTUINA.—The name of Lantinius Veltinius, expressed in short, as in the case of Aulus Veltinius afterwards, and in the nominative case—governing a verb at the end of the sentence, the intermediate words, THURAŚ, ARAŚ, &c. being in the accusative. All after NAPER XII to the end of this first division of the inscription is written without the slightest break whatever.

22. THURAŚ—in the nominative case THURA—must be identified, I think, with *twer, quer, querh,* implying transverse, oblique, or opposite, but in the special sense here in which we find *die quere* used for ' ripa obliqua, adversa, opposita,' the opposite banks or ' shores' of a stream or river. The river in this case may be presumed to be the Tiber, which lies to the N. and N.E. of Perugia, on that side of the town where the inscription was found; and we shall see further evidence to support this presumption. Q (or k) and t are letters constantly interchangeable, as in *quist, twist,* ' ramna,' a bough, as already shown. The word THURAŚ answers here to that which occurs in the clause " cum . . . ripis, rupinis, montibus," &c. in the feudal charters of medieval Italy, as above stated.

23. ARAŚ.—To be read as the Latin ' areas,' explained by Ducange as open spaces, neither ploughed nor cultivated. The word corresponds with the " terris . . . incultis," and " cum terris, . . . ortis, aroia, et terris," &c. of the middle-age charters referred to.

24. PERAŚ.—Compare *fores, foret, forst,* wood or forest. In the charters as, " cum . . . silvis, salectis, sationibus," &c.

25. KE.—The words from this point to the end of the clause are so crushed together that it appears hopeless at first sight to arrive at their signification. But KE, if I mistake not, is equivalent to the medieval ' gaia, gajum, gagium,' implying " sylva densissima," very thick wood, and, I think, high up in the hills. " Silvâque et gajo" are linked

together, and in the same order as ᛈᛖᚱᚨᛊ ᚴᛖ here, in one of Muratori's charters.

20. ᛗᚢᛚ.—Evidently, I think, our common *mill*, the right to which is constantly reserved even now to the lord of the manor. Such passages as "molendinosque ibi sitos duos, seu et gajum unom," &c., and "vaccariciis, alpibus" (*i.e.* cattle pastures, the proper sense of *alp*), "gajis, molendinis," in a charter of Hugo, King of Italy in 927, and in the 'Chronicon Farfense,' both cited by Ducange, show that the mill and the 'gajum,' forest or thick forest, were usually contiguous and (as I inferred) high up in the hills, the water that fed the mill descending probably through the 'gajum,' or as it is here abbreviated, ᚴᛖ, *g* being represented by *k* in Etruscan orthography. The sequence of ᛈᛖᚱᚨᛊ, ᚴᛖ, ᛗᚢᛚ, as above explained, is thus natural, and the interpretation of each word supports that of its neighbour.

27. ᛗᛚᛖᛊᚴᚢᛚ.—A compound word, divisible—not as ᛗᛚᛖᛊ-ᚴᚢᛚ, but ᛗᛚᛖ-ᛊᚴᚢᛚ—i. ᛊᚴᚢᛚ may represent either the Teutonic *scalh*, *scalck*, 'servus,' from the obsolete *schul-en*, to minister or serve, the compound thus implying 'the mill-slaves,' or serfs, attached to the soil, and answering to the "et familiis utriusque sexus," and the "servi et ancillæ," so frequently found in Muratori's charters; or it may more probably be the Etruscan and ancestral representative of the medieval 'sequela,' synonymous with the "secta ad molendinum et secta montis," implying the customary obligation of the feudal tenant to grind his corn at the lord's mill. The word *sequela*, used in a somewhat different sense but in connection with the *multures* of the miller, is common in Scottish leases. ᛗᛚᛖᛊᚴᚢᛚ therefore expresses, broadly, the 'mill-rights' or 'dues,' reserved by the Lar, or Superior, from his concession to the Conductor—in this case, L. Veltinius.*

28, 29. ᛉᚢᚴᛁ ᛖᚾᛖᛊᚴᛚ—These two words occur twice in this

* Even the modern *mahlgelt*, used for multure in the sense of a 'pensitatio' due from the corn to the landlord of a mill, might have been represented by this old Etruscan compound, divided as ᛗᛚᛖᛊ-ᚴᚢᛚ,—the final *t* of *gelt* being, as usual, omitted, and ᛗᛚ taken in the genitive case. But the objection meets us here that the 's' is written with the *sigma*, whereas it would have (presumptively) been the ᛊᚨᛊ if ᛗᛚᛖᛊ formed the first half of the compound.

inscription,—with the sense in the present clause of the right of 'hunting with dogs,' or 'sporting,' and in a later one, of 'sporting dogs.' The two words would equally express both meanings, but there was probably a slight modification in the actual speech which is not preserved in the written record of it. These words carry us back into very remote antiquity, and their full discussion would occupy many pages. Briefly, —i. ZUKI appears to me an ancient form of our modern *jagd*, 'venatio,' or hunting, the proximate root being found in *ruck-*, *zuck-en*, 'capere,' and the old Aryan *as* (Zendic), ἄγ-ω, whence the Zendic *azra*, 'venatio,' the Greek ἀγρ-εύω, 'venari,' and 'Zagreus,' the title of Dionysus, denoting 'the hunter,' which preserves the original initial 'z,' like ZUKI. ZUKI was probably pronounced ZUKTI (*jakti, jagd-*), the second consonant being omitted in writing. It must be added that although *jagd* and ZUKI properly and distinctively denote 'venatio' or the chase, the idea of that chase being with dogs is implied in it, the word *huni, hund*, 'can-is,' and even 'dog,' deriving by independent descent from the same original root.—ii. ENESKI, on the other hand—pronounced, as it doubtless was, ENTESKI—is evidently derived from this ancient *huni, hund*, as its proximate root, with a sense akin to that of the Latin 'index,' and which might be rendered 'indicator,'—but whether the termination -ESKI is adjectival, like *hündisch* (but in a noble sense), is not so clear. Either way, I think it denotes a leader or (rather) 'pointer,' that being the special signification, if I mistake not, both of our English 'dog,' the Teutonic *hund*, the Latin 'can-is,' and of the root of the Etruscan ENESKI. While 'dog' is simply the *togo*, 'dux,' leader, the Sanscrit analogue *sûdaka*, implying 'indicator,' as applied to the dog, is derived from the root *súd-*, which is a mere variety of the Egyptian *teka* and Pelasgian δεικ-, 'dic-,' the root of 'in-dic-are, in-dex,' in which last word we may discern, I repeat, a very close analogy to END-ESKI, EN-ESKI.* — ZURI ENESKI thus signifies here, 'Rights

---

* The resemblance of the Greek κυνηγέτης to ENESKI is striking but superficial only. That of κυνηγεσία, the chase by dogs, is closer, but still not so near as the approximation suggested in the text. All these words are indeed akin.

of chase with dogs,' or 'of coursing.' The phrase coincides with the "cum venationibus" of the charters.

30, 31. EPLT ULARU,—two separate words.—i. EPLT is a contraction, as I take it, for *aufhalt-et*, signifying 'protects' or 'defends'—as *sich aufhalten der gewalt*, 'tueri se contra vim;' and ii. ULARU I read as the ablative case of *vler*, *vlur*, 'damnum,' injury—the same word as PHLER, with which we are already familiar. Reverting to the nominative 'Velthina' at the beginning of the sentence, and which governs the whole, the clause reads therefore thus,—'Veltinius shall protect the banks or shores, &c. &c., from damage,'—the rights to these being thus reserved by the Superior, Aponia, in granting the lease.

The first section of the Perugian inscription thus runs substantially as follows:—" Legal notice" of " Agreement. Lord's Court," or " Exchequer. Lautinius Veltinius, steward" or seneschal, " farms " (or " is farmer of") " the Dominical land of Aponia, *ad pretium fixum* " (or in *affitto*), " in vassallage:"—[To pay, viz.] " From the income of the holding, as rent, twelve *nummi* monthly:"—[On the other hand,] " Veltinius warrants the river-banks, open spaces, forest-ground, highland copsewood, the mill, the milldues, and the right of coursing over the manor, from *damnum* "—infringement or injury on his part.

§ 2. *Illegal alienation of two-thirds of the Farm.*

The second portion of the inscription records an attempt by Aulus, the son and heir (I presume) of Lautinius, the original 'conductor,' to alienate a portion—two-thirds—of the *feudum*. This must now be dealt with:—

1, 2, 3. AULESI VELTHINAS ARZNAL.—The name, in full, of the son and heir in question. I say the son, because apart from that relationship he could not have had a right to the holding except by a special disposition, which is not mentioned. He is not styled ESTLA, like his predecessor, from which I infer that Aponia had not renewed the office in his person.

4. KLENŚI.—This is the third person singular, present tense, active, of the verb akin to *linden, gelinden*, 'lenire,' and *klein*, small, which we have already met with, and which implies *in genere*, 'to diminish,' and, in a special and legal sense, to 'mitigate' damages as in the plea of an advocate, or to atone for guilt and 'extenuate *pœna*' as incurred by a culprit. Here, I think, the special sense is that of 'diminution' or 'depreciation' of value through an act of Aulus Veltinius by which he had lessened the security of the 'dominus' for the duty payable under the 'locatio' of the farm, by alienating a portion of it.* The extent of diminution or depreciation is next specified:—

5. THIITHIIŚ.—THII and THIIŚ must be taken together, as one word, notwithstanding that THIIŚ and the word which follows, viz. KUNA, are written without break in the inscription. The peculiar s in THIIŚ denotes the end of a word, or of a word the constituent element of a compound. THII-THIIŚ appears to be a compound, in the genitive case, answering to the German *zwey-theil*, 'duæ tertiæ,' two third-parts, especially of an 'ager,' or farm. I read it as 'to the extent of two-thirds.'

6, 7. KUNA KENU.—i. KUNA I should read as KUNTA, the *t* being omitted, answering to *kunde*, 'cognitio, notitia;' and ii. KENU as *ana, ani*, 'sine,' *ἄνευ*, without—the original *k* having been abraded in the German, Latin, and Greek dialects, and, as we have seen, in the more peculiarly Pelasgian inscription analysed at the beginning of this memoir—ANA MINETHU, without *meineid*, or perjury. KUNA KENU thus signifies 'without notice to' or 'knowledge of' Aponia the Lar, —an alienation surreptitiously, or at least illegally effected,

---

* I am not sure whether 'alien-are' be not derived from a common source with KLEN, KLENŚI—the hard 'k' or 'h' having been rubbed off in the Latin equivalent.

and which rendered the perpetrator liable to judicial punishment.*

8, 9. EPLK PHELIK.—I am inclined to think that FP and PHELIK answer to the modern *abfällig*, the older German *faellig*, denoting 'deficiens à fide pacti,'—the intermediate LK either representing *lik*, 'similis,' *like-as*; or, more probably, '-liq,' '-lict,'—in the sense of 'delictum' or 'delinquency,' the LK being introduced between the two elements of the compound word in a manner of which other examples occur in Etruscan. On the other hand, EPLK may be a distinct word, a compound of, i. *é*, *ehs*, 'fides, lex;' and ii. *pflicht*, *plight*, 'jus, fides, cura, tutela,'—thus signifying 'plighted faith,' 'legal engagement,' which would equally suit the sense. I lean to the former alternative.

10, 11. LARTHALŚ APHUNEŚ.—These words (like PHELIK) might appear at first to be proper names, but they are not so. They should be divided as LAR THALŚ-APHUNEŚ, these last two words being used as a compound. LAR denotes 'dominus,' or lord, *ut supra*. THALŚ-APHUNEŚ corresponds, or rather is identical with the Teutonic *pfund-zoll*, 'vectigal, pensio,' rent, that is, properly, weighed money. The position of the constituent elements is reversed as usual. The words are in the genitive, governed by PHELIK, *abfällig*, deficient—*i.e.* of the 'Lord's rent.' The genitival termination -EŚ, it will be observed, is not that of the feminine name, APHUNAŚ.

The sense of this second portion of the inscription is therefore this:—" Aulus Veltinius Arznal alienates" or "diminishes" the farm by "two-thirds without notice; failing likewise," or "culpably failing, in paying the rent due to the Lar's Court, or Exchequer."

* I feel pretty sure of the reading given in the text; but it is worth mentioning that THII THILŚKUSA would give the same signification as THIITIULŚ, viz. 'two-thirds,' if TRILŚKUNA were identified with *zelgen*, a word explained as 'tres partes, in quas dividitur prædium rusticum (*eine hube*) in Suevia,' the portions being discriminated as '*sommer-, winter-*, and *brachfeld*.' But no such economic cause for division existed in the present instance; and the context seems to prescribe the interpretation I have adopted.

§ 3.—*Action at Law.*

We proceed to the action at law brought by the proprietor in consequence of this alienation and its consequences:—

1. KLEN—is apparently the same word which we have already dealt with, implying suit or petition for justice—but as of a plaintiff, not a defendant. It is possible indeed that although written by the same letters, KLEN may here stand for the old *be-langen*, 'desiderate,' now *ver-langen*, with the sense of accusation. There are cases numberless in which words and names absolutely identical in shape and sound, but of different significations, derive from very different roots. *K* often represents *b* or *p* in Etruscan orthography. Either way the signification would be practically the same.

2. THUNCHUL.—This, as in other cases, would be more properly transcribed as THUNSCHUL. It might be read as *twangksal*, 'oppressio violenta,' masterful violence; but the sense here and the use of the word as recurrent in a subsequent part of the inscription show that it is a compound, of i. *thunch, ding, ting*, a court of justice, and ii. 'vel-,' 'vol-,' 'will,'—thus implying a 'placitum' or judicial sentence, sued for by a litigant,—nearly in the sense of *dingsal, dingnuss*, 'judicium.'

3. THEPHALAS.—Not, I think, to be connected with *zeppeln*, 'rixari, expostulare'—with the sense of kicking against the pricks: but with THUPHLTHAS, the Etruscan analogue of 'duplex,' which we have elsewhere met with, and with THITPHALSTI, which occurs *infra* in the judgment given by the court here in question. THEPHALAS would thus signify, 'Of fraud,' or 'double-dealing.'

4. CHIEMPHURLE.—A comparison of the two last syllables of this word with PHUSLENI, and the observation that the 's' is in each case expressed by a *san*, suggests *primâ facie* that PHUSLE and PHUSLENI represent the same word, the former being perhaps written contractedly. If so CHIEM must be a distinct element, and the whole a compound. On this con-

struction CHIEMPHUÉLE might be analysed as i. CHIEM, *chumpft*, or (the same word) 'comit-ium,' a convention or assembly; ii. PUCÉLE (for PUCÉLEM) 'of the vassals'—that is, a Manor-Court or Court-Baron. I should have acquiesced in this but for the light thrown (if I mistake not) on the word by what follows in the judgment, and which I shall explain in dealing with the word RANKZL. For the present I shall only state that CHIEMPHUÉ-LE, divided as I have here written it, appears to me to correspond — wholly in sense, and verbally in part — to the old Teutonic *Kemphisbuile*, i.e. (literally) the 'Hill of Contention,' the spot where points of dispute were decided by single combat or duel, according to a judicial practice of very primitive times. Such courts of combat were usually dedicated to the God of War, and thus we have the 'Campus Martius' of Rome (where the scene was, not a hill, but a plain), the 'Areopagus' or 'Mars' Hill' of Athens, &c., the idea of combat always underlying the name.* Whether hill or plain, the fundamental idea of *camp-*, *kemph-*, *chiemph-*, is that of *kampff*, 'bellum, certamen:' and it may be a question whether the contest was by strength of arm or eloquence of tongue in the earliest times. In those with which we now deal, when the influence of law pervaded the whole community, the spears were arguments and the shields the established law of the land; but the whole terminology of law and battle was interchangeable then, and is so even now. Space will not allow me to do more than suggest this. Applying a closer analysis to CHIEMPHUÉ-LE, it would appear that the final LE represents the old Teutonic *lé, lee, hléo, hlaiwe*, rather than *buile*,† — *lé* implying a 'tumulus' or grave, 'clivus' (as e.g. the 'clivus

---

* The 'Mons Sacer' of the Plebeians at Rome was possibly a hill or elevated ground of this description, although of natural formation, the indicative title 'Sacer' having probably a secondary signification in the sense of *dryad*, a word which links itself through 'ager' with the 'Campus Martius.' The secession of the Plebeians to the 'Mons Sacer' may have been simply to the original and superseded 'Moot-hill' of the Latin population, for consultation, &c.

† *Buile* is, however, I think, from the same root — a variation of *hlaiwe*.

Mamurii') being the Latin form of *klaiwe, lê*,—the word being in fact still familiar to us in Scotland as a *law*, e.g. 'Largo-Law,' 'North-berwick-law,' 'Dunse-law,' and the 'Law-hills' at various places. If this be the case, CHEMPH probably represents *kempe*, a champion or hero, and CHEMPHUŚ-LE should be read 'the Kempo's Law,' or 'tumulus'—which doubtless became the 'Moot-hill,' *chumft-lé*, or meeting-place, 'comitium,' of the inhabitants for purposes of public consultation and judgment—the place of judgment being always, whether hill or plain, a 'locus septus,' a place or court fenced in, viz. by *litze*, 'cancelli,' or 'lists'—the very word used in the language of the tournament. The two readings of CHEMPH as *chumft, kampf*, thus reflect the conjunction of purpose which time brought about in the use and destiny of these primitive seats of justice. CHEMPU, it must be remembered, should be written SCHEMPU; but such too was the case originally with *kampf*, and, I have little doubt, *chumft* likewise. This earlier form of *kampf* is preserved in *schimpff*, 'certamen,' (the Gothic *skimpe*),* *zu schimpfen reiten*, 'equitare in certamina, ludicra vel seria,'—and this word and its analogues show us that the Champion's Hill, or Plain, was used as a theatre likewise for jugglers, mock-combats, &c.,—*schimpfer*, 'histrio,' *schimpfen*, 'jocari,' and similar words, witnessing to what became ultimately mere degradation; while a series of corresponding words testify to this in parallel descent from *leika* (O. N.), analogous to δίκη, and from 'lud-o' in Latin, analogous to 'lis, lit-is.' The Etruscan word LUCAR, money paid for entrance to the theatre, or public 'palaestra,' is an illustration of the former of these categories.† I conclude, therefore, that the four words KLEN THUNCHUL THEPHALAŚ

---

* In an earlier stage still it was probably *schrimpe, schramp*, as preserved in *skirm-ish, scrim-age, ramp-ageous*, &c. I might cite many examples of a primitive 'r' having been softened down and obliterated in the growth, or rather disintegration of language. But the original sense is probably that of *schirm*, protection, whence the words for 'scutum, propugnaculum,' &c., and *schirmen*, to protect. These words all resolve ultimately into a common root with 'guerra,' 'war,'—and that too implies that the fundamental idea of warfare is defence, not offence, or aggression.

† See the Glossary in the Appendix.

CHIEMPIUŚ-LE are a sort of title or preface to what follows,—
'Suit for *placitum*' or 'judgment for fraud at the Areopagus'
or 'Moot-hill' of the district—necessarily in behalf of the
Lar, Aponia, against A. Veltinius Arznal, whose fraudulent
diminution of the farm by alienation of two-thirds of it is the
subject of the preceding section of the record.

5, 6, 7. VELTHINA HINTHA KAPE.—i. VELTHINA is the
name of the defendant, in the nominative case, written short,
without the final 's,' as in the case of his father—already
remarked upon.—ii. HINTHA is the Teutonic *hintz*, 'contra,'
as in *hintz einen clagen*, 'contra aliquem actionem instituere,'
and identical too with the Greek ἀντί, as in ἀντιλέγω, to
contradict.—iii. KAPE, again, may correspond either with
haben as used (in connection moreover with *hintz*) in the
phrase *rechtung und ansprach die wir hinz in haben*; or
otherwise with *kampfen*, 'pugnare,' to fight or contend—i.e.
HINTHA, in opposition,—an alternative which the analogies
indicated under the preceding word CHIEMPIUŚ-LE may
support. I think, upon the whole, that HINTHA-KAPE is a
quasi-compound, answering to 'contradicit;' and that VEL-
THINA HINTHA-KAPE signifies, 'Veltinius denies' the charge,
—thus meeting Aponia, not by an 'exceptio' as if it were a
case in equity, but by a 'contradictio,' the matter being one
of strict law.

8, 9. MUNIKLET MASU.—i. Of MUNIKLET—manifestly a
compound, and already noticed in association with the sepulchral MUNISVLETH, but in distinction from it—various
Teutonic analogues may be given which all point to the
same general signification, with one exception, viz. that of
gemeine leute, arbiters, which would not suit here, as the case
was not one of arbitration or equity, but of 'judicium.' *Mann*
is the Teutonic word for a vassal, or feudal tenant, and
mannrecht implied 'judicium feudale ex paribus curiae con-
stans, ad examinandas causas inter Dominum et Vasallos,'
exactly such a case as that between Aponia and Veltinius.
A compound *mann-leut* (*mann+leut*, 'populus') would
denote the vassals who composed this court; and this may
possibly have been the original form of the acknowledged
compound *mund-leut*, 'clientes,' although this latter word is

proximately associable with *mund*, 'advocatus' or protector. The older form of *leut, liut* is *hleut, hliut*, and MUNIKLET would thus correspond with either of these compounds, and signify a 'Vassal-,' 'Baron-,' or 'Manorial Court;' in which case it would be the noun governing the word which follows, MASU, as a verb. On the other hand it might be read as *gemein-hlôs*, i.e. 'common sentence,' 'lot,' or 'vote,' as an adjective agreeing with MASU.—ii. MASU may correspond with *mas, mase,* 'moderatio,' *massen, masen,* 'moderure, temperare,' as well as with the series of words expressing measurement, meting out—of justice from the scales of Themis, no less than in the case of other commodities. MUNIKLET MASU would thus be renderable, 'The Manor-Court adjudges,' 'decrees'—or, 'By common decree' or 'sentence,' MASU being read as in the ablative case; and this last alternative is upon the whole the safest, at least at present, as it does not appear for certain otherwise whether the Court on the 'Kempe's hill' was a Manorial Court or a public court of law for the whole Perugian district. The sentence was against Veltinius, and is given in the words that follow:—

10. NAPER.—As before, 'nummi.'

11. Ś.—I take this to be a contraction, standing by itself, and to be disconnected from the word that follows, viz. HANKZL. This may be inferred from its being written with a SAN, which is very seldom found at the beginning of a word. The context too prescribes a numeral; and we may supply it, I think, by ŚAS, the word that follows AVIL in an inscription to the memory of a lady given by Fabretti (No. 2104), and which, I presume, represents 'sex,' six—although, the lady in question having been an 'amke,' it may stand (there at least) rather for sixty. The number six is rendered by the numeral *s'* (the *s*, or 'stigma') in Greek.

12. HANKZL.—A compound of HANK and ZL—i. HANK I take to be the same word as the Teutonic *ring*, 'locus judicii olim sub dio cancellis munitus' (as in *an dem ringe oder an der schrannen*),—a space enclosed within rails, in which the combatants, whether at law or in single combat, disputed for victory—the word being still perpetuated in English

speech whenever a 'ring' is formed for a pugilistic contest. It is the occurrence of this word RANK, *ring*, in connection with CHEMPHCA-LE which confirms me in the belief as to the signification of the latter compound, as above stated. It was within this 'cancellaria,' 'chancel,' or 'chancery'—this *ring* —that orators or advocates spoke; and we have the word accordingly in the Italian 'arringatore,' and in the English 'harangue,'—the statue of Aulus Metellus illustrating, as we have seen *supra*, the oratory of the Etruscan bar. The judge and his assessors, I take it, sat on elevated seats, presiding over this 'chancel' (as was the case in the ancient basilicas, and in early Christian churches built on the model of the basilica, and in which the chancel is occupied by the choir), but within the outer *fossa* or *sepes* which fenced in the entire court of justice. RANK and *ring* are both abraded forms of an older *schranck*, 'consæptum, carcer' (*schranckzaun*, 'sepes ex lignis decussatim positis'), *schrannen*, 'cancellus, locus judicii,' *schrande*, 'cancelli, judicium,'—a form still familiar to us in our English *screen*. I should have read RANK as SRANK but for the peculiar initial *san* above remarked upon.—ii. ZI., as previously, signifies 'debitum,' debt or due, especially in 'told' money, 'numerata pecunia.' RANKZL must thus, I apprehend, be translated, 'dues to the Chancery,' that is, to the court which gave the 'judicium;' but, in a more special sense, 'fine to the *schranck*' or 'carcer'—which was practically in some cases and theoretically in all directly under the seat of the 'judex'—as a fine for exemption from imprisonment as the due of delinquency,—the amount awarded being, *ut supra*, NAPER 6., 'nummi sex,' six, or (possibly) sixty.

13, 14. THIPHALŚTI VELTHINA.—I read this as, 'to the defaulter' or 'fraudulent Veltinius,'—and the qualification additionally shews that the word RANKZL expresses the 'pœna' or fine for 'delictum' which was always inflicted in a case of 'judicium,' or strict law, such as that here in question. It was different in equity, as we shall see presently. The clause thus reads therefore, 'Six (or sixty?) *nummi* by way of fine to the Court on the part of the defaulting Veltinius.'—After this follows specification of

15, 16. HUT NAPER, *i.e.* 'One hundred *nummi*,' as
17. PENEZS.—This seems to be a compound of PENE-ZS,
answering to *pene-zeyss*, *-ziese*, or *pene-zins*. It may be thus
analysed:—i. PENE, our English *penny*, is a word of extensive
use among the Teutonic and Slavonic races, and is even found
in Hungarian, *pfennig*, *pfenning* being the later German form;
it signifies 'pecunia, nummus' in a general sense, and is
found in composition as *pene-geld*, 'pecunia mulctarum,'
pfennig-zins, 'census parata pecunia solvendus,' &c.—ii. ZS,
the second element in the compound, may be recognised in
zeyss, *ziese*, 'vectigal,' rent, which we have already met with
as TEIS in TESNS TEIS, *supra*; and, with the 'n' inserted, in
ZINS, 'reditus, census,' in which form we have it as *pfennig-
zins*, 'census.'—PENE-ZS and *pfennig-zins* being thus in fact
precisely the same word, and signifying, in its simplest sense,
'sum due.' HUT NAPER PENEZS therefore denotes, 'One
hundred nummi'—according to the census or calculation 'of
rent'—this sum being the balance due to Aponia on the
alienated portion of the farm, not hitherto accounted for,
and in which Aulus Veltinius is stated in the second portion
of the inscription to have become a defaulter—PHELIK
LAB THALS-APHUNES. The rent due and not paid was probably for a year and about three weeks, the rent for two-
thirds of the holding being 90 'nummi' *per annum*. The
Court disallowed and treated the alienation as *non advenu*, as
by one 'non habento potestatem' by the constitution of the
farm, while they punished the fraudulent infraction of that
constitution.

18, 19. MASU ARNINA.—With ARNINA we may compare
eigenen, 'convenire alicui' in the sense of what is befitting,
and *eigenen*, 'conferre, dare in proprietatem'—but here, if I
mistake not, in an extreme sense, analogous to that by which
the judge was wont 'judiciali auctoritate appropriare (*eigenen*)
creditori fundum vel bona mobilia debitoris per immissionem'
—that is, to make over the entire property of the debtor
or defaulter to the creditor—in this case to Aponia,—"his
wife and children and all that he had," in the words of
the parable, till payment should be made to the uttermost
farthing.

The entire record and sentence under this third division of the inscription would appear to run as follows:—" Suit " (at law) " for judgment of fraud," on behalf of Aponia against Aulus Veltinius, " at the Kempe's-law," or " Moot-hill " of the district. " Veltinius puts in a *contradictio*. The Court decrees, —Six (or sixty?) *nummi* as *pœna* against the defaulter, Veltinius:—One hundred *nummi* as rent due" and to "be refunded" to Aponia:—Further, " Decrees appropriation of his goods," as security, that is to say, " for payment."

§ 4. *Proceedings in Equity.*

The 'delictum' in the preceding case was, it is evident, a fraudulent alienation of land held under the lease, without notice to the Lar, or Dominus, Aponia, inferring the risk of manifest *damnum* to the latter whether the alienation was total or that merely of sub-letting. Aponia therefore took legal measures to replace the 'conductio' on its proper footing and punish the infraction of its terms, and, as we have just seen, with success. But the whole position of the farm appears to have required reconsideration, and personal annoyance had apparently been resorted to on the part of Aulus Veltinius since the death of his father Lautinius. Aponia therefore followed up the suit at law without delay by proceedings before a higher (but not, in this case, appellate) tribunal, that of the Prætor—proceedings in equity, not at strict law. The parties were heard; reason was found for enlarging the holding and readjusting the rent; but at the same time stringent restraint was imposed upon the annoyance to which Aponia had been subjected. No *pæna* is specified,—Veltinius meets the prosecution, not by a 'contradictio' but by a demurrer; and other points in the proceedings shew that the suit came before the Prætor in his capacity of ' Arbiter pro finiendis controversiis,' and that Aponia's suit was for an *Interdictum*, which was granted, proceeding upon an arbitration and adjustment of rights and wrongs equitable to both parties. I have little doubt that substantial justice was done,—at the same time I think we shall see that the Prætor proceeded upon a presumption which gradually grew up under the Prætorian jurisdiction, that long tenancy had established a *quasi-* or qualified ownership on the part of Veltinius, so that the effect of the award—while in a personal sense favourable to Aponia—was on the other hand to recognise Veltinius as holding by right of *emphyteusis* under the Dominus, thus in fact elevating him to a *status* of subordinate, it is true, but still co-proprietorship. I cannot think that his conduct had deserved this allowance; but the principle doubtless prevailed.—The following is the analysis of this last portion of the inscription :—

1. KLEL.—This word is followed by a point of distinction of the usual sort, but which may possibly indicate a technical abbreviation, as in cases previously noticed. I think it represents a legal vocable or phrase answering to the Teutonic *gelegenlicher tag*, 'dies ab arbitris cum consensu partium constituta,' i. e. on 'a day appointed by consent of both parties.' KLEL, thus abbreviated, would represent this phrase, or formula, as KLEknLk, which would answer to *gelegenlich*, 'by agreement,' even if the *tag* were not understood.

2, 3. APHUNA VELTHINAM.—I understand this as 'Aponia v. Veltinium.' Aponia had sued for the Prætor's intervention. Veltinius accepts the challenge.

4. LERZINIA.—A compound of LER and ZINIA.—i. ZINIA seems to be the Etruscan representative (although in a more primitive form) of *zank*, the modern *zink*, 'jurgium, altercatio, rixa,' quarrel or dispute—our English *taunt* and *twit*, and the Greek τωθασμός, sarcasm or bark,—the root, *zahn*, 'dens,' tooth, expressing itself in *zanen, zannen*, 'dentes ostendere,' 'mordicari,' to show the teeth, or bite; a verb which, under the influence of bitter feelings—the bite being symbolically vented (it would seem) on the legal instrument of agreement—produces *einzanen*, 'concordare' as by indenture, the root of TANNA, the word already analysed.—ii. The initial vocable LER is more difficult. Read as *lära* (S.-Goth.), *leren*, 'docere,' it would signify to 'instruct,' in the Scottish forensic sense of building up legal proof of a case. But *lära, leren*, is by general consent referred to the same origin as *läsa, lesen*, the letters 'r' and 's' being constantly interchangeable; and I suspect that LER here is the analogue of *lass-, lass-en*, 'permittere,' to let—but in the special legal sense of *an oder auf einen lassen*, 'permittere causam arbitro.' I understand LER-ZINIA therefore as 'Submission of matters of dispute by way of arbitration.' *

5, 6, 7. INTEMAMER.—Divisible into three words, i. IN, which I take to be a preposition answering to our English 'to':—ii. TEM, answering to *tuom, doom, deem* (Scoticè), 'judicium,' and the Greek (Pelasgic) τίμησις, 'æstimatio' awarded by a judge in law-proceedings,—and, iii. AMER, the Etruscan analogue of the Teutonic *amber, ambter, ambachter*, in its highest sense of 'prætor causarum civilium, præfectus loci vel judicii in loco,'—the three words thus implying, 'To the estimation,' or 'arbitration,' 'of the Prætor.' The title written in this diluted form in Etruscan—analogously to UM-ETH, that is ETH-UM, in the Pelasgian inscription, the

* LER, as *lassen*, might have had the sense of 'ostendere, manifestare' (*lisa, biim*, O. N.), if the matter had been limited to the exhibition of rights, and of 'rogare ad aliquid judicium sententiam.' But the context requires the interpretation given in the text.

first in this series, and to AMAT (*ambacht*) in the inscription of Montarozzi, near Tarquinii—is applied throughout the Aryan world to every grade of official life, but in law-proceedings specially to the supreme judge within his district, or even in the kingdom under the sovereign, and is thus used sometimes for 'prorex' under the German Emperors. Our English 'umpire' is merely AMEN, *ampter*, in a kindred language. But, I repeat, it was to an official umpire, and one of the highest rank, the Roman Prætor and his 'nobile officium' of equitable jurisdiction, that Aponia had recourse. —The words thus far given constitute the title of the record, and express Aponia's reference or submission of the matters in dispute, as plaintiff, to this ultimate authority.

8, 9. KNL · VELTHINA.—KNL is, I think, a contracted form of a word answering perhaps to *gegen-behelf*, 'exceptio' in the sense of a 'replica' or reply; or to the current *gegenlaut*, 'oppositio,' *gegenhalt*, &c. The meaning is, 'Veltinius excepts,' or 'demurs,' to Aponia's summons and charge. Compared with Veltinius's peremptory denial before the Vassal Court or judicial tribunal—VELTHINA HINTHA KAPE —in a case of strict law, the word KNL additionally marks the character of the present proceedings as being in equity, before the Prætor.—The matters in dispute being thus tabled and the parties in opposition, the Prætor proceeds to action. The first portion of his award, as we shall find, is Declaratory, as to what Veltinius shall enjoy and do, and thus of the nature of a 'Decretum,'—the second is Prohibitory, defining what Veltinius shall not do,—the two together forming a complete specimen of an Etruscan 'Interdictum.'

10, 11. ZIAŚATENE TESNE.—TESNE we have had already. For ZIA-ŚATENE, a compound, compare *zusatz*, 'assessor,' *zusetzer*, 'arbitri pari utrinque numero olim electi et additi superarbitro communi,' 'adjuncti partium,' with the relative verb, as in *eine sache zu einem setzen*, 'causam ad aliquem tanquam arbitrum decidendam deferre,'—and also *setzen*, *kesazta*, *kesezzan*, 'ordinare, disponere,' in the sense of the Greek τάσσειν, τάττειν, denoting *inter alia*, to impose a tax or any other contribution. The phrase ZIA-ŚATENE TESNE implies, I think, 'Let the holding (TESNE) be taxed, or valued, by arbitration,'—this being the ruling of the Prætor, either naming arbiters to value it, or acting himself in his office as such.

12, 13. EKA VELTHINA.—EKA may either represent the *ach, acht,* 'æstimatio, taxatio'—the revaluation and settlement of rent which immediately follows; or it may represent *eigen,* to possess, i.e. the *echt,* possession or usufruct (as distinguished from the *dominium* or superiority) of the holding. This last is more probable, partly because the order for the valuation has been already given, and partly because a verb is thus supplied to cover the words that follow. EKA VELTHINA thus would imply, 'Let Velthina hold,' or 'possess.'

14. THURAS.—The same word which we recognised previously as signifying the 'banks' or 'shores' of a river.

15. THAURA—if I mistake not, is to be read THABRA, that is, 'Tybris,' or 'Tiber,'—the *u* standing for the Latin *b*. *Tuber* in old German, 'tybrum' in medieval Latin, implied 'alveus,' the trough or bed of a river,—a word humbly represented in Scots by *dub,* and in English, although in a modified signification, by *tub!* These THURAS THAURA were the river banks which had been reserved by Aponis, and warranted free from encroachment by Lautinius Veltinius, at the original constitution of the farm; and part of which was now awarded to Aulus Veltinius towards the enlargement of his holding, in implement of the compromise.

16. HELUTESNE, a compound, HELU-TESNE.—For HELU compare *halba,* the A.-Sax. *healf,* half,—the *u,* as in the preceding case, representing *b*.—TESNE we are familiar with; and from the analogy of *halb-hube,* half the farm, as opposed to *haupt-hube,* an entire farm, I take HELU-TESNE to mean 'the half-holding,' i. e. of the opposite shores or banks of the Tiber.

17. RASNE.—'At the rent-payment of.'

18, 19. KEI.—To be divided, I conceive, as KE I, and understood—reading KE as *kuh,* (our Scottish *kye*)—'One cow'—that is, *per annum,* as appears by a subsequent word —as tribute for the right of grazing along the pleasant banks of the river, where the sweetest and freshest grass grows, as known to every farmer. There was probably not much of it,—but the value of the cow may have been com-

mensurate at the time.*—The entire clause would thus run:
—" Let Veltinius possess the half-farm of ' Banks of Tiber,'
at the rent-payment of one cow," *per annum*.—The succeeding
words describe modifications in the tenure and rent of (I
take it) the original farm:—

20, 21, 22. TESNŚ TEIŚ RAŚNEŚ,—RAŚNEŚ being apparently
in the genitive case:—That is,—' From the income (TEIŚ) of
the holding (TESNŚ), as' or 'of rent'—so much. TESNŚ
TEIŚ refers here (I repeat) to the holding proper, or original
farm, whole and entire, independently of the additional lease
of the half-farm of ' Banks of Tiber.'

23. CHIMTH.—This and the following words are run
together without break, but I think they may be divided
and interpreted as I shall proceed to show:—For CHIMTH—
which should be written in German as SCHIMTH, compare
SCHUMPF, KUMPF, CHUNF, ' mensura frumenti,' a measure of
corn, but—at least in ancient Germany—of a very minute
description;† and *schaub*, *sceaf* (A.-Sax.), ' garba,' a *sheaf* of
corn. Remembering the interchangeability of *b* and *m*, *th*
and *pf*, in the ancient languages, and taking the word that
follows into consideration, I am inclined to think that the
word SCHIMTH here means ' sheaves.'

24. SPELT.—Identical, I presume, with the Latin ' spelta,'
and German ' *spelt* (A.-Sax.), *spel*, *spelz*,' a sort of corn, the
most common grain in which payments in kind are made in
the old Italian charters. The word ' spelta' is not classical
Latin; it occurs first in a poem ' de Ponderibus' attributed to
Priscian, who flourished in the sixth century of the Christian
era; and I have little doubt that it is a purely Etruscan and
German word, Latinised as above shewn.

25. HUT.—As before, ' centum,' a hundred. ' One hundred
sheaves of spelt.'

26, 27. AŚKUNA.—Divisible as AŚ KUNA, and to be read, I
think, as *aus gang*, in the sense of the phrase *gäng und gebe*,
used ' de monetis et mercibus,' and signifying ' cursibilis,

---

* If I were read as the Greek ς, it would represent ten cows. But that
would, evidently, have been too much.

† The word may be the same as the Southern ' coppa,' which denoted a
larger measure.

usualis, usualiter dativus, legalis,'—that is, 'usual, or current.'

28. APHUNA. Here to be understood, from the context, as *pfund*, 'pondus, libra,' weight.

29. MENA,—the same word as *meyn*, *gemein*, 'communis, publicus.'—The entire phrase AS KUNA APHUNA MENA thus denotes (with the words that immediately precede), 'One hundred sheaves of spelt, usual or standard market-weight.'

30. MES.—*Ut supra*, 'annually.'

31. NAPER,—'nummi.'—'And in cash, nummi' so many.

32. KI.—Evidently a numeral, and probably abridged; but it is difficult to judge between alternate readings. KI may represent the Roman letters CI, 'one hundred and one.' —nummi, (and this would be in keeping with the use of the Roman letters as numerals in the statement of the original terms of the lease):—Or it may stand short for an Etruscan word representing 'quinque,' *cinque*, five, or even 'viginti,' although this is less likely.—The rent of the original farm, at first payable in money only, but now partly in money, partly in kind, was thus fixed at 'One hundred sheaves of spelt, standard weight, *per annum*, plus'—I will not undertake to say how many '*nummi*.'—And this is followed by the usual provision in awards of this nature:—

33, 34, 35. KNLHAREUTUSE. Divisible into KNL, the word, (or rather contraction) which has been already dealt with; HAR, and EUTUSE.—i. KNL implies, as before, 'the Opposition,' or 'Opponent,' i. e. Veltinius.—ii. HAR must be compared with *wer*, 'cautio,'—in composition (a very ancient form) *gewaer*, *gWer*, from whence *gar-*, and *guar-antee*, &c.; and with *war-en*, 'cavere, cautionem adhibere vel præstare,' as in law-proceedings, &c. 'Gare l'eau!' and 'Ware hawk!' exhibit the two varieties of the word in their simplest (compound) form. HAR thus signifies 'to give caution' or security; and this might be either for the proper use of a thing entrusted to one, or, abstractly, for due fulfilment of covenanted obligations.—Lastly, iii. EUTUSE is a compound of EUT- or EBT-USE, answering to *ambaht-*, *ampt-*, or *amt-hus*, or *haus*, denoting the 'curtis principalis,' the 'aula' or High Court, presided over by the *Amper*, *Amptmann*, or Prætor. The sense therefore is, 'The Opponent, or Exceptor, shall give *cautio*, or security, to the Court.' '*Cautiones*' were especially required in cases where the rights of parties were not in active litigation, but the subject of compromise, as here.—This first portion of the Prætorian award thus runs,—' Let the holding be taxed by arbitration. Let Veltinius possess the half-farm of " Banks of Tiber," at the rent-payment of One cow (annually);' and ' pay, from the income of the farm (proper), as rent, One hundred sheaves of spelt, of the current market-weight, annually ; and five,' ' twenty,' or ' one hundred and one,' '*summi*,' as the case may be. And, 'let the Exceptor Veltinius give caution (or guarantee) to the Court,' that he will fulfil these conditions.—From this point to near the end of the record, we have to deal with the second portion of the award, which is directed to the protection of Aponia, the motive party in the suit.

36, 37. VELTHINA ŚATENA.—VELTHINA is in the nominative case, as before. ŚATENA may represent *satten* in the reflective sense of *sich saettigen lassen*, ' acquiescere,'—' Let Veltinius satisfy himself' or ' acquiesce in ' the restriction to be imposed. Or, taking ŚATENA with the words EŚ TAK at the end of the sentence, it more probably answers to *satz*, a compromise by arbitration, *satzung*, ' conventio ' or ' pignus,' and the relative verb *satzen*, *setzen*,—thus implying, ' Let Veltinius agree, as a compromise, to keep only,' &c. &c.

38, 39. ZUKI ENEŚKL—' Dogs for hunting,' as already shewn.

40. IPA.—A preposition, already familiar to us,—answering more nearly perhaps to *bey*, ' per,' for, than to ' of.'

41. ŚPELANE.—Compare *spielen, spilen*, ' ludere,'—a word embracing many meanings, including that of ' venari, feras persequi, aves avibus capere,' in which latter sense Luther uses it in translating the third Book of Baruch. ' Sporting ' is our nearest English equivalent.

42. THI.—As before, *zwey*, two.

43, 44, 45, 46. PUULUMCHVAŚPEL.—Before attempting to analyse this uncouth-looking phrase, I would note that *federspil* implies in German either ' collective, omnes aves quibus fit aucupium,' birds, viz. that are employed in hawking or fowling; or 'venatio avium per aves,' i. e. 'the sport of hawking itself,'—the word being compounded, in either acceptation, of *spil*, 'ludus venatorius,' and *feder*, 'penna,' wing, feather, &c. "Wo sind die fürsten der heyden .. die da spielen mit den vöglen des himmels" are Luther's words in the translation of Baruch just referred to. CAPYS, too, we know to have been the Etruscan word for *hafuc, habicht*, an 'accipiter' or hawk, the prime minister of 'aucupium.' And the root of CAPYS, as of 'accipiter,' is manifestly 'capere,' *hab-en*, to take and hold with force. Assuming therefore that the phrase here in question may imply 'Hawks for the sport of fowling,' the question arises how to divide and identify the words. SPEL is, indeed, unmistakeable; and CHVA is probably CAPY-S, or hawk; UM may represent the Teutonic *umb*, 'for the purpose of;' and PHUL the root found in 'vol-are,' *fle-on* (A.-Sax.), to fly; from whence 'volucres,' birds, i. e. winged or feathered fowl. PHUL indeed, like *fowl*, would appear to be a softening down of the early and dissyllabic *vogel*, the hard *g* being wanting here.* And although CHFA, read as SCHFA, would become 'av-es' by eliding the *sch*—as in the parallel case of *schaf, ßis*, 'ovis'— the sense, assuming it to be such as supposed, requires an aggressive not a passive substantive in the place. With much hesitation therefore as to these particular suggestions, but with strong assurance as to the general sense, I read the passage as CHVA UM PHUL SPIL, or (in the order in which they are written, following a peculiar Etruscan grammatical form), PHUL UM CHVA SPIL, denoting, 'Hawks,' or falcons, 'for the sport of fowling.'—The number of these is by the decree, as in the case of the dogs, limited to

47. THI,—*twey*, two, as in former instances of this nume-

* That this should be the case ought not to surprise us; for the same work of disintegration and refinement was going on, it may be presumed, in Etruria as among ourselves North of the Alps, under the same grammatical laws, and under more harmonious conditions. 'Pullus,' a chicken in Latin, the modern Italian 'pollo,' is simply the Etruscan PHUL; but 'pullus,' used as the young of any animal—e.g. a 'foal'—is (I conceive) from a different root.

ral. Veltinius had, I fancy, poached on the preserves of his 'dominus,' the Lady Aponia; and, although she now granted him under the award of the Prætor rights of coursing within the limits of his own holding, this concession was fenced in by strict limitations in her interest.

48, 49, 50, 51. BENETHIESTAK. Divisible as BENE THI ES-TAK, and explainable as follows:—BENE, probably *rawa*, 'equus castratus,' a gelding, for following the game.—ii. THI, as before, *swey*, two.—iii. iv. ES TAK,—two words which apparently answer to *su dank*, in the sense of *su dank sein*. 'acceptum esse,' and, taken with SATENA at the beginning of the clause, would imply, 'shall content himself' with the number of dogs, falcons, and horses specified in the award. The clause would therefore run as a whole, 'Veltinius shall content himself with dogs for hunting, two; with hawks for fowling, two; and with geldings, or riding-horses,' for following up the game, 'two.' But Aponia's protection is still further to be secured:—

52, 53, 54. AKILUNE · TUR.—AKIL and UNE are two words. AKIL is the German *angel*, 'cardo,' hinge; UNE (probably pronounced, in full, UNDE) is our modern *und*, *and*; and TUR corresponds with *thur*, or *door*,—*thürangel* signifying 'door-hinge' in existing German. The three words here taken together may be recognised in the old Teutonic phrase, 'einen mit *thuir und angel* beschliessen,' 'alicui injungere ne domo suâ vel certo loco excedat, confinare, . . . januâ et portâ continere aliquem,'—to enjoin upon any one that he keep—or to restrain any one—'within door and hinge.' This proverbial phrase was thus common to ancient German and Etruscan.

55, 56, 57. UNESKUNEZEA,—divisible as UN ESKUNE ZEA, —the whole being written without break, and ending with ZUKI, this last being certainly, as we have repeatedly seen, an independent vocable. Postponing for the moment the initial UN, we may compare ESKUNE with *ausgang*, *ausgehen*, 'exitus, exire,' and with the similar combination in the phrase ASKUNA ATHENA MENA already analysed; and then, conjoining UN and ZEA, proceed to identify the compound thus presented to us with *einziehen*, implying to draw in, restrain, and even imprison (*einziehung*)—a sense inherent indeed in the very roots of the language. The phrase would thus run UN-ESKUNE-ZEA, *ein-ausgehen-siehe*, 'shall restrain from going out.' The separation of the verb and its affix here shown is familiar to us in the Germanic languages.

58, 59. ZUKI EMESKI.—'His sporting-dogs,' as before.

60, 61, 62.—ATHUMIKŚ. Three words are here conglomerated, ATH, UM, and IKŚ.—i. ATH must, in its primitive form, have been AZ, *s* being the original and fuller form of TH. It represents here *hetze*, 'venatio,' *hetzen*,' venari'—*caccia, chasse, chase* being the Latin, and *huntian, hunt*, the Anglo-Saxon form at the present day,—hunting, that is to say, with the *hund*, hound, or dog, which in its earlier form was probably written *hud* (*hud* = *huds* = *huz*) before the *n* was introduced for euphony. The old Francic form of the verb, *eez-en*, comes very near to ATH. ATH, *eez-*, *hetze*, 'cacc-ia,' *hunt*, all spring from the old Aryan *az* already spoken of, and are cousins-german of ZCHI, *jagd*, 'venatio.'—ii. UM is the Teutonic *umb*, 'à,' 'ab,' or 'de'—from.—And iii. IKŚ probably represents *icht, ichtes, ichts, ichsit*, 'aliquid,' and likewise 'aliquo modo.' I interpret the phrase therefore as 'from hunting in any wise.' UM, 'from,' is placed after the verb, which seems to have been idiomatic in Etruscan.

63. APHUNAŚ,—the genitive of APHUNA, 'Aponia.'

64. PENTHNA.—To be compared with *puindt, buinde*, plur. *buindina*, 'locus pascuus septus, fundus,' enclosed pastures; or, in a more general sense, with our English 'bounds.'*— The sense of the clause up to this point would be, 'Veltinius shall restrain his sporting-dogs within' (or by) 'door and hinge from hunting in any wise' (that is, from trespassing) 'upon Aponia's bounds'—I had almost written, 'preserves.' —The Prætor's award proceeds as follows:—

65. AMA.—This combination of letters must here, I think, answer to *sam, ἅμα*, denoting 'along with this,' 'at the same time,' or 'moreover.'

66. VELTHINA.—'Let Veltinius ——.'

* *Bundin, bunden*, had even the sense of 'agri dominicales,' at least in Nassau, which would more precisely tally with Aponia's character as *dominus*. See Brinckmeier's 'Gloss. Diplom.' in voce.

67, 68. APHUNTHURUNI. — Divisible as APHUN-THURUNI. APHUN and UNI form one compound word, with THUR interjected between them, according to Etruscan usage. The whole is governed by the verb EIN which follows immediately after them in the Etruscan.—i. THUR I take to be either *thor*, door, or *thurm*, 'turris,' tower, a word of the most ancient Tyrrhenian and Etruscan origin.—ii. APHUN-UNI corresponds with *offenunge*, 'jus aperturæ,' in feudal law, the 'castrorum tempore belli debita apertura,' the obligation of opening the gates of the vassal's castle or house to the Lord in time of war. The house of Veltinius is thus declared to be what was called in medieval Germany an *offenes haus*, *oder schloss*, 'castrum patens, apertum et aperiendum Domino in casu necessitatis'—an *oppen stott*; such a house as it is repeatedly covenanted in old German charters shall be 'domus aperta et domus lygia, vulgariter dicta *ein offen ledig hus*,' or, as more fully defined, "Domino nostro .. semper esse pro omnibus necessitatibus suis aperta municio contra quemlibet indifferenter,"—in short, a quasi-fortalice, held by free feudal service, and to be maintained against all men in the Lord's cause, the Sovereign only excepted.

69. EIN.—This word, divided from the preceding and attached to the ensuing cluster of words as EINZERIUNAKCHA, may be compared with *ein-en*, 'tribuere in proprium,' *eigenen*, 'concordare, pacisci,' &c. I think it signifies 'afford' or 'yield,' 'render,' 'fulfil, as of obligation,' &c.; and that it applies to both portions of the sentence, before and after it.

70, 71. ZERIUNAKCHA.—To be divided as ZERIUN AKCHA. —i. ZERIUN is formed from the very ancient *ser*, *sar*, *schar*,* a troop or band of soldiers, the fundamental element in the following compounds, (1.) *serianti*, *sariande*, *sariantus*, *sarianous*, *sergenter* (Goth.), *schariant*, implying one who renders military, or rather feudal service,—the same word as our

---

* The root *ser*, *schar*, has nothing to do originally with 'servus,' 'service.' Its analogies are with *schirm*, protection, *schrimpe*, the older form of *kamp*, &c. (as illustrated *supra*), and with *werre*, 'guerra,' war, between which and *ser* the Etruscan form SER affords, as in other cases, a common centre of connection.

familiar 'sergeant,' although its original sense is now lost; (2.) *scherwerch*, 'angarim,' and *scherwerchen*, 'angarias prestare,' that is, to pay the service agreed upon between lord and vassal—the vassal holding by what is styled in Anglo-Norman law 'serjeantry,' *grand* or *petit*,—and, (3.) *scharwacht*, 'manipulus vigilum,' a small body (handful) of soldiers, or armed men, detached as a watch, especially by night, and which is sometimes expressed as in the phrase *und hette des nachts wacht und skart gehalten*, the 'circuitores' or watch being styled *skart* or *skartleute*. I read ZERIUN as *serianti*, *schariant*, the final 't' being omitted in the Etruscan orthography.—ii. AKCHA, properly written AKSCHA, I take to be the *wachten* (in older, and especially Gothic and Saxon German, *wakan*, *wacha*), to wake, and in Low German generally, to watch for defence, in the sense of *warten*.* ZERIUN AKSCHA would thus signify, in its proximate sense, 'watch and ward by night,'—but with an ulterior signification of tenure by serjeantry, or as a military vassal. Either Voltinius had violated his duty in shutting his doors against Aponia, and neglecting his feudal obligation of 'watch and ward' in obedience to the provisions of the original contract as implied under the head of PHUSLERI, or vassalage; or the Prætor put the tenure now for the first time on a new, more liberal, and distinctly military footing, as of a *lediges haus*, held by the service of serjeantry,—and I think this last the more probable alternative.†—This second portion of the award

* *Wacha*, *wakan*, in the sense of watching, is recognisable—the result of Aryan and, I suspect, Tyrrhenian influence—in the Egyptian *malatara*, which is literally, as well as in signification, our English *watchtower*—the 'm' in Egyptian orthography constantly representing the Teutonic 'w,' and the word being thus tantamount to *wakataru*. The watchtower was adopted, I think, from the Tyrrheni alike by Phœnicians and Egyptians; and we have the *makutara* in a Semitic form in the 'Mag-dala' (Mig-dol) of Gennesareth and Abyssinia. The invention of towns is attributed to the Tyrrheni.

† It is just possible that AKSCHA may represent *ach*, *acht*, *acht-es*, 'Jus, possessio,' or *weg*, *weg-es*; and that ZERIUN-AKSCHA may thus signify 'by right of serjeantry,' or 'sergeant-wise.'—ZERIUN-AKSCHA, as above identified, considered as a compound, is fuller, it will be observed, than the more recent *scharwacht*. The immediate resemblance of this last word, and of the kindred form 'eschargaita,' 'scharmgmyta,' in medieval Latin, and the old

runs therefore, as a whole, thus:—' Let Vellinius content himself with two dogs for hunting, two hawks for fowling, and two riding-horses. Let him keep his sporting-dogs within doors, lest they trespass on Aponia's bounds. And let him keep open door' or ' render free entry ' (to his house in time of danger), 'and maintain watch and ward by night,' —acting, in short, as the dutiful castellan of a ' domus lygia,' holding (as aforesaid) ' in serjeantry,' by feudal service. We now reach the last clause in the judgment, which touches both parties equally:—

72-77. THILTHUNCHULTHL · ICH · HAKECHAZICHUCHE.— This last clause is the most difficult of all in the inscription. Its general sense seems to be, that the Court orders security to be given by both sides for observance of the award. Various explanations which might be offered in this general sense are met by the difficulty that the corrected orthography of ' ch ' as ' sch,' and the necessity of consistency in selecting the Teutonic equivalents for Etruscan words with regard to that condition, lay a veto on such words as *gegenseit-ig*, reciprocal, *sats*, compromise, and *schuts*, protection, which I have at various times thought of as answering to KAKE- CHAZI. The peculiar isolation of the word ICH, separated by points before and after from the rest of the clause, must be taken notice of, as it suggests that it denotes a formula of law, probably abridged. The interpretation that seems to me to be upon the whole most free from objection on these considerations, and most practical, and such as would justify the inscription of the clause on a public monument like this, may be set forth as follows:—i. THIL,—'statuit,' ordains; the third person singular, present tense, of *teilen*, ' statuere, sententiam ferre,' &c.—ii. THUNCHULTHL,—a compound of (1) THUNCH, *ding*, the ' thing' or court, and (2) ULTHL, for *urtheil*, ' judicium, placitum,' and signifying ' the decree of the Court:'—Or, if (1) THUNCHUL be read as THUNCH-WILL, *dingsal*, ' placitum,' as before ; and (2) THL as *teil*, ' pars litigans, adversarius in causâ litigiosâ,' the parties to a suit,

Norman ' escharmites,' to ESE... AESCHA made me think at first that the intermediate UN represented a connective *und, and*,—but I think the true rendering is as I have given it in the text.

then THIL THUNCHUL THL would imply, 'the *placitum* enjoins on the parties to'—do so and so.—iii. RAKECHAZI,—to be distinguished from the words that follow, although written without break, and to be read, properly, as KAKESCHAZI. It may be compared with *schanz*, 'cautio,' *gegenschantz*, 'cautio,' or security, with the sense of counter-protection, counter-security, the idea being that of fortifications reared in defence by two enemies opposed one to the other.—SCHAZI answering to *schanz*, 'cautio,' and KAKE to *gegen*, or perhaps *wider*, against,—the 'n' being omitted as usual in writing SCHAZI. —iv. CHUCH, or, written properly, SCHUSCH,—to be compared with *schach, schachen*, the French 'choquer,' our English *shock*; and with *quetschen*, 'contundere,' our *squash* and *quash*, —all having the sense of coming into collision, with the further qualification of 'jactura, damnum,' injury or skaith, thence accruing; while *schach* implies, in addition, the condition of 'check-mate' or 'dead-lock'—words fundamentally identical.—v. E.—Apparently *ehe, eo, é,* 'jus, fas, lex,' but with the sense of moral, eternal, or divine justice as contrasted with *gesets*, 'lex,' humanly imposed, or strict law,— *ehe*, I have little doubt, being the ultimate root (beyond 'æq-uus') of 'æquitas,' 'equity'—the mean, or compromise between severe 'jus' and 'indulgentia,' this last being the aim-point of the peculiar jurisprudence of the Prætors.— And, lastly, vi. ICH, properly written ISCH, stands, I presume, for *jezo, jetzt*, but practically in abbreviate as the first word of a formula well known in old Teutonic law, *jetzt als dann und dann als jetzt*, 'nunc prout ex tunc et ex tunc prout ut nunc,' the 'formula reciproca de continuatione æquali'— imposed, that is to say, on both parties in an agreement or award, viz., to adhere to it, without interruption, *in perpetuum*. —The clause would thus run, 'The judgment ordains,' or 'the judgment imposes on the parties to the suit'—to give 'counter-securities against' any 'shock to,' or breach of, 'the equitable award' just pronounced, and to be binding 'now and henceforward' unbrokenly for ever. This concludes the entire record. The point I am most doubtful about is the reading of ISCH. It might be interpreted *heisch* —'seeks,' 'requires'—'the judgment orders the parties to

seek security,'—and this would be more in conformity with
the force of the letter scn, as above insisted upon; but the
peculiar isolation of the word, and the importance of the in-
junction of continuity, induce me to acquiesce in the interpretation now given.*

The entire Perugian inscription may now be
repeated in sequence:—

I. "Legal Notice of Indenture," or Agreement.
"Lord's Court," or Exchequer. "Lautinius Veltinius, Seneschal, farms the Dominical Land of
Aponia, *ad pretium fixum*, in vassalage:"—Paying, to
wit, "from the income of the holding, as rent, twelve
nummi per month, annually :—Veltinius," on the
other hand, "warrants the river-banks, open (or uncultivated) spaces, forest-ground, highland copsewood, the mill, mill-dues, and the right of coursing
with dogs over the manor"—in other words, the
game—"from *damnum*" or injury.

II. "Aulus Veltinius Arznal diminishes the farm
by alienation of two-thirds without notice, defaulting
in the rent due to the Dominus."

III. "Suit (at law) for judgment of fraud" against

---

* An entirely different interpretation of KAKENCTIAEI SCHUSCH-E once
suggested itself to me, viz.—'The judgment awards the SCHUSCH-E,' the
'schutz-ice,' or 'costs of the defence,' that is, the public 'costs' incurred by
the litigant parties, each of which was the subject of the 'defence' or
'præsidium' of the tribunal in a case of equity—(or possibly it might be
read *schatz-é*, the 'sacramentom' or sum of money deposited by the rival
parties)—' to the KAKENCTIAEI,' or '*bona-caduca* chest,'—KAKE being read in
connection with 'cad-o,' 'coc-idi,' and SCHAEI identified with *schatz*, treasury
or 'ærarium.' This interpretation is the easiest of all; but the consideration that such an award—a mere matter of course—could not have been a
subject for public enrolment on marble determined me against it. Had
this interpretation been unobjectionable, it would have fixed the date of the
inscription as prior to the appointment of the 'Advocatus Fisci' in the
reign of Hadrian, up to which time the attribution of such windfalls to
particular uses was at the discretion of the local authorities.

Veltinius "at the Kempe's Law," or Moot-hill Court. "Veltinius contradicts the charge. The Court decrees,—Six (sixty?) *nummi* as fine to the Court," or *pœna*, "against the defaulter, Veltinius: One hundred *nummi*, as rent due, to be refunded" to Aponia: And "decrees appropriation of his goods" as security for payment.

IV. "By agreement of the parties on the appointed day: Aponia *v.* Veltinius,"—Suit in Equity. "Submission of matters in dispute by way of arbitration to the award of the Ampter," or Prætor. "Veltinius demurs." Decision:—"Let the farm be taxed." Award:—i. "Let Veltinius have the half-farm of Banks of Tiber," hitherto reserved to Aponia by the original lease, "at the rent-payment of one cow annually:"—Let him pay "from the income of the farm" (the original holding, proper) "as rent, one hundred sheaves of spelt, of the current market weight, annually; and five" ("twenty," or "one hundred and one") "*nummi*:—Caution" (or security) "to be given to the Court by the exceptor" Veltinius.—On the other hand, ii. "Veltinius shall content himself with two sporting-dogs, two hawks for fowling, and two riding-horses (geldings). Veltinius shall keep his sporting-dogs within door and hinge" (within doors), "that they hunt not within Aponia's bounds; and shall keep open-door and watch and ward by night, in serjeantry," as an observant vassal in future.—Finally, "The judgment orders the parties to find counter-security for perpetual observance of the equity," the equitable award, thus pronounced.

And thus the proceedings ended; and we can only hope that Aponia and Veltinius were better friends afterwards. As there is no further inscription on the stone, I presume that on the death of Veltinius the farm lapsed to Aponia or her representatives on failure of his male issue, to which the charter or original grant probably restricted it.*

* At the end of Conte G. Conestabile's 'Monumenti di Perugia,' he gives a very valuable synopsis of the different interpretations which have been rendered of this great inscription, in its individual parts, and as a whole. But to English readers the observations of Dr. Donaldson will be the most interesting; and they extend beyond the Inscription itself to general positions on which, as the reader will have seen, I cannot agree with him. "The facility," he says, "with which the philologist dissects the Etruscan words which have been transmitted to us, either with an interpretation or in such collocation as to render their meaning nearly certain, and the striking and unmistakeable coincidences between the most difficult fragments and the remains of the Old Norse language, might well occasion some surprise to those who are told that there exists a large collection of Etruscan inscriptions which cannot be satisfactorily explained. One cause of the unprofitableness of Tuscan inscriptions is to be attributed to the fact that these Inscriptions, being mostly of a sepulchral or dedicatorial character, are generally made up of proper names and conventional expressions. Consequently they contribute very little to our knowledge of the Tuscan syntax, and furnish us with very few forms of inflection. So far as I have heard, we have no historical or legal inscriptions." Historical Inscriptions are certainly as yet the grand desideratum; but such may perhaps be found hereafter, and the old Teutonic will be, we may now feel assured, the key to unlock them with. "If we go through this inscription," continues Dr. Donaldson—that, viz. of Perugia—"and compare the words of which it is composed, we shall find that out of more than eighty different words there are very few which are not obviously proper names, and some of these occur very frequently; so that this monument, comparatively copious as it is, furnishes, after all, only slender materials for a study of the Tuscan language." He supports his assertion of the Scandinavian character of the Etruscan by connecting ARAS with *ari*, 'junior,' —ENESKI with *eski* (O. N.), ashes, or *eski*, 'pyxis,'—EPL with *epli* (O. N.), 'progenies,'—ETH, as "a demonstrative pronoun and affix," with "the Old Norse idioms,"—HUT, with the "*hut* in the Runic inscriptions, as *thir huaru hut til Orika*, i. e. *isti proferti sunt in Græciam*,"—KUNA with the Runic *kuna*, wife,—LAT, with the O. N. *lit*, let,—LAUTN, with *laut* (O. N.), grave,—NAPER, with *knapr* (O. N.), son,—PENTHNA, with *phant*, *pantr* (O. N.), and *pantas* (Lith.), a pledge,—SLEL, with *súla*, *súl*, a column,—SRANEZL with the Icelandic *orsl*, 'tuber,'—and SUKI, with *sök* (O. N.), 'causa,' dat. pl. *sökum*, 'propter,' Engl. *sake*. "It would be easy to found a number of conjectures on the Old Norse assonances which may be detected in almost every line, and which I have noticed . . . , but until a complete

I have said nothing as yet of the date of the inscription, but it must be comparatively recent among those of Etruria. It is presumably later than the first institution of the Roman Prætor, B.C. 366. If we could ascertain the period when the Prætors

collection of all the genuine Etruscan inscriptions shall have furnished us with a sufficiently wide field for our researches—until every extant Etruscan word has been brought within the reach of a philological comparison—above all, until we get some sufficiently extensive bilingual monument—we must be content to say of this great Perugian inscription, that it appears to be a *cippus* conveying some land for funereal purposes, and commemorating the family connexions of certain persons bearing the names of *Rasius*, *Aponius*, *Atinius*, and *Velthina*,"—" Larthius, a member of the family of the *Rcza* (*Rasii*)" being " the donor," and " Velthina .. the person in whose honour this *cippus* was erected." "If," he adds, " I do not undertake to interpret all that Lartius, the son of Rasia, has thought fit to inscribe on this *cippus* for the gratification of his own immediate relatives, it must not be supposed that this in any way affects the results at which I have arrived respecting the ethnography of the Etruscans. That an inability to interpret ancient monuments may be perfectly consistent with a knowledge of the class of languages to which they belong, is shown, not merely by the known relationship between the language of the Egyptian hieroglyphics and the Coptic dialects more recently spoken in that country, but still more strikingly by the fact, that, although we have no doubt as to any of the idioms spoken in ancient Britain, no one has been able as yet to give a certain interpretation of the Runic inscriptions on the pillar of Bewcastle and on the font at Bridekirk, which are both in Cumberland, and which both belong to the same dialect of the Low-German language, (see Palgrave, *Hist. of the Anglo-Saxons*, Lond. 1850, pp. 146 sqq.). The really important point is to determine the origin of the ancient Etruscans; and the Perugian inscription, so far from throwing any difficulties in the way of the conclusion at which I have arrived, has furnished some of the strongest and most satisfactory confirmations of the Old Norse affinity of the Rasena."—*Varronianus*, pp. 215 sqq.

Although differing from Dr. Donaldson in so many points of detail, I cannot but recognise the clear insight into the Teutonic character (in the broadest sense) of the Etruscan speech exhibited by that distinguished and lamented scholar. But his proofs were less felicitous; and had I to choose between them and the arguments in favour of the Armenian as urged by Mr. Ellis, I should hesitate which side to take. That the Etruscan was Scandinavian in the paramount sense asserted by Dr. Donaldson the reader will agree with me in doubting; and such affinities as really exist are accounted for, I submit, by the original unity of the various branches of the Thuringa or Thuringian family.

first began to rule in favour of the right subsequently
known as that of 'emphyteusis,' this would lead us
nearly to the true date, for the process is evidently
in progress as between the original and the subsequent grant of the holding under Aponia. This
period is unfortunately as yet unknown to us. A
limit on the other hand as regards modern times is
imposed by the very fact of the record being written
in Etruscan. The question is, when did the language
die out? K. O. Müller thinks that it was in a moribund state when Volnius wrote his tragedies with the
view, he conceives, of reanimating its waning vitality,
shortly before the time of Varro, who was born B.C.
116. He observes that "Latin inscriptions gradually
supplanted" the Etruscan "in every possible manner.... The right of citizenship in Etruria and
the merciless desolations of Sulla may have driven
out the native tongue, and imposed the Latin. Yet
the Haruspices continued to read their 'Etruscos
libros' in Cicero's time. Dionysius speaks of the
Etruscan as a living language in his day,"—he died
shortly after B.C. 7; "and many urns with Etruscan
legends shew us from the style of their decorations
that they belong to imperial times. At this period,
however," he concludes, "the language became extinct; and even the Etruscan seers used in their rites
the Tarquitian translation, instead of their ancient
Ritual and Fulgural Books."* With these facts and
views before us, we have to consider that the
language appears in this inscription in full vigour and
quite uncorrupted, without any infusion of Latin

* I quote from Mrs. Hamilton Gray's translation in the third volume
of her 'History of Etruria.'

words. It is not a little remarkable, indeed, that none of the inscriptions—of those, at least, that I have examined—exhibit the mixture of language which generally takes place before extinction. And yet various words which we have recognised as Etruscan, and not Latin, linger on in the speech of modern Italy. The calligraphy of this inscription is, it is to be observed, remarkably regular; the more modern forms of the letters 'm,' 'n,' and others are used only, and, although the words are agglomerated together, the orthography is settled and consistent. My impression, upon the whole, therefore is, that it cannot be much later than the days of Volnius and Varro.

SUMMARY.

It is now for yourself, MY DEAR ANNE, and others, to decide whether or not I have made out my proposition, viz. that the Etruscan was a Teutonic language. In guidance towards such decision, I may be allowed to point out that Jacob Grimm, in his argument from language to prove that the Dacians and Getæ were Teutons, writes thus,—"If only six or eight of my interpretations be correct, and the remainder more or less probable, there needs no further proof that the races in question are of the German stock."* This is spoken of isolated words transmitted to us as Dacian, and I might have claimed your verdict accordingly on the score of the Etruscan words preserved by the classical and other ancient writers—words *in pari casu* with those of Dacia and the Getæ—and which I analysed and explained by ancient German long ago. But no one should be content with second-hand evidence when primary is accessible; and, applying Grimm's standard therefore to the original inscriptions which we have now examined, I venture to think that you must have recognised many more words than "six or eight" among them as pure German. What I would lay greater stress upon, however, are the facts; 1. That these words thus interpreted form in their current concatenation consistent sense throughout, and sense

* *Geschichte der Deutschen Sprache*, Leipzig, 1868, 3rd edit., vol. I. p. 150.

too in which no word is superfluous and no idea occurs which is not naturally warranted by the apparent purpose of the inscriptions in which they occur:—2. That many of these words present themselves in particular clusters, or rather in sequences closely agreeing with similar familiar sequences, not only in German but other Indo-European languages; such, for instance, as ARITIMI PHASTI RUIPURIM, 'engagement confirmed by striking hands;' IPA MURZUA KER, 'per manum mortuam;' AŚ KUNA APHUNA MENA, 'current market-weight;' and AKIL UNE TUR UN-EŚKUNE-ZEA, 'shall keep at home within hinge and door,' where the AKIL UNE TUR is the very phrase of the vernacular Teutonic idiom; to which may be added, in similar illustration, the correspondence of the clause TUURAŚ, ALAŚ, PERAŚ, KE, MUL, MLEŚKUL, ZUKI ENEŚKI, 'shores, areas, forest, upland-copse, mill, mill-dues, rights of chase,' &c. with similar clauses including the same subjects in the old Italian charters of the ninth and tenth centuries cited from Muratori:—And 3. That a parallel line of proof is afforded by the identity of the Etruscan CHIS-VLIKŚ, or as it should be written, SCHISVLIKŚ, with the Teutonic *zu geschoss und pflicht*; 'jure ac more,' Legal and Customary; and by the correspondence between such compound words as TRUT-VEKIE and *weg-strassen*, PHANU-ŚATHEK and *pfand-satzung*, KŚ-UATHA and *wette-schatz*, EŚ-TLA and *gas-told*, PENE-ZŚ and *pfennig-zins*, THAIŚ-APHUNEŚ and *pfund-zoll*; as also, I may add, between the Pelasgian VENE-KEVE-LTHU and the Teutonic *weinkauff-leuthe*,—these compounds bearing the same signification in both languages, although the position of the component elements is usually reversed, as has been repeatedly illustrated. It is incredible, I submit, that such coincidences as the preceding should exist unless the Etruscan language was really, as I contend it was, archaic German. I may add to these considerations the striking fact that the primitive figure by which human obligation was conceived of as a 'bond' or 'chain' linking parties together as by a physical union—an idea which may be traced backwards (although this is not the place for it) to the earliest moral conceptions of the Aryan world, and to the original sanction of faith and dependence in the character and relations of God to Man—is expressed—and not only the idea, but the symbols which shadow forth that idea—in Etruscan and in Teutonic by the same words, as already shewn in speaking of the Will and 'Fidei-Commissum' of Lautinius Pompey, and I may also add, in the article upon the 'Pontifex Maximus' (abridged as it is) in the Appendix to this Memoir.

It is but right that I should state that in hardly any case have I taken up an inscription—least of all the great one of Perugia—with a foregone conclusion as to its meaning. The meaning that dawned on me, as I proceeded in the analysis, was, on the contrary, in repeated instances, the reverse of what I had anticipated. This is not saying much; but I have at least attempted in my own practice to hold rigidly by the rule that should govern all such inquiries, viz. to abstain from coming to any positive conclusion till all the words have been analysed and their possible significations ascertained,—it is then only that, upon a review of the whole, the exact purport can be approximated to. In fact, after a

P

certain point in the process the true meaning usually opens on the perception like a flash of lightning.

I do not, let me further say, overlook the maxim that mere resemblance or even identity of words between the speech of two nations is insufficient *per se* to establish identity of race; nor do I assign the Etruscans to the Teutonic stem on the bare ground that they spoke a Teutonic language. Although affording a strong *primâ facie* argument, identity of speech does not necessarily infer identity of race. There are many instances, both in Europe and Asia, of whole populations losing their original and adopting a foreign vocabulary,—although, when this is the case, the grammar or skeleton (as it were) of the language usually remains unaltered below the change on the surface. Now, in the case of the Etruscan language, we find that not only the vocabulary but the inflections and grammatical structure are, as has been shewn in repeated instances, identical with the Teutonic; and by this supreme test in the application of language to questions of ethnology I count myself justified in the conclusion I have come to as to the German origin of the Etruscans. You will recollect moreover throughout, that the proof from language here given is merely the coping-stone of an induction laboriously built up from an accumulation of historical evidence all tending to the same conclusion.

It will be for others to work out the theory and practice of the Etruscan grammar, in due scientific method, after the whole of the accessible inscriptions have been analysed and translated; and I shall add nothing therefore to the few observations on this point scattered over the preceding pages. But, in looking back on the inscriptions now before us as materials for history, I may observe, first, that they throw a very pleasing light on some points of character in the old Etruscans—on their domestic affection, on their high respect for women, on their temperance, their honesty, their abhorrence of fraud, and their addiction (so like the English) to amicable composition of dispute by compromise. It is interesting, in a legal point of view, to recognise notices of a system of pledge and pawn, with its accompanying forfeits (a system introduced into Rome from Etruria and systematised, as I believe was the case, under the special protection of the Pontifex Maximus)—the actual words (I may almost say) of a last Will and Testament, constituting a trust—the foundation-charter (as I may call it) of a mortuary-chapel; a lady in that case, as in others, acting with an independence hardly known to Rome, but in perfect keeping with the high estimation of women so abundantly testified to as existing among the Etruscans— the public notification of a mortgage of land to a religious College, and its subsequent foreclosure—and the history of a farm, held under feudal tenure, and the subject, as has just been shewn, of two lawsuits, the first by *judicium* under strict law, the second in equity—all recorded in the ancient language of Etruria, the mother of Rome in so many of her most important institutions. There is an especial touch (I may observe) of feudalism in the relations of the Dominus and the Vassal as described in this last-named record, which bespeaks a Northern people domiciled in the South, as well as in the glimpses of manners brought out by the narrative. We should hardly think of Cincinnatus or Publicola hunting and hawking on horseback along the Volscian slopes or on the Latin plain. The Mamilii of Tusculum may have done so, in company with Porsena. On the other hand, the inscription of Perugia mirrors, as it were, in its successive dramatic scenes, the change of feeling through which the tenure of a farm held by vassalage at a fixed rent becomes invested in the eyes of the tenant himself first, and afterwards of the law, with a qualification of property, ownership, tenant-right, or 'emphyteusis'—subordinate indeed to that of the Superior, but equally the subject of legal protection so long as the conditions of the contract are observed, and to which Equity is always on the watch to give undue preponderance,—a generous proclivity not unknown to our own day, and which we may recognise, I think, in the favour with which Aulus Veltinius is treated by the Amper, or Prætor, although it must be allowed that the dues of Aponia also receive fair consideration. All this drama is at least as much Etruscan as it is Roman; and my impression is that the Law of the Twelve Tables in the first instance, and the Equity or Prætorian law of later Rome, was mainly inspired by the more liberal doctrines of Etruria. When I add to this enumeration the revelation of the 'Dies Viridium' or *Hohe Donners-tag*, the Holy Thursday sacred to TUNCR, Tinia or Thor, as the great festival of the Etruscans no less than of the Teutons—and take into account the peculiar ideas suggested by the choice of that particular period for the commemorative rites to the memory of the departed—it appears hardly possible to doubt that they looked forward to that yearly recurring epoch, and beyond it too, with hopes of immortality and happiness for themselves and the friends they loved on earth akin to those which we ourselves cherish—although with a fuller assurance than could have been shared in by Lautinia Prekutia and the sisters of San Manno.

All this will, I doubt not—and much more—stand out clearly in some future day when the inscriptions— that of Perugia and others, to say nothing of those not as yet discovered—shall have been fully elucidated and their shades of technical meaning ascertained by some one qualified for the task (which I am not) by familiarity with the old Teutonic languages and with the laws and customs of ancient Germany and Scandinavia. Enough has in the meanwhile, I think, been done to establish a fact of the gravest importance for historical science, viz. that the great nation, whose institutions exercised so powerful an influence over the development of Rome, and through Rome on existing society, was of the Germanic stock. Niebuhr professed himself willing to devote the best part of his fortune as a prize to the man who should solve the problem 'Who were the Etruscans?;' inasmuch as the ascertainment of that fact would throw, as he says, an entirely new light over the ethnography and history of ancient Italy. But the solution now offered does more— illuminating, as it will be found to do, many dark places of history, bridging over many difficulties which have hitherto proved impassable, linking the nationalities of Europe in closer bonds of consanguinity than they have been aware of hitherto, and leading us many steps onward toward the remoter sources of the pre-historic civilisation of the West. It may appear daring to base such hopes and beliefs on a few fragmentary inscriptions imperfectly interpreted like the preceding; but such fragments are for the historian what the fossil relics of extinct organic life are to a Cuvier; and the Hebrew belief that a particular bone, surviving of every man, is the destined germ of his future corporeity, is but a shadow of the truth that one single line of Etruscan proved to be genuine German is sufficient to resuscitate and animate and identify as such for the purpose of history a great multitude which no man may number—an exceeding great army—an entire nation, including all its successive generations—of which the forgotten hand that traced that line was a representative. I may conclude with one or two observations illustrating these later positions.

The identity of the Etruscan with the German language (now, I think, proved) carries back our positive or literal knowledge of German to an extremely remote period—that, namely, when the two branches of the common race, Teutons and Etruscans, were living together, as one people, before they parted in the East. It may be affirmed—if only I have proved my main point—that, unless still earlier Tyrrhenian or Pelasgian—I will even say, purely Lydian records, are discovered by Mr. Dennis in Asia Minor, where he is now exploring, these Etruscan or Tyrrheno-Pelasgian inscriptions of Italy—distinct grammatical compositions as they are, and not mere isolated words—must stand henceforward at the head of Teutonic literature in point of antiquity. In a word, we now have connected writings,

I am entitled to say by Germans in a German
dialect, earlier in point of composition and calligraphy than the Gothic Gospels of Ulphilas—earlier
than the Dacian and Getic words preserved by writers
of the second century of Christianity—earlier than
the lost verses which Ovid wrote during his exile,
"pæne poeta Getes,"* in the Dacian, that is, if
Grimm be right, the German tongue of Thrace—and
earlier (to take a still further flight) than the capture
and binding of Dionysus by the Tyrrhenian mariners
on the Icarian Sea—writings, in fact, in a language
which was the familiar speech of the Tyrrheni-
Pelasgi when they first quitted the shores of Asia
Minor and rounded Mount Athos in pre-historic time,
and which must have been spoken in substantially
the same dialect and idiom by them and by the
ancestors of the Germanic tribes of Tacitus, and of
the Mœso-Goths of Ulphilas, when living as one
people (I repeat) in their latest Asiatic home before
starting — the latter to proceed directly Westward
towards the Atlantic and the setting sun, the former
to seek their fortune, like their kinsmen, the Northmen
of later times, along the coasts of the Mediterranean.

But it is not only identity of speech that is demonstrated through this unexpected approximation,—a
consideration of what the preceding inscriptions reveal
enables us to refer much in thought and civilisation
that is usually considered comparatively modern, or
dating at least within historic times, to the same
archaic antiquity, the same ethnological origin,—and
it is in Law principally, that most constant witness to
human progress, that this reveals itself. When, for

* *Ex Ponto*, lib. iv.; Epist. 13; v. 18.

example, we find such compound words as PHAND-
SATHEK, or *pfand-satzung*, KS-UATHA, or *wette-schatz*, as
above noticed—such phrases as IPA MURZUA KER and
AKIL UNE TUR UN-ESKUNE-ZEA — such descriptive
qualifications as VENE-KEVE-LTHU, or *weinkauffleute*,
identically the same in Etruscan and German; when
we find the technical phraseology of a primitive
conveyance, or will, *per æs et libram*, expressed in
Etruscan by the same words which express it in
German—those words echoing the symbolism and
being clearly intelligible in the two languages, while
the corresponding words in the Roman conveyance
are each different from the other, obscure in etymology, and in no sense echoes of the symbolism sanc-
tioning the transaction,—the title of the Pontifex
Maximus, the guardian of contracts, himself, being
moreover significant only in Etruscan and German,
not in Latin;* when we consider that this all-
pervading identity could not have arisen from the
various words and phrases in question being independent translations from the Latin by the Etruscans and medieval Germans at any period subsequent
to the original separation of the two latter races, because—and I would beg your especial attention here
—because in that case, at such great intervals of
time—the Etruscan language too having been in a
moribund state—in the opinion, at least of Müller—
even before the commencement of the Christian era
—equivalent words different in composition although
not in meaning would infallibly have been used in
many instances; whereas the words, and what is of

* See, once more, the article 'Pontifex' in the Glossary, *infra*.

more importance than the separate words, the very compounds and the sequences and phrases, are, as we have seen, identical in Etruscan and German,—when, I say, we consider all this, it is impossible not to put such queries as the following—and with a strong assurance, I venture to submit, that they must be answered in the affirmative :—1. Was not the law of Rome, like her religion and civil institutions generally, borrowed in great measure from that of Etruria —its harsher features exaggerated, its milder depressed, till through the 'Jus Gentium' and the influence of the Prætors, the Etruscan Equity prevailed over the more rigid Quiritian Law, and prepared the way for the legislation of modern times, —Etruria still, be it remarked, sending forth, almost within our own times, her plea in favour of mercy (I praise the spirit, not the particular utterance of the oracle) through the voice of Beccaria ?—2. Must not "the credit of inventing the Will—the institution which, next to the Contract, has exercised the greatest influence in transforming society"—I quote the words of Sir Alexander Maine in his profound yet most lucid essays on 'Ancient Law,' which have suggested more than one of the problems here submitted to you *—must not this great credit be attributed to Etruria rather than Rome; or, rather, must not the Conveyance or 'Mancipium,' out of which the Will and the Contract both sprung, have been in full development and common use among the ances-

---

* *Ancient Law*, p. 195.—He adds, "It is doubtful whether a true power of testation was known to any original society except the Roman :"—And, "whatever testamentary law exists" in the *Leges Barbarorum* "has been taken from the Roman jurisprudence."—*Ibid*., p. 190.

tors of the Etruscans and Teutons before they separated?—3. Must not those portions of the 'Leges Barbarorum' which, through their resemblance to Roman law, have been supposed to betray a Roman origin, and to have been absorbed through contact with the Romans while the Goths, Lombards, and other Germanic tribes were hovering on the frontiers of the Empire—must not these portions be esteemed indigenous—relics of the same original legal system which the Etruscan branch of the common race had preserved and improved under more favourable conditions in Italy, and perhaps at an earlier period in Greece?*—4. Is not, again, the feudal system and law of the middle ages the mere perpetuation, in the main, of the old Etruscan and Teutonic system and law, as existing in Etruria, in the case, for example, of the Salic land and farm at Perugia, and in Thessaly and Northern Greece (as it appears to me) in the days of the Aleuadæ and the Pelasgi—a system strongly contrasted with that of Rome, although Rome in her Imperial days found herself obliged to adopt it partially in those military benefices which have been supposed to exhibit the original model of the feudal fief?†—5. Must not the description of the

---

* On this point see the note appended to the query next to be suggested.

† Sir A. Maine repeatedly speaks of "a considerable element of Roman law" in the codes of the German conquerors of the Roman Empire as "absorbed by them during their long sojourn on the confines of the Roman dominion," "probably borrowed at widely distant epochs and in fragmentary importations."—*Ancient Law*, p. 282. He then observes, a few pages further on, "If Roman jurisprudence had any influence on the barbarous societies, it had probably produced the greatest part of its effects before the legislation of Justinian ... It was not the reformed and purified jurisprudence of Justinian, but the undigested system which prevailed in the Western Empire, and which the Eastern *Corpus Juris* never

Germans by Tacitus be considered as that of the outlying and uncultivated branches of the great Teutonic

succeeded in displacing, that I conceive to have clothed with flesh and muscle the scanty skeleton of barbarous usage. The change must be supposed to have taken place before the Germanic tribes had distinctly appropriated, as conquerors, any portion of the Roman dominions, and therefore long before Germanic monarchs had ordered breviaries of Roman law to be drawn up for the use of their Roman subjects. The necessity for some such hypothesis will be felt by everybody who can appreciate the difference between archaic and developed law. Rude as are the *Leges Barbarorum* which remain to us, they are not rude enough to satisfy the theory of their purely barbarous origin; nor have we any reason for believing that we have received in written records more than a fraction of the fixed rules which were practised among themselves by the members of the conquering tribes. If we can once persuade ourselves that a considerable element of debased Roman law already existed in the tartarian systems, we shall have done something to remove a grave difficulty. The German law of the conquerors and the Roman law of their subjects would not have combined if they had not possessed more affinity for each other than refined jurisprudence has usually for the customs of savages. It is extremely likely that the codes of the barbarians, archaic as they seem, are only a compound of true primitive usage with half-understood Roman rules, and that it was the foreign ingredient which enabled them to coalesce with a Roman jurisprudence that had already receded somewhat from the comparative finish which it had acquired under the Western Emperors."—*Ibid.*, pp. 297, 298. It is on this view that Sir A. Maine derives the feudal system, through the 'beneficia' of the Emperors, from the earlier tenancies in right of 'Emphyteusis,' pp. 298, 302; while "we have," he observes, "in the Emphyteuta a striking example of the double ownership"—illustrated, I may again remark, by the history of the farm at Perugia recorded in the inscription analysed *supra*—" which characterized feudal property." *Ibid.*, p. 301.—I venture, with the utmost deference, to suggest, that the queries expressed in the text, based as they are on the series of considerations previously noticed, furnish a solution for the various problems proposed, and in a manner not irreconcileable with Sir A. Maine's hypothesis, but rather tending to place it on a broader and more secure foundation. The germs of the feudal system, as well as of the chivalry which is frequently misunderstood as hostile to it in principle, may be recognised at the present day among the Rajpoots of India, of the Royal or Kshatra caste; and these were equally cherished, I imagine, in the institutions of the Royal Scythæ and early Teutons—although it was the destiny of their Thoringa and perhaps Pelasgian kinsmen to give them development in the West, at first in the days of Porsena, and afterwards in those of Godfrey de Bouillon. Let me further add, that the German contemporaries of the Roman Emperors were not, as I think I have shown, "barbarians," much less "savages." To the former epithet I take no

stock, remote from the centre of its civilisation; and do not the grammar and speech of the Goths of Mœsia, as represented by Ulphilas, direct us to the great Gothic race, comprehensive alike of Grutungi and Tervingi, Rhæti and Tyrrheni, as the representatives in the North of the identical civilisation which the Etruscans represented in the South—thus accounting for the continuity in descent of common laws and usages, and identical technical forms of speech, through two separate channels, but derived from one and the same source?—6. May we not, further, attribute the superior respect for women, the absence (according to the negative testimony of Gaius) of the 'Patria Potestas' (at least in its narrower form) from the domestic institutions of Etruria, the importance assigned to ETH, faith, or credit, in the inscriptions,— and, on the other hand, the peculiar severity exhibited against violation of trust—justice and mercy thus balancing each other in the scales of the Etrurian Themis—to the influence of that extended commerce which the Tyrrheni carried on in pre-historic times along the coasts of the Mediterranean, bringing them into contact with men of every race and character, and preparing the way for that more general and cosmopolitan view of life from which the 'Jus Gentium' or 'Jus Naturale' drew its original sanction?

exception, so long as it is used in a classical sense; but "savages"—if the word be used in its usual signification—they were not, even as described by Tacitus.*

* The name 'Scythæ' is, I suspect, a variety of 'Kshatra,' with the 'r' abraded; and with this their title of 'Royal Scythians' agrees. The same title in Gothic (and kindred dialects), *thiudans*, interpreted as Βασιλεύς, may probably have given their name to the 'Teutons,' whether the name 'Deutsch' be derived from the same root, or not.

—I have little doubt, in fact, that the Tyrrheni and their kindred of the Thoringa and Hruinga stock had made permanent settlements at a very early period on the Eastern and Southern shores of the Mediterranean, ranging between the coasts of the Euxine and the Pillars of Hercules.—Finally, do not the preceding considerations, taken as a whole, direct us—as the Homeric Poems equally do—to a period of early civilisation in Eastern Europe and Western Asia which fell to ruin and rose up again under altered conditions and taking a new start, even as the modern life of Europe did under the latter days of Rome and through the subsequent period of the so-called middle ages? We lose sight of that early period beyond the days of Solon and Thales in Greek history; we see the shadow of it, not in the story but the manners incidentally depicted in the Iliad and Odyssey; mythology, and the rites and ceremonies, religious and civil, preserved from early times, supply much to assist us towards the resuscitation of those ancient days; language, critically examined, does even more:—But I must not dwell on the subject here.

It may at least be said that answers to the foregoing queries in the affirmative would be in consistency with the evidence of these Etruscan inscriptions—would be contradicted by them in no point—and would contribute towards the solution of very obscure historical problems. But it requires an effort of the mind like that of Cuvier, as above suggested, to conceive of historical truths revealed, not by actual records, but by comparison and induction from the language used in such records,—and the time for such generalisation is hardly ripe as yet. I therefore make no demand on your belief on these latter points, but merely turn over the turf, shew you the metallic fruit germinating beneath, lay the turf back, and ask your sympathy in the hope that, however immature now, it may ripen into "gold another day."

There is but one thing that has troubled me throughout these investigations — anxiety lest the results should hurt the patriotic feelings of those with whom we have ever entertained such warm sympathy — the Italians. It looks as if I were attempting to rob them of their great men, ancient and modern. But a little reflection will shew them that, while all the greatest races of humanity have sprung from the marriage (as it were) of two stocks — Hindu and Persian, Celtic and Teutonic, Pelasgian and Hellenic, Latin and Etruscan, it has been the prerogative apparently of Italy and Greece to generate the greatest thinkers and actors among mankind; and Italy need feel no susceptibility therefore in recognising the claim to kindred blood now preferred on behalf of those 'Tedeschi' who have, in truth, not only in the Etruscan but the medieval times of Italy, exerted such influence upon her fortunes — and far more for good than for evil — as one of the two great factors of her political life and being. With this word of deprecation — and in protest against Müller's unqualified denial of 'genius' to the race to whose history he devoted so much learning and acuteness, I may claim, not only "the all Etruscan three" of Christian times, but Virgil himself, as paternally at least, of the old Teutonic and Thoringa race.

I have somewhat diverged, in these concluding pages, from the main object of this inquiry, which was, simply, to strengthen a weak link in my original chain of argument by shewing that the native inscriptions of Etruria, as well as the words recorded as Etruscan by the classical writers, are in the Teutonic language. The argument in question is only one, although the most important, among many; and it is the concentration of the whole upon one conclusion that (to speak with humility) commands conviction. I shall therefore wind up these remarks by stating—more fully than I did at the commencement of this Memoir, yet still in a very abridged form—the main points of the proof, as originally worked out, and now, I trust, sufficiently vindicated, of the German origin of the Etruscans:—

I. I demonstrated in a memoir entitled 'The Thoringa,' and which preceded that on 'The Etruscans,' i. That the 'Thoringa' were a family of Aryans divided into many branches, all bearing the same patronymic under varying forms as derived from an ancestral 'Thor,' whom I shewed to be identical with the classical Hercules,'—ii. That wherever the Thoringa race were found, they were in association with tribes of earlier development, bearing under various forms the general patronymic of Hruinga, derived from an ancestor named 'Hru,' whom I shewed to be identical with the eponymic 'Hlu,' 'Æol-,' from whom they were in one particular (classical) branch called 'Æolidæ,' or 'Pelasgi,'—and iii. That, in the background of both these races there towered a still remoter ancestral stock named everywhere, with the like superficial variations, 'Iotunga,' or Jötuns, after their patriarch 'Iot.' The Tyrrheni, or Etruscans, found their place by necessity under the first or latest of these three genealogical categories, and the Rhæti or Grisones, the next neighbours of the Etruscans, and their kinsmen by blood (the Etruscans themselves bearing, it is affirmed, the alternate name of 'Rasena') —under the second. The presumption necessarily was that all were nearly related to each other, and that the Tyrrheni were a branch of the great Thoringa family on the same footing as the Dorians of Greece and the Thuringi of Germany. They figured to that extent only—as one among many—in the memoir upon 'The Thoringa' here spoken of.

II. But in my essay on 'The Etruscans,' starting from the basis laid down in 'The Thoringa,' I showed at large, i. That the Tyrrheni-Pelasgi—whether as Pelasgi or Tyrrheni—were in religion, in political character, in manners (especially in the point of their respect for women), in their commercial instinct, and in their singular love for technical and legal proceedings, and so far as I had then traced it, in language, closely allied to the Teutonic or German race, especially in its Gothic, Low German, and Scandinavian branches,—the identity of Tages with Tuisco and of the Manes with the Mannus of the continental Germans giving a predominance of probability to the alternative of their Gothic extraction:—And, ii. That, as the nearest neighbours of the Tyrrheni and Rhæti in Italy and Germany were the Tervingi and Grutungi—the two great branches of the Gothic nation, subsequently styled Visi-Goths and Ostro-Goths, with whose language, as Goths, their own stood in near connection, the probability was that the

Tyrrheni were identical with the Tervingi and the
Rhæti with the Grutungi, although come off from
the Gothic stem at a far more remote period—the
'Rotnno' of Lydia, whose wars with the Pharaohs
are pictured in the Egyptian bas-reliefs, being, in
fact, primitive Grutungi, out of whom the Tyrrheni-
Pelasgi in all probability originally sprung. After the
close of the wanderings consequent upon the original
separation, and on their settlement in Greece and
Italy, the Tyrrheni, I argued, came once more into contact with their long-estranged Rhætian and Thuringian
kinsmen, who had pressed steadily Westward, North
of the Alps, and whose rusticity had naturally received
none of that polish and enlightenment from Lydia,
Phœnicia, Egypt, and Hellenic Greece, which had
civilized their Southern brethren. I founded further,
strongly, upon the identity of national character
exhibited by the piratical warfare waged at an interval
of two thousand years along the coasts of Europe by the
Tyrrheni-Pelasgi and by the Tyrki vikings of Scandinavia—as well as on the ready adoption by both races
of a high civilization after settlement, and their generation thereafter of mixed races of high intellect and
indomitable energy in ancient Greece, in ancient and
modern Italy, and in Northern and Hesperian Europe.
I observed too that the points of resemblance between
the Etruscans and the Thoringa of continental Germany were probably only less salient because the
original records of the Tervingi and Grutungi have
for the most part (with the exception of the Visi-
Gothic law, in its Latin translation*) utterly perished.

* A few most precious words and phrases of the original are preserved
in this translation as well as in that of the Salic Law.

III. These conclusions have, I presume to think, been confirmed by the results which have emerged from the analysis of the inscriptions given in the preceding pages. The Teutonic character of the Etruscan language has been (I trust) satisfactorily ascertained. It might have been doubtful, as the argument was left in 'The Etruscans,' whether they were more nearly akin to the Tervingi or the Tyrki of Scandinavia, but the fact (*inter alia*) now ascertained, that *pfand* was used rather than *wad*, for 'pignus,' and that the God worshipped as Thor in Scandinavia and as Donar and Thunner by the ancient Saxons and Thuringians, appears as 'Tunur' in the inscription of S. Manno—taken in connection with the argument from Tuisco and the Manes above noticed—weigh down the scale in favour of continental Germany. The closest link would appear to be with the Thuringi,—but the Thuringi were merely an outpost of the Tervingi, and their dialect still exhibits nearer affinity to the Gothic than any other. The link with the Tyrki and Asiani, or Asa, of Scandinavia was only less near, for they too were Thoringa and Asa—*i.e. Visi*-Goths. The historical fact that stands out from the whole inquiry is, that the Etruscans and Rhæti of antiquity, the Tervingi and Grutungi (Visi-Goths and Ostro-Goths), the Thuringi, and the Tyrki, or original Northmen of Scandinavia (the ancestors of Ivar of the Uplands, Rognvald the Magnificent, Rollo, and the highest families of the Normans), formed a group of tribes, branches of one and the same Thoringa or Tyrrhenian stock, dwelling in almost uninterrupted geographical contiguity; and the pulse of kindred blood beat continuously throughout the vast community. The presumption must be that the members of this family group used a language mutually intelligible, even to the latest date when the Etruscan was a living language. We have seen what the Etruscan language really was; and I feel certain therefore that the Emperor Claudius, the historian of Etruria, could have made himself understood without an interpreter had he met the great Hermanric face to face in early life.

ENVOI.

And now, my dear Anne, let me revert once more, ere laying down my pen, to the "two white days" commemorated in the Dedication which I have prefixed to these pages. It is pleasant to recall such sunny hours, and to take note of the contrasted sensations of by-gone times through the telescope of retrospection. The first occasion, that of our visit to Volterra, the queen-like capital of Northern Etruria, was in very early days—before Pio Nono had raised the cry of revolution in Europe—when he was still a simple monk in his cell at Imola—and when Gregory XVI. slumbered on St. Peter's chair at the Vatican. Mr. Dennis's work had not then been published, nor indeed that of Mrs. Hamilton Gray, which first and powerfully aroused the interest of England in the relics of Etruscan greatness. We had left our friend and fellow-traveller, the gifted and loyal Félicie de Fauveau, at San Gimignano—San Gimignano of the 'Bello Torri' and of Santa Fina—revelling among the frescoes of Benozzo Gozzoli and Domenico Ghirlandajo. We had spent a long day among the antiquities of Volterra, and we were sitting in the evening on the Cyclopean walls to the North of the town, inhaling the breeze, and admiring the shadows stealing over the vast extent of rolling wilderness, when the tinkle of a guitar and the pleasant voices of two young girls, gradually nearing us, dispelled the silence. They stopped when they saw us, to return our greeting. We spoke of their music, of their old songs, of the flower-draped ruins which formed our resting-place, but which to them conveyed no thought of their Etruscan forefathers; and then they offered to sing to us—to improvise—on whatever subject we might please to dictate. ONE was then with us, since gone to his rest—One most gentle, most wise, yet strong as he was gentle, and merciful as he was wise—whose genial temper added brightness to the fairest day—whose graceful genius lent an ideal charm to every aspect of material nature—and whose inspiring sympathy drew forth, like the lyre of Orpheus, the divine spark from the dullest natures with whom he came in contact. HE—whom no one has such cause to remember and to mourn for as yourself—said to these young Etruscan Muses, 'Sing to us of this fair Lady!' And they sang accordingly, to the music of their cithern—alternate strophes in your praise; much in the same strain doubtless as the minstrels depicted on the walls of the old sepulchres near us had piped and sung to the Etruscans of three thousand years ago—crediting you with every charm and wishing you every blessing, and a happy return home when your pilgrimage to their Southern land should have been accomplished. And here I point my contrast. We thought little then of the ancient possessors of the fair region we were sojourning in; or, I should rather say, their tombs, their paintings, their sarcophagi, their mirrors, their candelabra—the old walls themselves we sat upon—in a word, everything connected with the old Etruscans interested us except—themselves; they, the

creators of everything around us, were personally
stranger and more remote from us (so we thought)
than the old Egyptians,—we were aware of no special
tie between us and them except that of our common
humanity. So passed the hour.

It was otherwise when the Second Day marked
with white chalk in this Tuscan calendar dawned
upon us. Our friend above commemorated, the
ruling spirit of that visit to Volterra, had indeed
departed to the land—not of Etruscan interlunar
shadows, but of Christian realities; and the fine gold
of our enjoyment had thus been dimmed of its former
brightness; but Time, the Healer, had laid his hand
tenderly on the survivors, and they sought to be
cheerful because He would have wished them to
be so. It was a peaceful rather than an exciting
time that we passed among the tombs of CASTEL
D'ASSO—peaceful, at least, as regarded the seniors of
the party; for a generation had sprung up, undreamt
of by us at Volterra, and its eldest representative was
in full activity among us. Our caravan was a picturesque one as we left Viterbo, in charge of our
friend the Campagna farmer—or rather lord—of the
district we were bound to,—his attendants, horsemen
and foot, scouring the country on either side as we
advanced—over a far-extending plain, with the blue
hills that shelter Toscanella in front of us. Suddenly
we paused, brought up unexpectedly by a deep gulf
at our feet—rifted in the plain; its rocky walls (as
we looked down into it) sculptured into pillar and
pediment, with yawning apertures below, half visible
through brushwood—the necropolis, in a word, of an
ancient city that once crowned the adjacent table-

land, but of which not one stone now rests upon
another,—a ruined middle-age castle towering over
against us on the opposite side of the chasm. We
descended by a precipitous path and spent a long
summer's day in the winding valley, alternately
exploring the tombs, deciphering the inscriptions, and
resting under a shadowy rock when the sun was
powerful; while lizards rustled round us, the cicada
sang from the trees, and the distant shots of our
cacciatori occasionally came up the vale. Nor were
songs wanting, but proceeding from our own party;
for no fair Etruscan maidens volunteered their company,—the place is an absolute desert. Knowledge,
however, had brought to us a new sympathy which
had been wanting at Volterra, but now coloured the
entire scene with its warmer and peculiar hue. We
no longer felt, as formerly, strangers to those who
had streamed up the valley of yore in so many
long and sorrowing processions, and who still people
the yet unprofaned sepulchres. We had learnt to
believe, from the investigations which have suggested
the preceding pages, that these old Etruscans were
our own near kinsmen, blood of our blood and bone
of our bone, Thoringa of the South, as we, through
our distant Norwegian ancestry, were Thoringa from
Northern Thule. At Volterra our old-world sympathies had been excited by the simple epitaph of the
Roman girl preserved in the Museum,

'FELICULA VIXIT XIX ANNOS, DULCIS SUIS,'

rather than by the thought of the illustrious Cecinæ
ensepulchred under its walls,—speculating on her

early death and simple sweetness, Roman and Briton did not appear so far asunder—the tie of consanguinity, though distant, was still appreciable. But now it was different; the veil had been removed from our eyes,—and at Castel d'Asso we felt almost as if we were visiting the graves of our own ancestors. It was something surely for archæology thus to have re-knitted the broken links of time, brought us face to face with the old Etruscans as near kinsfolk, and invested their last resting-place with the pure, and homelike, and almost filial associations we then experienced. Nor can I think that the vision we thus indulged in—and which I venture to hope I have now substantiated—was as unreal and transient as that of the bridge of a thousand arches in the long winding valley of Bagdad,—or, to revert to Mr. Dennis's warning simile—a Sabine dream!

It was night;

"A dewy freshness fill'd the silent air,"—

the last song of the *contadino* had sunk to rest—the stars were shining brightly over us—the moon was rising over Monte Cimino—and a deep calm was in our own hearts, as we re-entered Viterbo.

APPENDIX.

No. I.

THE BILINGUAL INSCRIPTIONS.

(See p. 64, *supra.*)

I.

LEUKLE PHISIS LAV(I)NI
L · PHISIUS · L · LAUCI
(*Fabretti*, no. 794 *bis.* Clusium.)

The names 'Lavini' and 'Lauci' are, according to Fabretti, 'incertissima.'

II.

SENTI · VILINA
L · SENTIA · SEX · F
(*Fabretti*, no. 979. Chianciano.)

III.

L · F · TIITIA GNATA
MIISIA · ARUN
AR : MESI
(*Fabretti*, no. 1888. Perugia.)

IV.

L · KAE · KAULIAŚ
LART · CAI(I) CAULIAS
(*Fabretti*, no. 935. Montepulciano.)

The Etruscan seems merely rewritten here in Latin, or rather Old-Italic characters.

V. VI.

Tʜᴀɴɪᴀ ' ꜱᴜᴅᴇʀɴɪᴀ ᴀʀ · ꜰ
ᴛᴀ ꜱᴀᴅɴᴀʟ

ᴛᴀɴɪᴀ · ꜱᴜᴅᴇʀɴɪᴀ · ꜱᴀᴅɴᴀʟ

(*Fabretti*, no. 958 and 285.)

These evidently relate to the same lady, and come, I presume, from the same tomb, although the former (on a sepulchral tile) remains at Montepulciano, and the latter (on an *olla*) is now in the museum at Florence. Both are written in the Latin character; but ꜱᴀᴅɴᴀʟ is the Etruscan form of the matronymic in both.

VII.

Kᴜɪɴᴛᴇ · ŚɪNᴜ ᴀʀɴᴛɴᴀʟ
Q · ꜱᴇɴᴛɪᴜꜱ · ʟ · ꜰ · ᴀʀʀɪᴀ · ɴᴀᴛᴜꜱ

(*Fabretti*, no. 980. Chianciano.)

This has been discussed in the text, *supra*, p. 64.

VIII.

Vʟ · ᴀʟᴘʜɴɪ · ɴᴜᴠɪ ' ᴋᴀɪɴᴀʟ
C · ᴀʟꜰɪᴜꜱ · ᴀ · ꜰ · ' ᴄᴀɪɴɴɪᴀ · ɴᴀᴛᴜꜱ

(*Fabretti*, no. 792. Chiusi.)

See p. 71, *supra* in regard to 'Velus' and 'Caius.' ɴᴜᴠɪ appears to correspond with 'A. F.,' which last is to be read 'Auli Filius.' ɴᴜᴠɪ is probably *knabe, nefi,* 'nepos,' the word usually used for grandson, and which was not unknown to the Etruscans, although used (according to Roman testimony) in a disparaging sense. We have it in Greek as νῆπιος; but I suspect it is here used in the sense of 'junior,' νεώτερος.

IX.

AELCHEPHULNIAELCHES KIARTHIALISA
Q · FOLNIUS · A · F · POM FUSCUS
(*Fabretti*, no. 251. Arezzo.)

Already discussed in the text, pp. 67 *sqq.*

X.

. . . . SPEDII · TULLIO
LAUTNATA . . . .
SERTURUS . . . .
(*Fabretti*, no. 934. Montepulciano.)

This inscription (on a sepulchral tile) is very imperfect; and I think that as many letters are wanting after LAUTNATA and after SERTURUS as before SPEDII TULLIO. It will be remembered that, the Etruscan being written from right to left, the deficient portions in the original are wholly to the left-hand of the reader.

The first line doubtless records the husband's name, part of which, 'Tullius,' is clearly given. The dative case is unusual; but in another sepulchral inscription of Montepulciano, a Latin one, (no. 951 of Fabretti,) the name is similarly given, 'Aullo · Larci.' 'Spedo' also occurs as a surname—'Ar. Spedo,' 'Vel. Spedo,' in Latin inscriptions of the same locality (no. 956 and no. 957 of Fabretti). The S in SERTURUS identifies LAUTNATA as the -SA or wife of SERTUR, or SERTURU; and the presumption is, that the names 'Tullius' and 'Sertur' correspond. ANNIA THANA occurs in Fabretti, no. 953, and THANIA SUDERNIA as in the preceding page, all three inscriptions being at Montepulciano; and I read LAUTNATA . . . . therefore as LAUTNA THANA.

With these facts before us, and in the view of what will follow, I should suggest 'Mr. and Mrs. Tailor' as the equivalent of the respective names in English. The accepted etymology of 'tailor' and of the cognate 'tailler,' 'tagliare,' 'tallare,' from the Latin 'talea'—the branch of a tree, cut and sharpened like a stake, and planted in order to produce a new tree—is quite insufficient. The word proceeds, I think, from *theil-*, *theil-en*, to divide, in the sense of a 'cutter out;' and that this is the primary conception, the central idea of tailorship may perhaps be supported by the lexicographical rendering of *theilchen* as a 'snip,' to say nothing of *schneider* having the same signification. TULLIUS thus appears to me, in the present case at least, equivalent to 'Tailor.' SENTUR, on the other hand, may be a word formed from *smerz*, *smerz-en*, to smarten up, or botch—the precise signification of the Latin equivalent, 'sartor,' and the noun formed from this would be *smerz-dri*, 'sart-or,' SENTUR. That I am serious in these suggestions (although I cannot resist a smile) will appear when I point out that the surname SPEDO is apparently formed from 'suo,' to sew or stitch, whence 'sut-um,' what is stitched, and 'sutor,' a sewer,' or—as by accepted usage, a shoe-maker or cobbler,—'su' being equivalent to 'sp' in 'sp-edo,' while the Teutonic *fadam*, thread, must have originally been written *sfadam* or *spadam*. The two elements in the name, 'Spedo Tullius,' thread and snip, thus speak for each other. I suspect he was a tailor; but the gentle craft of 'souters' may have been represented by 'Thania Sudernia,' whose bilingual epitaph is given *supra*. 'Monto Follonica' rises to the N.W. of Montepulciano, and seems to reflect the kindred idea of fulling-mills. And those who have noticed the extraordinary tenacity with which old associations cling verbally to certain localities through every change of time and circumstances will not scout the suggestion before testing it, that the idea of 'botching' which lies at the root of the preceding etymology may perhaps survive in the name 'Bucelli' attached to the palace where the inscriptions here commented upon are preserved. My impression is that Montepulciano was a great settlement of fullers, tailors, and (possibly) shoemakers; and that the town derived its Etruscan name—as yet unknown—from the root *fleck-en*, *flick-en*, 'sarcire,' to 'botch,' in German,—that Etruscan name having been handed down to us (I conceive), substantially unchanged, in the medieval name of the place, 'Castellum Politianum.'

The calligraphy of Montepulciano is marked by many peculiarities.

XI.

Arth · kanzna | varnalisla
·c · cæsius · c · f · varia ; nat

(*Fabretti*, no. 252, tab. xxiii. At Florence.) *

Discussed in part at p. 66. I cannot at present account for Autu · and C · as equivalents. The 'C · F ·' only occurs in the Latin inscription, in accordance with the usage noticed under the second result enumerated in the section upon 'Sepulchral Inscriptions,' p. 62, *supra*.

XII.

C · vensius · c · f · caius
vel : venzile : alphnalisle

(*Fabretti*, no. 700. Chiusi.)

This inscription relates to husband and wife, or concubine. While the Latin *prænomen* 'C ·' agrees with the Etruscan vel · through the affinities noticed in the preceding Memoir, the *agnomen* 'Caius' must, by analogy, have been formed from the mother's name Alpnsi, or 'Alpinia;' and a point of connection may be suggested in both 'gaia' and *alp*—the latter denoting the upland pastures and thickets of the mountain, which the Etruscans, I suspect, called 'alps' and the Romans 'gaia,' as shewn *supra*, p. 72. Here, again, 'C · F ·' is unrepresented in the Etruscan.

XIII.

C · licini c · f · nigri ·
v · lekne v · | thapirnal

(*Fabretti*, no. 253. Siona. Now at Florence.)

Discussed in the text, p. 70.

---

* The Etruscan surname given as Kazzna in Fabretti's text appears to read rather as Kiszzna or Kiszzpia in the engraving. But it occurs distinctly as Kaszna on an 'arca' at Montepulciano. *Fabretti*, no. 887.

XIV.

C · CASSIUS · C · F · ' SATURNIKUS
V · KAZI · K · KLAN

(*Fabretti*, no. 460. Arezzo.)

The word KLAN has been discussed in the text, p. 65. The isolated K · in the Etruscan version does not represent 'C. F.,' the proper equivalent for which would be v, but the initial of V. Kazi's matronymic, which is represented by the agnomen 'Saturninus' in the Latin version. 'Saturninus' appears to point to that city of almost primeval antiquity, Saturnia, as its origin.

XV.

PUP · VELIMNA AU KAHATIAL
P · VOLUMNIUS · A · F · VIOLENS CAFATIA · NATUS

(*Fabretti*, no. 1496. Perugia.)

Already discussed in the text, pp. 70 *sqq.*

XVI.

A · TITIUS · A · F · SCAE · CALIS
A · TITI · A · VANIAL

(*Fabretti*, no. 936. Montepulciano.)

By analogy with other cases, the Latin 'Scae · Calis' must be viewed as an *agnomen* formed from the name of 'Vania,' the mother of A. Titius. The idea common to the two names—at least, as conceived of by the personage commemorated or by the friends who composed his bilingual epitaph—is that of wandering, with the moral idea superinduced, of defection, error. 'Van-ia,' in this point of view, would represent our *wandern, wandeln*, with the associated idea of defect, diminution, falling away, or starting aside, as derived from the root *van, wan*, one of extreme antiquity. 'Scae · Calis' I take to represent 'Scæva Callis,' a combination analogous to the 'devius calles' spoken of e.g. by Livy,—'callis' denoting a narrow path or track going off from the main road, but with the particular sense affixed here by 'Scaeva,' viz. to the left hand. The left hand was fortunate according to the Roman auspices, but unlucky according to those of other nations, including, I presume, the Etruscan; and 'Scaeva Callis' would thus be a metaphorical equivalent to 'Van-ia' in the sense of defect or aberration, as above suggested.

XVII.

ATH · UNATA · VARNAL RA
M · OTACILIUS · RUFUS · VARIA · NATUS
(*Fabretti*, no. 794. Clusium.)

Discussed at large in the text, pp. 74 sqq.

XVIII.

... F · ATIUS · L · F · STE · HARUSPE(X) | FULGURIATOR
KAPHATES · LR · LR · NETSVIS · TRUTNVT · PHRONTAK
(*Fabretti*, no. 69, tab. vi. bis. Pesaro.)

Fully discussed likewise in the text, pp. 82 sqq.

XIX.

Fragments exist of a bronze tablet, discovered at Chiusi, on which a bilingual inscription exists, but in so mutilated a state as to be quite unintelligible. Two of the fragments are given by Fabretti, no. 801 bis, and tab. xxxii.; but the plate and the transcript do not entirely correspond. Another fragment was bought by Mr. Clarke at Chiusi, and a fourth was in the possession of P. Matranga when Fabretti wrote.

No. II.

GLOSSARY (*Abridged*) OF ETRUSCAN WORDS KNOWN TO US OTHERWISE THAN THROUGH THE INSCRIPTIONS.

The following are the results (abridged) of an examination of four distinct classes of words positively or presumptively Etruscan, and now shown to be akin to, if not identical with ancient Teutonic. The first class consists of Etruscan words transmitted to us as such by the classical writers, with their equivalent meanings in Latin or Greek,—the second, of words designative of persons, offices, insignia, or things miscellaneous, in use among the Romans, but which are expressly stated to have been adopted from the Etruscans, and the names of which are therefore presumptively Etruscan, and especially so in cases where those names are manifestly not immediately derived from Latin roots,—the third includes the names of deities and other supernatural beings belonging to Etruscan mythology; and the fourth, the proper names of cities, districts, &c. reported, or which are reasonably held, to have been founded and named—in some cases, re-named— by the Etruscans. I have not attempted to keep the words belonging to the two first of these classes separate in the following enumeration. In each instance where a word is transmitted to us as Etruscan by a classical writer, the authority is added within brackets.

I would remark on the threshold that, although in a few instances the etymology of an Etruscan word may bear an equal resemblance to the Teutonic and to Greek or Latin, still the mere fact of its being cited by the Greeks or

Romans as Etruscan, and foreign (as they understood it) to classical speech, transfers it to the Teutonic side of the argument, and entitles us to found upon it (if we choose to exercise the right) in proof of the nationality contended for. Occasionally we find a compound word of which one portion is common to Teutonic and to Latin, and the other peculiar to the North; and such compounds are of course *à fortiori* to be dealt with in the like manner. But the greater number of the words recorded as Etruscan will be found, I think, to be purely Teutonic.

You must not misunderstand me as proposing to derive these Etruscan words from the Teutonic or German language proper, but from roots and verbal formations which I infer to have existed in the mother Teutonic tongue from which both German and Etruscan are descended. I do not, for example, when I approximate the Latin 'diribitores' (v. *infra*, under 'Senatus') and the Teutonic *droppetári*, intend to derive the Latin from the German word, but to point out that the two words are derived from one original root through different lines of descent, under the influence of the genius of the original, generative, but superseded mother-tongue perpetuating itself throughout the lines of its descendants. The parallelism in question affords a proof that both these words and the languages they belong to spring from a common stock and origin. I do not, as a rule, compare these Etruscan words with those in the other Aryan languages, as the Teutonic is sufficient for my purpose, and is the nearest in consanguinity to them. But this rule has its exception.

I would protest, however, on broader grounds, against the prejudice, at first sight most natural, that Teutonic or German must be reckoned as a modern language, far more recent and young than Greek or Latin, and that it would be absurd therefore to attempt to explain Etruscan words by the light of Teutonic etymologies. We are apt at all times to think of nations as beginning to exist only from the time when we first hear of them through history,—and still more apt are we to forget that the antiquity of a language is not to be measured by that of its existing literature. Least of all, ought these fallacies to be allowed in relation to such a language, such a stock, as that of the Teutons. There were Germans before Tacitus, and there must have been a German literature before Ulphilas. It would not be difficult to prove that in very many instances German (in the broadest sense), even as spoken at present, preserves the primitive forms of Aryan and Japhetan speech with a purity and precision which is entirely abraded and worn down even in Sanscrit. German is, to say the least, the contemporary and sister of Sanscrit, Zendic, Latin, and Greek, and is thus a sufficient touchstone for the purpose to which I now apply it.

FIRST GROUP.—*Words expressive of the Relations of Life and Society.*

[LANS, AL, KLAN, SA, and SLA, words originally noticed under this group of the Glossary, have been discussed in the text, pp. 143, 64, 65, 68, and 66, *supra*.]

1. AGALLETON, a child (*Hesychius*).—The same word as *agaleizi*, or *agalleizir*, one that is careful and attentive, the roots being, i. *aga*, *aki*, discipline, and, ii. *leitj-an*, *led-ian*, *led-a*, to lead—equivalent to 'one led along by discipline,' i.e. a youth, or to use the exact etymological equivalent, a 'lad '—in the state of pupilage.

2. ATRIUM,—the inner court, open to the sky, and provided with an 'impluvium' or pond for the reception of rain-water in the centre, which formed the usual entrance-hall (as it were) of Etruscan and afterwards of Roman houses. From i. *wato*, *waetr*, *udr*, *wasser*, water, and ii. *heim*, implying a dwelling.—Equivalent therefore to the 'water-tank,' or 'place for water.'

3. DRUNA,—government (*Hesychius*).—From *drott*, lord, and *at drottna*, to govern, according to Dr. Donaldson.

4. LUCUMO, plur. LUCUMONES,—the title of the chief magistrates of the twelve Etruscan cities.—From i. *lag*, law, and ii. *guma, gomo*, 'homo,' a man, but in the sense (preserved chiefly in the Old-Northern or Scandinavian languages) of 'custos' or guardian (as in *brútigomo, brydguma*, bridegroom),—the compound 'Lucumo' thus signifying 'the guardian of the law,' or chief magistrate. The title is thus analogous to that of 'lag-madr' or 'lag-man' of the North, which was attached to an office strongly resembling that of 'Lucumo' in Etruria.

SECOND GROUP.—*Words descriptive of Dress, martial and domestic.*

1. BULLA,—the plate or boss of metal worn as an ornament by the sons of the Roman patricians, and which was adopted from the Etruscans.—From *balg-an*, or *belg-an*, to swell or boil, like a bubble—which 'bulla' also signified in Latin.

2. CASSIS, originally CASSILA. (*Festus*.)—A helmet, made of metal, as distinguished from the 'galea,' which was only of hide. (Adopted from the Etruscans, according to Isidore.) The same word fundamentally as our English 'hat.' From *huotj-an*, 'custodire,' to guard in the sense of covering; from whence *huotil*, a protector, in a martial sense, and *huotila*, a mitre or tiara, evidently the same word as CASSILA, the letters 'c' and 'h,' 's' and 't' being constantly interchangeable.

3. BALTEUS,—the military girdle, or belt. (*Varro*.)—From *fald-an*, to fold, or bind.

4. LÆNA,—a woollen cloak.—Like the Greek χλαινα and the Latin 'lana,' wool, from *liuhhan, lyccan*, 'vellere,' to tear—as the fleece, 'vellus,' was (formerly, it would seem) torn from the sheep.

5. STROPPUS,—a fillet (*Festus*).—From *strouf-en*, to bind. Hence our English *strap*.

6. TOGA,—the well-known robe of the Romans, borrowed from the Etruscans.—A Latin form of the Teutonic *deki, thecki, decha*, implying anything worn as a covering. *Dok* is

the existing name for the black *peplus* worn by women at funerals in Sweden. (*Ihre.*)—From *theckja*, 'tegere,' to cover. These words represent merely dialectic varieties of one language.

THIRD GROUP.—*The Chariot; and Amusements, public and private.*

1. ΩΑΓΟΣ,— ὄχημα, a chariot. (*Hesychius.*) — Considered by Dr. Donaldson a short Pelasgian form for ἀπήνη, a chariot. But its root must be sought further off. The ἀπήνη was a car made of wicker-work, and is described by Homer as four-wheeled and drawn by mules. It was essentially a vehicle of peace, and distinct from the δίφρος, or ἅρμα, the chariot of war.—From *web-an*, to weave, *gaWeb-an*, to weave together, *ga Web, gWeb*, a ' texture,' or weaving together.—Equivalent to a ' basket-carriage.'

2. SUBULO,—a 'tibicen' (*Festus* and *Varro*), or player on the Etruscan or double flute, made of the reed—a character constantly introduced in the festive ceremonies of the Etruscan tombs.—From i. *sub, sæf, sif*, a reed, (a word of Egyptian * and Semitic as well as Aryan antiquity,) and ii. *bláhan*, to blow.—Equivalent to a ' reed-blower.'

3. LANISTA,—a ' gladiator ' or ' carnifex ' (*Isidore*), one who keeps and trains gladiators.—From i. *lón*, hire, and ii. *hazus* (that is, *hatrus*, or *hastus*), in the sense of an athlete.— Equivalent to a ' keeper of athletes for hire,' or ' one who professionally trains athletes.' The Old-High-German *hazo-sun* is rendered ' palæstritæ,' that is directors of the ' palæstra,' to wit, of the wrestling-school, or place for practising athletic exercises. This gives the further sense of LANISTA as he teacher or trainer of his ' familia ' or school. There is no intimation of gladiatorial combats (strictly so called) in this etymology; and I therefore infer that they were of subsequent introduction.

4. HISTER,—a pantomimic actor.—From *gasa, jasa*, to

* *Sb, sba*, implies a flute in old Egyptian.

jest—a word corresponding to the character of the 'hister' and (Latin) 'histrio,' from its original dignity of pantomimic action through all its successive shades of degradation.— Equivalent to our English 'jester'—*gasdri, jasdri*—alike in etymologic formation and signification.

5. LUDUS, LUDII, and LUDIONES,—play, players, &c. (*Dionys. Hal.*).—From *leitj-an, led-ian*, to lead,—their character being originally that of leaders in public processions, religious and civil. The armed dance, the mock fight, the josts and mockeries, scurrility and grossness that succeeded (the latter perpetuated to us in the words 'ludibrium,' 'ludicra ars,' &c.), are all secondary to this dominant idea. The 'ludio,' like the 'hister,' was introduced into Rome from Etruria.

6. LUCAR,—the price of admission to the public plays and shows performed by the *ludiones, histriones,* &c. As these were Etruscan, the word LUCAR is probably so likewise.— From i. *laik-, leik-, laich-*, play (especially of a martial character), and ii. *er, ar, eyr,* money.—Equivalent to 'play-money.' As in the case of *jasa* and *hister,* the word *laik-* corresponds to 'ludere' in all its successive shades of meaning.

FOURTH GROUP.—*Words descriptive of Animals, Plants, the Heavens, the Elements, &c.*

I. *Animals, Quadrupeds, Birds, &c.*

1. DAMNUS,—ἴππος, a horse. (*Hesych.*)—"This," observes Dr. Donaldson, "seems to be an Etruscan, not a Pelasgian word, and suggests at once the O. N. *tam=domitus*, assuetus, cicur; N. H. G. *zahm.*" It is one of Donaldson's happiest approximations. The specific character of the DAMNUS is to be gathered from the root *zahm*, 'frenum,' *zahmen*, 'frenare,' giving the sense of 'bridled;' and *zaumen*, according to Wachter, "dicitur proprie de jumentis." DAMNUS thus signifies a pack-horse, or horse of burden. But DAMNUS is itself, I think, the identical word *jumentum* in an Etruscan form; the initial 'd' representing 'j,' as 'Di-anus' represents

'J-anus;' while the final 'n' is omitted according to Etruscan usage, as illustrated in the text of this volume, *passim*. If so, DAMNUS must be reckoned as a word common alike to the Pelasgians and the Teutons proper.

2. CAPRA,—a she-goat. (*Hesych.*)—I should rather think this word of Celtic origin, and connected with the *gafr*, *gauvr* of the Breton, the *gavyr* of the Welsh, and the *gabhar* of the Gaelic dialects, all implying 'goat.'

3. ARIMI,—τίθηκοι, apes. (*Strabo.*)—Probably a Phœnician word, and derivable from the Hebrew *charúm*, 'simus,' snub-nosed, as shewn by Dr. Donaldson.

4. ANTAR,—the eagle. (*Hesych.*)—This has been discussed sufficiently in the text, p. 74 *supra*.

5. ARACOS,—the hawk. (*Hesych.*)—The same word as the Greek ἱέραξ, 'accipiter,' and the Icelandic *haukr*; and either from *aro*, *arao*, greedy, or (which is more probable) from a common root with 'capys' and *habuh*.

6. CAPYS,—'falco' (*Servius*), the falcon. The Greek γύψ and Teutonic *habuh*, 'accipiter.'—From *haban*, *hafa*, *haben*, 'habere,' 'capere,' to have—that is, to possess oneself of, by taking or seizing.

7. GNIS,—the crane. (*Hesych.*)—Evidently, I think, the Teutonic *gaNós*, *gNós*, *genoss*, implying a 'sodalis, collega, commilito,' or 'companion,'—in allusion to the gregarious habits of the bird, its peculiar characteristic as noticed by Pliny and the ancients.

II. *Plants, or Vegetable Substances.*

1. ATÆSON,—ἀναδενδράς, (*Hesych.*), the wild vine, which climbs up trees, or 'vitis arbustiva.'—From i. *at*, equivalent I conceive to 'vitis,' the vine, and ii. *as-*, *as-ón*, to creep.—Equivalent to 'the creeping' or 'climbing vine.' Pliny's advice, to prune the (cultivated) vine well "ne in altitudinem repat,' lest it creep up into height, illustrates the appropriateness of the latter half of this rendering.

2. APLUDA,—the chaff of corn, or froth of pottage, which is blown off by the breath or wind. Used also for anything

light, unsubstantial, and worthless. (*Aulus Gellius* and *Festus*. Gellius is uncertain whether the word is Tuscan or Gallic.) From i. *ob*, from or away, with the sense of detraction, and ii. *lidan*, to go—a word connected with a host of terms expressive of what is worthless and execrable.—Equivalent therefore to 'that which flies off, and is vile and unprofitable.'

3. FLOCES,—the inferior wine made by squeezing the fleshy or gross part of the grape, which had been left as dregs in the wine-press. (*Aul. Gellius.*)—From *fleisc*, flesh, fat, or pulp.

III. *The Heavens, Elements, &c.*

1. FALANDUM,—'cœlum' (*Festus*), the heavens.—From i. *uf*, up, and ii. *land*, region.—Equivalent to 'the upper region,' like the O. N. *uppheimr*, the name by which heaven was known to the Jötuns, or giants, who, I apprehend, were, in an historical sense, Juthungi and Goths, and ancestors of the Tyrrheni and Tyrki. FALANDUM may be the same word as 'Olympus,' the *nd* taking the form of *m* or *mp*, as is often the case, e. g. in *limo, linde, Flamand, Flandrensis*, &c., the *nd* usually prevailing in the northern dialects of the common language.

2. AUKELOS,—ἕως, the dawn. (*Hesych.*)—From i. *augj-an*, to manifest, and ii. *lios*, light—or, possibly, ἠλ-, the sun.—Equivalent to 'the revelation of the light' of day.

3. ANT.E,—ἄνεμοι, the winds. (*Hesych.*)—Noticed in the text, p. 75, *supra*.

4. ANDAS,—'Boreas,' the North, or the North wind. (*Hesych.*)—This word has been dealt with in the text, p. 75, *supra*.

FIFTH GROUP.—*Words expressive of Matters of Common Life; and Miscellaneous.*

1. MANTISSA,— a make-weight; that which is added to the weight in the retail of provisions or other merchandise,

but which is of an inferior description, and valueless. (*Festus.*)—From i. *meinida*, that which is 'propositum,' proposed or offered, and (perhaps) ii. *wahsan*, to increase; or possibly, simply, the Gothic *mein-aiths*, perjury, in the sense of a fraudulent proffer.

2. NANOS,—πλανήτης, a wanderer, in the Tyrrhenian speech, according to Tzetzes in his commentary on Lycophron, who applies the epithet to Odysseus or Ulysses.—Dr. Donaldson views this interpretation as "only a guess based on the πλαναῖοι of Lycophron," and considers the name equivalent to the Greek νάνος and Latin 'nanus,' a pigmy. (*Varron.* p. 191.) He supports this identification with great ingenuity, basing it on the conjecture of Dr. Kenrick that Ὀλυσσεύς implies ὀ-λυγος, λιτός, little. (*Ibid.* p. 171.) But I know of no authority for degrading the brave and sage hero of Ithaka to the stature of a Lilliputian. Mazochius, in his additions to Voss's 'Etymologicon,' argues that NANOS is a corrupt reading for 'natus,' or 'nadus'—a word he supposes to have been derived from the Hebrew and Phoenician *nad*, 'erro,' a wanderer,—and, were this admissible, Dr. Donaldson's suggestion that the 'Tyrrheni' of Tzetzes should be read 'Tyrii'—the people, not of Tyrrhenia but of Tyre—would be singularly happy. But it is not necessary, I think, to go to such a distance. NANOS appears to me to be simply NAN-TOS or 'navita,' ναύτης, i. e. 'the sailor,' with the last letter, 't,' omitted, a frequent practice in Etruscan inscriptions,—and this was a character constantly attributed to Ulysses by the ancients. In a secondary sense, indeed, as a wanderer "per mare, per terras," he figures on a coin cited by Lanzi as a beggar, with the inscription 'Natis,' which corresponds with the Etruscan word, read as I read it, NAN-TOS. The coins, again, of the Mamilii, lords of Tusculum, the reputed descendants of Ulysses, represented that hero in the dress of a traveller, with his staff in his hand, and accompanied by his dog—unless indeed (as I suspect) the representation be that of Hermes, the remoter ancestor (through Ulysses) of the Mamilii. The name 'Ulysses' or 'Odysseus'—'Ulysses' being, in fact, the older, at least the Æolic form—tracked to its ethnological origin

in remote antiquity, associates itself, it is true, like the kindred forms 'Pelasgi' and 'M'loch'ha,' (and we may even suggest the name of 'Peleg,') with the idea of 'wanderer,' although not ultimately founded upon it.

3. NEPOS,—a spendthrift. (*Festus.*)—The same word, I conceive, as the Latin 'nepos,' a nephew or grandson, but with a further moral signification, as collaterally developed in the Teutonic dialects proper; and identical in both respects with our familiar *knabo, knapi,* boy—or knave.

4. AQUILEX,—a discoverer and collector of springs for aqueducts, a peculiarly Etruscan profession, the "Tuscus aquilex" of Varro.—From i. *aha, á, ahwa,* water, and ii. *gaLesan, lesa,* to collect.—Equivalent to 'a water-collector.'

5. VORSUS,—a field one hundred feet square, so called by the Etruscans and Umbrians, according to an old writer 'De Limitibus.'—From *fior,* four; *fior-ise,* four-ish, or square.

6. QUINQUATRIA, or QUINQUATRUS,—a festival celebrated on the fifth day after the Ides.—From i. 'quinque,' five, and (perhaps) ii. *aftar,* after. The TRIATRUS, SEXATRUS, and SEPTIMATRUS of Tusculum, and the DECIMATRUS of the Faliscans, celebrated respectively on the third, sixth, seventh, and tenth days after the Ides, form one category with QUINQUATRUS.—Equivalent to 'of, or belonging to, the third, fifth, sixth, seventh, or tenth' day 'after' the Ides.

7. DURNUS,—κάνθαρος, a drinking-cup, with two handles. (*Hesych.*)—Like *einBar,* the Teutonic equivalent of the Latin 'amphora,' from *beran,* to bear or carry.

8. ARSE VERSE,—words inscribed on the threshold of a house, and explained by Festus as signifying 'averte ignem,' 'avert, or ward off, fire!'—ARSE would appear to correspond to *vard, vairths,* implying watchfulness against, and VERSE to πῦρ, *fiur,* fire.

9. RIL AVIL.—Already discussed in the text, p. 04, under 'Sepulchral Inscriptions.'

SIXTH GROUP.—*Names of Etruscan Deities, celestial and infernal, including the Genii, Lares, &c.*

I. *The Gods,—general name.*

1. ÆSAR, the name of 'Deum,' God, among the Etruscans, according to Suetonius; and Αἰσοί, 'Æsi,' signifying θεοί, gods, among the Tyrrheni, according to Hesychius.—K. O. Müller and Donaldson connect both titles, and justly, with the Scandinavian *As*, 'deus,' pl. *Æsir*. Donaldson further compares them with the *Aīsa*, the Fate, or Destiny, of the Greeks. It is clear from the passage in Suetonius that the word 'Æsar,' translated as 'Deum,' gives but a part of its Etruscan meaning, while the words of the oracle "inter deos," as reported by him, supply the omission, and prove that 'Æsar' implied, not the Supreme God, absolutely, but 'the Gods,' generally—answering, letter (almost) for letter, to the 'Æsir' of Scandinavia. It may further be noted, 1. That the Goths, according to Jornandes, styled their 'proceres' or heroes 'semideos, *i.e.* Anses;' and 2. That the O. N. *ás*, A.-S. *ós*, 'numen' or deity, the singular of 'Æsar,' takes the form of *ans*, likewise, in O. H. German. These forms *as* and *ans*, but more especially the latter, and the feminine form *ana, anna*, in the sense of 'numen,' occur continually in the composition of the names of Etruscan and Latin deities, as will be seen hereafter. Perhaps these words are all connected with the Assyrian and Babylonian, that is, the Semitic and Hamitic *Ana*, implying, originally, Deity. (*Rawlinson's Five Great Monarchies*, vol. i. p. 144.)

II. *The Three Great Gods of the Etruscans.*

1. TINIA, or TINA,—otherwise Ζήν, 'Zeus,' or 'Jupiter'— the ruler of the material heavens and wielder of the thunderbolt. The 'Dii Complices' and 'Dii Consentes,' twelve in number, were his assessors or councillors in heaven.—The name TIN-, Ζήν, stands in etymological regard to 'Thor,' as

the Assyrian 'Asshur' does to the Samaritan (Cushite) 'Astun,' the 'r' and 'n' being interchanged. The name TIN-IA, again, is akin to that of 'Thun-ar,' the name under which Thor was worshipped by the Thuringi—the Tyrrheni or Thoringa of the North.* Ζην and TIN-IA may, in remoter antiquity, be identical with 'O-din,' 'Wo-den,' whose name corresponds with that of 'Va-Dana,' 'the Lord Dana,' the Babylonian equivalent of the Assyrian 'Thourras' or Thor,— the 'O-,' 'Wo-' in the name of the German and Scandinavian God answering to the honorific prefix 'Va.'—The association of Tinia, Thunar, Thor, with the thunder-bolt is through the assonance of the root *tan-*, *ton-*, as in *stanayitnu* (Sansc.), *tonitrus*, thunder.

2. KUPRA, or CUPRA; the Greek 'Here' or Ἑρρα, and Latin 'Juno,'—worshipped under her Etruscan name, according to Strabo, at 'Cupra Maritima,' on the coast of the Adriatic. KUPRA is primarily (I conceive) derived from 'Hra,' Ἑρρ-ος, through the archaic form 'Ηρerr-,' producing 'Hpr,' 'Kupr-a.' But, in a special sense, KUPRA expresses the character of Juno as presiding over contracts and obligations of every description involving good faith among mankind, and especially that of marriage—answering thus to the Teutonic *koupári*, formed from the primeval root *kp*, *koupen*, to bargain or covenant. It is, moreover, in the name of KUPRA, thus understood, that we find the significance of the 'æs,' or *copper*, which played so important a symbolical part in the ancient 'mancipium' or contract. The Etruscan 'KUPRA' is evidently the same name as 'Cybele' of Phrygia, the 'r' taking the place of 'l' in the final syllable.

4. MENERVA, MENURKA, MENERUKA,—the Minerva of Rome, and analysable as 'Men-erva, -rka, -eruka.'—A compound, I think, of i. *çpenta* (Zendic), holy—the 'ç' being elided and the 'p' changed to 'm;' and ii. *urva* (Zend.), soul, or spirit, —although the 'k' in 'Men-rka' indicates a distinct root expressing itself in the second portion of the name. This root is represented in parallel descent in the Greek title of

* Since this was written, I have met with his name as TUNUR in the Inscription of S. Manno. See p. 118, *supra*.

Athene, 'Ἐργάνη, the 'Worker,' — Minerva being thus viewed as the Goddess of practical ability. This secondary character of Minerva has been influenced by association of the initial title 'Min-' with μην- (as in μηνύω), 'mene,' mani, and with the Teutonic mah, mag-an, 'posse,' to 'may,' or be able. Every characteristic of Minerva, or Atheno 'Ἐργάνη, is reflected and represented by Teutonic words derived from the root mah. The name of 'Athene' proximately connects itself with átman (Sanscr.), soul, the exact equivalent of urva; but has a remoter origin which I need not discuss here. The character of 'Pallas' does not appear to attach to the Etruscan and Roman Minerva.

III. *The Dii Complices and Dii Consentes—general names for the twelve principal Gods of Etruria, Councillors of Tinia.*

1. DII COMPLICES.—From gaPlegan, to act as ministers, —formed from plegan, to take counsel, care for, or govern. 'Ga' becomes 'con' or 'cum' in the Latinized form of the particle.—Equivalent to 'the Gods Councillors.'

2. DII CONSENTES,—so called from their common origin, pilgrimage, fate, and destiny, rising and setting together, as Varro describes them.—'Consentes' is a Latinized form of the Teutonic gaSiathya, gaSinda, kaSinde, 'comites, satellites,'—the root being sind, sidh, a path, journey, fate.— Equivalent to 'the Gods Companions.'

IV. *The Dii Novensiles, or Nine Great Gods who had the privilege of hurling thunder-bolts.*

1. DII NOVENSILES,—so called, proximately, from i. niun, nine, and ii. sello, colleague; and thus far equivalent to 'the Nine Colleagues' or 'Companions.' But, more remotely, the final -SILES appears to me to point to the root sphil, to split or splinter, whence 'sil-ex,' flint, and πελ-, the root of πέλεκυς, an axe, spear, or arrow-head, which I take to have been the primitive symbol of lightning; while NOVEN

similarly may be connected with νέφ-ος, 'nub-es,' a most ancient root, which we have in a fuller sense in Erse as *neamh*, heaven. But, I am inclined to think, it ascends as high as the title 'Num,' 'Nef,' that of the 'Spirit'-God, whom the early Japhetans worshipped in common (as I think may be shewn) with the old Egyptians. If this be so, the idea of 'Nine' colleagues is of subsequent aggregation.*

V. *The Dii Involuti—the Shrouded, or Hidden Gods.*

1. DII INVOLUTI.—The title has its root in the Teutonic *falh-an, fal-a*, to veil or conceal; with its derivative *falth-an, fald-an*, to fold or bind; whence *ana-gaFaldan, in-gaFaldan*, to wrap up, or infold. These deities, unnamed and nameless, ruled over Gods and men; and even Tinia bowed to them in obedience.

VI. *The Etruscan Gods proper,—exclusive of the Three Great Gods, Tinia, Kupra, and Minerva, and omitting those whose names are not strongly marked as Etruscan.*†

1. ANIL, Atlas,—so named in paintings representing him supporting the globe symbolical of the heavens.—From *hvarb*, the root of *hvarbo, hverfla, hverbalón, hrirvil, whirl*, and a host of other words comprehensive of all the conceptions entertained respecting Atlas, and having an especial

---

* It must be very ancient, however, and before the Lithuanians separated from the Etruscans, if, at least, I am justified in comparing the Nine Norensikes with the Nine Sons of Perkons, of whom, according to a popular rhyme, we are told, "Father Perkons has nine sons; Three strike, three thunder, Three lighten."—Ralston's *Songs of the Russian People*, p. 90.

† These are, Apollo, Camillus (as a name of Hermes), Ceres, Charun, the Dioscuri, Eileithuia, Fatuus, Hercules, Janus, Latona, Lucina, Mars, Ops, Pales, Saturn, Sylvanus. All of these deities were worshipped by the Etruscans and are reckoned as Etruscan by Mr. Dennis, or by authorities cited by him; and I treated of them accordingly at length in the original of this abridged Glossary, shewing that their names are Aryan except when they ascend into primeval antiquity. But I am anxious to shorten this abridgment as much as possible, and therefore omit them.

connection with the ideas of the globe, or earth, the seasons and changes of the material heavens, &c.* BIL in BIL AVIL is a similar derivative.

2. DEA, the Etruscan name of Rhea.—The same word as θεά, 'diva,' and the Teutonic *dia*, *tifi*, all implying 'the Goddess' *per excellentiam*. She is doubtless identical with the 'Dea Dia' of the Arval Brothers.

3. FEBONIA,—the goddess of freedom and liberty.—From i. *frei*, *fri*, free, and ii. *anna*, mother or nurse,—but used likewise, as above suggested, in the sense of deity.—Equivalent to 'Mother, or Goddess of the Free.'

4. HORTA,—the goddess, it is supposed, of gardens.—Either from the primitive *g-rd*, *g-rt*, implying an enclosure, from which the Latin 'hortus;' or a variety of 'Hertha,' the Teutonic goddess of the Earth.

5. LOSNA,—the name attached to the figure of a goddess with the crescent, on an Etruscan mirror, supposed to represent Diana,—the Goddess of the Moon. (*Dennis*, *Cities*, &c., vol. i. p. liv.)—As such, it might represent '*lios-anna*,' i.e. Goddess of Light; but I rather think she was Juno, in the character of Lucina, the midwife.

6. MANTUS,—the Dis Pater, or Pluto, of Etruria (*Festus*). The name is connectible with the 'mundus,' the pit in the Comitium at Rome, which was popularly considered to be the 'mouth' of Orcus; and with the 'Manducus,' the effigy with gaping jaws and chattering teeth, which was carried in the Roman processions. 'Mantus' may be identified, in this aspect and phase of development, with the Teutonic *muntha*, *munt*, *mund*, 'the mouth'—that is to say, of Hades. Remotely indeed, 'Mantus' may be a form of the Egyptian and Semitic 'Amenti' and 'Mu-t.' See the text, p. 100, *supra*.

7. NETHUNS,—the Etruscan Poseidon, or Neptune. Both NETHUNS and the Roman name resolve into 'Nept-un-a,' the

---

* *Heirud* has the sense, not only of the heights or crown of heaven but of the deeps, hollows, and whirlpools (*wirbel*, *hvirbil*) of the sea—with which Homer, be it remarked, represents Atlas as familiarly acquainted; a strange qualification for an earth-born Titan, but which is rendered quite intelligible by the Teutonic affinities and the actual signification of his Etruscan name Aar.

'Spirit-Deity,' formed from the Egypto-Aryan 'Num,' 'Kneph,' πνεῦμα, 'Spirit,' and 'ana,' Deity.

8. NORTIA,—the goddess of Fate, or Destiny. This deity has been discussed in the text, page 86, *supra*.

9. PHUPHLUNS,—the Etruscan Dionysus, or Bacchus. Compounded of i. PHUPHL,—a name—the same as 'Apollo'—common to both Japhetan and Shemite, denoting 'Son' in a divine sense; and ii. *ans*, deity,—the title signifying 'The Son-God:'—But proximately, it takes its character, through symbolical association, from i. ἄμπελ- or, as it must have been pronounced in Pelasgian times, Fαμπελ-ος, the Latin 'pampinus,' and ii. *ans*, deity (*ut supra*),—being thus equivalent to 'God of the Vine.'

10. POMONA, wife of Vertumnus, and the goddess who presided over the fruit of trees. From i. *baum, poum*, a tree; and ii. *anna*, nurse or mother, *ana*, goddess.—Equivalent to 'Mother' or 'Goddess of Trees.'

11. SETHLANS,[*] the Hephæstus or Vulcan of Etruria.—A compound of i. SETHL, and ii. *ans*, deity. Ultimately, from the root *sk*, or *ska*, implying separation; whence *sceit-*, and *sceit-il-ôn*, signifying to divide or discriminate, and, in one marked direction, through analysis and epuration by fire. But *sceit-, sceitil-*, are abraded forms of a more primitive *schmeit-, schmeitl-*, a trace of which is preserved in the Egyptian *smy*, to strike, and in our English *smite* and *smith*—this last being the central type in this analysis. The original form of SETHLANS has thus been SCHMETHL-ANS. The ideas connected with *sk* and epuration had a moral as well as physical significance; and thus we may interpret SETHL-ANS as 'the Subtle,' 'Searching,' or 'Refining God.'

12. SUMMANUS,—one of the Novensiles; the God who emitted such lightnings as flew by night. The early Romans held him in higher reverence than Jupiter himself.—The title is divisible as SUMM-ANUS, 'the God Summ-,'—'Summ' being identifiable, I presume, with 'Soma,' the Lunus of the Hindus, proximately, and more remotely with 'Yama,' or

---

[*] Both the initial and final 's' are written with the *san*, as *ś*, on a mirror described by Fabretti under no. 450. On another, no. 2492, the first *ś* only is so written.

'Yima,' the Aryan ruler of the dead. Ultimately, Sommanus is, I think, a form of the One Supreme God.

13. THALNA,—a goddess represented on Etruscan mirrors as assisting at the birth of Minerva, of Apollo, &c. She has been identified with Juno, but this can hardly be, as she appears in attendance on Latona, the object of Juno's especial hatred and malevolence. The name could only have been applied to Juno as an epithet, in the same manner as that of 'Lucina' was in regard to her presidency over marriage. From i. *tal*, implying separation, division,—a root found in special connection with marriage and parturition in the classical languages; and ii. *anna*, nurse or mother, and in composition, *heo-anna*, midwife. Equivalent, therefore, to 'the nurse'—or, if -NA be read as *ana*, 'the goddess'—'who divides,' or 'separates,' the child from the womb. THALNA may perhaps be Lucina or Eileithuia *in propriâ personâ*.

14. THANA, apparently the same as 'Diana,' goddess of the moon and protectress of slaves.—Connectible, proximately, with i. 'di-,' 'di-es,' and ii. *anna*, or *ana*; and thus equivalent to 'Mother,' or 'Goddess of Day'—the 'dies' or day beginning with the Romans, it will be recollected, at midnight:—As protectress of slaves, connectible with *deo*, *dis*, a slave, *dionôn*, to serve as a slave, &c. Remotely THANA is a feminine reflex of 'Janus,' 'Dianus,' Zην, Tinia, &c.

15. THESAN,—Aurora. Perhaps from i. *tos*, gen. *tows*, the dew, and ii. *an*, *ana*, or *anna*; and if so, equivalent to 'mother' or 'goddess of the dew,' in accordance with the mythological legend. 'Ros,' 'roris,' the dew, stands in similar relation to the name 'Aurora.'

16. THURMS, or TURMS, the Etruscan Hermes or Mercury, the god presiding over limits and boundaries, and all the relations of life that are dependent on their inviolability. THURMS is evidently a more primitive form of 'Hermes.' —From i. *drum, thrôm* (O. N.), a frontier, limit, or boundary, the border or margin of anything, especially at its circumference; and ii. *as*, deity,—THURM-s thus implying 'the God of limits or landmarks,' and being identifiable so far with the Latin 'Term-inus' ('Thurm-an-as'); although he bears a more important character in the Etruscan mythology, co-

extensive with that of Hermes and Mercury. The names of Hermes and Mercury are connected etymologically with that of 'Thurms' through this central idea of fixed terminal boundaries, physical and moral. I need not ascend to the higher *origines* of these titles.

17. TURAN,—Venus or Aphrodite; also worshipped as MURCIA at Veii, and styled on Etruscan mirrors MALAVISCH and TIFANATI.—TURAN is resolvable into TUR-AN, signifying 'the Goddess' or 'Mother Tur.' TUR is, I think, the same name and person as the Egyptian 'Athor'—the pure and holy 'Urania' of the Greeks—'Urania' being identical again with TURAN, although with the initial 't' abraded. The title 'Pandémos,' applied in classical times to Aphrodite or Venus in her degraded aspect, is in that later sense a mere corruption of what I believe to have been the original title, 'Çpent--amma,' 'Holy Mother,' as applied to 'Aphrodite Urania,' 'Turania,' or 'Turan,' throughout the Aryan world. TUR is a worn down form of *Sicartz*, the 'Black,' or 'Hidden,' a title of the Supreme God among the primitive Japhetans.—MURCIA and MALAVISCH seem to be connected with *maro, marawi*, tender, delicate, graceful, the 'l' changed to 'r,'—but in this character Turan approximates more nearly to the classical Aphrodite.—TIFANATI is, I have no doubt, a compound of, i. *tiji*, θεϜa, goddess, and ii. *Anait-is*, or *Anta*, the Oriental deity, probably the same as Astarte, whose name is given by the Persians to the planet Venus. Astarte and Athor were originally one and the same deity. 'Anait-,' or 'Anta,' is probably itself a corruption of 'Çpenta,' the 'Holy,' and identical with 'Bendis,' the Thracian analogue of Cybele and the Etruscan Kupra.

18. USIL,—a name given to the Sun.—Perhaps the same word as the Greek ἥλ-ιος, ἠέλ-ιος, the Cymric *haul*, the M. Gothic *uil* and *sauil*, and the Latin 'sol.' U may represent the Oriental prefix 'Va,' but I suspect that USIL is simply SUIL by metathesis.

19. VEJOVIS, or VEDIUS,—an infernal God, whose thunderbolts deafened or stupified his victims before actually striking them. Also described as adjudging for impiety, and as identical with Dis and Pluto.—VEDIUS corresponds proximately

s

with *wudl, eód,* our Scottish *wode,* stupified or (to use another Northern word) demented; and may be an Etruscan form of 'Hades' or 'Aides'—which again, considered as a locality, expresses, like the Teutonic *öli, authis,* wasteness, emptiness, desolation,—*öli* and *wuöl* being, in fact, varieties of the same original word and idea. I need not trace the etymology higher.—VEJOVIS, VEDIUS, as the 'judge,' corresponds with *wiz,* the root of *wissd, witoth,* law, *wizi,* judgment, &c. The Oscan 'meddix' is collaterally akin to this same root.

20. VERTUMNUS, or VORTUMNUS,—styled by Varro "deus Etruriæ principalis,"—the God of wine and gardens, presiding over the transformation of plants and their progress to blossom and fruit; and thence, derivatively, among the Romans, over every conceivable description of change and exchange, the vicissitudes of the seasons, the return of rivers to their proper beds, matters of sale and purchase, &c.—Not, immediately, from 'verto,' as commonly supposed; but from *herta,* gen. plur. *hertono,* implying vicissitude (of time), alternation (of seasons, of germination, &c.), and proceeding from the same root as *hwarb, hwarbo,* already mentioned as implying revolution. The Latin 'ordo' has the same signification and etymology as *herta,* and, with the prefix of the digamma, might have originated the name 'Vertumnus;' but the roots of the word can only be found in the old Teutonic, although they extend far beyond it into the primeval language.— VERTUMNUS is thus the compound HERTON-ANS, the 'God of the Seasons,' the prior 'n' being changed to 'm' for the sake of euphony, as in 'alunnus, alumnus.'

21. VOLTUMNA,—the wife of Vertumnus, and the goddess at whose shrine, in the heart of the Ciminian forest, the Etruscans held their great annual council.—Perhaps from i. *wald,* forest, and ii. *anna,* mother,—(Pomona, who was also the wife of Vortumnus, deriving her name, as has been shewn, from *baum,* a tree); but connectible, in her character of presiding over the national council, with the root of *walz-an, walt-an, welt-a,* to deliberate, and thus signifying 'Mother, or Goddess, of Counsel.'

VII. *The Fates, or Female demons, friendly and hostile, attendant on death in the Etruscan mythology, as represented and named on ancient mirrors, &c.*

1, 2. LASA and MEAN,—the "mild or decreeing Fates" (as they are described by Mr. Dennis), who take note of and record the destinies of men. They are usually figured with a *stylus* and a sheet of paper, recording the judgments of destiny, or (in a few instances) with a hammer and nails, the attributes of Nortia.—Respectively from *las*, whence *lesan, lesa, laisa,* implying to collect, gather, and ascertain by examination; and from *mein,* as in *meinj-an, mein-a,* to record or commemorate, but with the affection of memory and love associated with it in the Teutonic dialects. LASA is thus the 'Inquirer into' and MEAN the 'Recorder' or 'Remembrancer'—in both cases in an official sense—of Fate or Destiny.

3. LEINTH,—the goddess, apparently, of Fame.—Probably identical with *hliumunt, liumunt,* praise, reputation, fame, &c.

4. KULMU,—a demon represented in the death-scenes of Etruscan art as issuing from the gate or mouth of Orcus, sometimes with a flaming torch on her shoulders, and carry-

---

* The name LASA is frequently associated, as a generic title, with other epithets denoting varieties of duty, as in the case of L. LASA PHRSU,—PHRSU being associable with *vach* (Sansk.), *spec-,* to speak, as in *vogt, fogot* (O. N.), and 'ad-vocat-us.' The demon in question may personify either the summons to judgment or forensic advocacy before the judicial tribunal after death:—2. L. SITMIKA, in which SITMIKA is probably akin to *scihl,* fate, or *scrid-, scritunga,* 'scissura,' separation as by the shears, the idea thus corresponding exactly with that of the Greek Μοῖρα:—3. L. TIMRAE,—connectible with *tomj-ári,* judge, or *dumpfan,* to extinguish, developable into *dampf-ári,* 'one who extinguishes'—i.e. the torch of life:—And, 4. L. REKUSETA, whose name resolves into l. *rach,* as found in *rakka, race, racu,* a cause, plea, or sentence; in *róka,* the act of (legal) procuration or advocacy; and in *rech-an, rachnj-an,* to reckon,—and il. *not, need,* necessity. REKUSETA thus expresses either the inevitability of the call to reckoning or judgment, or the need of an advocate. All these titles have a forensic sense, responsive to the prevenient idea and apprehension of citation to judgment after death. They are respectively interpreted by Gerhard as 'Victoria,' 'Semele,' 'Thymbraea,' and 'Graecanica.'

s 2

ing a pair of shears.—Evidently a personification of *qvalm, cvalm*, death; with a latent etymological suggestion of impending punishment, or at least, suffering. The idea of the flaming torch is involved in the root *qual* (Sansc. *jval*, 'flagrare,' *jvar*, 'ægrotare'); and the shears may have been suggested by the resemblance between *qual, kul*, and *kliuban*, to cleave or shear, in the same manner in which they are attributed (if I mistake not) to Clotho, the Greek form of the Teutonic *hlós*, 'sors,' lot or fate.—KULMU is thus equivalent to the angel, or demon of 'Death.' I suspect that KULMU represents the original form of the Scandinavian 'Hela;' and the Hindu '*Kali*' and Greek '*Kora*' (Proserpine) may be perhaps of kindred origin.

5. VANTH,—a demon likewise attendant frequently on scenes of death.—Probably identical with *weinót*, 'ululatus, fletus, planctus,' and a personification of Grief, or Tears.

6. NATHUM,—a demon, fierce and truculent, attending on scenes of violent death.—Compounded of i. *nót*, 'necessitas,' and ii. *tóm*, judgment or doom.

VIII. *The Genii.*

1. The GENII,—spirits, the offspring of the Great Gods, who were the efficient cause of human life, and attended mankind throughout their lifetime, and even to the world of immortality.—Derived, like a host of kindred words in Latin, Greek, and old Teutonic, from the Japhetan root *jan, jin,* γεν, *gen*, and *kan*, implying generation and birth.

IX. *The Lemures; and their subdivisions, the Lares, Larvæ, and Manes.*

1. The LEMURES,—a generic term (in its original and proper sense) for the spirits of the dead, whether Lares, Larvæ, or Manes.—From *lam, lamer, lamr*, a root implying the deficiency and weakness arising from deprivation of vital or physical force.—Equivalent to 'the weak,' 'the maimed,' the 'lame,' or in the dialect of Lancashire, the 'clemmed' ones. In later times (only) the idea of malignancy was attri-

buted to them. The noun *ela*, souls or spirits, is to be understood.—Under the 'Lemures' are to be ranked,

 i. The LARES,—the spirits of virtuous ancestors, who presided over the hearth and home of their descendants.—From *lári*, 'inanis,' empty or void, as characteristic of disembodied spirits — the idea being the same as that at the root of the preceding epithet 'Lemures.' The Lares were associated with the family dwelling-place through the resemblance of *lári* to *lári, giLári*, the house, or domicile. The 'Lar Familiaris' more particularly was looked upon as a 'Lars,' lord, or 'paterfamilias'—a distinct character and name.

 ii. The LARVÆ,—the spirits of evil men, having no longer a happy home, but wanderers abroad, in exile from the domestic hearth.—From i. *lári*, 'inanis,' empty, or void, as before, with a strong influence collaterally from *lári*, 'domus;' and ii. *dwiggi*, 'avius, devius,' wandering and errant,—a compound of *â*, privative, and *weg*, the Latin 'via,' way,—that is, errant from the way and home of virtue and peace.—Equivalent (to use a word of kindred origin and exactly correspondent sense) to 'the souls of the wick-ed.'

 iii. The MANES, or DII MANES,—the souls of the departed, generally, although frequently used as synonymous with 'Lares.' Connected likewise in tradition with the lower world and with the moon, the souls of men being supposed to have emanated from that planet.—From *mein, mân* (Ital. *mancare*), implying defect, deficiency, *défaillance*, as from privation of the body, of animal life and strength, as in the case of the Lares and Lemures. The connection with the moon has been suggested (partly) by the resemblance of *mân* to *mani*, the moon. The 'Manes,' ancestors of the Etruscans and Romans, correspond ultimately with 'Mannus,' ancestor of the Teutonic tribes, the son of Tuisco; as also with Menu, Minos, Menes, and other patriarchs—the primary signification of all being *mana*, 'homo.' Tuisco again, the father of Mannus, is the same personage as the Etruscan Tages, of whom presently,—each stands (as it were) as a towering shadow behind the dead ancestors of his nation; and the parallelism affords a strong argument in favour of the original identity of the two races.

X. *The Dii Penates.*

1. The DII PENATES,—the household Gods, dwelling in the 'penetralia' of the house or city. The images of the ancient Roman Penates, said to have been brought from Troy, bore the inscription ΔΕΝΑΣ, DENAS.—Proximately associable with the Pelasgian word represented by ἔνδ-ον in Greek, and 'end-u' or 'ind-u' in Latin, signifying 'within,' and, as of ἔνδον, 'those of the family, or household;' and which, with the digamma prefixed (as represented in the Teutonic *pfund*, enclosure), and in composition with *as*, deity, would give us Fενδ-ας, 'Fend-as,' 'Pinnt-as,' whence 'Penat-es,' equivalent to 'the Gods Indwellers.' The remoter root, intimately associated with it, is, I conceive, *indu*, the moon, in Sanscrit—the 'Penates' being thus connected with the gods and heroes of the race styled 'Induvansa' or 'Children of the Moon' in India and elsewhere.—The word DENAS is either a transposition of 'End-as,' or a compound of i. *tèn*, an enclosure, whether in the case of a house or a town, and ii. *as*, deity,—thus implying, proximately, 'Gods of the house, or city.' More remotely, remembering that the Penates of Rome were represented as two in number, with the attributes of Castor and Pollux, we may recognize in 'Den-,' 'Denas,' a form of *twin*, twin, and the name would thus imply 'the twin Gods,' in other words, the Dioscuri. Both DEN- and PEN-T- find, in fact, their ultimate reconciliation in ZWIN, 'd' representing 'z' and 'p' the 'w,' even as δελφὶν and its dialectic variety βελφὶν find their common origin in the older but forgotten form of δϝελφιν.

SEVENTH GROUP.—*Words connected with Divination, Public Worship, &c., among the Etruscans, and (as derived from the Etruscans) among the Romans.*

I. *The revealers, teachers, and guardians of Divination.*

1. TAGES,—the mysterious being, half boy, half sage, the son of Jupiter, or according to another legend, of Hercules and Minerva, who sprang out of the earth when Tarchon was ploughing the foundations of Tarquinii, and revealed the science of divination and the 'Disciplina Etrusca,' which formed the foundation of the political and religious observances of Etruria.—The same word and name as 'Tuisco,' or 'Tuisto,' above spoken of, the "doum e terrâ editum," put forth by the earth, and whom the Germans celebrated in the time of Tacitus as the father of Mannus, the ancestor of the three tribes of their nation. 'Tages' and 'Tuisco,' as thus known to us, seem to reflect the influence of the Teutonic *zwiski*, *tuix*, literally two-ish, or double, which also has given its signification in classical mythology to the name Diosc-uri. The original root of all three must be referred to a still earlier date in etymology.

2. BEGOE,—a nymph who taught the Etruscans the art of interpreting the signs given by lightning.—From *spihi*, wise through intuition, like a seer—the Scottish 'spaowife,'—the initial 's' being abraded, as (to cite one among many examples) the 's' in 'speht,' the oracular bird of Mars, is abraded in the Latin 'pic-us.' The nymph-like character of Begoe reflects the ancient '*piga*,' a pure virgin, the origin of our familiar 'Peggy.' The 'book' of her writings has been suggested by the resemblance of her name to *buch, book*, a word derived from the *buocha* or *beech, laminæ* or tablets of the wood of which tree served (among other mediums) as paper to the early scribes of the Japhetan race.

3. The SIBYL.—The word SIBYLLA is simply the Teutonic *spella*, the feminine of *spello*, a spokesman. Compare the Latin 'fatum,' the 'libri fatales,' the 'fata Sibyllina.'—Equivalent to 'the Saga,' 'the Spokeswoman.'—The legends of the 'books' of the Sibyl, of the 'leaves' on which she wrote

her prophecies, and even of her 'cave,' all find their origin in the remoter root *aphal, phal* (Sanscr.), 'dissilire,' to split, from which the words *spella*, 'sibyl,' are derived.*

4. The DUUMVIRI,—the guardians of the Sibylline Books, and to whom the office of consulting them was exclusively confided. There were several bodies of Duumviri, but all were magistrates; and this their function gives the clue to the interpretation of the title.—From *tuom, dóm*, judgment; whence *tuomo*, and (probably) *tuomári*, a doomer, dempster, or judge.

II. *The Ministers of Divination.*

1. The HARUSPICES,—the diviners who ascertained the will of the Gods, generally through inspection of the entrails of victims offered in sacrifice. Their Etruscan name appears to be connected with the word TRUTNVT, of which I have treated at page 83 of this volume, as well as of the etymology of 'Haruspex.'

2. The AUGURS—originally, it is said, named AUSPICES,— diviners whose duty, like that of the Haruspices, was to ascertain the will of the Gods, principally through the flight and sounds of birds. They seem to have been described in Etruria by the name of NETSVIS. This, as well as the titles 'Augur' and 'Auspex' have been discussed in the text, p. 85, *supra*.

III. *The Insignia of Divination.*

1. The LITUUS,—the wand with which the Augur drew or marked out the 'regiones,' or boundary lines on the expanse of the heavens before taking an observation.—From *leit*, the root of *leitj-an, led-ian*, to lead, *gaLeit-jan*, to lead or draw—

* The idea of the *leaf* is more closely connectible with the Sibyl than that of *book*, which last, as composed of *laminæ* of beech-wood (*ut supra*) attaches rather to Begoe. The connection between 'folium,' a leaf, and 'Sibyl' is seen more nearly in the Irish or Gaelic words *duil*, a leaf, *duil-leach-an*, a little book, or pamphlet,—*duile* passing immediately—by the exchange of *d* for *s* (component elements of *s*), and of *u* for *b*—into *sbile*, 'Sibylla.' *Leabhar, liber*, points to the bark of trees as a third material for writing. It is remarkable how we still speak of the 'leaf' of a book, as if contemporaries of the Cumæan Sibyl.

in Latin, 'regere,'—this Latin equivalent being the very word by which, as 'regere fines,' the operation in question was expressed.

2. The TRABEA, or robe of honour. See *infra*.
3. The TUDA. See *infra*.

IV. *The Templum—the connecting link between Divination and worship; and the Pomœrium.*

1. The TEMPLUM,—in its original signification, the place in the sky circumscribed, marked out, and separated by the Augur with his 'lituus,' or staff, from the remainder of the visible heavens, and within which he proposed to take his observations. The word afterwards expressed (in Greek as τέμενος) a piece of land marked off as sacred to the Gods, from which the building erected within it for divine worship received the name of 'temple.'—Proximately from *tum*, the root of *tŭm-ón*, and of *túmil-ón*, to encircle or go round,—the letter 'p' being introduced in *túmil-* for euphony, as we have it, for example, in the English form of *túmilón*, to 'tumble.'—Equivalent to 'a place encircled,' or 'circumscribed,' to the effect of distinction and separation, according to the original meaning of the word, as above stated.

2. The POMŒRIUM,—the symbolical wall, or rather the hollow space or trench, its course marked by stone pillars erected at intervals, which was made by the Etruscans and Romans when founding a town, and within which only the city auspices could be taken. The city walls might be either on one side or the other of the 'Pomœrium.'—Compounded of the preposition i. *bi*, governing the dative, and implying 'by,' 'at,' 'beside,' or 'close to,' and ii. *múrom*, the dative plural of *múra, múri, múr*, a wall,—POMŒRIUM thus resolving into the '*Bi-múrom*,' the space 'at,' 'by,' or 'near the walls.'*

---

* The article 'De sulcis extra villas' in the 'Indiculus Superstitionum'—the list of heathen ceremonies and observances denounced by the 'Concilium Liptinense,' A.D. 743—may perhaps have had reference to the 'Pomœrium,' or something akin to it. We have, alas! nothing but a few meagre headings, like that 'De sulcis,' to instruct us as to the rites against which the censures of the Council were directed. 'Sulcus,' as used in old German-Latin, is explained by *linie*, a line; such a line, I presume, as was

V. Public and Private Worship; rites, ceremonies, officials, &c.

i. Service of the Gods in general.

1. SACER and its derivative compounds, SACRIFICIUM, SACERDOS, the REX SACRIFICULUS, &c.—SACEU is the old Teutonic *seir*, implying bright, shining, pure, free from alloy, not inherently but through refinement and purification by fire—the ultimate root being *sk*, implying (as noticed under SETHLANS) separation or division. This root *sk*—common, I may observe, to the Japhetan and the Hamite race, governs and accounts for all the significations (otherwise irreconcilable) of the Latin 'sacer.'

ii. Service of the Gods in particular.

1. The FLAMINES,—the priests of particular deities.—From i. *pleg-an, plaga*, to care for, or minister to, used with reference to religion; and ii. *man*, as in 'lagman,' 'landamman.' —Equivalent to 'the Minister' of such or such a God. The word may perhaps be the same originally as the Hindoo *Brahman, br-* being read as *pl-*.

2. The SALII, the priests of Mars, at Rome, the guardians of the ANCILE, or sacred shield that fell down from heaven— who marched in procession through the city on the festival of Mars, singing their hymns, the AXAMENTA, in alternate verse, to the clashing of their shields, in honour of the illustrious armourer MAMURIUS VETURIUS—and dancing in a measured step described by the words AMPTRUARE, AMPRUATIO, TRIPUDIUM,—the day concluding with a solemn feast held in the temple of their god. The SELLI too were the priests of Jupiter at Dodona. 'Salii' and 'Selli' are apparently the same word as *sello, gesello*, companion, in the sense of fraternity, or as a college. A further signification is imported from the root *hal*, importing to cover, protect, and defend, especially in a military sense. The dance was probably suggested by

---

drawn by the augurs in their rites. (*Brinckmeier, Gloss. Diplom., in voce.*) The trench of earth corresponds—whether in the case of Romulus on the Palatine or of Tarchon at Tarquinii—with the lines which mark out the *templum* in heaven.

the resemblance of these roots to the Greek and Latin ἅλλομαι, 'saltare.' The word ANCILE is compounded of i. *hag*, city, and ii. this same *hal*, protection, and is equivalent to 'palladium.' The AXAMENTA are derivable from i. *wig*, gen. *wiges*, war, and ii. *mund*, memory, or commemoration. TRIPUDIUM is a mere Latin form of the Teutonic *trift* (*trifl*, *tripd*, *tripad-ium*), implying impulse or 'affectus,' from *triban*, *drifan*, to impel or drive—in allusion to the divine 'afflatus;' and AMTRUATIO and AMTRUARE spring from the same root, with the prefix of *ambi*, ἀμφί, the Teutonic *um* or *umb*, implying 'round, or in a circle.' MAMURIUS VETURIUS appears to me to combine a tradition of Weyland Smith with the name of Weyland's master, the illustrious armourer 'Mimer'—who moreover is associable with the Mimor (himself the father of a band of 'Salii') celebrated in Scandinavian tradition. VETURIUS—otherwise written VETUSIUS—implies in old Teutonic and Zendic, 'the wise,' or 'skilful,' a common epithet of the hero-smiths of early time. Both names are indeed traceable to eastern Iran. And, finally, the whole institution of the 'Salii' appears to me a reflection in Italy of the life and conversation of the Æsir and of Odin in the celestial Asgard, as depicted in the Edda. The 'Salii,' I should add, were the priests of Mars (Ἄρης) under his title 'Gra-divus' and of 'Quir-inus'—that is of the God 'Gra' and 'Quir.' But 'Gra,' 'Quir,' and Ἄρης are the same name as Ἔρρος, the Æolic or Pelasgic Jupiter, of Dodona. The 'Salii' and the 'Solli' (above-mentioned) were thus branches of one and the same priestly community. There are many curious points of connection between Dodona, Rome, and Scandinavia.

iii. *Certain particular religious festivals.*

1. The FEBRUA, LUPERCALIA, &c.,—festivals of lustration or purification.—FEBRUA is evidently derived from *furb-*, as in *furbj-an*, *furb-ish*, to cleanse, purify, and renovate—the root being *fiur*, the 'fire' which refines and purges all things. The Teutonic *hlouf-an*, *hloup-a* to run, or leap, accounts for many characteristics of the god 'Luporcus' and the 'Lupercalia.'

2. The LUSTRATIO, and the SUOVETAURILIA, otherwise termed SOLITAURILIA, the great sacrifice of appeasement.—The words LUSTRARE, LUSTRATIO, LUSTRUM, are connected with *hlútar, lútur,* signifying washed, purged, pure, *hlútarjan,* to expiate, &c. The word SUOVETAURILIA is a compound of i. *suovetaur,* i. e. *sauthr* (originally *suauthr*), a ram or lamb; and ii. *-ilia,* the usual suffix denoting religious service,—the name thus signifying 'the lamb-sacrifice.' The bull and the boar-pig were, I take it, additions to the original and central offering, the "sacer agnus." The alternate name SOLITAURILIA expresses the cause and object of the atonement, viz. *skhal, scol-o, sculd,* 'delictum,' crime—the Latin 'scel-us'—with the same termination *-ilia.*

3. The COMPITALIA,—the ancient festival of the 'Lares Compitales'—that is (as commonly understood) of the Lares who presided over the 'compita,' or places where two or more roads met. Also mixed up with the legend concerning the miraculous birth of Servius Tullius. From *chumft, kumft,* implying 'the [fact of] coming,' used substantively as a noun, whether applied to events in prospect, to progeny or posterity, to the meeting of persons (whence the Latin 'comitium'), the crossing of roads, &c.,—the root being *cumen, koma,* to come. The suffix *al-,* implying procreation, gives prominence to that idea in the case of these particular Lares, in connection, however, with the sense expressed, as just shewn, in *-ilia.*

iv. *The insignia of the Ministers of Divine Worship.*

1. The APEX, or conical hat worn by the Flamines and Salii, in shape exactly like a bee-hive.—From i. 'ap-is,' the Teutonic *bia,* a bee, and ii. *uahs, vex, vax,* implying increase.—Equivalent to 'a bee-hive,' after the analogy of *win-wahs,* a 'vinetum,' or vineyard.

2. The TUTULUS,—the conical knot, or pile, into which the hair of the Flaminica, or wife of the Flamen Dialis, was bound.—Similarly, the O. H. German *tidal,* a bee-hive.

3. The RICA,—the square, fringed, and purple garment worn by the Flaminica, as a mantle or hood.—The same

word as the Teutonic *rok*, the Celtic *rhuchan*, &c. The root is *rih*, as found in the Anglo-Saxon *vrig-an*, to cover.

EIGHTH GROUP.—*The Pontifices, the Pontifex Maximus, the Calends, Ides, Calendarium, Iduarium, the Dies Fasti, &c.*

1. The functions of the PONTIFEX MAXIMUS and of the Pontifical College have all of them reference, ultimately and essentially, to the enforcement of obligations—of 'bounden duties'—of what the Romans in a special sense called 'nexus' and 'nexum.'—There are two significations of the word 'bounden,' the first that of being meted out, the second that of being attached, ourselves or something else, to each other reciprocally as by a chain. Of these significations the first is the oldest, and expresses the essence or reality of the conception; the second is the more recent, and gives utterance to the symbolism by which the conception is rendered palpable to our apprehension. The root of the whole series of words which express this oldest sense—of measurement or definition—is that found in Egyptian as *ma*, truth, and which in the commutable form of *wa, ve*, gives origin to 've-rns,' 've-rit-as,' *wahr-heit*. By the association of *ma* with χa, to measure, $\chi \chi$, to balance, the old Egyptians formed *maχa*, a balance or pair of scales—the scales of justice. By the exchange of χ for *t, d*, *maχ-* is found in Latin as *met-, met-iri*, to measure; while, *m* taking the form of *p*, and the letter *n* being introduced by 'annswara,' *maχ-* becomes 'pe-d-,' 'pend-,' 'pend-ere,' 'pond-us' in the same language. In the North, on the other hand, through the interchange of *m* and *w*, which constantly obtains in the Egyptian analogues of Aryan roots, *maχa* is found as *wage, wagan*, and *weigh* in the German dialects; while *pfund* also figures among them through a process of descent analogous to that which has produced 'pond-,' 'pond--us,' in Latin. It is at this point, of the clear theoretical consciousness of moral duty, as meted out by Themis, that the root *band, bind*, the Sanscrit *bandh*, to bind, is (as it were) called in to give practical sanction to the sense of duty by the symbolical idea of enchainment, which the Roman expresses by 'obligatio' and by 'nexus' (*ut supra*), and the

Teuton and other Japhetan tribes by 'bond' or 'bounden'
—'bounden duties,' as above used. The third step was the
introduction of pledges for the redemption of such obligations—and these were expressed by the *wage, wager, gage,*
and *wad* in Teutonic, and '*vadium*' in Latin; and by *pfand,
bond,* in Teutonic, '*pignus*' and (perhaps) '*sponsio*' in Latin.
—Applying these premises to the etymology of the title
PONTIFEX, I should therefore derive it from, i. $M = P\text{-}nt$,
denoting 'bounden duty,' as stated; and ii. *fyka, fiks, ahs,
acht* (as in *amb-acht*), signifying in old Teutonic ' the being
occupied or busied with anything ministerially or officially,
in the way of duty,'—the compound PONTI-FEX thus implying, 'He who presides officially over matters of bounden
duty and obligation,' whether towards God, or between men.
For this reason I rank the 'Pontifices'—not, as hitherto,
under the religious polity of Rome, but in a position by
themselves, intermediate between Church and State, or
rather appertaining to both, although, if I mistake not,
originally and properly a branch of the Civil legislature.
It is hardly necessary to observe that this remoter etymology
of the word PONTIFEX was totally lost sight of by the
Romans; while in Teutonic it survives *in viridi observantiâ*.
The derivation of PONTIFEX from the 'Pons Sublicius,' of
which the guardianship was confided, on symbolical and
mystical grounds, to the 'Pontifex Maximus,' is quite in-
adequate, and on a par with innumerable etymologies suggested by Varro and others, in classical times, who had not
the advantage (which we now possess) of judging from the
point of view of Comparative Mythology and Language.
It was from this lofty and primitive moral sense of justice,
as the equal admeasurement of rights and duties, that, in
later times, when the symbolism had obscured the reality,
debt—*schuld*—however incurred, was invested, so long as
unsettled, with the taint of *seel-us,* or criminality, and punishment by imprisonment, slavery, and even death.

2. The CALENDARIUM.—This had nothing to do originally
with religion, but was purely a secular institution, and a
means and memorial for the transaction of what the Romans
called 'negotium,' or business. The whole system of the

CALENDS and IDES turns, if I mistake not, upon the system of money-lending and pledging, as practised in early times. The Calends were the first, the Ides the middle day of the month. Money lent became due, with its interest, on the Calends. But it was the usage to indulge the debtor with a delay till the Ides, after which he became liable to the law in case of non-payment. The CALENDARIUM was a book or ledger in which creditors noted the names ('nomina') of their debtors, the sums of money lent, the rate of interest, and the times when principal and interest became due. The IDUARIUM, in like manner, recorded the names of those to whom indulgence till the Ides had been given, on the 'promise to pay' of the debtor.—I derive, therefore, CALEN-DÆ from i. lehan, lân, to lend; partic. past, gaLâned, what is lent; and ii. dag, tag, day,—the compound kaLâned-dag, 'Calendæ,' signifying 'the day of money lent upon loans,' or interest. The word IDUS proceeds from eid, aiths, an oath or promise (the Latin 'fides'), and signifies 'the day of faith,' 'trust,' or 'credit'—the root being wet-an, vith-an, to join, or bind. The DIES FASTI are in like manner derived from the Teutonic fas, the Sanscrit paç, to bind, whence the participle fasti, fast—that is, 'what is bound, fixed, and immoveable.' And the words CALENDARIUM and IDUARIUM are formed from the combination of the words above mentioned, 'Calendæ' and 'Idus,' with the root war, implying custody—the respective compounds thus signifying, 'the repository,' or place of registration 'of loans,' and 'promises to pay.' The process by which the register of private obligations became that of the State is very interesting, but not to the purpose for the present argument.

NINTH GROUP.—*Words connected with the Public Civil Ceremonial of the Etruscans, and (as derived from the Etruscans) of the Romans.*

I. *The Rulers—the Executive.*

1. The LUCUMO.—See the First Group, number 4, *supra*.
2. The REX,—supreme both in civil and ecclesiastical

matters.—A word rooted in primeval speech—the Sanscrit 'Raj,' Babylonian 'Ra,' and Egyptian 'Re,' (titles of deity,) being all derivative from the ancient root *Ursa*, already cited.

3. The CONSULS,—the two great officers on whom the civil power of the kings devolved after the establishment of the republic,—said to have been originally termed PRÆTORS, as commanders of the army.   PRÆTOR and IMPERATOR— this last title written by Ennius 'Enduporator'—appear to me to be the same word, and compounded of i. *umb*, *ὀμφί*, and it. *rit*, *ris*, the root of *ritan*, *risen*, signifying 'to ride,' but with the especial sense of 'on a military expedition.' *M* and *nt* are constantly interchangeable, as already observed; and thus *umb* and 'endu,' are identical. The Teutonic *fartári*, denoting leader of a *fart*, or military expedition, is probably of cognate origin. CONSUL is *ga-Sello*, signifying 'sodalis,' 'collega,' the colleague—in the plural, 'the colleagues,'—the well-known title of the Consuls.

4. The PRÆTOR.—See the preceding article.

5. The TRIBUNI PLEBIS.—See the articles 'Tribus' and 'Plebs,' *infra*.

II. *The Nation.*

1. *The Patricians.*

1. The PATRICII,—a name resolvable into 'Atr-inga,' pronounced with the digamma,—'ϜAtr-inga,' 'Patr-inga,' 'Patricii;' and thus probably the same patronymic (although disguised) as that of 'Tyrrh-eni,' or Etruscans. 'Atri' and 'Tyr' are two forms of the same name, and the Scandinavian Tyr corresponds to the Roman Gradivus, or Mars. The digamma and consonant thus restored are preserved in the corresponding title 'Eupatridæ,' at Athens. 'Tyrrh-' is not the oldest form of the eponymic title.

2. The POPULUS,—not the 'people,' or 'populace,' in the modern sense, but the conquering or dominant class, as opposed to the 'Plebs,' or commons,—identical in fact with the Patricians.—From *afl*, *afla*, implying, first, strength; secondly, generation or procreation; thirdly, acquisition and conquest. Pronounced, with the digamma, 'Ϝafl,' and sub-

sequently developed, by substitution of the kindred 'p' for 'f,' into 'papl,' 'popl-us' (the older form), 'populus.'—Equivalent, originally, to 'the strength' of the nation, in the sense in which a son, 'fil-ius' (from the same root), is said to be 'the strength' of his father's loins; and, in a later conception, to 'the conquerors,' in the sense in which William of Normandy is styled 'the Conqueror,' that is, the 'acquirer' of England.

3. The EQUITES,—the knights, or equestrian order.—From i. 'equus,' a horse, a word akin to the Celtic *each*, the Greek ἵππος, the Zendic 'açpa,' and Sanscrit *asva*; and ii. the root 'it,' implying motion.

4. The CELERES,—originally, the three hundred horsemen forming the body-guard of Romulus (according to the legend) —all Patricians.—From a common root with *held*, *helder*, and implying likewise 'fighters' or 'warriors.' The ultimate root is closely akin to that of 'Populus,' *afla* and *afl*.

ii. *The Plebeians.*

1. The PLEBS,—the commons of Rome, chiefly of the Latin race.—The same word, I think, as the Gothic *biLaifs* and Greek λεῖψις, derived from *biLaibj-an*, λείπειν, and signifying 'the remnant'—the remains, that is, of the original population, 'left' so by the conquering race, the 'Patricii' or 'Populus.' The name 'Eleusis' is, I think, of similar origin.

2. The CLIENTES,—members of the Plebs, dependent on, or attached to, members of the Patrician order.—From *ga-Laub-jan*, to trust; part. present, *keLoub-endo*, *geLoubenti*, trusting, confiding,—an etymology involving the ancient metaphor of dwelling under the shadow of one who is as a tree of shelter and protection.

iii. *The Tribes.*

1. The TRIBUS,—the three Tribes of the Patricians.—Like 'stirps,' from *trib-an*, *trif-an*, to drive, *uzTrib-an*, to drive out, in the sense of a tree thrust or driven forth out of the earth,

T

by the force—*trift*, impulse—of its inherent vitality and growth. I take it that each 'tribus' constituted originally one family, and that the current arrangement of three branches under one 'tribus,' was suggested by the resemblance of the word to *dri*, τρεῖς, τρία, 'tres,' the numeral 'three.'

III. *The Deliberative Assemblies.*

i. *The Forum.*

1. The FORUM,—in its original signification, an open space or area in front of a building.—From i. *fora*, 'præ,' 'pro,' 'ante,' 'in conspectu,' and ii. *heim*, a home, or city,—the 'forum' thus signifying 'the [space] in front of, or before the city.' The ideas of market-place, place of assembly, place of deliberation, &c., are all posterior to this.

ii. *The Curiæ.*

1. The CURIA,—signifying any one of the ten divisions into which each of the Roman tribes was partitioned, or the place of assembly where the division in question held its religious and civil meetings. This last I should think the original meaning.—From the root *gar, kri*, implying appropriation, enclosure, the mother of many Japhetan words, including the Teutonic *chur*, a court; and, in a more developed form, *gart, gard, yard*,—the widely extended root already mentioned under 'Horta.'—Equivalent to the 'chur,' or 'court' (*gart*), the place of assembly for the transaction of public business. The tribal division probably acquired its name from the 'curia,' just as the Court of the Queen, or the High Court of Parliament, is so styled from the *gart*, 'court,' or palace in which it resides.

iii. *The Comitia.*

1. The COMITIA (nom. pl.), and the COMITIUM,—originally COMITIA, plur. COMITI.E,—the assemblies of the Roman people, and the place where they met.—From *chumft*, *kumft*,

the noun already mentioned as implying 'the [fact of] coming.'

iv. *The Senate.*

1. The SENATUS and the SENATORES.—From the root *san, sinn-, sadh, sidh,* signifying ' to go for the accomplishment of a matter;' and from which descend two distinct streams of verbal thought, which include all the peculiar characteristics of the Roman Senate, their mission or delegation, as 'sent' from their different 'curiæ'—their fellowship, as *gaSinda,* companions—their general office of counsel, deliberation, and 'consensus' (*sinn, sinna*)—their fulfilment of embassies (*sind* and *senden*)—their peculiar office of ministers of peace, and habitual assemblage in the Templo of Concord (*sónida*)—their equally peculiar character of reconcilers and arbiters for the settlement of disputes (*sónari*)—and, finally, their judicial office, as a sort of Committee of Privy Council (*sónjo*). The crescent or half-moon on their 'calcei,' or shoes, that well-known badge, was, I suspect, an emblem and reminiscence of ' San,' the God of the Moon among the Assyrians, and, I think also, the Lydians. The connection between *sinn,* the mind, and 'San,' the moon, on the one hand, and 'mens,' the mind, and μήν, *mani,* the moon, on the other, is to be remembered here. And ' Tyr'—originally identical with Thor—with whom I have connected the Patricians as ' Atr--inga,' 'Tyrrheni,' was God of the Moon as well as of war among the Scandinavians—the Senate originally consisting, you will recollect, exclusively of Patricians. Legislation and the moon have been associated in all the oldest traditions of mankind.

2. The SUFFRAGES,—including the SUFFRAGIUM; the ROGATORES, the TABELLÆ, the CISTA, the SITULA, the DIRIBITORES, and the CUSTODES.—The votes were given originally either *vivâ voce* or by a stone or pebble, ψῆφος, dropped into an urn; and SUFFRAGIUM, it appears to me, is a compound of ψηφ- and *frag-, frag-en,* the Latin ' rogare,' to ask for,—thus implying a ' request for one's vote,' which you give—give as your suffrage in the form of a pebble—to the candi-

date, or in favour of the measure proposed to you. The 'Rogatores,' 'Tabellæ,' &c., all have their exact meaning in old Teutonic; and I will merely add, as an example, that the DIRIBITORES, the tellers (as it were) of the Roman division, exhibit a merely Latinised form of the Teutonic *droppetiri*, a dropper—in the sense of the 'dropping' of the votes, the ψῆφοι or 'tabellæ,' one by one, out of the 'cista' or 'situla,' for the purpose of ascertaining on which side lay the majority—this being the especial function of the officers in question.

IV. *The Fetiales.*

1. The FETIALES,—a college of priests who acted as guardians of the public faith, and as heralds in cases of dissension between Rome and other states. The title was sometimes written 'Fetiales,' sometimes 'Feciales.' In the former case I should connect it with i. *eid, adh*, an oath,—the root which, in the digammatised form, becomes in Latin 'fides,' whence 'fœdera,' treaties, the especial care of the 'Fetiales;' and ii. *heil-, heiljan*, 'servare,' to keep or preserve. 'Fetiales' would thus be equivalent to 'Conservators of Faith.' But the older form was, I think, *Feciales*. I should derive this from the Sanscrit *vach, vachas*, the Latin 'vox,' the Teutonic *spec-an, speak-er*, and interpret the title as the 'Spokesmen,' literally, of the State. In keeping with this, we learn that the technical word for their demand for redress and proclamation of war was 'clarigatio'—(a word reminding one of "the lark's shrill *clarion*," the early horn of the herald of day); and this word points too to what must have been the older form of the Greek κῆρυξ, viz. κλῆρυξ—the root being καλ-, *kall-*, to call or summon. The title of the chief of the heralds, "pater patratus," and the flint-stones (stone-axes evidently) with which they slew the victim in whose blood the missile lance was dipped before hurling it into the denounced country, connect the institution with remote antiquity—with Jupiter Feretrius, with the oath by Jupiter Lapis, and the stone held by the man that swore that oath,—and, beyond Rome, with the Pelasgi.

V. *The insignia of Authority—at first Lucumonian and Royal, afterwards Consular, Senatorial, &c.*

1. The SELLA CURULIS, or Curule Chair,—the seat of dignity or honour *per excellentiam* among the Romans.—Primarily from *gar-*, *chur*, 'curia'—as the 'seat' in which the president of the 'court' sat. The 'chair' and the 'chairman' of our English popular assemblies spring from the same root. But in its more general signification of a chair of state, 'curia' reflects an influence from *hru*, glorious, the ancient word from which proceed so many epithets of majesty and honour.

2. The LICTORS,—officers who went before, or in front of, the Consul or magistrate, one by one, in a line, processionally.—A Latinised form of *leitári*, 'dux,' a leader—as leading the way.—From *leitj-ian*, *led-ian*, 'ducere,' to lead.

3. The FASCES,—rods bound in bundles, and containing a 'securis,' or axe, in the middle—carried by the lictors.—From *fas*, the Sanscrit *paç*, to bind.—'Securis' is the old Teutonic *scur*, an axe; and the 'securis' must have been adopted as an ensign of royalty through its resemblance in sound to *scir*, distinguished, illustrious, the origin of our 'Sir' and 'Sire.' The root is *sk*, signifying separation, distinction—for good or for evil.

4. The TRABEA,—the ancient official robe, sacred to Gods, to the Augurs, Kings, &c., according to its varieties of colour.—The same word as *streif*, *streif-ig*, stripe, striped, in allusion to the transverse stripes with which the robe was decorated. The root is *dwar*, *thver*, transverse, oblique, or athwart.

5. The PRÆTEXTA, or TOGA PRÆTEXTA,—the toga of white, bordered with a purple stripe, originally the Royal robe of Etruria, and afterwards that of the Roman Kings—worn by certain high magistrates during the Republic, and to the latest times by boys and girls of the Patrician order—by the boys till they attained the age of sixteen, by the girls till marriage, when they dedicated it in the Temple of 'Fortuna Virginalis.'—Probably, I think, a Latin form of *toga wirdigsta*, literally, 'the robe of highest honour,'—*wirdigsta*

being the superlative of *wirdig*, 'dignus,' 'augustus,'—the ultimate root *ward*, *vridh* (Sanscr.), including the idea of growth or increase. 'V' and 'p' are, I need scarcely insist, interchangeable letters—none more so. The subject of the 'Toga Prætexta' is a very intricate and interesting one.

6. The CLAVUS—whether 'latus,' broad, or 'augustus,' narrow—the former being a broad purple band or stripe which ran down the centre of the tunic worn by the Senators—the latter consisting of two narrow purple slips, which extended from the top to the bottom of the tunic,—this was worn by the Equestrian order.—The same word as the Teutonic and Lithuanian *lappa* and *lopas*, implying the edge, border, or fringe of a garment; and derivable from the Sanscrit 'lup' and Teutonic *kliub-an*, to cleave or divide; which exactly expresses the manner in which the 'clavus' or purple stripe 'clove,' or divided the tunic. It will be observed that the 'c' in 'clav-us' preserves the 'k' in the old Teutonic *kliub-an*.

7. The CALCEUS, or high shoe worn by the Senators.—Perhaps from *gaLegj-an*, 'ponere,' 'inducre,'—in the sense of putting on clothes or shoes.

8. The CLASSICUM,—the trumpet by which the people were called to the Comitium.—Either from *kallasj-an*, derived from *kall-ôn*, to call; or from *gaLes-an*, to collect together. 'S' and 'r' being interchangeable, the word 'classic-um' is probably connected with 'clarig-atio.'

9. The collective word INSIGNIA.—Proximately from 'in,' upon, and 'signum,' a sign,—the latter word being ultimately identical with the Teutonic *zeichen*, *teken*, plur. *zeichena*, our English 'token,' with the δόκανα of Sparta, and with *tχn*, an obelisk, in ancient Egyptian,—all from a common primeval root.

TENTH GROUP.—*The Sæculum.*

1. The SÆCULUM.—Ten 'Sæcula,' according to the Etruscan doctrine, were to comprise the life of their nation; and the close of the 'Sæculum' *per excellentiam* was to witness the extinction of the Gods themselves,—a doctrine resem-

bling that of Scandinavia, as remarked by Mr. Bunbury in his valuable article on 'Etruria' in Dr. Smith's *Dict. of Greek and Roman Geography.*—S.ECULUM is the same word, if I mistake not, as the old Teutonic *syle*, *skal*, implying a separation or distinction between any two things—the ultimate root being the particle *sk*, of Indo-Teutonic and indeed primitive antiquity, already noticed. 'S.ECUL-UM' thus implies 'the division' or 'separation' between periods of time, between generations or centuries. The 'Ludi Sæculares,' the expiatory games of Rome—which, contrary to the usual impression, were not celebrated at any fixed period—are nowise, I think, connected with the word 'sæculum' except through common derivation from the original root, *sk*. They were so named from *scul-an*, 'debere,' our English 'shall,'—from whence *solo*, 'debitor,' a debtor, and *sculd*, debt, or guilt—the root from which I have already derived the games named 'Solitaurilia.'

ELEVENTH GROUP:—*Miscellaneous Words, presumably Etruscan, as descriptive of things borrowed by the Romans from Etruria.*

1. AGER,—a field, a territory.—The Teutonic *akra*, *akr*.—From *ak*, the Latin 'ag-ere,' to drive.'—Equivalent therefore to 'land tilled by cattle.'

2. ARCUS,—the arch.—From the ancient Indo-Teutonic root *eipy-*, 'arc-,' *werj-*, to hold together by pressure.

3. C.ESTUS, or CESTUS,—the boxer's glove.—Like 'custos,' 'custodire,' akin to *huotj-an*, the root of 'cassila,' *ut supra*,—implying guardianship or protection, as for the boxer's fist.

4. CIRCUS,—the same word as κύκλος, a circle, 'l' and 'r' being interchangeable letters, and thus implying a round or circular space, or ring.

5. CLOACA,—a sewer.—Compare the Teutonic *loh*, 'foramen,' 'burntrum,' 'os (inferni, putei, &c.); ' *loe*, 'clausum;' *lucha*, 'apertura.'

6. The CORNU, invented, according to Festus, by the Etruscans.—The same word as the Teutonic *horn*, the Celtic 'carn,' and the Greek κέρ-ας.

7. FAVISSA.—the ditch or fosse which surrounded a temple,—inferred to be an Etruscan word by Dr. Donaldson. Connectible with 'puteus' and 'fossa,' and thus belonging to one of the most wide-spread roots existing.

8. MURUS,—a wall.—The old Teutonic *múr*, as shewn under 'Pomœrium.'

9. TESTUDO,—a vault.—From i. *tuo, tu*, to, or against, and ii. *stedian*, 'applicare, condere,' to put together, build, join, or attach, forming the compound *tuoStedian*, 'applicare,' in old Teutonic; and akin to *státi*, firm, stable, and *stán*, to stand. Equivalent to 'that which is firm through counter attachment or pressure'—as is a vault in architecture.

10. TUBA,—the Greek σάλπιγξ, the war trumpet of the Etruscans.—Probably the same word as *s-b, s-f*, (originally, as in Hebrew and Arabic, *s-ph*.) a reed—although the 'Tuba' in later times was made of brass. Σαλπ-, the root of σάλπιγξ, is in like manner, I conceive, the Teutonic *halm* or *seiluf*, a reed—*s* and *h*, and *m* and *p*, being convertible letters.

TWELFTH GROUP.—*Proper Names, Etruscan and of Etruscan origin.*

I. *The National Surnames of the Etruscans.*

1. TYRRHENI, otherwise *Tyrseni*, Τυρρηνοί, Τυρσηνοί.—A form, as elsewhere stated, of the patronymic which the Etruscans bore in common with the Tervingi, Thuringi, Tyrki (or early Aryan Northmen), and others, and which may be generalised as 'Thoringa,' i. e. 'Children of Thor.' Thor is Hercules, and Thoringa is thus an equivalent of Heraclidæ. By some accounts Tyrrhenus, the eponymus, was son of Hercules,—according to others he was son of Atys, king of Lydia, and son of Manes—the Mannus of the Germans, Menu, Menes, &c. I have little doubt that Tyrrhenus represents in Etruria the patriarch known (under a more archaic form of the name) as Thraotaona (Feridun) in Persia, whose fathers were styled the Athwya—a title corresponding with At-ys, as it does in another direction with

Jöt-un and Goth. The name of Tarchon, the founder of Tarquinii, is a mere variety of that of Tyrrhenus, the double -ρρ- hardening into '-rch-,' as in the opposite direction it softens into '-rs-.'

2. HRASENA, 'Ρασένα or 'Ρασέννα,—stated by Dionysius of Halicarnassus to have been an alternate name of the Etruscans, and more especially that by which they styled themselves. I should doubt the latter assertion, or that 'Hrasena' was more than an alternate name, inasmuch as, although 'Porsena' was their hero, the glory and traditions of Etruria centered at Tarquinii. The title 'Hrasena' belongs rather to the earlier, the Pelasgic stage, or component element, in their genealogy; and it is evidently the same as that of the GNISONES or RHÆTI, the inhabitants of Rhætia, who were, we know, of the same stock as the Etruscan, and spoke according to Livy, the same language, although corrupted— and as that of the 'Grut-ungi,' the sister tribe (with the Tervingi) of the great Gothic family in Germany. HRASENA, RHÆTI, may be analysed as i. HRAS- or HR.ET-, and ii. -ENA, a termination akin to the -ηνοί in Τυρρηνοί, and similar patronymics. But I suspect that 'Hrasena' and 'Porsena' were originally the same name as 'Tyrs-enus, -i,' although dialectically distinguished afterwards. It is noteworthy that 'Hrosar' and 'Thursar,' titles of the Jötnns or Giants of Scandinavia, answer very nearly to 'Hrasena' and 'Tyrseni,' the children of Atys, as these again do to the 'Grutungi' and 'Tervingi' of the German Goths. All these fit into a much larger scheme. As 'Hrasena,' the Etruscans were, so to speak, Æolidæ, or Pelasgi; as 'Tyrrheni,' Heraclidæ, Dorians, and Hellenes; and, in a more extensive sense, they formed a mixture of Suryavansa and Chandra-, or Induvansa, Children of the Sun and of the Moon, according to the nomenclature of Oriental Aryanism. A variety of collateral attributes of the Tyrrheni or Etruscans, connect themselves with the title HRASENA through secondary resemblance, as, for example, their character as builders of Cyclopean walls (compare the German *riesenmaur-*, from *reso*, 'gigas,' Cyclops'),—as lovers of horses, *hros, ros, redz, ret,* (conf. the horse's head on the coins of Larissa in

Thessaly, and the fact that 'Resen' in Mesopotamia is rendered 'Larissa' by Xenophon and 'Aspa' by the Samaritan Pentateuch),—as the 'equites' at Rome, *reiter, reisener*, &c. &c.

II. *Names of Etruscan Cities.**

1. *Of the Twelve Confederated Cities of Etruria.*

1. ARRETIUM, now Arezzo,— celebrated for its red pottery and its walls of brick; and called the 'City of Potters.' On its coins there is the inscription UPN.—From i. *rôt*, red, and ii. *heim*, forming 'Rôi-heim,' 'Arretium'—emphatically, 'The Red City,'—unless indeed the original root be 'Rus-' or 'Rhæt-,' as denoting a city of the Rhætian branch of the Etruscan race.† The site of the ancient 'Arretium' is on a barren hill called 'Poggio di S. Cornelio' (not an Italian Saint), and 'Castel Secco,' both of which names point to the colour of red (the latter through aridity) as the characteristic of Arezzo.‡ UPN I should identify with *ofun*, *uphan* (our English *oven*), a furnace or kiln, the same word, in fact, as the Greek ἰπνός. This may have been the original Pelasgian name of the city, thus signifying 'the Brick Kilns;' and I am the more inclined to think so, as one of the symbols used on the coins is an anchor—probably then known as εὐνή, the word applied by Homer to the great boulders used to retain ships at their moorings in primitive times before anchors (in the usual sense of that word) were invented. Even the prow of a ship, likewise exhibited on the coins, may refer to this; while the wheel, 'rota,' *rad*, also found there, may typify the potter's wheel. The family of Mæcenas, the 'Cilnii,' may perhaps have derived their surname from

---

* Some of these are discussed more fully than is the case in other articles of this abridged Glossary; but this I cannot avoid, the evidence for their etymology being more multifarious and complicated, and the results important.

† The association of 'Ares,' Mars, with Arretium may support perhaps this latter suggestion. But the former is, upon the whole, more probable.

‡ *Erde*, earth, as the material of brick and pottery, is almost too vague, but it deserves notice.

cyln, 'fornax,' or kiln, as the great brickmakers or potters of Arezzo. It was through that manufacture probably that the "atavi reges" acquired their historical wealth and greatness.

2. CÆRE, or CISRA (as Müller reads it), the city of Mezentius and the Tarquins,—seated, according to Mr. Dennis's description, on a table-land united by a rock to the highland adjoining, and thus forming a sort of peninsula.* We are thus reminded, in the first instance, of the Greek χέρσος or χέρρος, a continent or waste, as in 'cherso-nesus,' which denotes a peninsula or similar projection, connected by a narrow tongue of land with a continent. But the name CÆRE has a signification behind this. The Pelasgian and thus, presumptively, the older name of the place—or that, at least, by which the Pelasgi who formed such an important element in the Tyrrhenian or Etruscan population must have known it—was AGYLLA; and the etymology of this word must be taken into consideration along with that of 'Cære.' AGYLLA may be connected, proximately, either with i. *eih*, 'quercus, ilex,' and ii. ὕλη, 'silva,' wood, in allusion to the spontaneous growth of ilex which now, according to Mr. Dennis, covers the site of the city and the entire district; or with the Teutonic *igel (blut-igel), echel, egil-, egala, ecala*, 'hirudo, sanguisuga,' the leech—with which little beast the wooded and swampy valleys probably abounded in the early ages. The existence of a streamlet named (now) 'La Sanguinara' in the neighbourhood, and the statement of Livy that on one occasion the waters of Cære flowed mingled with blood, induce one to pause on this etymology as possible; and further inquiry shews that it can be strongly supported. The derivation of the name 'Agylla' from the ilex-groves finds no echo in χέρρος, χέρσος, nor that of 'Cære' from χέρσος any echo in 'Agylla.' It does not follow that when a place has two names derived from different languages or races they must each denote the same characteristic feature; but, when they do, the coincidence can hardly be accidental. That this coincidence exists in the present instance may be shewn thus. The word for 'hirudo,' leech, in Greek is βδέλλα,

* *Cities and Cemeteries, &c.*, vol. ii. pp. 27 sqq.

βδέλλα χερσαία,—βδέλλα being derived from βδάλλω, to suck or draw off by suction; while χερσαῖος, if derivable from χέρσος, can only be so in the sense that that word bears of 'waste,' and must find its root rather in the Teutonic kaerr, kiar, 'palus,' itself formed (I conceive) from an earlier kraerr, or kmaerr, whence 'marsh.' Βδέλλα χερσαία thus signifies 'marsh-leech'—or what we now call, by corruption, a 'horse-leech,' 'horse' answering to χερσ-, and signifying, not the noble creation of Poseidon, but the swamp in which the 'hirudo' lives.* I think we may assume at this point that 'Cære' or 'Cisra' is the same name as χερσ-αία or χερρ-αία, as found in this compound. But βδέλλα, when analysed, is the same word as the Teutonic egil, and, as we shall find, the Pelasgic 'Agylla,' leech; its earlier form (as ascended to by etymological induction) having been ζυδελλα, whence, the ζ being elided and the letter υ taking the form of β, we obtain in the descending line, first, βδέλλα, and then, β being replaced by a and δ by 'g' or 'k,' egil = 'agella' = 'Agylla.' The result is, first, that βδέλλα χερσαία corresponds verbatim with AGYLLA-CÆRE, or CISRA; and, secondly, that the double name of the town under discussion is thus tantamount, strange as it may appear, to 'the marsh-leech.' 'Agylla' is doubtless the Pelasgian, and 'Cære,' 'Cisra,' the Etruscan name; and I suspect that 'cære' or χερσαία was used for the horse-leech as an independent noun by the Etruscans as the Latins used 'hirudo,' which is of cognate origin. But further:—Ζυδελλα, the original form of βδέλλα, is modifiable as Ζυγελλα, and must have passed through that stage in order to become Ἀγέλλα; and this leads us to the earlier etymology of the word in 'sugo,' to suck, or draw by suction—the Latin and Teutonic equivalent of βδάλλω, the peculiar characteristic of the βδέλλα, egil, or leech. The object of this particular suction is blood, and the next step in the process suggests the connection.—By insertion of 'n,' according to the rule of 'anuswara,' 'Agylla' becomes 'Angilla,' and by restoring the initial 'z' in the softened form of 's,'

---

* We have, however, the combination in Gaelic, as deal-each, horse-leech; deal being the Celtic form of βδέλλα, (the β abraded,) and each of 'equus.'

'Sangilla'—that is, 'Sanguilla;' while, 'l' being exchanged for 'n,' it becomes 'Sanguin-,' 'Sanguinea,' whence the present name of the streamlet 'Sanguinara,' the 'Bloody,' above spoken of, and the current tradition of the waters of Cære having become mingled with blood—both thus supporting the proposed etymology. Mr. Dennis approximates the name and the tradition, and inquires, with his usual sagacity, "May not the tradition be preserved in the name of this stream?" But both tradition and name bear reference, I think, to the preceding Pelasgo-Tyrrhenic etymology.— Lastly, and in consonance with all this, the name of Mezentius, the tyrant of Agylla, bears the same signification. I had long been convinced that Mezentius and Turnus in the Æneid were identical with Modsognir and Durinn, the princes (the first-created) of the Dvergar or Elves in the Scandinavian mythology, the respective names being etymologically identical, and other coincidences leading me to the identification. But, while pondering over this etymology of Agylla, it occurred to me that we have in 'Modsognir' the identical name of 'leech,' or what comes very near to it. The signification and etymology of the name given by Finn Magnusen is this,—" vigorem sugens, sive succum attrahens, . . à τῷ modr (*mothr*), succus, vigor, et verbo *suga*, sugero (Dan. sue, Germ. *saugen*, Angl. *suck*, &c.)." Comparing the lines of Virgil,

"Mortua quinetiam jungebat corpora vivis,
Componens manibusque manus atque oribus ora,
Tormenti genus; et sanie taboque fluentes
Complexu in misero longâ sic morte necabat,"—*

the conclusion seems evident that, whatever be the primitive signification of the names 'Mezentius,' 'Modsognir,' that of 'Mezentius,' the ruler of 'Agylla-Cære,' was, in the mythical age, identical with that of his city, and equivalent to 'the marsh- or horse-leech,' and therefore that the etymology above suggested is correct.† Both 'Modsognir' and

* *Virg. Æn.*, viii. 485.
† The tribute of the entire annual vintage—the 'blood of the grape'— demanded by Mezentius from the Latins, and which gave rise to the Roman

'Mezontius' (in older orthography this name would be 'Medsentius') must have been written with an initial 'z;' and in the syllable Zmod-, Zsod-, Zmed-, Zsed-, thus restored, and which is evidently identical with the ϝδ- or βδ- in βδέλλα, we at once recognize the familiar 'sud-or,' ἰχώρ, and 'sang-uis,' blood. The importance of this identification, not merely as regards 'Agylla-Cærre,' but as bearing on the entire argument in favour of the Teutonic origin of the Etruscans, cannot be overlooked. Virgil was himself an Etruscan, and we can now hardly doubt that traditions of the Dvergar and Alfar were familiar to him and his race, derived by independent descent from the ancestors of the Etruscans and Teutons when both were living together as one people. The subject cannot be pursued further here.*

3. CLUSIUM; now Chiusi,—originally named CAMAR, or CAMAR-TS; the capital of Porsena, and celebrated after that hero's death for his tomb, the glory of Etruria, of which such a curious description is given by Pliny after Varro.—The key to the signification of CAMAR-TS is afforded by the fact that there exists a double type of coins corresponding in all respects, except that the one bears the legend 'Ku,' or 'Kam,' the other 'Ku' and 'Ruet.' The former corresponds, I conceive, to kam, the latter to karte (ka-raed), both implying a

festival of the 'Vinalia' according to Ovid (*Fasti*, lib. iv. ver. 870 sqq.), is not out of keeping with the tradition which I believe to lie at the root of the etymology. His skill on horseback is noticed both by Virgil and Ovid. This may refer to the later sense of χέρσ-, marsh = horse.

* It is a curious fact that Agylla consulted the oracle of Apollo at Delphi, and dedicated treasure there. The βδέλλα, ζυδέλλα, above suggested as the original form of Agylla, may be compared with the alternate forms (already cited) of δελφίν, βελφίν, and with what must have been the early form of Delphi, viz. Ζβελφοί, Ζυελφοί. But Delphi appears under the name of 'Crissa' in the Homeric hymn to Apollo, just as Agylla is named also 'Cisra,' or 'Cære.' The word *lerch*, as 'medicus,' a physician or healer, is common to the Gothic, German (proper), Scandinavian, Celtic, and Slavonic languages; and I have little doubt that it gives character to the title 'Lycian' applied to Apollo, and that *λκέσιος*, *λκέομαι* were originally *λκκέσιος*, *λκκέομαι*. It connects itself also with *lerkra*, to lick, the sanative process which dogs apply to wounds or sores. But the question leads into intricate veins of exploration, even within the limits of Aryan speech.

'pecten,' or comb—the *karis* formed of the sharp spikes of the thistle ('carduus'), as used originally for carding wool. *Kam* further signifies the 'scapus,' or columnar stem of a plant, from which the fruit or berries hang, as it were, in a circle round it,—and the Greek word for this, καυλὸς, leads us within the associations of the CL-, in CLUSIUM.—This name CLUSIUM is a compound, I think, of, i. *hlaiv*, *hléo*, gen. *hléwes*, a tomb or mausoleum, and ii. *heim*, city,—implying the 'City of the Sepulchre.' Or it may be simply the Gothic *hlaivs*, 'sepulcrum,' the same word as the Latin 'clivus,' e. g. the 'Clivus Mamurii,' the hill, barrow, or tomb of Mamurius Veturius at Rome. It is noteworthy at this point that *keil* signifies 'cuneus,' a wedge, or, as applied to architecture, a building of conical elevation, like a pyramid,—the peculiar feature which distinguished the tomb of Porsena. The marvels attributed by Varro to the tomb are all echoed by Teutonic roots bearing more or less resemblance to *Kam*, *Ka-ruel*, *Camar-*, and *hléo*, and which have suggested evidently the separate features of the description,—*krumb*, 'curvus,' tortuous; *krumbi*, 'ambago, mæandrus,' and *krumba*, 'camiros, broves circulos' (the translations are Graff's), answering to the labyrinth within the basement of the tomb; and *klos*, *klot* (O. N.), *kliuwa*, to the compact and close masonry, to the bronze circle or 'orbis,' on which the four pyramids or cones stood, with a fifth in the centre (in regard to which the word *klot* in Ihre's Suio-Gothic Lexicon suggests an interesting approximation), and to the *clue* of thread by which only the labyrinth could be explored with safety. The *kam*, 'scapus,' καυλὸς, evidently suggested the bells which hung—like pendent berries—and like the bells round pagodas in China, or the tripod-caldrons around Dodona—from the *petasus*,—rung, like them, by the wind. Exaggerated as the tradition may be, the tomb must, I think, have existed; the very name, CLUSIUM, as above analysed, witnesses to its importance. The 'Poggio Gajella' has been identified with it,—but the Poggio is not 'below the city,' as Varro describes the tomb; on the other hand, the labyrinthine passages are of the character described, and the name 'Gajella' recalls the *keil*, or 'cuneus.' 'Poggio S. Paolo' has not yet been explored; and the name 'Paolo,' too, may be a reminiscence of *k'eil, keil*, 'cuneus.' There may have been other cuneiform or pyramidal tombs at Chiusi besides that of Porsena.

4. CORTONA,—the great Pelasgic stronghold, captured by the Etruscans (it is said) from the original inhabitants of the land, and from which they extended their sway over Western Italy.—Proximately, from i. *gard, gart*, the primitive word, implying an enclosed space, already cited, and ii. '-ona,' as in 'Vetulonia,' 'Populonia,' &c., connectible with *won-en*, to dwell, implying abode or residence. Originally, it may perhaps be derived from 'Rhæt,' the alternate surname of the Tyrrhenian race, and which resolves into that of the Pelasgi. The older name of the city is said to have been 'Corythus;' and this is etymologically the same as 'Corinth.' Its symbol is a wheel—*rat* and 'rota' in Teutonic and Latin, in evident echo of the name of the city; and such too was a numismatic symbol (one among many) of Arretium.

5. FALERII, the city of the FALISCI or ÆQUI FALISCI, said to have been a colony from Argos.—The name FALISCI, like that of VOLSCI, and that too ('l' and 'r' being interchanged) of 'Prisci,' is evidently (I think) an Italian form of 'Pelasgi.' The Æqui may have been 'Achæi,' of the same stock as the original inhabitants of Argos.—FALERII is resolvable into i. 'Fal,' the root of 'Fal-isci,' 'Pel-asgi,' and ii. *erbi*, patrimony or heritage, or ἔρα, the Pelasgian form of 'terra,'—thus implying 'the patrimony,' or land, the 'term' or 'patria' in modern Italian, 'of the Fal-,' or Pelasgi.

6. PERUSIA (PERUGIA),—in Etruscan orthography apparently, PENUSE.—A form of the old Teutonic and Indo-European *burz*, implying a 'burg,' burgh, or fortified city. The 'Bursa' of Carthage, for example, was (I conceive) the *burz*, the 'perusia,' the citadel, of that city. The Hellenic ἐφύρη is, I think, remotely, the same word.* The emblem of Perusia, a 'bipennia,' or two-headed axe, was doubtless chosen

---

* Mr. Gladstone suggests "that ἐφύρη and φεραὶ may properly denote, and may be the original and proper Hellic name for the *terræ* (Ital.), or walled places, founded by the Hellic races; as ἀργος signifies the open districts in which the Pelasgians were given to settling κωμηδὸν, for agricultural purposes."—*Homer and the Homeric Age*, vol. I. p. 513.

from the resemblance of the old Teutonic *bursa, byrs*, a 'bipennis,' to the name 'Bursa,' 'Perusia.'

7. RUSELLE,—a city of which the site is now completely overgrown (as it doubtless was before the settlement of any population there) by a beautiful, thorny, yellow-flowering plant, called by the Italians 'marruca,' and which renders the exploration of Ruselle, according to Mr. Dennis, "a desperate undertaking." Nowhere had that indefatigable explorer such difficulty in making his way to any Etruscan site; and the growth is of very old standing, inasmuch as Polybius probably refers to it (this is Mr. Dennis's observation) in describing a battle fought between the Romans and Gauls in the neighbourhood.* The name appears to me a compound of i. *ris, hris*, the Welsh *prys* and English *brush*—*gorse* being in fact the same word—but in the special growth of the Latin 'ruscus' and Greek ὀξυμυρσίνη, μυρσίνη being apparently the modern 'marruca,'—and ii. *halba*, a region or district,—RUSELLE thus implying, 'the region' or world 'of ruscus'—'gorse' (shall we say ?)—or whins,—unless indeed it be simply developed from the first of these roots analogously to the French *broussailles*.

8. TARQUINII, in Greek Ταρκυνία and Ταρκυνίναι, in Etruscan orthography perhaps TARCHNA,—the parent city of Etruria, founded, it is said, by Tarchon, the son of the Lydian Tyrrh-enus.—From 'Tarch,' the same root as Τυρρ- in 'Tyrrh-enus,'—with the termination *-uvia* or '-ona,' and thus implying 'the City of Tarch,' 'Tyrrh,' or 'Thor.' But the root *tarq*- had certainly the signification of 'rule' among the early Aryans; *targadh* exists as government, 'imperatio' (conf. the Etruscan DRUNA), in Erse; and the Greek "Αρχων is 'Tarchon' *minus* the initial. TARQUINII may thus have signified also 'the Ruling City'—in the south, more especially, of Etruria.

9. VEII,—the great fortress and bulwark of Southern Etruria.—The ancient *wik, wige, wick*, denoting castle or fortress, (whence the Latin 'vicus,') occurs to one at once; but I think that the name VEII is specially derived from

---

* *Cities, &c.*, vol. ii. p. 251.

weggi, wiga, 'cuneus,' a wedge, as representing its situation, —the ground which the earliest site of the city, afterwards the citadel, occupied forming a complete wedge, bounded by the two valleys of the 'Fosso di Formelle' and 'Fosso de' due Fossi,' which converge at a point below the citadel, where the two streams, uniting, form the Cremera. The legend of the 'cuniculus,' or mine, of Camillus has been suggested, I think, by the root in question.*

10. VETULONIA,—VATL (written abridged) on the coins; the town from which the 'fasces' and other symbols of power, the Curule chair, &c., were borrowed by Rome; while a naked athlete, an oar, and a pine-cone, are the emblems on her coins.—Ultimately, I think, from i. *wald*, a forest—in reference to the pine-woods still flourishing near the town, and ii. the suffix '-onia,' denoting habitation,—the name thus signifying 'the City in the Wold, wood, or forest.'—The connection with the idea of authority or power, and the various numismatic emblems just mentioned, are echoes of resemblances existing between the root 'Vetul,' 'Vatl,' and words —e. g. *wald*, *walt*, power; πίτυς, the pine; τίτυλος, the act of rowing, πιτυλίζω, to strike in boxing—in old Pelasgian Greek, and Teutonic.

11. VOLATERRÆ, VELATHRI (in Etruscan orthography), Volterra,—once the most powerful of the Etruscan cities.— Probably from i. *wald*, *walt*, power, and ii. *ipa*, or *erbi*, patrimony or district,—unless the name be *waltiri*, 'dominatrix' —the 'lady' or 'queen' of Upper Etruria. Her various symbols all find their echo in Teutonic words resembling the name VELATHRI in sound.†

---

* The nod of Juno, in assent to the invitation to Rome, has on the other hand been suggested by a word of similar sound, viz. *wey-an*, our English *wag*.

† The etymology given in the text is the broadest and simplest; but it is difficult to think of 'Velathri,' or Volterra, save in association with 'Alatrium,' now Alatri, near Ferentino, a most ancient city of the Hernici; or of both without remembrance of the three mysterious heads, the puzzle of Etruscan antiquaries, on the 'Porta dell' Arco' of the Etruscan city. If *Walt-ipa*, or *Waltari* be the oldest and most general title, I cannot at the same time but think that 'Velathri,' 'Alatri-,' (and I may add, conjecturally, 'Velitræ,') had, at some period, the more special sense of *dri-*

12. VOLSINII,—VELSINA, or VELSUNA, apparently, in Etruscan,—the modern Bolsena. The natural features of Volsinii consist, first, in its site—that, I mean, of the ancient Etruscan town, identified by Mr. Dennis as "the summit of the hill above the amphitheatre" which circles the Lake of Bolsena, "the loftiest height on this side of the lake, where the ground spreads out like a table-land, extensive enough to hold a city of first-rate importance;" and secondly, in the Lake itself, the 'Lacus Volsiniensis' of antiquity, filling the crater of an extinct volcano—its basin being of a nearly circular shape. The district has for ages been one of mystery and marvel. The lake, at all times bearing a changeful, unsteady, capricious character, was famous in pagan times for its floating islets covered with thick groves—sometimes taking a circular, sometimes a triangular, but never (a curious speciality) a square form; while in the days of Christianity it refused to receive into its bosom the little child-martyr St. Christina, when they threw her into the waters with a mill-stone round her neck, but bore her up, while she knelt in prayer (as Vincenzo Catena has depicted her in a beautiful picture at Venice),

---

falt, 'three-fold,' but with the position of the component syllables reversed, according to the peculiarity so frequently illustrated in the text of this Memoir. Volterra had under her wing two dependent and yet potent cities, Populonia and Luna, of both of which I shall speak presently; and a club and a crescent, which I believe to have been their respective symbols, are found on her own coins. The most memorable fact, moreover, in the history of Alatrium (nothing, it should be stated, of a similar nature, is recorded of Velitrae) is her joint refusal, along with Ferentinum and Verulli—(members like herself of the Hernican League, but which I should imagine to have been bound to her by immediate political ties)—to proclaim war against Rome,—which the Romans rewarded by permitting the three cities to retain their own laws and enjoy the mutual right of 'connubium,' and other immunities. We have thus the common point of a trifold (*drifaltig*) confederation attached respectively to Volterra and Alatri; and it is thus conceivable that the three heads over the 'Porta dell' Arco'—which in the ancient neuter plural form, as used by Ennius, would be expressed by 'Volta Tria'—represented the three Etruscan cities. This, indeed, may, as suggested, have been a symbol of more recent, although still ancient origin; and, as a general rule, I suspect that the Romans who ruled over Etruria frequently interpreted or played upon the Etruscan words and names according to Latin assonances and analogies, and invented symbols accordingly.

and bore her to the shore. The mill plays an important part in the traditions of Volsinii,—hand-mills, according to Pliny, were invented there, which turned of their own accord, by an innate vitality, reminding one of the living furniture with which Hephæstus supplied the courts of Olympus and the palace of Alcinous in Scheria, the land of the Phæacians. At a very early period, when Tinia still ruled the land, and probably before the town was founded, the monster 'Volta' —evidently, by the etymology of his name, a dragon—ravaged the surrounding country, till Porsena drew lightning from heaven and destroyed him. On another occasion the town was entirely consumed by lightning. Ages afterwards the marvellous element inseparably attached to Volsinii broke out again in the far-famed 'Miracle of Bolsena' immortalized by Raphael in the Vatican. The whole country was once, and still partly is, a vast forest—of exquisite beauty.—Before attempting to ascertain the etymology of the name, I may observe that 'Volsinii,' 'Felsina' (the Etruscan name of Bononia, or Bologna), and 'Fæsulæ,' or Fiesole, form a group etymologically and mythologically considered, and hang together, although distinguishable according to their respective leading characteristics. Volsinii was the most important member of this group, and the only one which had rank among the Twelve Cities of central or primitive Etruria. Assuming that the name of the Lake must be older than that of the town, its circular form, a marked characteristic, would naturally suggest the compound title, *Walbi-sèo*, the 'Round Sea,' or sheet of water; and this word, with its cognate *welbi*, 'vertigo,' and *walbi*, 'volubilis'—all from *wellan*, 'volvere,' would in time suggest its changeable character, as well as the spontaneous revolution of the hand-mills above spoken of. At the same time the situation of the lake, in a wood, and the idea of the floating islands (perhaps lacustrine habitations), would correspond to *wald*, forest, and the Greek ἄλσος, which we have in the Æolic form of ἄλτις in the name of the sacred grove of the Peloponnesian Olympia,—suggesting an alternate title *Falo*—or *wald-sèo*, that is, 'the Lake in the Forest.' When the primitive settlement developed into a town, it would naturally be called by a combination of the name of the lake with the local word, *heim* in Teutonic, -UNS in Rhætian, and -ENA in Etruscan, the name becoming *Walhi-æo-heim*, or ϝαλϝ-æo-ena, shortened into VELSUNA, or VOLSINII, the 'City on the Round Sea,' or 'Lake in the Forest.' But upon this foundation, a purely Pelasgic one, a more special character, etymological and mythological, was imposed, I think, at a very early period, and probably by the Thoringa or Tyrrhenian settlers. Keeping in view the composition of the name—its three elements VOL, æo, and ENA,—considering that 'v' is interchangeable with 'm ;' and that the presumption is that VOL or MOL must have been preceded by a primitive 'z,' commutable as 'k' or 'q,'—remembering in this connection the tradition about mills and mill-stones, the dragon Volta, and the legends (to be noticed hereafter) connected with Folsina and Fæsulæ—my impression is, that the initial VOL- represents, according to the Etruscan nomenclature, an earlier QVUL-, or KUL-, and that it is, in fact, the name of the goddess *Qual*, or Death, the Etruscan KULMU, whom we have identified with Kali and Hela, or Hel; and that the name 'Vol-æo-ena,' 'Volsinii' thus came to signify 'the City of the Sea of Hela,' 'Culmu,'—or possibly, if the 's' be viewed as a genitival inflection, 'Kulmu's-' or 'Hela's City' or dwelling,—being thus tantamount to the Scandinavian *Hel-heim* and Greek 'Elys-ium.' The floating islands and groves, quasi-islands of the blest, will at once recur to us here. I can but suggest the identity of the sacred ἄλτις of Olympia, with its lofty wall built by Hercules, its spacious gates, and the great πομπική εἴσοδος, or 'Path of Processions'—those, I believe (symbolically) of the Dead, marshalled by the ψυχοπομπός—with the walls and gates of Helheim, and the road trodden by Odin and Hermode to the halls of Hela. The topography of Helheim, as recorded in the Edda and that of Elis have many points of singular resemblance; and —as shewing connection with Volsinii—Elis was originally written with the digamma, 'Velia.' * Even the very -ENA in

* Elis, the 'holy land,' stands in etymological as well as mythological contrast to the rest of Peloponnesus, and especially to Laconia,—Alphæus, the river of 'life,' or 'white' river, flowing in its chequered course past Olympia and the sacred ἄλτις, as through paradise; and Eurotas, the river

the local name may possibly, in this particular instance, have the signification of 'Euna' in Sicily, where Cora, or Persephone, the Greek analogue of 'Hela,' was sporting when carried away; and Mr. Dennis's description of the site of the city corresponds with this suggestion. It is possible, on the other hand, that the lake may have derived its mythological name—or had a new sense imported into its original designation—from the dog of Hell, either Garmr (the classical Cerber-us) or the wolf Fenrir, the brother of Hela, and been thus called *Ulf's sö*; and this derives some plausibility from the consideration that it was on the shores of an *Ulf's sö* in the north that Völundr (or Weyland Smith) passed his early years; while Völundr was pupil of the wise smith Mimer, whom (as already stated) I take to be identical with the Mamurius Veturius so celebrated in the songs of the Salii, the priests of Mamers or Mars at Rome, Mars being the Southern analogue of Tyr, whose hand the wolf Fenrir bit off. But Felsina was the sacred city (I conceive) of Fenrir, and, although Fenrir may have been commemorated at Volsinii, Hela or Kulmn was, I think, the ruling spirit there. The great serpent Jörmundgand, or Midgards-örm, the other brother of Hela, is more recognisable perhaps in the dragon Volta, whose name reminds us at once of *walzan*, 'volvere,' and may perhaps be connectible with that of Ladon, FLadon, the dragon of the Hesperides. I lean therefore to the identification of 'Volsinii' with 'Hel's-heim,' 'Hel-heim,' or 'Elys--ium.' The legends respecting the mills and mill-stone have evidently sprung up from the commutability of the letters 'v' and 'm,' vol- and mul-, as above stated.* Whether the great name of the Völsungr is connected with Volsinii may

of 'death,' past Sparta, the 'black' and stern representative of annihilation—to their several bourns at opposite extremities of the peninsula.

* The root *vol-*, implying will, volition, spontaneity, probably exerted a collateral influence on the tradition. The hand-mills must have been of the primitive species familiar to us as 'querns,'—but this word would connect them with Hela through another channel. *Quern* perpetuates an older form than the Gaelic *braithean* and Welsh *breuan*; and its fundamental element, the Sanscr. 'jri,' to grind, must be taken in connection with *Quer = χείρ =* the obsolete Latin 'hir,' hand. 'h' and 'l' being interchangeable, 'hir,' *quer*, associates itself with 'Hel-a,' 'Kora.'

be subject for inquiry. I may at least suggest the identity of *Nibel-* with *Nifl-* in 'Nifl-heim,' and of *Giuki* with *Aki*, and thus, through Hela, with every district where her awful home was localised. It is in keeping with the preceding suggestions that the river which flows from the Lake of Bolsena to the sea is called the 'Marta,'—whether it allude to 'Mars' (Tyr), or 'Mors,' Death; and that the ancient name of GRAVISCÆ, the sea-port of Tarquinii, which lies towards its mouth—a place as pestiferous in ancient times as it is now—stamped, as Mr. Dennis remarks, with the "curse on Moab and Ammon—salt-pits and a perpetual desert"—suggests the idea of the 'grub,' or grave. Volsinii and Graviscæ probably existed before Tarchon built Tarquinii on an intervening spot,—and even there, when he ploughed his first furrow, the element of marvel, attached to the region, broke forth in the apparition of the mysterious Tages. But these last may be merely fanciful approximations. The preceding explanation of 'Volsinii' cannot be fully appreciated till after perusal of what has yet to be said regarding Felsina and Fæsulæ.

ii. *Of other Etruscan Cities.*

1. ADRIA, in the older orthography ATRIA,—founded by the Etruscans on the Eastern coast of Italy, at a confluence of rivers, and among vast marshes. The Etruscans who settled there connected the rivers by canals, drained the marshes, and became a great maritime and commercial people, and the adjacent gulf derived its name from ADRIA, as the 'Adriatic.'—From *watr, udr, ὕδωρ*, water, (the root of *Atrium*, as elsewhere shewn,) and signifying 'The City of Waters.'

2. ALSIUM,—either from ἅλς, the sea, (literally salt), or ἄλσος, *hols*, a grove.

3. CAPENA,—perhaps from i. *kamp, kam*, a comb, or mountain-ridge, in allusion to its position, and ii. *ena*.

4. CAPUA,—perhaps, proximately, from *hof*, as the court, capital, or chief city (which it was) of Campania. But the idea of *kamph*, battle, *kampho*, warrior or champion, was equally present to the memories of the place, as shewn by a

coin of Capua representing two warriors shaking hands,—the idea of compact, or reconciliation, thus indicated, finding its expression likewise in *kp*, the hollow of the hand, and the whole tribe of words of which *kaupen*, *kaufen*, is the general representative. The oldest affinity of the name, however, is with CAPYS, γύψ, the vulture; and this I infer from the name VOLTURNUS conferred on Capua by the Etruscans after the conquest,—VOLTUR- evidently answering to CAPYS, the latter being probably the Pelasgian and the former the Tyrrhenian equivalent.

5. CLAVENNA, now Chiavenna, in Rhætia; situated at the foot of the pass over the Splügen.—From *kliuban*, *kliufa*, to cleave, or separate, in the sense of a cleft or pass in the mountains. The word 'Splügen' derives, I suspect, from the corresponding form found in Sanscrit as *phal*, 'findi,' *sphal*, 'dissilire'—to split, or cleave asunder. But *su*, *sp*, being interchangeable with *k*, 'Spl-ug-' and 'Cl-av-' themselves both resolve into one root.

6. COSA, Κόσσαι, now called 'Ansedonia;' a marvellous Cyclopean fortress of Pelasgic antiquity, erected on a conical hill overlooking the Tyrrhenian Sea.—The Roman 'Consus,' whose character is defined as 'Neptunus Equestris,' and 'Poseidon' were the same deity. COSA, I imagine, reflects the former, and 'Ansedonia' the latter title. Ossa, in Thessaly, now called 'Kissavo' (conf. COSA), is also of conical shape; and I believe was originally sacred to Poseidon. The idea of the wedge, or 'cuneus,' was also connected with 'Consus.' The port of Cosa, 'Portus Cosanus,' was named the Ἡρακλέους Λιμήν, or 'Portus Herculis.' This suggests an influence from Egypt through the Greeks, Khonso being the Egyptian analogue of Hercules; and the connection of Hercules with Cosa is thus apparently accounted for.*

* Porto d'Ercole stands on the peninsula of 'Mons Argentarius,' a name sufficiently appropriate to the silver expanse of waters, but which rather, I should think, points to the metal silver having been found there at some remote period. The tradition of silver—or at least of metal; for the same word seems to have been applied at different times alike to silver and iron—as expressed in the Gothic *silubr* and Lithuanian *sidabras*, has evidently, I think, given its name to the ancient town facing Mons Argentarius, and

7. FÆSULÆ, the modern Fiesole, situated on the summit of a hill, an advanced post or buttress of the Apennine. The coins attributed to FÆSULÆ bear a winged gorgon holding serpents in each hand, with the inscription PHESC in Etruscan letters. The goddess 'Ancharia' was worshipped there,—of her we know nothing, but the goddess 'Angitia' was the protectress from serpents; and, taking this fact in connection with the initial syllable of 'Anch-aria,' the presumption is that they were identical, and that at all events Ancharia is represented by the gorgon on the coin. In approaching the etymology of FÆSULÆ the first thing that strikes us is the fact that 'ancharius,' denoting an ass in the Latin, is equivalent to *esil* in Teutonic. *Esil, Fesil,* or *Fesil,* and 'Anchar-ia' are thus brought into connection with a special reference to that animal. The ass is the symbol of 'Set,' or 'Tet,' the Syrian and Egyptian God, once held in the highest honour, but afterwards dreaded and hated as Typhon, and who is identical with Azhi Dahâka, the demon out of whose shoulders grew —not wings, but serpents, in Iranic tradition—Azhi Dahâka, again, being identical with Asa-Lok, or Lok, of our Scandinavian mythology.* I cannot pause upon the proof of all this. Further, the wife of Lok was Angur-boda, the 'messenger of ill,' a giantess from Jarnwid, the 'forest of iron;' and she became by him the mother of the goddess Hela, of Fenrir the wolf, and of the great serpent, worm, or 'anguis,' Midgards-örm. I would suggest, therefore, that FÆSUL-Æ was named after Lok under the symbol of an *esil,* or ass; and that 'Ancharia,' represented by the gorgon with her snakes

now named Orbitello, but in which the root *s-l-b, o-r-b,* has been the prime constituent element. The same root *silb-* appears in the river 'Alb-inia.' Moreover, the port of Telamone, looking straight on Mons Argentarius from the North, recalls the tradition that Æacus, father of Telamon, was the first discoverer of silver. Here too the etymologies melt into each other, *s-l-b* = 'Telam-on,' and likewise 'Salum-is.' Silver would appear to be more especially connected with Poseidon through the Lithuanian *sidabras*. The prevalence of silver, 'argentum,' along this coast may have contributed to the development of the poetical legend that the Argonauts visited it on their return from Colchis.

* I think that our familiar 'Jack-Ass' is a corruption of 'Dahâka-Azhi,' or 'Lok-Ass,' the titles being reversed. Thus are the mighty fallen!

on the coins above mentioned, is his wife 'Angur-boda.' We thus have the father and mother established at Fiesolo; while Hela, their daughter, with their son, the great dragon 'Volta,' rules as we have seen at Volsinii. Here too—as at Volsinii, and in the river Marta—we have the idea of death present, if I mistake not, in the name of the 'Arnus,' or Arno—which I take to have been originally 'Marun-' in old Etruscan—the black, sorrowful, or (in French) 'morne' river of hell. Lower down on its banks we have 'Pisa,' answering to the 'Pisa' of Elis, but with this difference, that the 'Pisa' of Elis is on the banks of the Alphæus, the river of light and life; whereas the Etruscan 'Pisa' is on those of the river of darkness, corresponding to the Eurotas. This would appear to shew that the essential spirit and import of the name 'Pisa' had been lost sight of before the Etruscan town was founded.*

8. FANUM VOLTUMNÆ.—Respecting this city *vide supra*, under the goddess 'Voltumna.'

9. FELSINA, the Latin 'Bononia,' now Bologna, styled by Pliny "princeps Etruriæ,"—the "city of puppy-dogs and sausages," as Mr. Dennis calls it—the puppies being the "dogs of Bologna, so celebrated in the middle ages, which still figure in the city arms, and are alluded to in the epitaph of King Enzius;" while, as regards the sausages, we may recall the etymological resemblance of the 'ventres Falisci,' and those of 'Fels-inn,' and the Latin name of a sausage, or black-pudding, 'botulus'—from the same root evidently as the Greek μύζα. The dog-symbol is of Etruscan antiquity,—a coin exists with the legend VELSU, exhibiting a woman's head and a dog as its device, which Niebuhr assigns to Volsinii and Sestini to Bologna, but which the heraldic symbolism so long perpetuated may satisfy us belongs to the

* Pisa, in Elis, had originally the presidency over the Olympian festival, but lost it through the usurpation of the Elaians. Tantalus and Pelops were kings of Pisa, and it was there that Pelops was slain and served up to the gods as food by his father Tantalus. I believe this legend to be a perverted form of a very ancient and universal tradition of eucharistic sacrifice; and that the name 'Pisa' records this, as derived from *ps* (Egyptian), to cook, —an ancient word cognate with our familiar 'foss-t,' and other words in the Aryan tongues.

latter city. My belief is that, as Hela was the lady of Volsinii, and Lok and Angurboda were the patrons of Fæsulæ, so FELSINA completed the mythological group as the ULF'S--ENA, or 'Wolf's-heim'—the 'City of the Whelp,' 'Wolf,' or 'Dog'—to wit, Fenrir, the son of Lok; and who, although not identical with Garmr or Cerberus, may be presumed to be the dog that Odin (Vegtam) met coming from Helheim as he rode to consult the Vala concerning the dreams of Balder. The association of dogs and sausages would almost suggest that the 'offa' flung to Cerberus by Æneas was a 'botulus,' in the opinion of Felsina; and certainly it would have been a more acceptable morsel—at least in the opinion of the dogs of the present day. If, then, the dog on the coin be Fenrir, the woman is probably either Hela, his sister, or Angurboda, his mother. The special interpretation of which the names of these three cities, Volsinii, Fæsulæ, and Felsina are thus susceptible—while they all echo the same general idea of 'Helheim'—confirm, I submit, the general accuracy of the approximations offered. It may be added in corroboration, that Mantua, a daughter of Felsina, derives her name from another peculiarly Etruscan deity of the infernal regions; while, as Felsina was herself a daughter of Perusia, it is not improbable that some tradition of Persephone had been superimposed by the Pelasgi on the original and simple name of that fortress, as above alluded to.*

10. FESCENNIUM,—a dependency on Falerii. It derived its name, I think, from the character of the soil on which it was built. Its area is now, according to Mr. Dennis, "covered with dense wood," and he describes himself as forcing his way "through pathless thickets." This, however, is merely Nature vindicating her own, triumphing over the ploughs and pride of man,—as it is, so it was before Pelasgian or Etruscan set

---

* It may have occurred to the reader that a combination of L. *felis*, (*hella*, *hallr*, O. N.,) '*petra, promontorium,*' or of *hals*, '*collum,*' neck; and il. *ena*, would produce a word akin to the German '*Felsenberg*' and give intelligible meaning to the names Felsina and Volsinii. But the sites of those two towns do not answer to the idea of a *fels*; and, although that of Fæsulæ meets the requirement, the letters '*s*' and '*l*' must be transposed to make the etymology suit, a liberty not to be taken without sufficient cause.

foot there. I should therefore derive the name from *busc*, pl. *buscen*, implying low trees and scrub, in our colonial phrase, 'the bush,'—'Buscen-heim,' 'Fescenn-ium,' the 'Town in the Bush.' In keeping with this, the site is now occupied by a church dedicated to S. Silvestro; and the whole plain takes its name accordingly. 'Silvestro' is an exact translation of the original appellation. Modern names are constantly translations of old ones, and should never be neglected, as they often furnish clues to the identification of forgotten sites.*

11. HORTANUM, or HORTA, now Orla,—named after the goddess Horta.

12. LUNA,—the celebrated sea-port, so called—situated in the Bay, now termed, of Spezia. Müller thinks that Luna was named so from the shape of the port, as resembling the moon, but it has no resemblance at all to that luminary; and Mr. Dennis rightly observes that we have no ground for supposing that 'Luna' implied the moon originally in Etruscan. He suggests that, inasmuch as '-luna' occurs as a termination to the names of other Etruscan towns — of Populonia and Vetulonia—all situated on the sea-side—it signifies 'Port.' I have no doubt that it does in the particular case of 'Luna'—but not so, I think, as regards the

* Let me add, for the credit of Etruria, that the 'versus Fescennini,' the ribald rhymes of Rome, did *not*, I am convinced, derive their name from Fescennium, but from their own native characteristics. They were sung in irregular, extempore, doggrel, alternate verses, dialogue-wise, by the peasants, bantering and rallying each other, not in malice but in the indulgence of the coarsest fun and humour—the regular amusement of the harvest-home among the Oscan villages; from whence they were introduced into Rome and sung, especially at weddings. The root of the word is evidently the Teutonic *hön*, explained as 'nuggs, nænia,' light or scurrilous discourse, but with a strong collateral influence from *bis*, the root of *bisjan*, *bisön*, 'lascivire,' to wanton or frolic as cattle do, and of *bisa* or *bræs*, the Scandinavian word implying the rushing of cattle to and fro, from one side to the other, when persecuted by the hornet or gadfly. The former of these roots would express the general character of the song, wanton and free,—the latter its alternate or antiphonal character, and the venom of satire which animated it. *Bita, beissen*, to bite, and *byta*, the Northern word expressive of interchange, literally 'chaff,' (kindred forms to *bisjan*, *bisa*,) may equally be noticed in this connection. 'B' and 'F' are letters, I need not say, closely akin and interchangeable.

other towns, which I account for differently. Towards ascertaining the root of LUNA we must consider the analogy between that word and the Latin 'portus.' 'Port-,' whether in 'porta' or 'portus,' is akin to 'opertus,' and implies that which is 'clausus,' shut up or enclosed—as distinguished from that which is 'apertus'—expanded or open. Thus 'port-' in 'portus' originally meant the house, as in the Law of the Twelve Tables. Its secondary meaning is the gate, or barrier, —'port-,' 'porta,' 'portus,'—by which the entrance of the house, or of any place, is shut up and defended. Hence 'portus' came to signify a port, or sea-port—that is, a place in which ships are sheltered and defended against the tempests of the sea—the house, in fact, of the navy. 'Importunus' is thus used to describe a shore where there is no port for refuge, 'opportunus' for one where there is. Now LUNA appears to me to be derivable from the old Teutonic by precisely the same analogy as 'portus.' The verb *lúhhan* and its compound *biLúhhan* (derived, like the kindred *liuhhan*, 'vellere,' 'frangere,' from the root *luch*), are equivalent to 'claudere,' to shut up; while *antLúhhan*, on the contrary, implies 'aperire,' to open; and *lun* in old Teutonic—which appears to me directly derived from it—signifies 'paxillus,' 'obex, 'humerulus,' a stake or pile, a bar or bolt, or any obstacle used for the purpose of impeding or shutting up. The Etruscan LUNA therefore—assuming the word to be, like *lun*, a softened derivative from *lúhhan*—is the precise analogue to the Latin 'portus;' and implies, like that word, 'a place shut up and protected' from the rage of the winds and waves—in fact 'the Port' *per excellentiam*. The port of Luna is emphatically *the* port of the whole coast of Etruria; and the lines of Silius Italicus descriptive of the place, as cited by Mr. Dennis, equally illustrate the preceding etymology,—

> " Insignis portu, quo non spatiosior alter
> Innumeras cepisse rates, et *claudere portum*."

I may observe further that *lúhhan* is explained in modern German by *schliessen*, to lock; while *schloss* implies both a lock and a fortress or castle, *i.e.* a place shut up and protected—in fact, a 'fort,' which may be in reality the same word as 'portus.' We have the same ideas expressed by *lukhan* and *lus*, 'claudere' and 'obex,' in close approximation in the—

"*Ecce maris magni claudit nos objice portus*"

of Virgil, and the

"*portasque petunt quas objice firmá
Clauserat Iliades,*"

of Ovid.* I may add in conclusion, that Portumnus, or Portunus (the Greek Palæmon), the God of Ports, "deus portuum præses," had the custody of keys ('clavium')—the Teutonic *schloss*,—and was usually represented with a key in his hands; while Janus, in his character of president over the doorway, was also sometimes named Portumnus. Portumnus or Portunus is evidently a combination of i. *Port*, and ii. *ana*, deity. In later times *Luna* doubtless was symbolised by a crescent, and is figured so on the coins of her mother state, Volterra.

13. MANTUA,—a colony (as has been stated) of Felsina, and the birth-place of Virgil—or, at least, the mother town of 'Andes,' where he was actually born.—Named (according to Mr. Dennis, and I have no doubt he is right †) after Mantus, the Etruscan personification of Hades; which is in keeping with the etymology which I have suggested for Volsinii, Fæsulæ, and Felsina. The peculiar character of Mantua as a *mund*, *munt*, or fortress, is of modern date.

14. PISÆ,—named after the old Pelasgian city in Peloponnesus. I have spoken of the etymology of the latter in a note, *supra*.

15. POPULONIA,—in Etruscan orthography, PUPLUNA; the port of Volterra, and "the grand depôt and factory of the iron of Elba." ‡ Of the devices on her coins some, as the head of Vulcan with the hammer and tongs—that of Mercury with the caduceus—and that of Minerva with the owl, appear to point to her staple article of commerce. The head of a gorgon

---

* *Virg. Æn.* v. 377; *Ovid, Met.* xiv. 780; *Sil. Ital., Punic.* viii. 483.
—And see Dennis, *Cities*, &c., vol. ii. p. 81.

† *Cities and Cemeteries*, vol. I. p. lvi.

‡ *Ibid.* vol. ii. p. 242.

is another very peculiar symbol. We have also the wild boar; and a coin with a female head covered with the lion's skin, and a club on the reverse, which evidently points to Hercules, the female head being identified by Müller with that of Omphale, although he suggests a doubt whether it may not be that of Hercules in youth. Of these types I should assign the four first to the dominant idea of ἔργ, *work*, as embodied in the Greek 'Εργάνη, the title of Athene, ' Men-eruca' in Etruscan, as has been shewn,—handiwork at the smelting-furnace and forge on the exported iron of Ilva, or Elba. The wild boar, 'aper,' *aphul*—the animal that peculiarly strikes, may, in the stage of the digamma, have been used as a symbol of PUPL- in PUPLUNA. That 'Omphalo,' with the digamma, equally answers to PUPL- is evident; but the same connection exists with Hercules also through his symbolical tree, the 'populus,' and the primitive *afl*, *Fafl*, *popl*-, denoting strength. Mr. Dennis connects the name with that of 'Phophluns,' Dionysus; but I see no direct trace of connection between the town and that God.—I think we must resort for the etymology to the character which POPULONIA must have presented during the earliest times of its existence—that of a smithy, gradually of course developing into a factory, for the smelting and working of the imported iron. I have already spoken of *ak*, *smy*, *schmeil* as an ancient root implying separation, as of the ore from the dross, and have derived from it the name of Sethlans, originally (as suggested) *Schmethl-uns*. Abrading the initial 's' in Smethl-, and applying the well-known rules governing the intermutation of letters, we obtain on the one hand the Latin 'faber,' smith, and on the other an Etruscan constituent root, PUPL, which may be presumed to have the same signification as 'faber.' PUPL, with the suffix UNA (from *wonēn*, to dwell), would then give us the sense of 'smithy' as that of Populonia. It is not a little curious, I may add, that the Latin 'papilio' signifies both a butterfly and a tent—that the butterfly, lightning, the Telchines, and the smithy generally, have a close etymological relation in the Celtic and Teutonic languages—and that PUPLUNA, or POPULONIA, read as a word of cognate development with 'papiliones,' would exactly describe the sheds, or tents, which must have been exhibited by the original encampment of workmen when the first cargoes of ore were shipped from Elba. Through 'papilio' as a butterfly—the ϝαιϝολος, or variegated—we have a connection with Phuphluns under this latter conjecture; but that with Hercules on the coins is more immediate, through ϝαϛ, and ΡϹΡΛ. The club must, I think, be viewed as a πίτυλος in this connection, as it certainly is to be understood in the case of Vetulonia. The word is used for the movement of the hands and oars in rowing, for the succession of blows planted in boxing, and for an athletic exercise which seems to have corresponded with our dumb-bells (although no clubs are mentioned in connection with it); but it is equally appropriate to the succession of strokes given by the smith at the anvil; and thus πίτυλ-, or, with the restoration of the lost initial σ, σπίτυλ-, brings us back literally to the original form, Schmeitil-, or Sceitil-, whence 'Sethlans.'

16. SALPINUM,—now represented, as it is believed, by Torre Alfina, a fortress on a lofty height ten miles west of Bolsena.—From i. *halba*, the flank of a mountain (whence the familiar *alp*), and ii. *heim*, or *ena*. 'H' and 's' are constantly interchangeable.

17. SATURNIA,—from the name of the God known in Italy as Saturn, but recognisable in many kindred forms elsewhere.

18. SUTRIUM,—where the Goddess Horta had a temple.—Perhaps a compound of 'Hort-a' and *heim*, the 'City of Horta.'

19. VULCI,—not properly an Etruscan name; it was the town of the Volcentini, who were neither Volsci, Falisci, nor Pelasgi, but, I think, Bolgæ, of the same stock as the Volcæ Aricomi and Volcæ Tectosages in Gallia Narbonensis, and the Volcæ Tectosages of Asia Minor,—all of them branches, although scattered, of one great Cymric and (comprehensively) Celtic race.

iii. *Of Rome, as an Etruscan City.*

1. ROME,—built, as we are told, with Etruscan rites, and distinctly recognised by Mr. Dennis as "an Etruscan

city."*—This, however, can only apply to what I conceive to
have been the re-foundation of Rome by the Patricians, or
conquering race—'Atringa,' or Thoringa, akin to the Tyrrheni
or Etruscans—who formed for so many generations the ruling
class there, but commingled ultimately with the Plebeians,
the descendants of the conquered Latins and Sabines. It
was these latter races who constituted the bulk of the Roman
people under the name of Quirites, and it is to them that
the name 'Roma' exclusively attaches itself.—ROMA is a
compound of i. 'R,' and ii. *heim*; and thus equivalent to
the 'City of R.' Mars, it will be recollected, was the tutelary
God and supposed ancestor of the Roman people. Mars was
otherwise styled 'Gra-divus,' and 'Gra' (as has been stated)
is the same word with 'Quir,' the root of 'Quir-inus' and the
patronymic 'Quir-ites.' I therefore identify 'R' with 'Gra'
or 'Quir'—with ̓Αρης, the God of War of Thrace and Greece
—and with the Teutonic and Indo-European 'Hra,' the ̓Ερρος
or 'Herr' of Æolic or Pelasgic antiquity, the ancestral eponymus of the entire race whom I have qualified as 'Hrainga.'
'Gra,' again, is probably the same as the 'Va-Gur,' or 'the
Lord Gur,' the Babylonian title of Nergal, the God of War
and planet Mars of Babylonia and Assyria, and who stands
in close relation with Thourras, the Assyrian Hercules, and
(as well as the deities previously enumerated) with Tyr, the
Mars or Ares of Scandinavia. The Quirites and Patricii of
Rome were thus fundamentally of the same stock, but in the
same manner and relative antiquity as the Rhæti and the
Tyrrheni, the Grutungi and the Tervingi, the Pelasgi and
the Hellenes—branches severally of the older Gothic, Jötun,
Teuton, and Titan race; and that both Latins and Quirites
were Pelasgi is further shewn by the epithet 'Prisci' at-
tachable to both, a word which, in its oldest signification, is
a mere variety (as already observed) of the name 'Pelasgi,'
the 'l' and 'r' being interchanged. 'Latium' again and
'Latini' are mere varieties of the names 'Rhætia' and
'Rhæti' through the same interchangeability. And the
Lydians, the Eastern kinsmen of the Etruscans, the rulers

* *Cities, &c.*, vol. ii. p. 490.

over an Oriental Latium or Rhætia, are described as ' Rot-n-no ' in the Egyptian inscriptions—the same patronymic, I doubt not, as ' Grot-ungi.' It follows from these considerations that the Etruscan rites above mentioned as attending the foundation of Rome must have sanctioned the building—not of the original, but of a new Rome on the ruins of an older one, which yet transmitted its name and its population to historical times; and the secret name of the city, respecting which there has been so much controversy, was that, I take it, of this Patrician or Thoringa city, standing in the same relation to that of the earlier Rome as the name of ' Cære ' to the original one of ' Agylla ' and that of ' Arretium ' to ' Upn.' It would be out of place here to go into details respecting the original tribes and primeval antiquities of Rome, seeing that they belong to pre-Etruscan times. But the Latin, Sabine, Oscan, and other races connected with early Rome were all of the Japhetan stock; and almost every point connected with them, in manners or in history, may be elucidated by the help of the old Teutonic—to say nothing of its sister Aryan languages.

CONCLUSIONS FROM THE PRECEDING SURVEY.

It remains for us to estimate the evidence afforded by the preceding words and etymologies as affecting the thesis, that the Etruscans were a Teutonic people speaking a Teutonic language—a very ancient branch of that people, speaking a very ancient dialect of that language.

The first process in the investigation must be to clear the ground of every word that can be considered doubtful or questionable—in other words, not demonstrably Etruscan. I have necessarily included in the survey all the words without exception which are stated to have been Etruscan, or which express, according to trustworthy testimony, Etruscan offices, *insignia*, or things in general. I have thus the broadest footing to stand upon, and could afford to be generous in concession, even to the most carping critic. I should make him a present in the first instance of a number of words unquestionably in use among the Etruscans, but which, as being common to the Etruscan, the Greek, and the Latin languages, may be fairly described as Pelasgian. It might be shewn that the Pelasgi themselves were, if not Teutons, nearly allied to the Teutonic race; but this would complicate the matter; and the simplest course is to exclude such words altogether from the argument.* And further, there are many words which are the same, or nearly the same, in the Etruscan and in the group of languages to which the Sabine, Oscan, and Latin (in its Oscan element) belong. That these latter tongues and the races that spoke them were likewise closely allied to the Teutonic stock, I firmly believe. But my object at present is to avoid controversy, and I will therefore dispense with these words also.

An ample store of materials remains for consideration notwithstanding these deductions. We have, for example, among the words expressive of the relations of life and society, *Lars* or *Larth*, implying the 'pater-familias,' or house-father; *al*, implying mother's son; *clan*, eldest child; *agalletor*, a boy in a state of pupilage; *atrium*, the open or hypæthral hall of the family residence; *druna*, government; and *Lucumo*, the guardian of the law, or chief magistrate:— Among words descriptive of dress, the *bulla*, worn by the sons of the Etruscan and Roman Patricians; the *cassila*, or helmet; the *balteus*, or military belt; and the *toga*:—Under the group of words referential to public amusements, the *gapos*, or basket-carriage (a word essentially Teutonic in its Etruscan form); the *subulo*, or flute-player; the *lanista*, or keeper of gladiators; the *hister*, or pantomimic actor; the

* This was written long before the examination of the Pelasgian inscriptions of Cære, treated of in the preceding Memoir.

ludio, or player; and the *lucar*, the price of admission to the public shews—every one of the words grouped under this head being purely Etruscan and Teutonic:—Among animals and birds we find the *damnus*, or pack-horse; *antar*, the eagle; *aracos*, the hawk; *capys*, the falcon or vulture; and *gnis*, the crane:—Among plants and material substances,—*ataeson*, the wild, or creeping vine, and *apluda*, the chaff of corn or froth of pottage:—Surveying elementary nature, we have *falandum*, the heavens, or sky; *aukelos*, the dawn; the *antæ*, the winds; and *andas*, the North Wind, or North generally:—Among words expressive of matters of common life, and of miscellaneous import, I may enumerate *mantisa*, a makeweight; *nepos*, a spendthrift; *aquilex*, a spring-finder: *vorsus*, a square field; *quinquatria*, the name of a festival, together with kindred words, compounded of the numerals three, five, six, seven, and ten, all Indo-Germanic; and *burrus*, a cup, or drinking-vessel,—together with the familiar invocation *Arse verse*, 'averte ignem,' and the sepulchral *Ril avil*, 'he lived' so many 'years:'—Under the category of deities, we have *Æsar*, the collective term for 'Gods; *Tinia*, or Jupiter; *Kupra*, or Juno, at least in her character of guardian of contracts; and *Menerva*, or *Meneruca*, Minerva; the Dii *Complices, Consentes, Novensiles,* and *Involuti; Aril,* or Atlas; *Horta*, the goddess of gardens; *Mantus*, the Etruscan Pluto, or Hades; *Nortia*, or Fate; *Phuphluns*, or Bacchus; *Pomona*, the goddess of fruit-trees; *Sethlans*, or Vulcan; *Summanus*, the God of the nightly heavens; *Thalna*, the goddess of childbirth; *Thesan*, or Aurora; *Thurms*, or Hermes; *Turan*, or Venus Urania; *Vejovis* or *Vedius*, a form of Dis, or Pluto; *Vertumnus*, the god of the revolving seasons; *Voltumna*, the goddess of will, or counsel:—And among dæmons, or deities, of lesser dignity, the *Lasas* or *Means*, the mild or decreeing Fates; with *Leinth*, the goddess of Fame, *Kulmu*, of Death, and *Vanth*, of Tears; and the

demoniac *Nathum*, the Destiny of the Etruscan mythology:
—Passing from the world of deity to that of departed spirits,
we have the *Lemures*, the *Lares*, and the *Manes*:—Under the
head of divination are to be reckoned the genius *Tages*, the
revealer of the Etruscan discipline; *Begoe*, the beautiful interpretress of the lightning,—and, I think we may add, the
Sibyl, and her books of fate:—The *Haruspices* were unquestionably derived from Etruria, and probably the Roman
Augurs likewise; while the *lituus*, the *templum*, and the *pomœrium* are certainly Etruscan:—Among words appropriated to
public and private worship, we have *sacer*, pure through
refinement, with its derivatives *Sacrificium*, *Sacerdos*, and the
Rex Sacrificulus; and the *Flamen*, or private priest:—
Among religious festivals, the *Compitalia*, or feast of the
Lares Compitales:—The whole system of the *Calendar*, the
Calends and *Ides* of the month, &c.—and, I think also, the
Pontifex Maximus and the College of Pontifices, rank among
the institutions originally derived from Etruria; while the
system of *Sæcula*, or ages, was a doctrine peculiarly Etruscan:—Among words expressive of civil office and ceremonial,
the title *Lucumo* (already mentioned); that of *Rex*, or king;
that of *Consul* and of *Prætor*—with the *lictor*, the *fasces*, the
sella curulis, the *trabea*, the *toga prætexta*, and the *laticlave*,
the attendants and *insignia* of authority — were certainly
Etruscan,—and so too (or at least of Patrician or Thoringic
institution) were the *Senate*—the *Comitia*—and probably the
Fœtiales (*Feciales*), or guardians of the public faith:—Among
proper names, those of the twelve confederate Etruscan cities,
*Arretium, Cære, Clusium, Cortona, Falerii, Perusia, Rusellæ,
Tarquinii, Veii, Vetulonia, Volterra, Volsinii*, are important
witnesses; as well as those of other towns of Etrurian origin,
but not members of the confederation, such as *Adria, Fæsulæ,
Felsina, Luna, Mantua, Populonia*, and *Salpinum*. The
patronymic *Tyrrheni*, 'sons of Tyrr,' or 'Thor,' bears similar

testimony. But that of *Hrasena*, as well as the name of *Rome* (the original city, before its refoundation with Etruscan rites), can only be noticed as testifying to the Rhætian or Rasenic affinities of the Etruscans proper.

Confining, then, our attention to the words just enumerated, I think we are entitled to affirm that they are Teutonic, and that the Etruscan speech as represented by these words, covering as they do the most essential elements and features of the national life, thought, and polity, was a Teutonic language. —[My original impression (as stated at the beginning of the text of this volume) was that, taken in combination with the converging arguments from the national patronymic, and from the correspondence in manners, civil and religious, and in national character, between the Etruscans and the Teutons, the identifications above submitted afforded sufficient proof of my thesis. That original impression may have been right,—and yet I do not regret having been induced to make the further researches among the original inscriptions recorded in the pages preceding this Glossary, through an anxiety to leave no stone unturned that could reveal truth. 1872.]

I have not, of course, forgotten the wise and established rule, that mere resemblance of words is insufficient by itself alone to infer identity of race, unless it can be shewn at the same time that the grammatical structure of the language exhibits a corresponding similarity. It is a well-known fact that in certain instances a people have lost the greater part of their original speech, and substituted foreign words in almost every instance for those originally native to them; and yet the grammatical structure, the skeleton (as it were) of their former language, survives, and betrays the foreign importation. But in a case like this, where not only the roots and words correspond throughout, but the correspondence of language is confirmed by correspondence in manners, polity, religion, and surname, all in perfect harmony, the rule in question loses (I conceive) a great part of its stringency and significance.*

We are not, however, without proofs that the grammatical structure of the Etruscan was similar to that of the Teutonic languages. In the nominative case, singular, of nouns, for example, we have *as*, necessarily the singular of *Æsar*; *lemur*, the singular of *lemures*, evidently the same with *lamr*, the Old Northern or Scandinavian form of *lam*, deficient or lame; *vanth*, identical with *weinöt*, weeping, *leinth* with *hliumunt*, fame, *compit-* and *comit-* with *chumpft*, the fact of 'coming' or assembly. We have *hister*, formed from the verb *gasa*, like *gasiri* and our English 'jester,'—and *lictor*, corresponding with *leitiri*, a leader, formed in like manner from *leitjan*, *lediun*. In the genitive case we have the Teutonic form in *avils* answering to 'metatis;' in *Clus-*, i. e. *hlévo-es*, the initial syllable of *Clusium*; in *Thes-*, answering to *tou-es*, the component portion of *Thes-an*, the Goddess of the dew; and in *ar-*, the initial syllable of the *azamenta* or war-songs of the Salii, originally, as I conceive, *wiges*, the genitive of *wig*, 'bellum,' war. In the nominative plural we have *Æsar*, corresponding to the Scandinavian Aesir; in the genitive plural, *heriono*, as found in *Vertumnus*, and *buschen*, as in *Fescennium*. The dative plural, as governed by the preposition *bi*, is recognisable in *Pomœrium*, or (as I have analysed it) the *Bi--múrom*. The name *Sibylla* bespeaks the feminine gender, agreeable to its analogue, the Teutonic *spella*. The adjectival termination *isc* is found in *vorsus*, i. e. *fiorisc-us*, and in *Tages*, equivalent, I believe, to *Tuisc-o*; and that of *-inga* in *Tyrrh-eni*, Thoringa. The preterite form in verbs is seen

* A passage nearly to the same effect as this will have been noticed *supra*, towards the conclusion of the text of this volume. But the observation is appropriate here also. I leave it, and the paragraph that follows, as written many years ago.

in *ril*, 'vixit;' the participle passive in *Calende* (*gaLined-dug*), and in the Dies *Fasti* (from *fas*, to bind, *fast-*, that which is bound, or fixed). The prefix *ga* is observable in *gapos* (*gaWeb-*), *gnis* (*gaNöz*), *aquiles* (*gaLes-*), in the Dii *Complices* (*guPleg-*) and *Consentes* (*guSinde*), in the *Augur* (*eó-gu-Wári*), in the *Calends*, and in the *Consul* (*gaSello*).—These are but a few instances, and yet sufficient, I think, to meet the demand above indicated.

[Some slight discrepancies may be detected between the forms of ancient Teutonic adduced in this Appendix, and those brought forward in the text of this volume. This has arisen from the accidental circumstance that I used Graff's 'Althochdeutscher Sprachschatz,' Ihre's 'Glossarium Suio-Gothicum,' and Finn Magnusen's 'Lexicon Mythologicum' (appended to the third volume of his edition of the Edda), as my fireside manuals while working out the preceding vocabulary, but Scherz and Oberlin's Glossary when translating the greater number of the Inscriptions. The discrepancy is merely superficial. And it is possible that a true instinct guided me in my resort to counsel in each instance. It is certainly remarkable at first sight, that while the common vocabulary of the Etruscans in practical life, as shewn in the Inscriptions, has nearer relation upon the whole to the languages of continental Germany than to the Old-Northern or (what would be a better name) the Norræna speech, of Iceland and Scandinavia, the names and attributes of deities and matters connected with the services of religion receive illustration rather from the Old-Northern than from the Germanic proper. But this—and there are considerable exceptions to qualify it as a general rule—will be accounted for when we recollect that, while we possess the Edda of Scandinavia, the precious repository of her early Asa or Odinite faith, we have inherited nothing of a corresponding nature from the Goths or Thuringians. The early conversion of these latter nations to Christianity consigned their mythological records to oblivion, but the probability is that if those records had been preserved, we should have found the same deities and the same legends in central Germany as in Scandinavia, and recognised the faith of the Edda as that of the entire Teutonic people. Meanwhile, the loss of these records has a tendency to give undue prominence to Scandinavia in any argument as to the origin of the Etruscans based upon the analysis of words and names pertaining to the class of religious or ceremonial observance; but it is corrected by the results arrived at through the examination of the Inscriptions, dealing as they do, for the most part, with matters of law and practical life. The real fact is, that the Etruscan language and people represent the ancient Teutonic or German stock in both the great branches of that stock, High-German and Low-German, at a period so extremely remote that elements in custom and speech subsequently disintegrated, and specialised so as to become the characteristic heritage of particular peoples, are in them found in original harmony and observance.—1872.]

INDEX
OF
ETRUSCAN WORDS

DISCUSSED IN THE FOREGOING PAGES.*

-ACHE   AMER

A.

-ACHE, in LES-ACHE, page 51.
-ACHEN, in KIL-ACHEN-ER, 95, 102, 103.
-ACHEIŚ, in TLEN-ACHEIŚ, 51. Conf. -AKEŚ.
ACU-ŚUN, 31. Conf. ESTER, EŚ (in EŚ-TLA), KECHA.
.... ACHS, 105, 106.
AELCHE, nom. pr., 61 sqq.; AELCHES, 67.
Æpui, 288.
Æsar, 8, 250.
-æśa, in al-æśos, 210.
agalletor, 242.
ager, 279.
Agylla, 223.
AMERAS, 48.
-AK, in PHRONT-AK, 82.

-AKCHA, 164, 192.
-AKES, in TLEN-AKES, 52. Conf. -ACHEIŚ.
AKIL, 164, 195. AKIL UNE TUR UN-EŚKUŚE-ZNA, 208, 210.
AKŚINA, 164, 185.
AL, 31. Conf. -AL.
-AL, 64, 67, 70, 71, 74, and passim. Conf. AL.
-ales, in Feti-ales, 276.
-alia, in Compit-alia, 268,—in Laperc-alia, 267.
ALPAN, 45, 54, 55; ALPNAS, 17.
Alsi-um, 295.
AMA, 164, 191. Conf. AMI, AM- (in AM-ER), MAM-, com-, con-.
AMA-HEN, 164, 172. Conf. MA · ANI.
AM-AT, 31. Conf. AMER, AME-VACHES, AVIF-, EUT-, -UM (in ETH-UM), &c.
AMER, 164, 188. Conf. AM-AT, &c.

---

* Words found in the Etruscan inscriptions, and of which an interpretation is given in the text of this volume, are printed here in CAPITAL letters. Those recorded by the ancients, as well as others, treated of in the Appendix, are in Italics. Proper names of persons are omitted except when an attempt has been made to explain their meaning. In compound words the component elements are distinguished by hyphens, and the elements found last in such compounds are inserted as independent words, but with a hyphen prefixed. The letters B, C, D, F, G, O, and Q, are wanting in the Etruscan alphabet; and such words therefore as begin with those letters in the Latinised or Græcised forms of Etruscan words are placed under the letters which correspond to them in Etruscan, those beginning with B and F under P PH; those commencing with C, G, and Q, under K; and those of which the initial is O under U. Words that begin with the Etruscan character usually rendered CH will be found in a group immediately after S, as the character in question has properly, I think, the force of SCH. I have not separated the words which begin with the sigma and the san, ś and ś, as it is not clear that they were distinct letters, and words are sometimes written with one, sometimes with the other character. The references for comparison are to varieties of the same word or words proceeding from the same root. These are given usually under the first of the words to be compared; and reference is made backward to that first word afterwards.

AME-VACHER, 164, 167. Conf. AM-AT, &c.
AMI, 17. Conf. AMA, &c.
AM-KE, 07, 105, 106. Conf. AMA, &c.
am-truatia, 207. Conf. AM- (in AM--AT), &c.
-AN, in THEM-AN, 256; in TUR-AN, 257, and passim. Conf. -ANH (in TH-ANA), -ANS, -ONUS, -IRUS, -NA, -NNA, -ONA, -S, -WIRAG, -UNA.
ANA, 19. Conf. KENU.
-ANA, in TH-ANA, 256, and passim. Conf. -AN, &c.
-ANATI, in TIF-ANATI, 257.
-AKI, in MA · ANI, 125, 129. Conf. AMA HEN, | -NF, -NEA.
ane-ile, 207. Conf. KE, in KIL--ACHEN-KE.
Anibia, 74.
-ANB, in SETHL-ANS, 255. Conf. -AN, &c.
Anta, 74.
ANTAR, 74.
-ONES, in SANIN-ANES, 255; and passim. Conf. -AN, &c.
Ap-ex, 208.
APHUN-UXI, 164, 107.
APHUNA, 164, 192; -APHUNES, in THALI-APHUNES, 164, 178.
ap-luda, 216.
aqui-lex, 240.
-ar, in Ine-ar, 245. Conf. -ER.
arucca, 240.
ABAS, 164, 173.
ABABA, 150, 154.
-ABABI, in PERKUTH-ABABI, 110, 113; in KLEH-ABABI, 110, 111. Conf. ABBA.
arcus, 270.
ABHI, 27.
Aril, 251. Conf. E., aii, Verti--EMBAUL.
arimi, 240.
ARITIMI, 66.—ARITIMI PHASTI RUI--THRIM, 208.
-arinus, in culend-arinus, ide-arinus, 271.

Aruns, Arno, 294.
Arreti-um, 282. Conf. Oru-divus, Quir-inus, Quir-ites, R-omu.
ABBA, 113. Conf. -ABABA.
ore crre, 242.
AS, 164, 191. AS-KUNA APHUNA HENA, 208, 210. Conf. KS- (in KI-KUNE).
-AT, in AM-AT, 33. Conf. -af, ETU--UM, EUT-, -fex, -vacher.
ai-crss, 216.
ATH, nom. pr., 74, 70, 81.
ATHIR, 125, 133.
ATH-LIR, 42.
-ATHRI, in VELATH-RI, see l'alterra.
ATH-UM-IK6, 164, 196.
Adria, Atria, 295.
-atria, in quinqu-atria, &c., 240.
atri-um, 240.
au-gur, 02, 312.
auk-elos, 247.
au-spex, 02.
AV, 19.
AVEN-KE, 105, 106.
AVIL, AVILS, 94, 97, 99, 105, 106.
AVIP, in AVIP-ABOL, 27. Conf. am- (in am-truatio), &c.
-af, in bpm-af, 20. Conf. -AT, &c.
axa-menta, 207.

E.
E, 164, 200.
EIN, 104, 197.
EIN-UB, 116. Conf. IN.
EITVA, 101. Conf. ETVE.
EITH-PHANU, 125, 126. (See ETH-PHANU.) Conf. idus.
EIT-VAPIA, 105, 108.
EKA, 95, 102.
EKA-NAR, 32.
ELI, 125, 134.
-elos, in ank-elos, 247.
ENAE, 125, 134, 136.
ENEAMI, 164, 175, 193, 196.
EN-ORUNA, 125, 137.
EN-VE, 97, 101.

EP-PUBLIK, 164, 176.
EPLT, 161, 176.
equites, 273.
-ER, in NAP-ER. Conf. -AR.
-*erii*, in *Falerii*, 288.
-*erra*, in *Volterra*, 290.
ERBER, 34. Conf. HAR, VER.
-*erura*, -*erea*, in *Men-erura*, 251.
-*erra*, in *Men-erea*, 251.
ERERE, 33. Conf. ACH-, in ACH-RUM, &c.
ES-EUNE, 164, 195. Conf. a6.
ES-TLA, 164, 168, and see 228. Conf. ACH-, in ACH-RUM, &c.
ETERA, 65, 66; -ETERI, in LAUTN-ETERI, 113.
ETH-PHANU, 110, 114. See ETH-PHANU.
ETHERSAI, 18.
ETU-UM, 16, 17. Conf. -AT, in AM-AT, &c.
ETVE, 110, 112. Conf. EITVA.
R-CLAT, 164, 166.
EURAS-VELE, 34. Conf. EITESAN.
EUT-UÓE, 104, 192. Conf. -AT, in AM-AT, &c.
EVRPIIA, nom. pr., 28.
-*ex*, in *up-ex*, 268.

H.

HAPIRNAL. See THAPIRNAL.
HAR, 164, 192. Conf. ER-RE, &c.
haru-spex, 85.
HER-Z-RI, 110, 117.
HELEPHU, 19.
HELU-TERNE, 164, 190.
HEN, 164, 192. Conf. AMA-HEN, &c.
(H)ERER, 125, 132.
HISTRA-HAPE, 164, 182.
HINTHIO, 110.
hister, 245.
Horta, 254, 300, 304. Conf. *Cort-ona*, *curia*, *curulis*.
Hortanum, 300.
Hruvna, 251.
HUT, 164, 185, 191. Conf. HUTH.
HUTH, 150, 151. Conf. HUT.

I.

ICH, 164, 200.
ida-arinm, 271.
idus, 271. Conf. EITU-, ETH-.
IK, 16.
-IKLA, in THUPHLTH-IKLA, 43.
-IKS, in ATH-UM-IKS, 164, 195.
-*ile*, in *anc-ile*, 267.
-*ilia*, in *snoveluur-ilia* and *oliduur-ilia*, 218, 268.
imperator, *induperator*, 272. Conf. *prator*.
IN, 125, 129; and 164, 188. Conf. EIN.
-INA, in VELS-INA, 234; -*ina*, in *Feb-ina*, 290. Conf. -*inii*.
-*inii*, in *Tarquinii*, 280. Conf. -INA.
insignia, 278.
-*inum*, in *Salpinum*, 304.
-*inus*, in Quir-inus, 267. Conf. AN, &c.
In-eduti, Dii, 252.
IPA, 110, 115, 125, 129, 130, 164, 172, 173, 208, 216. IPA MUSRUA KER, 208, 210.
IR, 23.
-*ista*, in *lan-ista*, 244.
IUKIR, 25.
IUUNA, 25.
-IVA, in ELUT-IVA, 110, 118.

K.

-K·, in [THT]AR-K·, 125, 136. Conf. KAKE-, KEN, ENL.
Care, or *Cara*, 283.
eradus, 279. Conf. *cassis*.
KAHATI-AL, nom. pr., 70, 71. Also written KAPHATI-.
KAKE-CHAEL, 164, 200. Conf. -K.
KAL·, 125, 129. Conf. *calen-da-*.
calecus, 278.
KALE, 150, 151. Conf. *Salii*, -*ilia*, -*sal*.
calen-da-, 270. Conf. KAL; ', *lan-ista*, LEN-ACHE.

calend-arium, 270.
KALU-SUBASI, 97, 100; KALUS..., 102, 101. Conf. KULMU.
Camar, Camar-ts, 286.
KAN-THKE, 102, 104. Conf. AMA, &c.
-KAPE, in TISTHA-KAPE, 164, 182. Conf. Capua, capys.
Capena, 265.
gapos, 244.
capra, 215.
Capua, 295. Conf. -KAPE, &c.
capys, 71, 216. Conf. -KAPE, &c.
KASU, 164, 170.
casia, 243. Conf. cassia.
KE, 164, 173.
KE, 164, 190.
-KE, in AM-KE, 105, 106.
-KE, in ZIL-ACHEN-KE, 95, 102, 103. Conf. unc-.
-KE, in AVEN-KE, 105, 106; in LUFU-KE, 97, 99.
KECHA, 55, 57. Conf. ach-, &c.
KECHASE, 125, 142. Conf. cnucn.
KEHEN, 110.
celeres, 273.
[KE]NAMUTRE, 125, 130. Conf. -NAM, in TH-NAM.
KEN. 59. Conf. -K-
genii, 290.
KENU, 101, 177. Conf. ANA.
KEM, 110, 116.
KEMASIN, 125, 131.
-EKVE, in VENE-KEVE-LTHU, 21. See p. 128.
-KIAI, in PUNE-KIAI, 45.
KIARTHI-AL-ISA, nom. pr., 67, 70.
KIKU, nom. pr., 85, 90, 91.
circus, 279.
KISUM, 105, 106. Conf. KIZI.
KIVEAAN, 31. Conf. BORAS-.
KIZI, 102, 103. Conf. KISUM.
KLAI-UM, 105, 106.
KLAN, 65, 97, 102, 105, 125.
classicum, 278.
Clavenna, 206. Conf. clavus.
clavus, 278. Conf. Clavenna.

KLE, 110, 113.
KLEI-, 164, 167.
KLEN, 51, 57, 110, 114, 161, 179;
KLENSI, 164, 177; KLESÂI, 59.
-KLET, in MUNI-KLET, 161, 182. Conf. -LTHU.
-KLETH, in MUNI-KLETH, 99, 102.
clientes, 273.
clones, 279.
KLTE, 125, 131. Conf. KUL-, cn[L-T].
Clusi-um, 280. Conf. -IE, in CHEM-PHUÈ-LE.
KLUTHI, 21. Conf. LEINTH.
KLUT-IVA, 110, 118.
gnis, 246.
KNL-, 164, 189, 192. Conf. -K-
Κόγξ όμπαξ, 20.
comitia, 274. Conf. compit-alia.
compit-alia, 268. Conf. comit-in.
Com-plices, 181, 252. Conf. ANA, &c.
Con-entes, Dii, 252. Conf. ANA, &c.
con-sul, 271. Conf. ANA, &c.
cornu, 276.
Cort-ona, 288. Conf. Horta, &c.
Cosa, 290.
Gra-divus, 305. Conf. Arretium, &c.
Grasinur, 295.
Grisones, 231.
KÉ, 150, 153. See Ké-UATHA.
KÉ-UATHA, 150, 156; and for 208, 216. Conf. [CHAEI-U]ATA, -CHAEI-.
quinqu-atria, 249.
Quir-inus, 267, 305. Conf. Arretium, &c.
Quir-ites, 305. Conf. Arretium, &c.
KULMU, 110, 116, 259, 291. Conf. KALU.
KUL-PIANSI, 45. Conf. KLTE, &c.
KUNA, 164, 177, 191.
KUFEA, CUPEA, 149, 157, 251.
-gur, in au-gur, 312.
curia, 274. Conf. Horta, &c.
KURIEAS, 25.
curulis, sella, 277. Conf. Horta.
KUMACH, 27.
KVEE, 52.

L.

lærna, 253.
-lundum, in fa-lan-lum, 217. Conf.
 LETEM, -LETII.
lān-iala, 244. Conf. calen-lar, &c.
LAPIITHI, 25.
LAPH . . . , 105, 106. Conf. LUPU,
 ZELATV.
lar, 104, 168, 178, 261. Conf.
 LARIS, LASTE, LAETHIA, larva.
LABEA, 261. Conf. -LEBI.
LARE-ZUL, 164, 166.
LARIS, 125, 142, 143. Conf. LAR.
LARKE, 61. Conf. LUSI.
LAETH, nom. pr., 143; LAETHIA,
 ibid. Conf. LAR.
larne, 261. Conf. LAR.
LASA, 250. Conf. -lex.
Latium, 205. Conf. Rhæti.
-LE, in CHIEMPUUŚ-LE, 164, 180.
 Conf. Clusi-um.
LEINE, 94.
LEINTU, 259. Conf. ELUTHI.
LEKNE, 61.
lemures, 260.
LEN-ACHE, 54. Conf. calen-dar, &c.
-LEBI, in PHUŚ-LEBI, 171. Conf.
 larva.
LEB-ZINIA, 164, 188.
LEKAN, 150, 155.
LETEM, 150, 154. Conf. -lundum.
-letor, in aga-lletor, 212. Conf. lictor;
 lituus, ludus.
-LETH, in OLE-LETH, 161, 170. Conf.
 -landum, &c.
-lex, in aqui-lex, 249. Conf. LABA.
lictor, 277. Conf. letor, &c.
-LIK, in ATR-LIK, 43.
-LIK, in EP-LIK-PHELIS, 164, 178.
LIMIAI, 17.
lituus, 264. Conf. letor, &c.
LN, 97, 98. Conf. LNM.
LOENA, 254. Conf. LUENL.
LAR, 98. Conf. LE.
-LTHU, in wne-ken-lthu, 23. Conf.
 ELET?

luc-ur, 215.
luc-umo, 213.
ludus, ludii, ludiones, 215. Conf.
 letor.
Luna, 300.
lupero-ukia, 207.
LUPU, 102, 104; LUPU-KE, 97, 99;
 LUPUM, 105, 106. Conf. LAPH . . .
LURI, 97, 101. Conf. LARKE.
LUESI, 42. Conf. LOENA.
lustratio, 208.

M.

MA - ANI, 125, 129. Conf. AMA-HEN.
MALAVISCH, 257.
Manes, Dii, 261.
mantisa, 247. Conf. MINETHU.
Mantua, 302. Conf. Nantus, MUNI.
Nantus, 254. Conf. Mantus, &c.
MARAN, 17.
MAUREI, 25.
MAEKEM, nom. pr., 105.
MARUN, 298.
MASU, 164, 168, 185.
MATMU, 17.
ME . . . . . , 105, 106.
MEALCHEM, or MEALCHLAR, 105, 106.
MEAN, 259. Conf. MIN.
MEANI, 102, 103.
MENA, 164, 192. Conf. MUNI-NLET.
MEN-EBVA, MEN-ERUKA, 251.
 -menta, in aru-menta, 267.
MER, 150, 153; MUEI, 150, 155.
Mecentius, 285.
MI, 40.
MI, 60.
MIAKE, 97, 101.
MIN, 10. Conf. MEAN.
MINETHU, 10. Conf. mantisa.
MINI, 22.
MLE-SHUL, 164, 174.
-marium, in po-marium, 205. Conf.
 marus.
MTIS-US, 125, 130.
MUL, 23.
MUL, 164, 174.

MULETH-SVALASI, 99, 160.
MUNI-KLET, 164, 182.
MUSI-KLETH, 164, 182. Conf. MENA.
MUNI-SVLETH, 97, 99, 100. Conf. Alontun, &c.
MUNI-SUBETH, 99. Conf. MUNI-SVLETH.
murus, 280. Conf. -murinm.
MUBLUA, 110, 116.
MUTH, 51.

N.

-NA, in LOS-NA, 254; in THAL-NA, 256, &c. Conf. -AN, &c.
NE -, nom. pr., 85, 90.
-NAK, in EKA-NAK, 32.
-NAM, in TH-NAM, 125, 131. Conf. [EK]NAMUTNE
names, 219.
NAP-ER, 150, 153, 164, 172, 183, 185, 192.
NARE, 105, 106.
-NATE, in PHLENX-NATE, 125, 135.
NATHUM, 260.
-NE, in NAS-NE, 164, 190; -NES, in NAS-NES, 164, 172. Conf. -ASI, &c.
nepos, 249, and see 131. Conf. NUVI, -ENEVES.
NPSL, 96.
NASI, 19.
NETH-UNS, 264.
NETS-VIS, 82, 85.
Neverita, 86. Conf. Nortia.
NI, 125, 130.
Nortia, 86. Conf. Neverita.
Novca-siles, Dii, 252.
NUFFIZI, 102, 104.
NUVI, nom. pr., 234. Conf. nepos, &c.
-NUA, in Vertum-nua, 278.

P. PH.

bulinus, 243. Conf. voluti.
patricii, 272. Conf. Tyrrheni.
Bayer, 263. Conf. -aper.

Penates, Dii, 262.
PENE-ZA, 164, 185, and see 208, 216.
PESTHNA, 164, 166.
PERAS, 164, 193.
Perusia, 228.
Pirsulas, 236.
Pu-lundum, 247.
Pul-erii, 268.
Pul-izei, 269.
PHANU-SATHES, 125, 126; and see 208, 216. Conf. PHSIS-, -PHANSI, ponti-, PUAS.
-PHANU, in ETH-PHANU, 125, 126, and ETH-PHANU, 110, 111.
fasces, 277. Conf. PHASTI, fasti.
PHASTI, 57. Conf. fasces, &c.
fasti, Dies, 271. Conf. fasces, &c.
PHAVN, nom. pr., 28.
favisas, 280.
februa, 267.
feci-ales, or fetiales, 176. Conf. PHERU.
PHERU, LASA, 250. Conf. feci-ales.
-PHELIE, in EP-LIE-PHELIE, 164, 178. Conf. SVULASE.
Felo-ina, 280.
Fer-onia, 254.
PHES, 34.
Fescenni-um, 200. Conf. -VE, in 'versus Fescenninl,' 200.
PHESU, 247. See Firsalar.
fetiales. See feciales.
-fex, in ponti-fex, 200. Conf. -AT, &c.
flamines, 266.
PHLENENA, 125, 129.
PHLENE-NATE, 125, 131.
PHLER, 39; PHLERE, 51; PHLERES, 50, 52, 63, 60. Conf. PLEBES, PLANU.
PHLES-ENEVES, 125, 131, 136.
floers, 217.
PHSIS-NIAL, 45, 46. Conf. PHANU-, &c.
-fragia, in suf-fragia, 276.
PHRONT-AE, 82 sqq.
PHUL-UM-CHVA-SPES, 164, 193.

Phuphl-uns, 253. Conf. Pupliana.
phus-lsri, 104, 170.
-pianśi, in kul-pianśi, 45, 51. Conf.
 phanu-, &c.
Pisu, 298, 302.
plebs, 273.
plenrś, 50. Conf. philen, &c.
-plicrs, in Com-plices, Dii, 252.
po-merium, 265.
Pom-oen, 255.
pontifex, 269. Conf. phanu-, &c.
Popul-onia, 302.
populus, 272.
for-um, 274.
pratexta, toga, 277.
prutor, 272. Conf. impertor.
puan-tes, 50; and see 65. Conf.
 phanu-, &c.
puiam, 105, 100.
bulla, 213.
Pupliana, 23. Conf. Phuphluns.
Pupl-una (Populonia), 302.

R.

s -, 110, 110. Conf. Aun., &c.
Ra, nom. pr., 74, 80.
rank-zi, 164, 181.
raś-ne, 104, 190; raś-kvś, 104, 172,
 101.
Rekuneta, Lasa, 250.
resp, 164, 195.
rex, 271.
Rhoti, 281. Conf. lati-um.
-ri, in ree-e-ri, 110, 117.
ricu, 268.
ril, ril avil, 91. Conf. Aril, &c.
-rim, in ruipu-rim, 57. Conf. -rum.
R-oma, 304. Conf. Arret-ium, &c.
ruiph-rim, 57.
-rum, in ach-rum, 30. Conf. -rim.
Rusella, 289.

S.

s -, 125, 127. Conf. -śatheme, m-thi,
 śuthi-.
-s, in Thuhm-s, 250.

s -, 164, 182.
-sa, 02, 67, 08, 99, &c., 235.
sucer, and compounds, 266.
sorulum, 278.
Salii, 206. Conf. kale, &c.
Sulp-inum, 301.
śal-ths, 41.
san-śl, 52, 59.
śatrna, 164, 193; and see zia-
 śatrna.
-śather, in phanu-śather, 125,
 126; and see 204, 216. Conf. s -,
 &c.
Saturnia, 301.
sech, 105, 106. Conf. as.
-selari, in then-selari, 150, 154.
śelan-śl, 40, 42 (note). Conf.
 solitaurilia, -sevil.
senatus, 275.
-s ntes, in Con-sentes, Dii, 252.
Sertures, nom. pr., 235.
sethl-ans, 256, 301. Conf. sitmika.
-siané, in thues-siané, 110, 111.
sibylla, 263.
siekp, 18.
-siles, in Noven-siles, Dii, 252. Conf.
 kale, &c.
Sitmika, Lasa, 250. Conf. sethlans.
sk, 105, 107. Conf. secn.
-skul, in mle-skul, 164, 174.
-skuna, in ens-skuna, 125, 137.
skusu, 125, 126.
-skvii, in tin-skvii, 42. Conf.
 śelan-śl, &c.
śl, 50; -śl, in san-śl, 52, 159; -śl,
 in śelan-śl, 40.
-sla, 62, 66, 125, 136, &c.; -sle, in
 alpinali-sle, 237.
sle-letr, 164, 169. Conf. -zul (?).
solitaur-ilia, 268. Conf. śelan-śl,
 &c.
-śpel, in phul-um-chva-śpel, 104.
 Conf. śpelane.
śpelane, 164, 193. Conf. -śpel.
-sper, in su-sper, huru-sper, 85.
 Conf. Begr.
-śt, in then-śt, 150, 155.

INDEX

stroppus, 244.
-sludo, in te-sludo, 280.
sub-ulo, 244. Conf. tub-a.
suf-fragia, 275.
-sul, in con-sul, 272. Conf. kale, &c.
Summ-onus, 255.
suovetaur-ilia, 268.
-surasi, in malu-surasi, 97, 100.
Conf. -sureth.
-sureth, in muni-sureth, 80. Conf.
-surasi.
sutri, 40; sutri, 95; -sutri, 110;
sutri-tp, 126, 127. Conf. s·, &c.
Sutri-um, 304.
-svalasi, in mulete-svalasi. Conf.
-svleth.
svalei, 50.
svas, 34.
-svleth, in muni-svleth, 97, 98.
Conf. -svalasl.
svclase, 58. Conf. -phelie.

CH = SCH.

[chazi : u]aza, 125, 133. Conf.
ké-uatha.
-chazi, in kake-chazi, 164, 200.
chiemphus-le, 164, 179, sqq.
chimth, 104, 191.
chis-vline, 59; and see 208.
cb[lt], 125, 137. Conf. elte, &c.
chm[un], 125, 135.
chuch, 164, 200. Conf. xechase.
-chva, in phul-um-chva-apel, 164,
194. Conf. -hape.
chvacha, 35.

T. TH.

-dæ, in culen-dæ, 270.
Tages, 263.
tan, 104, 193.
tame ..., 105, 106.
tamera, 97, 101 (and note), 102
(note), 113.
damnas, 245.
tanna, 164, 166; tan[na] 125, 132.
Conf. -thn, -zisla.

Turquin-ii, 289.
Deo, 254. Conf. tif-, -divus.
teid, 164, 171, 191. Conf. zé.
teisnika, 125, 128.
tek, 52; tkke, 59.
tem, 104, 188. Conf. duum-.
templum, 205.
tenise, 50.
tenne, 164, 189, 190; -tenne, in
helu-tenne, 164, 190; tenné, 164,
171, 191.
te-sludo, 280. Conf. th-, in th-nam;
zia-, in zia-gatene.
tez, 46, 47 (note).
tezan, 164, 170.
Thal-na, 250. Conf. thil, -thilé,
-thl, zil.
thalé-aphunés, 164, 178; and see
208. Conf. -tla, tlee, tlen-,
[z]ele, feluce, -zl, -zul.
Th-ana, 42, 256. Conf. Thapna.
Thapien-al, nom. pr., 70; also
Hapien-al.
Thapna, 42. Conf. Th-ana.
Thaura, 164, 190.
Thaure, 110, 112.
Then-selari, 150, 154.
Then-st, 150, 155.
Thephalaé, 164, 170. Conf. Thi-
fraléti, Thcphltaé, &c.
Thes-an, 250.
Thi, 164, 193, 195. Conf. thii, thui.
Thiiphaléti, 104, 184. Conf. The-
phalaé, &c.
Thii-Thilé, 104, 177. Conf. thi, &c.
Thil, 161, 199. Conf. Thal-na, &c.
-Thilé, in Thii-Thilé, 164, 177.
Conf. Thal-na, &c.
Thifuresal, 17.
-Thke, in kan-thke, 102, 104. Conf.
zukl.
-thl, in Thunchcl-thl, 164, 199.
Conf. Thal-na, &c.
-tun, in sal-thn, 43. Conf. tanna,
&c.
Th-nam, 125, 133. Conf. te-, zia-.
thp, 34. Conf. -tp?

Y

TUBER, 38. Conf. THER, TURER.
[THT]AS : X ·, 125, 130. Conf.
TITE, [T]UTNL.
THURÉ-SIANÉ, 110, 111.
THUI, 150, 151. Conf. THI, &c.
-THUM, in NATHUM, 260.
THUNCH-UL, 104, 170; THUNCHUL-
-THL (or TRUNCH-ULTHL?), 104,
199; THUNCHU ...., M, 125, 136.
THUPHLTAŚ, 54; THUPHULTHAŚ, 55;
THUPHULTHAŚA, 49; THUPHLTH-
-IKLA, 48. Conf. THEPHALAŚ, &c.
-THUR, in APHUN-THUR-URI, 164, 197.
Conf. TUR.
THURA, 40.
THURAŚ, 104, 173, 100. Clause,
THUHAŚ, ARAŚ, PERAŚ, EE, &c. 208.
THURM-e, 256.
TIF-ANATI, 257. Conf. Des, &c.
TIMRAR, Lass, 259.
TINERI, 125, 129.
TINIA, 250.
TIN-SEVII, 42.
TITE, 17. Conf.{THT}AS : X ·, &c.
TITTÁI, 150, 151 sqq.
diribitores, 270.
-divus, in Ura-divus, 308.
-TLA, in EŚ-TLA, 164, 108; TLEŚ, 150,
151. Conf. THALŚ, &c.
TLEN-ARES, 53; TLEN-ACHEŚ, 55;
TLEN-ACHEEL, 53. Conf. THALŚ-,
&c.
TRA, 150, 158.
toga, 244.
-TF, in SUTHI-TF, 125, 127. Conf.
THP?
T[R], 125, 138.
TE ..., 125, 130.
trabea, 277.
TRE, 150, 155.
tribus, 273.
tripudium, 267. Conf. -truatio.
TRER, 57. Conf. THERE, &c.
-TEN, in PUAN-TEN, 60.
-truatio, in am-truatio, 267. Conf.
tripudium.
druna, 243.

TRUTX-VT, 82 sqq.
TRUT-VEKIE, 48; and see 209.
tub-a, 280. Conf. sub-ulo.
TURUR, 110, 118.
TUR, 104, 195. Conf. -THUR.
TUR-AN, 257.
TUSER, 45, 46, 48, 50, 51. Conf.
THERE, &c.
Turnnu, 285.
TUTRINEŚ, 55, 59.
[T]UTNL. See UTNL.
tutulus, 268.
duum-viri, 264. Conf. TEM.
Tyrrh-eni, 280. Conf. patricii.

U.

UATHA, 51; UATHA, in KŚ-UATHA,
150, 158; [U]ATA, in [CHAZI-U]ATA,
125, 133. Conf. VEITHL.
-UL, in THUNCH-UL, 104, 179.
ULARU, 164, 178. Conf. PULER, &c.
-ULAT, in K-ULAT, 161, 168. Conf.
-ulo.
-ulo, in sub-ulo, 244. Conf. -ULAT.
-ULTHL (?), in THUNCH-ULTHL, 104,
100.
-UM, in ETA-UM, 17; in KLAL-UM,
105, 100; in UR-UM, 110, 110,
in ATR-UM-IEŚ, 164, 108. Conf.
AM-, &c.
-um, in Alsi-um, 295; in Arreti-um,
262; in atri-um, 242; in Clusium, 298, &c. Conf. -oma, -ona,
-onia.
-oma, in R-oma. Conf. -um, &c.
-umna, in Volt-umna, 259. Conf.
-AN, &c.
-urna, in Iuc-urna, 243.
$ur-aŚ, 29. Conf. AM-, &c.
UX-EEA, 164, 105.
-ona, in Cort-ona, 268; -onia, in
Popul-onia, 302; in Vetul-onia,
290, &c. Conf. -um.
-ona, in Pom-ona, 255; -onia, in Fer-
onia, 254. Conf. -AN.
-una, in Pupl-una (Popul-onia).
Conf. -um.

UNE, 164, 195.
-UNE, in NETH-UNE, 254; in PHUPHL-
-UNE, 255. Conf. -AN, &c.
-UNE, (local termination, Illuetian,)
293.
UPN, (Arretium,) 282.
URLAN, 61.
-ui, in NTIS-UÁ. Conf. AS, &c. ;
-UIE, in EUT-UÁE, 164, 102.
UTNI (TUTNI?), 40. Cf. [TET]AS-E -,
&c.
UZIL, 257.

V. (Digamma.)

-VACHER, in ANE-VACHER, 164, 167.
Conf. AM-.
VANI-AL, nom. pr., 238.
VANTE, 260.
VASN-AL, nom. pr., 74, 80; VASNALI-
ELA, 60.
-VAPLA, in KIT-VAPLA, 105, 108.
VATL. See Vetulonia.
Veii, 280.
VEITHI, 50, 51. Conf. UATHA.
Vejovis, or Vedius, 257.
-VEEIE, in TRUT-VENIE, 48.
VEL · , nom. pr., 237; VELE, 71;
VELA, 55; VELCE, 102.
VELATH-RI. See Volterra.
VELS-INA. See Volsinii.
VELSU. See Felsina.
VENE-KEVE-LTHU, 23; and see 208,
210.
VER, 125, 135. Conf. ERSEE, &c.
serra, arse, 240.
Vertum-nus, 258. Conf. ARIL, &c.
VESIE, 33.
Vetul-onia, 200.
Veturius, Mamurius, 267.
-VIÉ, in NETS-VIÉ, 82.

-VELE, in EUBAS-VELE, 34.
-VLISÁ, in CHIS-VLISÉ, 50.
Volsci, 288.
Vols-inii, 201.
Volt-erra, 200. Conf. Volt- in Volt-
umna.
Volt-umna, 258. Conf. Volt- in Volt-
erra.
-voluti. See Involuti. Conf. brittens.
-VE, in EN-VE, 97, 101. Conf. Fes-
cennium.

X.

-XNEVER, in PELES-XNEVER, 125, 131,
138.

Z.

-E, in HER-Z-EI, 110, 117, and note.
-ZEA, in UN-ZEA, 164, 108.
ZELAVV, 97, 101, 102 (note). Conf.
LAPR ..., &c.
[Z]ELE ..., 125, 130. Conf. -THALÉ,
&c.
[ZE]LUPU ?, 104. Conf. LAPR ..., ;
&c.
ZELUTE, 110, 112. Conf. THALÉ-, &c.
ZERIUN-AMCHA, 164, 197.
ZIA-LATENE, 164, 189. Conf. TR-,
&c.
ZIL-ACHEN-KE, 95, 102, 103; ZIL-
ACHNU-KE, 99. Conf. THAL-NA, &c.
-ZINIA, in LER-ZINIA, 164, 188. Conf.
TANNA, &c.
-ZL, in RANE-ZL, 164, 181. Conf.
THALÉ-, &c.
zi, in PENE-zi, 164, 185. Conf. TRIS.
ZUEI, 164, 174, 193, 196. Conf.
-THER.
-ZUL, in LARE-ZUL, 164, 166. Conf.
THALÉ-, &c.

THE END.

www.ingramcontent.com/pod-product-compliance
Lightning Source LLC
Chambersburg PA
CBHW021204230426
43667CB00006B/544